Girls' Schooling during the Progressive Era

STUDIES IN THE HISTORY OF EDUCATION
VOLUME 10
GARLAND REFERENCE LIBRARY OF SOCIAL SCIENCE
VOLUME 1091

GIRLS' SCHOOLING DURING THE PROGRESSIVE ERA
FROM FEMALE SCHOLAR TO DOMESTICATED CITIZEN

KAREN GRAVES

GARLAND PUBLISHING, INC.
A MEMBER OF THE TAYLOR & FRANCIS GROUP
NEW YORK AND LONDON
1998

Library of Congress Cataloging-in-Publication Data

Graves, Karen.
    Girls' schooling during the Progressive Era : from female scholar
to domesticated citizen / by Karen Graves.
        p.   cm. — (Studies in the history of education ; vol. 10)
(Garland reference library of social science ; vol. 1091)
    Includes bibliographical references (p.   ) and index.
    ISBN 0-8153-2224-0 (alk. paper)
    1. Women—Education (Secondary)—Missouri—St. Louis—History.
2. Women—Education (Secondary)—Missouri—St. Louis—Curricula.
I. Title. II. Series. III. Series: Garland reference library of social
science. Studies in the history of education ; vol. 10.
LC1759.S8G73   1998
373.1822—dc21   98-29905
                                                                  CIP

Portions of Chapter 3 also appear in substantially different form in "A Matter of
Course: Curriculum Transformation and Academic Decline in St. Louis," *Journal
of the Midwest History of Education Society* 22 (1995): 161–177.

Portions of Chapter 5 also appear in substantially different form in "The Impact of
the Differentiated Curriculum on African American Women High School Students:
The Case in St. Louis," *Mid-Western Educational Researcher* 8 (Fall 1995): 3–9.

Portions of Chapter 6 also appear in substantially different form in "Women and
'Democracy's High School,'" *Journal of the Midwest History of Education Society* 23
(1996): 49–54.

Cover photograph of a botany class in Central High School, St. Louis, Missouri, 1900.
Permission obtained from St. Louis Public Schools Records Center/Archives.

Printed on acid-free, 250-year-life paper
Manufactured in the United States of America

Series Preface

Garland's Studies in the History of Education series includes not only volumes on the history of American and Western education, but also on the history of the development of education in non-Western societies. A major goal of this series is to provide new interpretations of educational history that are based on the best recent scholarship; each volume will provide an original analysis and interpretation of the topic under consideration. A wide variety of methodological approaches from the traditional to the innovative are used. In addition, this series especially welcomes studies that focus not only on schools but also on education as defined by Harvard historian Bernard Bailyn: "the transmission of culture across generations."

The major criteria for inclusion are (a) a manuscript of the highest quality and (b) a topic of importance to understanding the field. The editor is open to readers' suggestions and looks forward to a long-term dialogue with them on the future direction of the series.

Edward R. Beauchamp

To C.P.W.

Contents

List of Tables

Preface

This book represents my best efforts to understand a critical period in girls' educational history in the United States and to articulate the significance of the curriculum transformation that surged through high schools in the early decades of the twentieth century. Increasingly throughout this century, citizens in the United States have turned to schools as key institutions for shaping one's life possibilities. At the same time, educators have established the differentiated curriculum as the dominant form of curricular organization in public high schools. In providing different schooling experiences for different students, school personnel have helped to chart divergent destinies for students. The earliest proponents of the differentiated curriculum considered gender a major factor in determining one's appropriate course of study. Gender distinctions in academic study, largely absent from the nineteenth-century high school, materialized in U.S. high schools with the adoption of the differentiated curriculum.

My research on the transition, *From Female Scholar to Domesticated Citizen,* assesses the impact that a gendered ideology brought to bear on educational policy. Like the critical educational historians of the 1960s and 1970s whose scholarship forged new ways of knowing, I hold that the diffusion of ideas exerts influence on human behavior. It is the nexus between intellectual and social history as described by historian Paul Violas that lies at the heart of educational history. Analysis of educational philosophy and dominant ideas concerning women, therefore, are as important to this study as examination of curriculum data. By focusing on one school system in the years from 1870 to 1930, I am able to canvass changes in philosophy, curriculum, student population, course of study selection, and community reaction, to study in depth the effects of the differentiated curriculum on girls' schooling.

The long-lasting predominance of the differentiated curriculum has yielded many results. One consequence is described in this text as the eclipse of the female scholar.

The era of the female scholar was by no means a golden age in educational history. For example, only a small proportion of school-age youth attended high school, rote exercises characterized pedagogical methods, and teacher authority often dominated classroom interaction. Yet, the study of education is well served by revisiting the idea of schooling as intellectual development, a cornerstone of nineteenth-century educational philosophy. As educators embraced New Liberal conceptions of schooling for work and citizenship, intellectual development became extraneous to the schooling process. Without a commitment to development of the intellect, the ability of schools to contribute to human growth is attenuated.

As Jane Roland Martin and other feminist scholars have written, the history of educational thought and practice is diminished by the exclusion of girls and women. Reviving awareness of the history of the female scholar in U.S. high schools promises to advance historians' understanding of a major social institution. Introducing this history to secondary-school students and teachers puts them in contact with the forgotten educational achievements of girls of earlier generations. The knowledge that girls' success in all academic disciplines predated the 1970s women's movement helps to fortify those who challenge the educational barriers erected with the differentiated curriculum. By tracing the transition from female scholar to domesticated citizen, one can evaluate the impact of gender on a critical development within a key social institution.

It has been my good fortune to have studied with educational historians whose scholarship reflects a profound commitment to honest interpretation of evidence and an unaffected concern for humanity. Jim Anderson's exemplary scholarship helped me to delineate the standards of historical research. His encouragement and critical reading of early drafts of this manuscript provided immeasurable support. In my development as an educated person, I owe as much to Clarence Karier as to any other. I find that I cannot articulate adequately the depth of gratitude I carry for his example of professional and personal integrity. His insights regarding intellectual history are fundamental to my understanding of education in the United States. I initiated my study of women's educational history under Linda Perkins' careful guidance. Her efforts, as teacher, colleague, and friend, have played a crucial role in my professional development. Paul Violas has been a central figure in my maturation as a teacher, beginning in 1979 when I was an undergraduate student in his "Social Foundations of American Education" course at the University of Illinois. The learning I experienced in that class prepared me, more than any other undergraduate experience, for my nine years of work as a high-school mathematics teacher. The opportunity to teach with Paul and my fellow graduate students in EPS 201 as a teaching assistant from 1991 to 1993 provided valuable teaching experience that I took to my position as assistant professor of education at Denison University. I appreciate the attention Paul has given to a later draft of this manuscript. His evaluatory comments have pushed me to sharpen and polish the arguments presented here.

In addition to these scholars, others have read complete drafts or excerpts from this book, or have engaged in dialogue regarding its content. My work has been enhanced by the efforts of Lisa McDonnell, Lyn Robertson, Mary Tuominen, Carol Whitt, Arlette Willis, George Williamson, Jr., and an anonymous reviewer from Garland Publishing. Numerous colleagues in the Midwest History of Education Society, the History of Education Society, and the Women's Studies Department at Denison University have challenged and sustained me throughout the course of this study.

I am grateful for the support of Edward Beauchamp, Garland's History of Education Series Editor. His prodding, sufficient but never overbearing, fit well within a framework designed to allow me space to complete the manuscript alongside my teaching and other responsibilities. His confidence in my work helped to make the publication of my first book a pleasant experience. A special debt of gratitude is due Marie Ellen Larcada, Michele Zyracki, and Chuck Bartelt at Garland Publishing for their significant help in preparing the final copy of this book. Denison University provided support for this research in the form of grants from the Summer Professional Development Program. In the past few years many librarians and archivists have assisted my research efforts. I appreciate the interest in my study and the expertise exhibited by the archivists and librarians at Denison University, the Harris-Stowe State College, the Missouri Historical Society, the Saint Louis Public Library, the St. Louis Public

School Archives, the University of Illinois, and the University of Missouri in St. Louis.

Finally, I am pleased to acknowledge the enduring support of my family. My parents, Audrey Graves and Sam Graves, provided a foundation from which I first constructed an appreciation for education. And, they taught me a great deal about schools. Karol Mueller and Ken Mueller have pursued their life interests vibrantly, and have delighted in sharing in mine. Their encouragement for this study found expression in many ways, not the least of which was allowing me to stay in their home during trips to St. Louis. Lauren Mueller and Micah Whitt have helped me to remember why it is so necessary to make schools academically challenging for all children and young adults. Carol Phillips Whitt has bolstered my enthusiasm for this project at just the right times. Her example of an educated woman has served as an inspiration to my work as a teacher and as a scholar.

Introduction

The culture of the rational soul—the intellect, the will, and the affections—is the privilege of every human being, whether male or female.[1]
> —William Torrey Harris, St. Louis School Superintendent, 1873

We had found ourselves within this dear old Alma Mater. . . . We had enjoyed every moment spent in school.[2]
> —Cora Vinson, Sumner High School Student, 1931

Nineteenth-century educators in St. Louis conceived of the public high school as a place where students could develop foundations for life-long learning. In 1869, St. Louis superintendent William Torrey Harris, soon to become a national leader in education and a prominent proponent of coeducation, championed general education based on academic study.

> Thus High School studies follow the channels begun in the lower schools, and have in view the plan of giving to the youth the *command of himself* [sic]. Having this, the youth can safely be left to select his own avocation. Our national idea and the interests of humanity alike protest against a one-sided education that shall predestine the youth to some special art or trade.[3]

As public high schools began to proliferate in urban centers across the United States, St. Louis led the way in extending general academic education to African Americans. When the St. Louis Board of Education voted to establish the Charles Sumner High School as a first-

class secondary school in 1875, it became the first public high school in
the United States for African-American youth, according to the editor
of a history of the school.[4] Students in St. Louis espoused the notion
that a general high-school education prepared one for study throughout
the lifespan. In 1928, Mrs. W. R. Chivvis, member of the St. Louis
Central High School class of 1884, remembered that many of her
fellow graduates knew that they were not finished with their education
at commencement. She recalled the high-school principal as saying,

> We have not attempted to give you education. Happy will we be if
> you remember one thought: the use of books, and then perhaps in the
> future you will be educated.[5]

Chivvis noted that many in her own class became teachers, impressing
the value of education on others.[6]

Traditional education in the nineteenth-century U.S. high school
included the classics. By the turn of the century, however, this portion
of the academic curriculum was under fire. In a paper written for the
North Central Association of Colleges and Secondary Schools in 1905,
Gilbert Morrison, principal of McKinley High School in St. Louis,
argued:

> To insist on Latin and Greek being studied by any pupils except
> those preparing for the ancient course is a species of tyranny which is
> injuring our entire educational system.[7]

A national call for more "practical" studies in the high-school
curriculum joined the attack on the classics and led to the creation of
the differentiated curriculum. From 1853 to 1894, high-school students
in St. Louis selected either the General or the Classical Course of study.
The chief difference between the two courses was that the Classical
Course, designed for students who planned to go to college, included
Greek, and the General Course required more advanced classes in
mathematics and science. With just a few distinctions between the
Classical and General Courses, then, the high-school curriculum was
nearly uniform throughout most of the nineteenth century. Around
1900, however, more girls and boys began to attend high school and
educators expressed concern that the traditional academic curriculum
was inappropriate for all students. Starting in the 1890s, St. Louis
educators added new courses of study to the high-school curriculum, so

that by 1911, African-American and European-American students were graduating from eight different courses of study: General, Classical, Scientific, Art, Normal, Commercial, Domestic Art and Science, and Manual Training. The establishment of a differentiated curriculum meant that students within the same school did not experience the same education.

Educators who transformed the high-school curriculum were aware of a characteristic of the nineteenth-century high school population that has been lost to many in the late twentieth century: until 1930 most students and graduates of the public high school were girls. That is, girls comprised the majority of high-school students at a time when the academic curriculum was at its strongest. But the differentiated curriculum changed the course of public secondary education in the United States so forcefully that few today know of the educational legacy of high school girls in the period from 1870 to the early decades of the twentieth century. Harris' educational ideal of cultivating the rational soul is remembered, if at all, as a quaint, anachronistic practice.

The shift to the differentiated curriculum, with a corresponding loss of academic status for girls, coincided with an increase in women's participation in public affairs in the United States. Given the popular perception that the women's movement in the Progressive Era advanced a radical perspective, it is not surprising that many turned to the public school to "restore" traditional images of women. In *The American Girl; her education, her responsibility, her recreation, her future*, published in 1915, Anne Morgan explained that the girl "must feel that the home is the unit of life, the object for which all science becomes worth while [sic]; that, far from a limit or a hindrance to her development, it is the center from which all effort springs and to which each new interest and higher ideals must be brought in turn."[8] In high school, students absorbed a gendered ideology along with geometry. An 1898 issue of *The High School News*, published monthly "of the pupils, for the pupils and by the pupils" of St. Louis Central High School, featured Olive L. Gregory's essay on "The Influence of Woman." Gregory described women's influence as a silent power ever operating for good and stated that the winning graces of women found their most fitting display in the home. This wording, however, was not quite right; Gregory followed it up with the observation that "Display is not the word—the very absence of it is the secret of her strength."[9] Gregory equated the influence of women with the influence of mothers, whose authority was "silent, unpretending, unmeasured."[10]

The high school acted as a force in the construction of gender even more intensely as the differentiated curriculum was called upon to prepare girls and boys for their sex-specific roles as worker and citizen. Extracurricular activity in the school reinforced the emerging directive that girls' schooling should differ from boys'. For example, the College Club held a series of vocational teas for Soldan High School girls in 1924, featuring information on occupations deemed suitable for women such as social-service work, journalism, and secretarial work. During the same semester, an editorial prompt for a new column devoted to student opinion in the *Scrippage* (Soldan's newspaper) proposed a question for the following issue: "Should girls and boys have equal rights on the campus and in athletics?"[11] Perhaps the issue was not of great concern to many students, for the question is not revisited in extant issues of the publication.

From Female Scholar to Domesticated Citizen is a study of the impact of the differentiated curriculum on girls' education in St. Louis public high schools, spanning the years from 1870 to 1930. The advance of the differentiated curriculum eclipsed the "female scholar" and launched the ascent of the "domesticated citizen" as the epitome of the idealized female high-school student in the early years of the twentieth century. Conscious of the preponderance of female students in the nineteenth-century high school, educators used gender to legitimate the transition to the differentiated curriculum, which has governed the curricular structure of secondary schooling in the United States throughout the twentieth century. Upon its introduction, the differentiated curriculum led to academic decline in St. Louis, altering girls' high-school experiences, and it served to restrict girls' access to certain kinds of knowledge, most notably mathematics and science. Once society accepted that schooling ought to differ among students so as to prepare each for her or his place in the social order, educators across the United States maintained that sex differences were an important factor in determining one's appropriate course of study. This rhetoric found expression in St. Louis as girls and boys gravitated to different curricula in the high schools. The notion that girls' schooling should differ from boys' aroused little protest in St. Louis.

*   *   *

Although it eventually became the dominant form of curricular organization in public secondary schools across the United States, the differentiated curriculum was forged in urban high schools at the end of the nineteenth century. This study focuses on the development of the differentiated curriculum in St. Louis, a leading urban center in the United States from 1870 into the 1920s. During this period, St. Louis was among the most highly populated cities in the country with a strong industrial economy, and it was recognized as supporting one of the best public-school systems in the United States. St. Louis has long been a conservative city in politics, economics, and social reform. Chapter 1 provides a brief history of the city of St. Louis, the geographical context in which this study is set.

In examining the ways in which educators used gender to sanction changes in the high-school curriculum and the degree to which girls' knowledge was restricted as a result, this study finds a place in women's history. Chapter 2 revisits the development of women's history in the last three decades. Initially historians addressed women's equality with men, focusing their research on women's restrictive communities. Toward the end of the 1970s, historians began to interpret women's communities as supportive and nurturing; this led to a study of what some perceived as women's "special" qualities. More recently the exclusionary nature of women's communities has come to the fore as historians consider ways in which women differ from each other. The thematic emphasis has passed from women's rights as persons, to sisterhood, to issues of diversity. As this study of women's history in St. Louis proceeded, it became clear that more work is needed to understand the full history of St. Louis women. Chapter 2 concludes with a sketch of issues as they affected women in St. Louis: social control, work, social reform, and suffrage.

The implementation of the differentiated curriculum brought about academic decline in St. Louis public high schools. Chapter 3 involves an analysis of the shift in educational philosophy and the corresponding transition in curriculum that occurred in St. Louis high schools from 1870 to 1930. Educators' nineteenth-century commitment to students' intellectual and moral development was overcome by a zeal in the twentieth century to train students as workers and citizens. Academic decline in the curriculum was measured by the introduction of nonacademic courses of study, a weakened academic component in the general course of study, fewer academic classes common to different courses of study, and a decrease in the number of academic classes required for graduation.

A strong increase in the number of students entering St. Louis high schools produced a major growth in student population after 1900. Yet, throughout the period of this study, high school remained the domain of a select group, as fewer than 50 percent of the St. Louis school-age population enrolled in the public high schools. Other than a sheer increase in size, gender marked the most significant alteration in the student body between 1870 and 1930. A steady decrease in the proportion of female students paralleled the philosophic and curriculum changes outlined in chapter 3. Data in chapter 4 show that the European-American working-class proportion of the St. Louis high-school student population increased from 21 percent in 1890 to 26 percent in 1920, while the African-American working-class proportion of the St. Louis high-school student population decreased from 81 percent to 61 percent. With the exception of a 10-percent immigrant student population in 1905, the proportion of immigrant students in the St. Louis high schools remained at 2 percent or less between 1900 and 1912, and increased to no more than 4 percent in the years 1913 to 1920. The percentage of African-American high-school students in St. Louis increased from 11 percent in 1900 to 13 percent in 1930. While the working-class, immigrant, and African-American percentages of the St. Louis high-school population increased by no more than five percent, the percentage of girls decreased from 64 percent in 1900 to 50 percent in 1930.

With increasing frequency in the twentieth century, educators expressed uncertainties of the appropriateness of an academic curriculum for high-school girls. As social role expectations and training for the job market became increasingly influential in determining students' course selections, a sex-stratified labor market opened the door for a sex-stratified curriculum. Based on an analysis of students' course selection presented in chapter 5, one can see that the implementation of the differentiated curriculum led to an eclipse of the "female scholar" in St. Louis. Similarities between African-American and European-American female students' programs indicate that gender was a powerful factor in determining one's course of study; at the same time, differences between African-American and European-American girls' course choices illuminate the impact of race on one's high-school decisions.

In St. Louis gender ideology legitimated dramatic change in the high-school curriculum that altered girls' schooling experience. Chapter 6 outlines the roles that New Liberal ideology, vocationalism, the "boy problem," and domestic feminism took in ushering the differentiated curriculum into St. Louis high schools. A way of thinking that recognized specific social roles for women, distinct from the roles of men, permeated New Liberalism, vocationalism, discussions of the "boy problem," and domestic feminism. Once these perspectives entered the high school, the function of schooling for girls was inundated by pressures to create the "domesticated citizen." Chapter 6 closes with an examination of the St. Louis response to the differentiated curriculum.

* * *

Girls' Schooling during the Progressive Era: From Female Scholar to Domesticated Citizen spans six decades, from 1870 to 1930. Although the first public high school in the United States dates to 1821 and the first high school for girls was established in 1826, few public high schools existed until after the Civil War. By the 1880s, however, public high schools had become the dominant institution in the United States for secondary education. Eighteen-seventy, then, marks a time when high schools were beginning to flourish. Much of this study centers around the turn of the century, when the introduction of the differentiated curriculum transformed the curricular structure of the high school. The analysis is carried through 1930, the last year that St. Louis educators designated graduates by different courses of study. Finally, women's historians recognize the years between 1870 and 1930 as a period when images of women were undergoing considerable reexamination. Issues relating to suffrage, birth control, women's work, and women's place in society in general created a social upheaval surrounding the "woman question." [12] To be sure, this early-twentieth-century social upheaval effected changes in the high school that proved to be of critical import for girls' education for the remainder of the century. In 1925 psychologist Winifred Richmond captured the fervor with which scholars and others had turned to the adolescent girl as a subject of interest.

> The last half century, which has witnessed the movements for the rights of women and children, with their far-reaching social and economic consequences, has brought her into a prominence which she had never before enjoyed. Her ideas and opinions, her education, her activities, social, economic, and even political, have become matters of grave importance, objects of study and analysis and subjects for endless controversy. [13]

Novelist Fannie Hurst graduated from St. Louis Central High School in 1905. In an autobiography she wrote, "When people said, as they were wont, and still are for that matter: St. Louis is a slow town, give me Chicago or New York; it seemed to me they must know nothing about Grand Avenue."[14] The enduring conservative reputation of St. Louis, combined with a significant population loss and major deterioration of its industrial base after 1930, obscure the luster of the city in earlier days. Borrowing from Hurst, there is a history to St. Louis that many "must know nothing about." In point of fact, St. Louis provides a rich context for exploring the impact of the differentiated curriculum on female high-school students at the turn of the century. Coeducation was never seriously challenged in St. Louis, one of the premier school districts in the midwest. Thus, from the time students first began classes in St. Louis Central High School in 1853, girls and boys studied alongside each other. When the differentiated curriculum was established, it disrupted a forty-year period of academic study common to both sexes. Coeducation, however, was the dominant form of education in public schools throughout the United States, especially in the midwest. St. Louis is an important district to study due to two factors. First, the St. Louis school system gained national prominence under the leadership of Superintendent William Torrey Harris (1868-1880), an educator recognized for his study of philosophy who later became the U.S. Commissioner of Education. Harris' position as the foremost educator in the United States during the last decades of the nineteenth century, alone, make the St. Louis schools a system worthy of study. But even more germane to questions underlying this study, St. Louis established Sumner High School for African-American students in 1875, allowing for a comparison of the effects of the differentiated curriculum on African-American and European-American girls.

Under the administration of Oscar M. Waring, principal of Sumner High School from 1879 to 1908, Sumner earned a reputation as the best-equipped, best-housed, and best-administered African-American high school in the United States. Teachers who joined Sumner's faculty were highly qualified, counting among them "graduates of Harvard, Yale, Howard, and Dennison [sic] Universities."[15] Editor Bohannon of *The Negro Educational Review* printed in 1909 that St. Louis had the "best paid colored teachers of any city in the United States and a school system far in advance of most cities of this section."[16] Sumner High School attracted highly educated teachers and scholars (including Edward A. Boucher, the first African American to earn a Ph.D. in the

United States), in part due to the fact that colleges and universities would not hire African-American scholars, and in part due to the high regard African Americans held for education. A statement in the *142nd Commencement Program of Charles Sumner High School* honored faculty with the observation: "Teaching must be the highest calling."[17]

* * *

Public schools have long been powerful institutions in the construction of gender, able to limit as well as liberate. Scholars in recent years have documented evidence of a hidden curriculum of sex-role socialization that takes place in schools through textbooks, subject matter, teacher behavior, counseling, extracurricular activities, and the organization of school itself.[18] During the twentieth century high school became an important institution in the lives of most people in the United States. Yet women's historians have made few explorations of girls' high-school experiences. The contributions that *From Female Scholar to Domesticated Citizen* makes to women's history are twofold: it assesses the impact of gender on the process to restructure the standard high-school curriculum in the United States, and it examines the consequences of the curriculum shift for girls. This research comes out of the critical tradition initiated in the late 1960s by educational historians who focused primarily on the effects of social class on schooling. More recently scholars have examined the intersecting impact of forces such as gender, race, ethnicity, social class, or sexual preference on one's schooling experiences. The intersection of gender and race are central to my analysis of the impact of the differentiated curriculum in St. Louis.

This work addresses a void in curriculum history by targeting the effects of a major curriculum change on *girls'* high-school education. In some aspects, the curricular pattern that developed in St. Louis was much like that David Labaree found in Philadelphia with his research on Central High School (for boys). Social class was a significant factor in determining high-school attendance early on, the differentiated curriculum assigned different values to the various courses of study, and the introduction of the differentiated curriculum resulted in a dilution of academic content.[19] The St. Louis study augments the existing roster of histories of high schools in the midwest, a comparatively short list that includes Chicago, Cleveland, and Detroit.[20] This research expands upon some of the issues taken up by Selwyn Troen in his 1975 comprehensive text on the history of St.

Louis public schools, particularly the intersecting force of gender, race, and social class on high-school students' course selection.[21] Evidence confirms Troen's position that the curriculum changes that occurred during the first decade of the twentieth century transformed St. Louis high schools into fundamentally different institutions. How this major transformation affected girls is not yet fully understood; thus far secondary schools have garnered precious little attention in women's educational history.

The field of women's history has grown considerably in the last four decades. Gerda Lerner documented that prior to 1960 only thirteen scholarly works existed on the history of women in the United States. Between 1960 and 1975, historians produced twenty-one new titles, the next five years produced thirty-six, and from 1980 to 1986 scholars produced at least forty pieces on women's history.[22] Women's educational history has been a part of that growth; however, the history of gender in secondary schools remains a neglected area of research.[23] In the last twenty years, women's historians have broadened their original emphasis on the history of higher education for women, producing what Lynn Gordon calls a rich literature on normal schools, women's academies, women in the professions, women as teachers, gender and literacy, the educational activity of women missionaries, women's roles in institutions such as settlement houses, and community and religious groups.[24] Gordon does not include secondary schools in a rather extensive list of recent developments in women's educational history, although some contributions to work on topics such as the education of immigrants, the relationship of women's education to women's work, African-American women as students and teachers, and questions of race, class, and ethnicity as they interact with gender in women's education have centered on the high school.[25] David Tyack and Elisabeth Hansot, John Rury, and Jane Bernard Powers have published significant research on girls' secondary education. As Sally Schwager and others have documented, however, the relative dearth of research on secondary schools leads to an unevenness in our understanding of women's experiences across the range of educational history.[26]

Thomas Woody's 1929 classic *History of Women's Education in the United States*, which remains the only comprehensive survey of the history of women's education in the United States, heads a list of historiographical articles on the history of women's education provided by Elisabeth Hansot and David Tyack in "Gender in American Public

Schools: Thinking Institutionally."[27] Six years before Woody's publication, Willystine Goodsell wrote *The Education of Women: Its Social Background and Its Problems*. Almost half a century and a subsequent women's movement would pass, however, before historians returned to substantial study of women's education. Ann Gordon, Linda Kerber, and Anne Firor Scott made early contributions to the study of women's education in the early Republic.[28] A good amount of research has been conducted on the history of women's higher education. Roberta Frankfort, Barbara Miller Solomon, Helen Lefkowitz Horowitz, John Mack Faragher and Florence Howe, Lynn D. Gordon, and Patricia Ann Palmieri have produced key texts in this field.[29] Biographical work in the field of education has highlighted the efforts of women such as Catharine Beecher, Nannie H. Burroughs, Myrtilla Miner, Lucy Sprague Mitchell, Almira Phelps, and Emma Willard.[30] Geraldine Jonçich Clifford's oft-cited essay, "'Marry, Stitch, Die, or Do Worse': Historical Perspectives on Vocationalism in American Education," is a major contribution to research on connections between education and women's work. Other pieces to read in this field are "The Labor Market and the American High School Girl 1890-1928," by Susan B. Carter and Mark Prus, "Vocationalism for Home and Work: Women's Education in the United States, 1880-1930," by John L. Rury, and *Sisterhood and Solidarity: Worker's Education for Women, 1914-1984*, edited by Joyce L. Kornbluh and Mary Frederickson. A number of texts focus on women's roles as teachers and their work in other professions.[31]

Barbara M. Brenzel's *History of Nineteenth-Century Women's Education: A Plea for Inclusion of Class, Race, and Ethnicity* points to an area in women's educational history that, still, is underrepresented in the literature. In 1982 the *Journal of Negro Education* published a symposium on the "Impact of Black Women in Education." Groundbreaking work in the history of African-American women's education has been published by Linda M. Perkins, Jeanne Noble, and Patricia Bell Scott. Maxine Seller is the prominent historian of the education of immigrant women, and Robert Trennert has documented part of the history of the education of Native-American women.[32]

In analyzing the impact of the intersection of gender and race on St. Louis high-school students' education, *From Female Scholar to Domesticated Citizen* aims to advance what is known about girls' secondary schooling, an underdeveloped area in women's educational history. A central thesis of this text is that the most significant curriculum shift in U.S. public high schools in the twentieth century resulted in a decline in academic education for girls in St. Louis. The argument is supported by an examination of students' courses of study in the period from 1870 to 1930. As John Rury explains, there is little evidence that speaks directly to the question of what students and their parents thought about changes in educational policy. We do, however, have evidence regarding students' courses of study following the implementation of the differentiated curriculum.[33] Evidence concerning teachers' classroom practice is also hard to find. Hansot and Tyack acknowledge the likelihood of some degree of gender discrimination in U.S. schools, but their reading of the prescriptive literature addressed to teachers leads them to the conclusion that within the classroom girls and boys met with similar expectations regarding learning and behavior.[34] My understanding is that prescriptive literature written after 1900 was more likely to cause teachers to assess the educational needs of girls and boys differently. One St. Louis high-school graduate of 1905, a girl who yearned for her teachers' attention, recorded that toward the end of her first year at Central High School, boys "began to bother me. . . . By the mere fact of their maleness they were accorded a superiority which irked me."[35] It would be difficult for teachers to ignore the voluminous professional literature calling for educational policy designed to socialize girls and boys to sex-specific roles, especially since the new ideas in education were consistent with other social and political agenda of the time. "Pedagogues often have stressed their intent to help students adjust to 'life'; they have rarely stated that their goal is to oppress women."[36] Yet during the Progressive Era, helping high-school girls adjust to "life" amounted to narrowing their educational opportunities.

Another key objective of this text is to explicate the argument that schooling became a major instrument for gender socialization during the Progressive Era, in a way nineteenth-century educators had not imagined. This research supports the work of scholars who argue that even though the differentiated curriculum allowed for girls and boys to remain side by side in many classes, gender roles at home and work became increasingly powerful in shaping students' academic behavior and goals. At the same time, gender ideology worked to refashion educators' ideas concerning girls' education.[37] In an article entitled, "Schooling Women in Citizenship," Susan Douglas Franzosa demonstrates that civic education in the United States has had much to do with socializing students to accept existing social relations: "Civic education was designed to train both male citizens and female civilizers."[38] Franzosa based her argument in an examination of women's education during the Jeffersonian period and the common school era; she concluded that those concerned with developing a civic education committed to goals and practices of a modern democratic society must recover the educational history of women.[39] The process of "domesticating citizens" that was applied to girls via the differentiated curriculum at the beginning of the twentieth century has an important place in this history.

In relation to recent works in women's educational history, *From Female Scholar to Domesticated Citizen* approaches curricular issues addressed by Powers, Rury, and Tyack and Hansot from a local perspective within a single school district, in contrast to their national focus. In addition, the St. Louis case study allows for comparison to similar local studies in California, making it possible to examine similar questions in different geographic regions.[40] Unlike histories on the women's vocational education movement, this text examines girls' schooling across the entire high-school curriculum. The St. Louis findings correlate with Rury's conclusion that the differentiated curriculum reproduced a social division of labor within the female workforce. The differentiated curriculum, itself activated by gender ideology, increased the significance of gender in the high school, a point also established by Brown concerning Los Angeles high schools.

From Female Scholar to Domesticated Citizen confirms a detail that educational historians have pretty much already accepted: even within the same school district, the differentiated curriculum did not affect African-American students exactly as it affected European-American students. This study also sheds light on a point that many probably suspect is true, but one that shows up less in the literature: not all African-American girls were affected by the differentiated curriculum in the same way. It is well known, for instance, that the Washingtonian system of education, which emphasized an accommodationist type of industrial education, swept through the South in the years between 1895 and 1915. And work that has been written on leading African-American women educators, such as Lucy Laney and Nannie Helen Burroughs, emphasizes their rationales for including home economics in African-American girls' schooling.[41] The fact that African-American girls were more frequently required to take home economics than were European-American girls—and in some cases encouraged to take special courses in preparation for domestic service—should not obscure recognition that African-American girls in some settings chose other courses.[42] In St. Louis, evidence shows that a higher percentage of African-American girls graduated from the Domestic Art and Science Course than European-American girls. Yet, more African-American girls selected the General Course than the Domestic Art and Science Course, suggesting that in high schools with a traditional academic heritage, African-American girls were likely to reject the home-economics curricula. Analysis of African-American girls' high-school course selection is a substantial component of the argument presented in this book.

Marguerite Stockman Dickson published a book entitled *Vocational Guidance for Girls* in 1919. In it she wrote that the teacher "must be a student of the 'woman question' as a vital problem, always recognizing that the whole social structure inevitably depends upon the status of woman in the world."[43] The New Liberal notion that women were to take on sex-specific roles in society, and that the progress of humanity depended upon girls being adequately trained for their predetermined roles, provided a foundation for Dickson's thesis. With appropriate schooling the adolescent girl would be "ready for the specializing which shall place her in tune with the world of industry and help her to make for herself a permanent and useful place in society."[44] Another element of *From Female Scholar to Domesticated Citizen* that separates it from other histories of women's secondary education in the United States is the nexus secured between New Liberal ideology and support for the differentiated curriculum. Other scholars have established the critical impact that New Liberal thinking had on public schooling in the United States, but characteristic of the pioneer phase in critical educational history, gender issues were not typically given a great deal of attention.[45] Reflecting upon the intellectual underpinnings of New Liberalism, however, adds depth to current understandings of women's educational history during the Progressive Era.

From Female Scholar to Domesticated Citizen documents the process by which educators retooled the high-school curriculum in St. Louis between 1870 and 1930. With the addition of the differentiated curriculum, the high school became a more efficient site for the construction of gender. The conception of "female scholar" receded as a consequence of this action. This story of the genderization of the high-school curriculum cannot be told apart from the history of generations of high-school girls who established a sterling academic legacy.

NOTES

1. *Nineteenth Annual Report of the Board of Directors of the St. Louis Public Schools, for the Year Ending August 1, 1873* (St. Louis: Democrat Litho. and Printing Co., 1874), 19: 108.

2. Cora Vinson, "Senior Reflections," *Maroon and White* (1931), 41. Sumner High School Yearbook, John Davis Buckner Papers, Western Historical Manuscript Collection, University of Missouri-St. Louis.

3. William Torrey Harris, *Fifteenth Annual Report of the Board of Directors of the St. Louis Public Schools, for the Year Ending August 1, 1869* (St. Louis: Missouri Democrat Book and Job Printing House, 1870), 15: 116.

4. G.D. Brantley, ed., *A Brief History of the Charles Sumner High School Saint Louis*, 5. Julia Davis Research Papers, Western Historical Manuscript Collection, University of Missouri-St. Louis.

5. Mrs. W. R. Chivvis, "1900 at Dinner at Central High School Diamond Jubilee," unidentified news clipping, 12 Feb. 1928. St. Louis School Scrapbook, Missouri Historical Society Library.

6. Ibid.

7. Gilbert B. Morrison, "Social Ethics in High School Life," paper prepared for the North Central Association of Colleges and Secondary Schools, Chicago, 1 April 1905, 6.

8. Anne Morgan, *The American Girl; her education, her responsibility, her recreation, her future* (New York: Harper & Bros., 1915), 23.

9. Olive L. Gregory, "The Influence of Woman," *The High School News*, 1898. The High School News (1896-), Newsletters, 1898, Western Historical Manuscript Collection, University of Missouri-St. Louis.

10. Ibid.

11. "College Club to Hold First Vocational Tea, "*Scrippage*, 10 Oct. 1924; "College Club to Give Vocational Tea, Nov. 12," *Scrippage*, 31 Oct. 1924. Soldan High School Collection, 1923-1931, Western Historical Manuscript Collection, University of Missouri-St. Louis.

12. Sari Knopp Biklen, "The Progressive Education Movement and the Question of Women," *Teachers College Record* 80 (Dec. 1978): 316-317; Jane Bernard Powers, *The "Girl Question" in Education: Vocational Education for Young Women in the Progressive Era* (London: The Falmer Press, 1992), 2. See chapter 2 of this text for an overview of women's history during this period.

13. Quoted in James W. Lichtenberg, "The Adolescent Girl—1925," *Journal of Counseling and Development* (February 1985): 341.

14. Fannie Hurst, *Anatomy of Me: A Wonderer in Search of Herself* (Garden City, NY: Doubleday & Company, 1958), 46.

15. "Oscar Minor Waring (1837-1911)," UMSL Black History Project Collection, 1911-1983, Western Historical Manuscript Collection, University of Missouri-St. Louis. Other colleges and universities attended by members of the Sumner High School faculty included Alcorn University, Berea College, Bowdoin College, Chicago Art Institute, Columbia University, Harvard University, Kansas University, Kings University of London, Massachusetts Institute of Technology, Oberlin College, Stanford University, State University of Iowa, Smith College, University of California, University of Chicago, University of Cincinnati, University of Colorado, University of Illinois, University of Kansas, University of Michigan, University of Minnesota, University of Pennsylvania, and Wesleyan University.

16. David V. Bohannon, "Editorial Comment," *The Negro Educational Review : A Monthly Magazine Devoted to the History, Science, Art and Philosophy of Education and to the Professional and Business Interests of the American Negro* 4 (August 1909): 31.

17. *142nd Commencement Program of Charles Sumner High School*, 3. UMSL Black History Project Collection, 1911-1983, Western Historical Manuscript Collection, University of Missouri-St. Louis.

18. Maxine Schwartz Seller, "*A History of Women's Education in the United States*: Thomas Woody's Classic—Sixty Years Later," *History of Education Quarterly* 29 (Spring 1989): 104.

19. David F. Labaree, *The Making of an American High School: The Credentials Market and the Central High School of Philadelphia, 1838-1939* (New Haven: Yale University Press, 1988).

20. See, for example, David L. Angus, "Conflict, Class, and the Nineteenth-Century Public High School in the Cities of the Midwest, 1845-1900," *Curriculum Inquiry* 18 (1988): 7-31; and Jeffrey Mirel, *The Rise and Fall of an Urban School System: Detroit, 1907-1981* (Ann Arbor: University of Michigan Press, 1993).

21. Selwyn Troen, *The Public and the Schools: Shaping the St. Louis System, 1838-1920* (Columbia: University of Missouri Press, 1975).

22. Seller, "Thomas Woody's Classic," 95.

23. Victoria Bissell Brown, "The Fear of Feminization: Los Angeles High Schools in the Progressive Era," *Feminist Studies* 16 (Fall 1990): 494; Sally Schwager, "Educating Women in America," *Signs: Journal of Women in Culture and Society* 12 (Winter 1987): 335.

24. Lynn D. Gordon, "Introduction to Special Issue on the History of Women and Education," *History of Education Quarterly* 33 (Winter 1993): 493-494.

25. Ibid.

26. Schwager, "Educating Women in America," 335; David Tyack and Elisabeth Hansot, *Learning Together: A History of Coeducation in American Public Schools* (New Haven: Yale University Press, 1990); John L. Rury, *Education and Women's Work: Female Schooling and the Division of Labor in Urban America, 1870-1930* (Albany: State University of New York Press, 1991); Powers, *The "Girl Question" in Education*.

27. Thomas Woody, *A History of Women's Education in the United States*, 2 vols. (New York: The Science Press, 1929; Seller, "Thomas Woody's Classic," 95; Elisabeth Hansot and David Tyack, "Gender in American Public Schools: Thinking Institutionally," *Signs: Journal of Women in Culture and Society* 13 (Summer 1988): 741-742.

28. Willystine Goodsell, The *Education of Women: Its Social Background and Its Problems*. (New York: Macmillan, 1923); Ann D. Gordon, "The Young Ladies Academy of Philadelphia," in *Women of America: A History*, edited by Carol Ruth Berklin and Mary Beth Norton (Boston: Houghton Mifflin, 1979); Linda K. Kerber, *Women of the Republic: Intellect and Ideology in Revolutionary America* (New York: W.W. Norton & Co., 1980); Anne Firor Scott, "The Ever Widening Circle: The Diffusion of Feminist Values from the Troy Female Seminary, 1822-1872," *History of Education Quarterly* 19 (1979): 3-25.

29. Roberta Frankfort, *Collegiate Women: Domesticity and Career* (New York: New York University Press, 1977); Barbara Miller Solomon, *In the Company of Educated Women: A History of Women and Higher Education in America* (New Haven: Yale University Press, 1985); Helen Lefkowitz Horowitz, *Alma Mater: Design and Experience in the Women's Colleges from Their Nineteenth-Century Beginnings to the 1930s* (New York: Alfred A. Knopf, 1985); John M. Faragher and Florence Howe, eds., *Women and Higher Education in American History* (New York: W.W. Norton & Co., 1988); Lynn D. Gordon, *Gender and Higher Education in the Progressive Era* (New Haven: Yale University Press, 1990); Patricia Ann Palmieri, *In Adamless Eden: The Community of Women Faculty at Wellesley* (New Haven: Yale University Press, 1995). Also see the following articles: F. Howe, "Toward a History of Women's Higher Education; Symposium," *Journal of Education* 159 (August 1977): 5-64; Patricia Albjerg Graham, "Expansion and Exclusion: A History of Women in American Higher Education," *Signs: A Journal of Women in Culture and Society* 3 (Summer 1978): 759-773; David F. Allmendinger, Jr., "Mount

Holyoke Students Encounter the Need for Life-Planning, 1837-1850," *History of Education Quarterly* 19 (1979): 27-46; Joyce Antler, "'After College, What?': New Graduates and the Family Claim," *American Quarterly* 32 (1980): 409-434; Barbara Finkelstein, "Conveying Messages to Women: Higher Education and the Teaching Profession in Historical Perspective," *The American Behavioral Scientist* 32 (July/August 1989): 680-699; Helen L. Horowitz, "Does Gender Bend the History of Higher Education?" *American Literary History* 7 (Summer 1995): 344-349.

30. See Kathryn Kish Sklar, *Catharine Beecher: A Study in American Domesticity* (New Haven: Yale University Press, 1973); Opal V. Easter, *Nannie Helen Burroughs* (New York: Garland Publishing, 1995); Paul Phillips Cooke, "Myrtilla Miner: Determined School Founder with Frederick Douglass," *Negro History Bulletin* 45 (Oct./Nov./Dec. 1982): 104-106; Joyce Antler, *Lucy Sprague Mitchell: The Making of a Modern Woman* (New Haven: Yale University Press, 1987); Emanuel D. Pudolph, "Almira Hart Lincoln Phelps (1793-1884) and the Spread of Botany in Nineteenth-Century America," *American Journal of Botany* 71 (Sept. 1984): 1161-1167; Nina Baym, "Women and the Republic: Emma Willard's Rhetoric of History," *American Quarterly* 43 (March 1991): 1-23; Philip Sheldon Foner and Josephine F. Pacheco, *Three Who Dared: Prudence Crandall, Margaret Douglass, and Myrtilla Miner: Champions of Antebellum Black Education* (Westport, CT: Greenwood Press, 1984); and Audrey Thomas McCluskey, "'We Specialize in the Wholly Impossible': Black Women School Founders and Their Mission," *Signs: Journal of Women in Culture and Society* 22 (Winter 1997): 403-426.

31. Geraldine Jonçich Clifford, "'Marry, Stitch, Die, or Do Worse': Historical Perspectives on Vocationalism in American Education," in *Work, Youth, and Schooling: Historical Perspectives on Vocationalism in American Education*, Harvey Kantor and David B. Tyack, eds. (Stanford: Stanford University Press, 1982); Susan B. Carter and Mark Prus, "The Labor Market and the American High School Girl 1890-1928," *The Journal of Economic History* 42 (March 1982): 163-171; John L. Rury, "Vocationalism for Home and Work: Women's Education in the United States, 1880-1930," *History of Education Quarterly* 24 (Spring 1984): 21-44; Joyce L. Kornbluh and Mary Frederickson, eds., *Sisterhood and Solidarity: Worker's Education for Women, 1914-1984* (Philadelphia: Temple University Press, 1984; Sandra Acker, "Gender and Teachers' Work," in *Review of Research in Education*, Michael W. Apple, ed., vol. 21, (Washington, DC: American Educational Research Association, 1995): 99-162; Richard J. Altenbaugh, ed., *The Teacher's Voice: A Social History of Teaching in Twentieth-Century America* (London: The Falmer Press, 1992); Kathleen Casey, *I Answer with My Life: Life Histories of*

Women Teachers Working for Social Change (New York: Routledge, 1993); M. Fultz, "African-American Teachers in the South, 1890-1940," *Teachers College Record* 96 (Spring 1995): 544-568; Polly Welts Kaufman, *Women Teachers on the Frontier* (New Haven: Yale University Press, 1984); Ruth Jacknow Markowitz, *My Daughter, the Teacher: Jewish Teachers in the New York City Schools* (New Brunswick, NJ: Rutgers University Press, 1993); Donald Warren, ed., *American Teachers: Histories of a Profession at Work* (New York: Macmillan, 1989); Ellen Fitzpatrick, *Endless Crusade: Women Social Scientists and Progressive Reform* (New York: Oxford University Press, 1990); and, Margaret W. Rossiter, *Women Scientists in America: Struggles and Strategies to 1940* (Baltimore: The Johns Hopkins University Press, 1982).

32. Barbara M. Brenzel, *History of Nineteenth-Century Women's Education: A Plea for Inclusion of Class, Race, and Ethnicity* (Wellesley, MA: WC, Center for Research on Women, 1983); "Impact of Black Women in Education," *Journal of Negro Education* 51 (Summer 1982): 173-357; Linda M. Perkins, "The Impact of the 'Cult of True Womanhood' on the Education of Black Women," *Journal of Social Issues* 39 (1983): 17-28; Perkins, "The Education of Black Women in the Nineteenth Century," in *Women and Higher Education in American History* (Norton and Co., 1988); Jeanne Noble, "The Higher Education of Black Women in the Twentieth Century," in *Women and Higher Education in American History* (Norton and Co., 1988); Patricia Bell Scott, "Schoolin' 'Respectable Ladies of Color: Issues in the History of Black Women's Higher Education," *Journal of NAWDAC* (Winter 1979): 22-28; Maxine Seller, "The Education of the Immigrant Woman, 1900-1935," *Journal of Urban History* 7 (May 1978): 307-330; William A. Proefriedt, "The Education of Mary Antin," *The Journal of Ethnic Studies* 17 (Winter 1990): 81-100; Devon A. Mihesuah, "'Too Dark To Be Angels: The Class System among the Cherokees at the Female Seminary," *American Indian Culture and Research Journal* 15 (1991): 29-52; Robert A. Trennert, "Victorian Morality and the Supervision of Indian Women Working in Phoenix, 1906-1930," *Journal of Social History* 22 (Fall 1988): 113-128; Trennert, "Educating Indian Girls at Nonreservation Boarding Schools, 1878-1920," in *Unequal Sisters: A Multicultural Reader in U.S. Women's History*, Ellen Carol DuBois and Vicki L. Ruiz, eds. (New York: Routledge, 1990).

33. Rury, *Education and Women's Work*, (Albany: State University of New York Press, 1991),132-133.

34. Elisabeth Hansot and David Tyack, "Gender in American Public Schools: Thinking Institutionally," *Signs: Journal of Women in Culture and Society* 13 (Summer 1988): 757.

35. Hurst, *Anatomy of Me*, (Garden City, NY: Doubleday, 1958), 49.

36. Gail P. Kelly, "Response to Angus's 'Conflict, Class, and the Nineteenth-Century Public High School in the Cities of the Midwest, 1845-1900," *Curriculum Inquiry* 18 (1988): 89; see also Maxine Seller, "G. Stanley Hall and Edward Thorndike on the Education of Women: Theory and Policy in the Progressive Era," *Educational Studies* 11 (Winter 1981): 373.

37. Biklen, "The Progressive Education Movement and the Question of Women," *Teachers College Record* 80 (Dec. 1978): 324, 331; Brown, "The Fear of Feminization," *Feminist Studies* 16 (Fall 1990): 505, 511-512.

38. Susan Douglas Franzosa, "Schooling Women in Citizenship," *Theory into Practice* 27 (Autumn 1988): 276, 279.

39. Ibid., 280.

40. Powers, *The "Girl Question" in Education*; (London: The Falmer Press, 1992); Rury, *Education and Women's Work*; Tyack and Hansot, *Learning Together*; Brown, "The Fear of Feminization," 493-518; Millicent Rutherford, "Feminism and the Secondary School Curriculum, 1890-1920," Ph.D. diss., Stanford University, 1977.

41. Powers, *The "Girl Question" in Education*, 21-22; Audrey Thomas McCluskey, "'We Specialize in the Wholly Impossible': Black Women School Founders and Their Mission," *Signs: Journal of Women in Culture and Society* 22 (Winter 1997): 403-426.

42. Powers, *The "Girl Question" in Education*, 90-91.

43. Marguerite Stockman Dickson, *Vocational Guidance for Girls* (Chicago: Rand McNally, 1919), 80.

44. Ibid., 151.

45. Groundbreaking work in this area of educational history was that of Clarence J. Karier, Paul Violas, and Joel Spring in *Roots of Crisis: American Education in the Twentieth Century* (Chicago: Rand McNally College Publishing Co., 1973).

Girls' Schooling during the Progressive Era

CHAPTER 1

St. Louis: The Future Great City of the World?

> The first time I ever saw St. Louis I could have bought it for six
> million dollars, and it was the mistake of my life that I did not do it.[1]

Mark Twain's avowal in *Life on the Mississippi* required little
explanation for his late-nineteenth-century readers. St. Louis had grown
to national prominence during the steamboat era, from a major frontier
trade center to one of the preeminent manufacturing centers in the
United States. The 1870 population of 313,301 established St. Louis as
the fourth largest city in the nation, a title citizens were eager to claim.[2]
Concerning its position relative to other leading American cities, St.
Louis was reaching its zenith in the final three decades of the
nineteenth century. By the third decade of the twentieth century,
however, it was clear that St. Louis had not become the "great city of
the world" that had been prophesied by enthusiasts of the 1870s.
Nonetheless, the transformation that did occur was no less significant
than that recorded by Twain during the years of steamboat ascendancy.

Urban historians have held the premise that cities were the central
arenas in which major facets of life in the United States were shaped.[3]
The proposition was on the mark regarding public high schools. The
extension of the high school in the United States during the twentieth
century reached into most citizens' lives. As Erving Goffman wrote in
Asylums, every institution has encompassing tendencies. But during the
first decades of the twentieth century, the circumference of public-
school influence on students' lives expanded.[4] Along with the growth of
extracurricular activities and Americanization efforts, the curricular

form that has come to dominate the public high school was forged in urban schools at the turn of the century. In the style of a new direction in urban history that emphasizes the city as a locus for change, this book draws upon the canvas of St. Louis.[5] To begin, demographic etchings of the city are presented.

FOUNDING AND EARLY HISTORY

> The difference between St. Louis and Chicago, Cincinnati and New Orleans, is not only, or mainly, that of larger and smaller, but that of origin, of history, of relative constituent elements in the sources of pride and in the social and other problems to be met. . . . This city has a life, a history, an influence upon the Mississippi Valley all its own.[6]

With these words Bishop C.F. Robertson provided a prelude for inquiry into the city of St. Louis. Perhaps a more representative example of nineteenth-century development in the United States would be difficult to find. The lives of a diverse group of people converged in St. Louis as it grew from a frontier settlement to a key distribution center to a primary manufacturing city. Its location near the confluence of the Mississippi and Missouri Rivers allowed the city to become known as the "Gateway to the West" as, for decades, pioneering adventurers of European descent encroached upon Native American nations. Further, St. Louis was a major player in the culture and commercial maturation that were generated by Fulton's harnessing of steam. Economic progress in St. Louis continued as the riverboat gave way to the railroad. Slavery, which was probably first introduced to present-day Missouri by the French as early as 1719, strengthened its hold in St. Louis with the migration of American settlers from such states as Virginia and Kentucky.[7] In 1820 the area became the focal point of the national slavery debate, which ended, in that instance, with the Missouri Compromise.[8] Finally, like other United States cities of the nineteenth century, the growth of St. Louis was propelled by immigration. So it was that the people of St. Louis found themselves involved in the defining issues of the U.S. political economy of the nineteenth century: the frontier, slavery, industrialization, and immigration.

St. Louis was founded 15 February 1764, by Pierre Laclede Ligueste and other members of The Louisiana Fur Company. The majority of the early settlers were French Americans who had come to engage in fur trading with Native Americans along the Missouri River. Walter B. Stevens, in his two-volume work, *St. Louis, the Fourth City, 1764-1911*, was careful to distinguish these pioneers from their European counterparts.

> While branches of these families, at home in France, were thinking the way to republican theories, the American offshoots were breathing free air and practicing liberty by instinct. There was little that was Parisian, and nothing of degeneracy, physical or mental, in the first families that settled St. Louis.[9]

The first families--those who were European American--did, however, accept slavery as a mainstay of their economy. African-American slaves worked in lead mines owned by French Americans before St. Louis was founded. After the end of the French and Indian War, Missouri slaves labored, primarily, in agricultural work.[10]

Although French Americans maintained great influence in St. Louis, the territory actually was ceded to Spain by the Treaty of Paris at the time that St. Louis was settled. The treaty allotted land east of the Mississippi River, excluding New Orleans, to Great Britain, while New Orleans and land west of the Mississippi went to Spain. The government of Great Britain adopted a more active posture toward the pioneers than that of Spain and, as a result, many French Americans moved west of the Mississippi River to live in St. Louis under Spanish rule. Spain returned Louisiana to France in the 1800 Treaty of San Ildefonso prior to France's transfer of the territory to the United States in 1803.

At this juncture, American settlers from Kentucky, Tennessee, Virginia, Connecticut, and other states began making their way down the Ohio River to the Mississippi. A strong southern United States element soon challenged the French culture of St. Louis. Although black codes had been established under French and Spanish rule, the newer arrivals patterned a set of black codes in 1804 after those in Virginia. Under these slave codes, African Americans were not allowed to testify in court, could not own or carry guns, and were restricted from leaving a slave owner's farm without permission.[11]

During the frontier period, then, St. Louis was governed by France, Spain, and the United States. Culturally, French Americans were dominant until after 1800 when the Southern influence began to grow. African Americans were held in slavery throughout this period, and

Native Americans came into contact with the citizens of St. Louis only peripherally.

The first steamboat arrived in St. Louis in 1817 and with it was borne a surge of commercial activity that would last through the end of the century. St. Louis' economic expansion during this period was built on its strength as a distribution center. Utilizing the expansive river system, St. Louis businesses could ship goods south to the Gulf of Mexico, throughout the southwest, and into the newly explored northwest territory. As the economy grew, major manufacturing firms were established to complement the distributive activity. Blessed with access to an abundance of farm land, mineral deposits, and timber, by 1870 the city had established industries producing flour and mill stuffs, clothing, tobacco, wooden ware, brick and tile, bagging and bags, as well as foundries.[12] In 1849 the city was hit by a devastating fire and a cholera epidemic. The fire, which consumed property valued at over three million dollars, seemed to revigorate the city's economy rather than retard its progress.[13] Just eleven years later, in 1860, St. Louis boasted 1,126 manufacturing industries employing 11,737 workers. The value of products produced that year was estimated at $27,000,000 with an additional $12,733,948 in capital. This was enough to rank the city's economy as eighth in the nation on the eve of the Civil War.[14]

The national struggle over slavery was played out in full on the smaller stage of Missouri and often the people of St. Louis were thrust into the spotlight, for instance, with the Missouri Compromise and the Dred Scott decision.[15] The fact that St. Louis had drawn its citizens from the South and New England was reflected in the operation of both the largest slave market in the state and a central depot for the Underground Railroad.[16] The southern element exerted greater control, however, dating back to the days of the drafting of the first Missouri constitution when a ticket of antislavery candidates to the constitutional convention was defeated.[17] The abolitionist perspective found some expression in St. Louis, Elijah P. Lovejoy's voice among them, but the abolitionist movement did not congeal into a potent force in Missouri. William Greenleaf Eliot, Unitarian minister of the Church of the Messiah and founder of Washington University, argued for African colonization. As president of the Young Men's Colonization Society of St. Louis, Eliot contended that to give African Americans

> equal footing, to give them equal political, social, and civil privileges
> with the whites is quite an impracticable thing in our day, and

probably will be impracticable for many generations to come, if not forever. I am by no means sure that it is desirable. I am certain of its impracticability[18]

Racist pragmatism characterized the thoughts of members of the upper intellectual echelon in St. Louis.

In spite of a dangerously racist environment, free African Americans lived and prospered in St. Louis. The first list of taxpayers in the city was not a lengthy one, but it included African Americans who owned real estate.[19] By 1858, African Americans controlled several million dollars' worth of real and personal property in St. Louis. Freedman Cyprian Clamorgan identified a select social group of St. Louisans as "The Colored Aristocracy," similar in description to an elite class in Philadelphia. In 1860, most of the 1,500 free African Americans in St. Louis, however, worked as waggoners, blacksmiths, carpenters, house servants, cooks, waiters, draymen, stonemasons, watchmen, carriage drivers, painters, gardeners, hostlers, stable keepers, store owners, chambermaids, washwomen, ironers, and seamstresses.[20]

Although free African Americans made up a small percentage of the total population, Lorenzo J. Greene, Gary R. Kremer, and Anthony F. Holland have made the point that the "widespread fear of the free black class as a potential threat to slavery manifested itself in laws and social customs designed to institutionalize black, rather than merely slave, inferiority and subjugation."[21] In Missouri, African Americans were not considered legally free without a deed of manumission, certified by governmental authorities. In 1835, laws were passed that required African Americans to purchase a "license" to stay in a Missouri county and county courts were required to "apprentice" all free African Americans between the ages of seven and twenty-one. An 1847 law forbade schooling for all African Americans and required a county official to attend all religious services conducted by African Americans. Yet the church and the school became two of the most important institutional vehicles for confronting legalized oppression. A number of examples recount the efforts of African Americans to pursue education in St. Louis, which was the only city in Missouri in which the African-American church achieved any measure of success against the stringent legal codes.[22] John Berry Meachum was minister of the First African Baptist Church of St. Louis as well as a businessman who owned a barrel factory in which slaves worked to purchase their freedom. Meachum continued to operate a school (using the guise of a Sunday school) after the 1847 law banning education for African Americans. When the school was discovered, Meachum built a steamboat, equipped it with a library, and anchored it in the middle of the Mississippi River--which was under federal rather than state jurisdiction. The school continued under these arrangements until Meachum's death in the 1850s.[23]

Slaves in Missouri were not freed by the Emancipation Proclamation in 1863 since Missouri did not secede from the Union to join the Confederacy. Slavery was finally abolished in Missouri by the new state constitution in 1865, just a few months prior to the ratification of the Thirteenth Amendment. This, however, did not mark the end of discriminating laws or racist practices. In 1867, Caroline Williams, pregnant and holding a baby, was pushed off a St. Louis streetcar by a conductor. She won a suit against the company, but was awarded damages of only one cent. This was the type of struggle that faced the Missouri Equal Rights League, founded in St. Louis in 1865.[24] Although African Americans had contributed a vital part in the building of St. Louis since its founding, the specter of slavery and the reality of racism would plague all inhabitants of the city for decades to come.

The people of St. Louis helped to shape, and were shaped by delineating phenomena of nineteenth-century America: the frontier, industrialization, the institution of slavery, and immigration. When the steamboat altered the course of St. Louis' economy in the latter 1810s, it provided another option for the latest arrivals to the United States. There was work to be had, west, in St. Louis. Immigration rose steadily, decade by decade, hitting peak numbers in the period from 1840 to 1870.[25] The Irish were established in the city by 1818 and Polish immigrants made St. Louis their home in the 1830s, but the group that would exercise, by far, the greatest influence on nineteenth-century St. Louis were the Germans. Appraising the impact of German immigration to St. Louis (22,340 in 1850; 50,510 in 1860; 66,000 in 1890), Walter Stevens wrote in his 1911 history of St. Louis, "So strong in numbers and virile in character was the German infusion that some philosophic minds contemplated the theory that the Teutonic element might assimilate the Anglo-Saxon in St. Louis and Missouri." Stevens hastened to assure his readers of nativist bent with what had become a "convenient" solution to the debate on Anglo-Saxon-Teutonic rivalry for supreme dominance over the rest of humanity.

"The result had not been the Germanizing of St. Louis, but an assimilation which has given notable elements of strength to an American city."[26]

The first wave of German immigration to St. Louis occurred in the 1830s. These were primarily craftsmen and women, artisans, and individuals interested in creating religious or utopian communities. The group that came to be known as "Forty-eighters" came to the United States following the collapse of the German revolution of 1848. Generally, these immigrants were better educated, liberal thinkers, and more politically active than others. Forty-eighters established German newspapers, theatre companies, and literature and choral societies in St. Louis. They manufactured chemicals, furniture, and clothing and established prominent brewing, milling, shipping, and hardware industries, as well as banks. The German influence in St. Louis was so strong that historian David W. Detjen notes that even "after the turn of the century, native Americans in St. Louis conceded their intellectual and cultural debt to the German culture of the city."[27] The St. Louis Movement, founded by William T. Harris and Henry C. Brockmeyer in 1857, was based on Hegelian philosophy. It flourished until 1885.[28] Along with philosophy, gymnasium-trained individuals led in scientific and musical endeavors in St. Louis. Perhaps the most basic concern, however, and the area in which German Americans created the most lasting impact on St. Louis, was the school system.

A German-language school was established in St. Louis in 1836, two years before St. Louis public schools were initiated. The effort to preserve German language and culture transcended social background to include all German Americans. By 1860, there were thirty-five public schools in St. Louis, enrolling 6,253 pupils and thirty-eight German-language schools with 5,524 pupils. In order to shore up support for the public schools, the St. Louis school board allowed for German classes in the curriculum in 1864. By 1888 there were ninety-eight German teachers and seventy-four bilingual German-English teachers employed in the public schools. The German courses were soon eliminated, however, due to nativist political pressure.[29]

German, Irish, and other immigrants were forced to battle nativist activity, which mounted a concentrated effort periodically throughout the nineteenth century. The Know-Nothings won every St. Louis city office in 1846.[30] Ordinances passed against Sunday use of public transportation, the sale of intoxicating liquors, and theatrical performances as a direct assault on German culture. German Americans

met on Sundays for recreation in the parks, theatres, and beergardens.[31]
An 1850s resurgence of the Know-Nothing Movement, seething with
hostility toward Catholics, brought riots against German and Irish St.
Louisans in the election years of 1852 and 1854.[32] What turned out to
be a temporary turning point was reached during the Civil War. Many
German Americans used their service in the war to prove their loyalty
to the United States. Unfortunately, nativism promoted by the United
States government during a later war not only questioned the loyalty of
German Americans, but effectively silenced German culture in St.
Louis.

Most of the citizens of St. Louis in 1870 descended from early
French settlers, American pioneers, African Americans, or Irish or
German immigrants. Their collective past involved experiences of the
western frontier and steamboat commerce, but industrialization and the
dominance of the railroad economy were on the horizon. St. Louis was
entering its golden age of national distinction.

1870-1900

Historians observe that "On its upper levels, by the middle of the
century, St. Louis life was Southern; but there was a strong admixture
of Yankee."[33] European ethnic groups joined the southern-dominated
culture of St. Louis increasingly during the nineteenth century.
Approximately one-third of St. Louis' 313,301 residents in 1870 were
immigrants. The overwhelming number of these (50,640) were from
Germany. Another major group (32,239) came from Ireland. Lesser
numbers migrated from England, France, Bohemia, Canada, Italy,
Austria, Belgium, Denmark, and Hungary. A few immigrants came
from various locations in Africa, Asia, Australia, and South America.
In 1880 the population was recorded at 350,522 and by 1890 it had
climbed to 451,770.[34] The city could not grow quickly enough for those
who praised its commercial potential. An 1878 review of St. Louis
hailed it as "the commercial center, the natural mart of seven hundred
thousand square miles of territory, full of mineral and agricultural
resources, and capable of sustaining in vigorous life a population of a
hundred millions."[35]

This was the age of the robber baron and railroad king in the
United States. *A Tour of St. Louis* informed readers in 1878 that the
"mighty dollar is truly the ruling influence of the age, to which all
mankind bows in sweet subserviency . . . "[36] Contemporary accounts of

St. Louis in the latter decades of the nineteenth century were filled with descriptions of the city's economic structure. Pages were devoted to details concerning businesses, manufacturing industries, raw materials, and marketing availability. Subtlety was not the greater part of the author's craft in these publications, as in, for example, *Saint Louis: The Future Great City of the World*. This book was, however, on the mark in one statement:

> The leading feature of the present age is the strife for commercial dominion. In this development of civilization is enlisted more capital, talent, and men than in any other.[37]

St. Louis built much of its nineteenth-century economy on the 45,000-mile river network that organized trade primarily in a north-south direction. With the emergence of the railroad, major trade networks began to run on east-west routes. St. Louis became a significant rail center, with sixteen distinct lines by the late 1870s, but was hampered in the east-west trade by the Mississippi River, ironically, its great advantage until then. It is not surprising to note, then, the considerable acclaim that accompanied the opening of Eads Bridge on 4 July 1874. "No structure upon the American continent deserves any more unqualified praise for practical utility and architectural beauty than the great steel Bridge that spans the Mississippi River at St. Louis."[38]

Once the bridge opened, St. Louis engaged in what one historian has described as a brief, unsuccessful struggle with Chicago for the title of railway gate to the West.[39] The people of St. Louis, however, did not let Chicago's predominance on the rails slow down their own economic growth. In 1880 the city boasted 2,886 manufacturing industries, producing $104,383,587 worth of products. These firms employed 39,724 workers and listed $45,385,000 in capital, placing St. Louis sixth in the United States in terms of investments.[40] Diversity was the key to St. Louis' economic strength. By the latter decades of the nineteenth century, the city's manufactured products included major outputs of iron and steel goods, clothing, shoes, tobacco, chemicals, streetcars, stoves and ranges, clay goods, and lumber. In addition, stockyards, breweries, and mills flourished. By the turn of the century, St. Louis ranked fourth overall among United States cities in manufacturing.[41]

St. Louis can not be excelled as a residence city, considering the
accessibility to suburban regions, its cheapness of rents, the absence
of all speculative prices upon its real estate, the thoroughness of its
sewerage and other well-ordered sanitary measures enforced, the
ample supply of wholesome water, the healthfulness of its
geographical position, the moderate rate of taxation, and withal, its
good government.[42]

The pride of St. Louis was not limited to its economic sector, as is
evidenced by this glowing report on the city's residential environment.
Citizens in St. Louis during the latter nineteenth century had access to
six daily newspapers printed in English, four in German, and twenty-
three additional weeklies. The city displayed an array of churches and
temples to meet the religious needs of its diverse population. The
Roman Catholic faith had been established in St. Louis since the early
days of the French, and the numbers of Catholic parishes increased with
the successive Irish, German, Polish, and other European immigration.
The other major pillar of the religious community in St. Louis,
Protestantism, planted its roots with the American pioneers in the early
1800s. By the late 1800s the leading denominations included the
Methodist, Unitarian, Episcopal, Presbyterian, Congregational, and
Baptist.

Organized religion, however, did not corner the market on moral
issues. The building of moral character was considered a crucial
objective of the public schools. Further, the push for moral reform
spread beyond these institutions and into other community arenas. For
instance, the people of St. Louis loved their parks, and many were
pleased, no doubt, to learn that they had good cause for enjoying
nature.

As a general rule, a love of the beautiful goes hand in hand with a
practice of the good. As the average amount of soap used by any
district is proved to be the measure of the average amount of good
behavior, so the same laws, working in the same direction, prove that
people who are brought closely and frequently in contact with nature
are really better men and women than those who do not receive those
advantages. The advance in civilization and culture of any people
may safely be estimated from the extent and variety of its parks and
gardens.[43]

It seemed inevitable that the two great concerns of the day, economic development and public morality, would converge, sometimes illogically, as is illustrated in this acclamation for St. Louis breweries. "Our great breweries are a feature in which a native pride must necessarily manifest itself, not only because of the enormous capital invested or the magnificent edifices which stand as enduring monuments of individual enterprises, but because in the proportion people adopt beer as a beverage, drunkenness, and the crimes consequent, diminish."[44]

The contemporary records of life in St. Louis during the 1870s, 1880s, and 1890s provided detailed accounts of the city's fine residential areas, the arts and other avenues to high culture, the elements of city government, philanthropic institutions, and so on. This side of St. Louis certainly did exist, but there was another image of the city that drew far less representation in the glorifying chronicles. As the owners and managers of the burgeoning economic enterprises moved away from the center of the city, they left those whose work had created the wealth struggling for survival, earning wages that could not maintain even the lowest standard of living. Abandoned mansions were transformed into squalid tenements, in neighborhoods with names such as the Cross Keys, Clabber Alley, Wild Cat Chute, and Castle Thunder. After a review of such living conditions, a city health commissioner astutely remarked that "the rights of property are ever jealously guarded, but the rights and interests of the pallid children of poverty are not so closely looked after."[45]

The panic of 1873, which brought bankruptcy and unemployment in St. Louis as elsewhere, plunged a depressed economy downward throughout the decade. Yet St. Louis society appeared to continue on two distinct paths. Then, events in the summer of 1877 forced a confrontation. Over expansion of railroads during the 1860s and 1870s led to debilitating rate wars. Companies responded by cutting or ignoring safety procedures in an occupation that was already highly dangerous, and by implementing a series of wage reductions. Finally, workers were forced into action. On 17 July 1877, the Great Railroad Strike began in West Virginia and within a few days its effect had spread across the country. Reverend Henry Beecher's reaction typified the response of the upper stratum of the two-class system that was forming in St. Louis and throughout the United States.

Is the working class oppressed? Yes, undoubtedly it is. God has intended the great to be great and the little to be little. . . . I do not say that a dollar a day is enough to support a working man. . . . Not enough to support a man and five children if he insists on smoking and drinking beer. . . . But the man who cannot live on bread and water is not fit to live![46]

Workers in St. Louis seized the moment of the Railroad Strike to call for a general strike. Specifically at issue were the demands for an eight-hour workday and the prohibition of child labor. Historian David T. Burbank has called the action "one of the first strikes anywhere in the world to paralyze a major industrial city; and without doubt was the first general strike of the modern, industrial labor movement in the United States."[47] Government forces were able to quell the St. Louis strike after a week, ending an explosion of frustration that has yet to be equaled and preserving the interests of capital. Conditions for workers changed very little.

Another image of St. Louis society that was given sparse attention by European-American commentators of the nineteenth century involved race relations. While the city may be classified as "northern" in terms of industrial development, it was clearly "southern" regarding racial diversity. In 1879, for example, many African Americans were migrating from southern states to Kansas. Often the trip as far as St. Louis would exhaust all of a family's funds, so it was necessary to find jobs in the city in order to accumulate enough money to continue to Kansas. European-American St. Louisans refused to help, perhaps owing to Mayor Henry Overstolz's prediction that the offer of jobs would bring more African Americans to St. Louis. Most travelers were able to continue their journey, however, due to aid from African Americans in St. Louis. The official St. Louis response was not repeated in Kansas City where Mayor George M. Shelley encouraged citizens to support those in need of assistance.[48]

St. Louis was a segregated city long before the 1896 *Plessy v. Ferguson* United States Supreme Court decision in which justices declared the "separate but equal" doctrine constitutional. In 1889 the Missouri legislature passed a law requiring separate schools for African-American and European-American children; however, St. Louis had operated segregated schools for as long as the schools had been opened to African-American children.[49] The state did not pass segregation laws covering public accommodations, but custom allowed it.[50] St. Louis was a city that produced volumes beckoning the world to enjoy its growing splendor, yet it did not welcome all of its own people.

1900-1930S

In 1900, St. Louis' population had increased to 575,238 and by 1910 it stood at 687,029. Much of the increase was due to immigration, with Germany and Ireland still leading the list of countries of origin for immigrants. At the turn of the century, however, significant numbers of people began arriving from Russia, Italy, and other southeastern European countries. In 1910 more than half of the population of St. Louis were either immigrants or children of immigrants.[51]

Contrary to popular notion, historians have determined that immigrants rarely established distinct, homogeneous, separate residential areas. One prominent exception to this finding had existed in St. Louis since the 1880s, the Italian "Hill." Historian Gary Ross Mormino has described the Hill as "one of the most stable, immobile, and cohesive ethnic colonies in the United States."[52]

Most of the Hill's residents came from Cuggiono in northern Italy. At first, single men immigrated with the idea of working in St. Louis to make enough money to purchase land in Italy. When these plans failed, the money was used to bring family members to the Hill. The period of greatest immigration to this part of St. Louis occurred between 1905 and 1907. Hill residents built a reputation as a blue-collar community with work readily available in the clay mines and tile factories of southwest St. Louis. Family was the unchallenged foundation of the community on the Hill. The undisputed symbol of success was the privately owned brick home; almost one thousand of these were constructed in the Hill's fifty-two-block area between 1900 and 1920.[53]

In *Immigrants on the Hill,* Mormino discusses possible reasons for the resilient ethnic bond that was maintained by Italians in St. Louis. Rural backgrounds, large families, a generally apathetic approach to schooling, nativist attitudes from others in St. Louis, and a sluggish urban economy all contributed to a weak economic infrastructure on the Hill as well as the community's self-imposed isolation from other parts of the city. Mormino cautions one not to judge Italian Americans as unsuccessful by pointing out that there are different measures of success. Hill residents preferred stability over mobility and community over suburbia, patterns of life that enabled the culture of Cuggiono to continue well into the twentieth century in St. Louis. [54]

Blue-collar workers, such as those on the Hill, made St. Louis the fourth-largest manufacturing city in the nation by 1910. In that year, 125,087 workers produced goods valued at $327,676,000 in industries with capital investments of $234,199,358. St. Louis claimed the largest shoe house, tobacco factory, and brewery in the United States. In fact, twenty-seven breweries made the city the second-largest beer-exporting center in the country. St. Louis industries produced more chemicals, streetcars, and twice as many stoves as any other city in the United States. One hundred sixty foundry and machine shops provided jobs for seven thousand people. In its manufacture of pipe, pottery, fire brick, terra cotta, and tiling, St. Louis easily led every other clay- manufacture center in the United States in 1910. Wholesale dry-goods houses sold a volume valued at more than seventy million dollars. St. Louis claimed the distinction of being the largest inland coffee- distributing point, the second-largest millinery market, and the largest hardwood lumber market in the U.S., along with boasting the largest horse and mule market in the world. Obviously, the strength of St. Louis' economic development remained anchored in its diversity.[55]

Characteristic of a capitalist economy, profits accrued by management in industry did not trickle down to the workers. Neither did the gains that were documented in the commercial sector influence any progress in social relations in St. Louis. There were 3,224 recorded lynchings in the United States from 1889 to 1918, eighty-one of these in Missouri (more than in the neighboring states of Illinois or Kansas, and more than in the southern states of North Carolina or Virginia). That this horrendous activity was not unfamiliar to St. Louisans may be suggested by the fact that on 31 May 1892, a national day of "humiliation, fasting, and prayer" was observed by fifteen hundred in the city to bring attention to the national atrocity.[56]

Evidence of discrimination against African Americans abounded in St. Louis. During the crowning period of industrial success, over 90 percent of African-American wage earners in St. Louis worked as personal servants, common laborers, and factory workers. Factory work was denied African Americans until labor shortages during World War I required a temporary end to job discrimination. After the war, employers returned to racist and sexist limitations in hiring practices. Racist attitudes permeated every social arena. In 1905, pastors of five European-American churches banned together to stop the sale of Central Presbyterian Church to the African-American congregation of Memorial Methodist Episcopal Church.[57] In 1916, St. Louis became the first city in the nation to pass, through the new initiative-referendum process, a residential racial-segregation ordinance. The law passed by a three-to-one margin.[58]

A few years previous to this action a progressive contingent of citizens concerned itself, not with the apportionment, but with the condition of St. Louis housing. A 1908 housing survey conducted by the Civic League of St. Louis paved the way for a 1913 New Tenement-House Law, which provided for, among other things, running water on every floor, lighted hallways, a mandate to keep tenements free of rubbish, dirt, and refuse, a prohibition on cellar-dwelling, and a maximum number of occupants per space.[59] The graphic detail of the housing survey may have helped to prod the citizens of St. Louis toward this action. Before the release of the survey many may have been inclined to accept the testimony of New York's Archbishop Farley's 1908 comparison between his city and St. Louis.

> In St. Louis the workingmen and poorer classes are much better taken care of in their homes than similar classes in New York. This results in contentment and prevents social troubles. I have seen no districts in St. Louis that I could call squalid. In fact, there seems to be no real squalor in the city.[60]

In the same year as the Archbishop's pronouncement, however, the committee conducting the housing survey documented a lack of running water, faulty drainage, unhealthy toilet and bathing arrangements, poor fire protection, and drastic overcrowding in the homes of thousands of St. Louis residents. In block after block, numerous families occupied dilapidated two- and three-story houses that had been abandoned by the elite in their mass exodus west of Grand Avenue. Multi-family dwellings that had been converted from single-family homes faced the streets, with rows of buildings behind them facing the alleys. Conditions there were even worse.

> Dilapidation, misery and dirt reach their depths in the rear buildings. The people who live in them are poorer, more sickly . . . than those who live in the front.[61]

The only water supplied in the majority of the dwellings researched in the survey was a lone hydrant in the inner yard of each block. When the water would freeze, or had been turned off due to leaks, renters had to carry it from neighboring yards. The yards also contained privies that were intended for common use. In the forty-eight blocks surveyed, 1,818 privies were counted to serve 12,251 persons. These poorly drained yards were the playgrounds of thousands of the city's children, but Charlotte Rumbold, author of the housing report, found a more piercing way to reach the progressive citizens of St. Louis.

> It is hardly necessary to insist . . . that such conditions breed fevers, tuberculosis and hideous unnamable diseases, and that such things spread. In the democracy of the street-car jam we come in perilously close contact with it all.[62]

The tenements were terribly overcrowded. People spilled over into wooden sheds originally constructed for livestock and basements that were often filled with water and infested with rats and roaches. Usually, the cellar-dwellers were elderly men and women. Again, Rumbold appealed to something other than readers' compassion or sense of justice. "Mostly when an old woman lives in a basement she takes in washing. Yours?"[63]

The wooden-frame structures, packed so closely together and cluttered with piles of trash, were continuously a spark away from disaster. Rumbold's comment on the fire hazards revealed an awareness of the skewed priorities in St. Louis during the early twentieth century. "Such conditions would never be permitted if these were warehouses sheltering merchandise instead of dwelling houses sheltering men, women and children."[64]

Of course, in St. Louis, as was the case throughout the nation in the early years of the twentieth century, housing reform was just one of a plethora of urban issues that came under examination. Some legitimate attempts at improvement surfaced in the area of civil rights, the women's movement, and labor. Yet, altruistic efforts were often clouded by self-serving interests in the cries for better government, better schools, and federal "protections."[65] One social reform that exerted a tremendous impact on St. Louis was prohibition. This movement, which had been fermenting in United States society throughout much of the nineteenth century, became more intense starting in the 1880s. St. Louis, with its vast economic investment in breweries and ethnic groups whose cultures included social drinking, remained wet, while one by one, the rural areas of Missouri were voted dry. German Americans took an active role in the fight against prohibition, which ended on 15 January 1919 with Missouri's ratification of the Eighteenth Amendment. Many in St. Louis joined in an effort to maintain this aspect of German culture. Detjen notes that "even more than the assimilative forces at work in the public schools, most German-Americans saw the temperance movement as a fundamental and, more important, an immediate threat to those elements of the German culture still embraced by the greatest number of German-Americans."[66]

The attention of St. Louis' German community abruptly turned to another scene in 1914. Pro-German sentiment was expressed by those with a cultural connection to Germany in the early years of World War I. Action such as a protest against the United States government providing economic aid to the allied nations was politically acceptable since the official U.S. position was one of neutrality. Yet the response to hold the United States within its neutral limitations was labeled as flagrantly pro-German.[67] St. Louis Germans maintained their allegiance to the United States throughout, and when the U.S. entered the war, public support for Germany ended. Yet anti-German hysteria that was whipped up throughout the country made its appearance in St. Louis. As a result, public schools and many churches abandoned the use of German language, German newspaper subscriptions declined markedly, and German theatre, which had been a mainstay of the arts in St. Louis, was silenced. The culture that had taken such a commanding role in St. Louis was deserted instantaneously. Detjen writes that "Never in United States history has an ethnic group so large and so well established suffered such a sudden and complete reversal of fortunes in time of war."[68]

By 1920, the population of St. Louis had climbed to 772,897. Slightly fewer than half of all St. Louisans, 46.5 percent, were native-born European Americans of native parentage. Thirty-one percent were native-born European Americans of foreign or mixed parentage. There were 103,239 immigrants who accounted for 13.4 percent of the population. The number of African Americans in St. Louis had risen since 1900, accounting for 9 percent of the total population in 1920. The census figures for this year, however, showed the lowest percentage increase since 1870, a harbinger of St. Louis' relative decline in population among major United States cities.[69]

Although declining in population growth, St. Louis, a city with 3,500 factories, 10,000 retail businesses, 26 steam railroads and 4 electric lines, still claimed to have "the most balanced situation of any great American city." St. Louis continued to define its economic character in diversity while other cities were building empires in particular industries. Pittsburgh, for instance, employed 35.5 percent of its workforce in the iron and steel industry and Detroit steered 33.5 percent of its labor to automobile factories. The largest employers in St. Louis, however, shoe manufacturers, accounted for only 8 percent of the city's total workforce.[70]

In St. Louis in 1920, 372,618 persons were employed, accounting for 57 percent of the population ten years old and older. Manufacturing claimed the largest proportion of the workforce, 40.7 percent; trade also supplied many jobs, at 15.4 percent; clerical work followed with 14.4 percent; domestic labor accounted for 12.6 percent of the workforce; transportation, 9 percent; professions, 5.2 percent; public service, 2 percent; and 0.7 percent were engaged in other occupations. Women made up 26.8 percent of the St. Louis workforce in 1920, about half finding jobs in factories. Twenty percent were domestics, while another 20 percent engaged in trade, communications, and clerical work. Less than 10 percent of employed women were professionals; most of these were teachers.[71]

Roman Catholics remained the most numerous religious group in St. Louis, attracting 38.9 percent of the population. Protestants accounted for 34.4. percent of St. Louisans. The city had a relatively small Jewish community in 1920, 2.6 percent of the population. Greek Orthodox and other faiths comprised 0.4 percent of the population, and 23.7 percent claimed no religious affiliation. In a 1924 church survey, H. Paul Douglass concluded that

> religion in St. Louis is socially more conservative than progressive. Its power to comfort people under conditions which must be borne at least temporarily had been greater than its impulse to remedy the conditions.[72]

St. Louis boasted a number of recreational facilities by the 1920s. The 1914 Pageant and Masque ushered in the Municipal Opera in Forest Park, home of the 1904 Louisiana Purchase Exposition. (Nineteen-four was also the year that St. Louis hosted the first Olympic games in the United States.) Henry Shaw's Botanical Gardens provided a pleasant place for some respite during the humid summers in St. Louis. Altogether the city owned 5,500 acres of parks and playground property, hosting thirteen community centers and a zoological park.

There were four swimming pools and four municipal baths equipped to serve thousands.[73] The Cardinals, the Browns, and the Giants (an African-American team founded in 1909) scored big with baseball fans.

In 1930, St. Louis had a population of 821,960. The African-American percentage of the population had risen to 11 percent, reflecting a nationwide trend in migration from the rural South to urban areas. Restricted immigration legislation in the 1920s kept the foreign-born population at 10 percent. The overwhelming majority of St. Louis citizens, native-born European Americans, accounted for 79 percent of the city's population. While nearing its peak in population growth, St. Louis was beginning to register a relative decline in the economic sector. By 1936 it had dropped to seventh place among United States cities in manufacturing. Exhibiting a desire to be "first" at something, a publication of the *St. Louis Post-Dispatch* relied on a well-established theme, the strength of industrial diversity in its (almost hopeful) statement: "St. Louis probably leads all other American cities in the volume of diversified production." It remained true that less than 10 percent of the workforce was concentrated in any one industry.[74]

The prime location for distribution and transportation, which in an earlier period led to St. Louis' emergence as a leading city, no doubt helped to sustain a place among the top echelon of cities in the early decades of the twentieth century. In addition to operating the second-largest railroad terminal in the country and serving as the focal point of the Mississippi waterway system, St. Louis added the Lambert-St. Louis Municipal Airport, and became an important crossroads in the developing interstate highway network.[75] Nevertheless, the 1930s were not years of economic prosperity, and in this regard, St. Louis was no different than any other American city.

The suffering brought on by the Great Depression was widespread, but it affected the poor and minority groups most forcefully. These were the individuals who were the first to lose their jobs and, generally, had access to fewer economic resources. The severity of the differences between economic classes was accentuated by a 1935 study based on census information in St. Louis. One of the more striking statistical results showed a positive correlation between the corrected death rate and indices of low economic status, such as relief and family service cases, medical-social cases, child-welfare cases, and juvenile court cases. At the same time, there was a negative correlation between the corrected death rate and indices such as median rentals, homes owned, homes valued at over three thousand dollars, and number of radios owned, all of which suggest higher economic status.[76]

Practices of discrimination that had been nurtured by custom and strengthened by law continued unabated in St. Louis during the depression years of the 1930s. The 1935 census report implicated the 1916 residential segregation law in causing the African-American community to experience the highest correlation of any group in St. Louis with population density and multiple-dwelling living.[77] Of the twenty-one higher-educational facilities in St. Louis in 1934, only one normal school and one institution for nurses' training were open to African Americans. All but ten of the city's eighty-four recreational centers, and seven of its seventy swimming pools and playgrounds were barred to African Americans.[78] Prejudice was part of the St. Louis social fabric throughout the period of this study. In preparation for World War II, the United States Air Force attempted to establish a training program for African-American pilots at Jefferson Barracks, near St. Louis. Pressure from St. Louis citizens prompted the Air Force to transfer the African-American unit, which distinguished itself in service during the war, to Tuskegee Institute in Alabama.[79]

CONCLUSION

St. Louis started to slip from a position of national prominence during the latter years covered in this study. Yet for most of the years from 1870 to 1930, the city ranked among the leading urban centers in the United States in terms of population and economic development. Although never a cultural giant, St. Louis was home to the foremost Hegelian philosophers in the United States, and, until 1914, cultivated an intellectual and artistic German community. In 1903, Harvard President Charles Eliot declared the St. Louis school system the "best organization of public education in the United States."[80] Although readers of Joseph Rice's exposé published ten years earlier might disagree, educators in St. Louis did create the first public-school kindergarten in the United States, pioneered in manual training in the schools, and established one of the outstanding public high schools for African Americans in the country.[81] St. Louis hosted a number of national political conventions and the general strike of 1877 broke new ground in the modern labor movement. In 1904, the Louisiana Purchase Exposition coincided with the third Olympic games in modern history to make St. Louis a focal point for the world.

St. Louis filched the title of America's fourth-largest city in 1870; presumably without the efforts of aggrandizing census takers, it placed behind New York, Chicago, and Philadelphia in 1890, 1900, and 1910. In 1920, the rate of population growth decreased and actual reductions in population occurred in 1940. In the next few decades St. Louis experienced the highest urban population loss of any city in the United States.[82] In the present day, then, it is difficult to imagine that St. Louis was once one of the most populous cities in the nation.

During the nineteenth century, St. Louis established a strong industrial economy. The "Gateway City" developed as a major rail center in the 1870s, which extended the vast range of trade already available via the Mississippi River system. By the turn of the century, workers and business owners in St. Louis had created the fourth-largest manufacturing center in the United States. This history, too, has been overshadowed by economic conditions that developed in the 1930s. During that decade, the St. Louis economy declined in relation to other cities. By the early 1970s, the St. Louis metropolitan area was marked as one of the weakest economies in the United States.[83]

In a sketch of St. Louis, conservative strokes dominate. The people who carved a city upon the banks of the Mississippi River in the nineteenth and twentieth centuries were conservative in politics, conservative in economics, and conservative in social reform. Notwithstanding tensions produced by opposing points of view, the political terrain of St. Louis was defined by its "southern character."[84] The black codes of 1804, Missouri's entry to the Union as a slave state, and laws intended to institutionalize African-American inferiority (1835 and 1847) framed an oppressive environment. Before the Civil War, representatives of an intellectual elite worked for African colonization and St. Louis courts ruled on Dred Scott's case. After the war, laws passed in 1889 and 1916 sanctioned the long-held custom of racial segregation. In a well-argued essay, Bourgois traced St. Louis' economic demise to the "Stranglehold of the Southern Oligarchy." Dealing effectively with other interpretations, Bourgois supported the theory that the general conservatism of St. Louis capitalists was rooted in an aristocratic atmosphere derived from Southern traditions.[85]

Douglass reported on the conservative dominance in St. Louis religious organizations in 1924, contrasting the situation with a progressive alternative. But even reform efforts that carried the progressive label exhibited conservative concerns. Charlotte Rumbold threaded her 1908 report on poor housing conditions with threats to the physical well-being of middle-class readers. The "democracy of the street-car jam" carried specific meaning for "West-Enders" who constituted the majority of progressive reformers in St. Louis. Working-class citizens identified the progressive elite as a "Big Cinch," motivated by self-serving interests. The working-class perception of progressive reform in St. Louis was that "Big Cinch" efforts were not designed to benefit the entire community.[86] Even in the midst of the Progressive Era, St. Louis generated a conservative climate.

In 1917 a social critic noted, "St. Louis is a melting-pot of different character from most large cities. It is a meeting place of the North and the South."[87] The unique character of St. Louis was shaped by intersecting forces. At the confluence of two great rivers, European cultures met the American western frontier. Defenders of slavery struggled against its demise for a century and a half. Industrialization impulses of the Northeast converged with traditions of the South. The process forged a conservative community—not the "Great City of the World"—but a city primed for study.

NOTES

1. Quoted in Gary Ross Mormino, *Immigrants on the Hill: Italian-Americans in St. Louis, 1882-1982* (Urbana: University of Illinois Press, 1986), 13.

2. St. Louis' fourth-place ranking was based on counting New York and Brooklyn as distinct cities. In sources that combine the boroughs of New York, St. Louis ranked third. Later evidence found the St. Louis 1870 census to be in error. William McKee, publisher of the *Missouri Democrat* recruited census workers with instructions to inflate the St. Louis total in order to edge out its midwestern rival, Chicago. See Mormino, *Immigrants on the Hill*, 14; Walter B. Stevens, *St. Louis, The Fourth City 1764-1911*, 2 vols., (St. Louis: S.J. Clarke Publishing Co., 1911), 2: 688-689; *Graphic Facts about People in St. Louis and St. Louis County*, Research Bureau Social Planning Council of St. Louis and St. Louis County (1947), 16-17.

3. Howard Gillette, Jr., "Rethinking American Urban History: New Directions for the Posturban Era," *Social Science History* 14 (Summer 1990): 205. Historiographical essays by Raymond Mohl and Dana F. White focus on urban history. See Raymond A. Mohl, "The New Urban History and Its Alternatives: Some Reflections on Recent U.S. Scholarship on the Twentieth-Century City," in *Urban History Yearbook* (Leicester: Leicester University Press, 1983): 19-28; and Dana F. White, "'The Underdeveloped Discipline':

Directions/Misdirections in American Urban History," *American Studies International* 22 (October 1984): 122-140. For updated evaluations of the state of urban history, see Gillette, "Rethinking American Urban History," and Margaret Marsh, "Old Forms, New Visions: New Directions in United States Urban History," *Pennsylvania History* 59 (January 1992): 21-28. The *Journal of Urban History, Urban Affairs,* and *Social Science History* are good sources for the study of urban history. No comprehensive history of St. Louis has been written. Noteworthy nineteenth-century texts include J.A. Dacus and James W. Buel, *A Tour of St. Louis; or, the Inside Life of a Great City* (St. Louis: Western Publishing, Jones & Griffin, 1878), J. Thomas Scharf, *History of St. Louis City and County* (Philadelphia: Louis H. Everts and Co., 1883), and Stevens, *St. Louis, The Fourth City* . The most prominent work of recent years is James Neal Primm, *Lion of the Valley: St. Louis, Missouri* (Boulder: Pruett Publishing, 1981). See also, Lawrence O. Christensen, "Black St. Louis: A Study in Race Relations, 1865-1916," Ph.D. diss., University of Missouri, 1972; Ernest Kirschten, *Catfish and Crystal* (Garden City, NY: Doubleday, 1960); and George Lipsitz, *The Sidewalks of St. Louis: Places, People, and Politics in an American City* (Columbia: University of Missouri Press, 1991).

　　　4. Erving Goffman, *Asylums: Essays on the Social Situation of Mental Patients and Other Inmates* (New York: Doubleday, 1961), 4. Developments in public schools at the turn of the century brought them into alignment with some aspects of what Goffman describes as "total institutions." School officials went beyond traditional academic concerns to organize play, in the form of extracurricular activities, and work, through vocational education. The various activities were rationalized as support for the stated aims of the school. It is accurate to describe schooling as the "handling of many human needs by the bureaucratic organization of whole blocks of people," Goffman's key fact of total institutions. See Goffman, *Asylums*, 6, 4-12. I am indebted to Paul Violas for bringing this interpretation to my attention. See Paul Violas, *The Training of the Urban Working Class: A History of Twentieth-Century American Education* (Chicago: Rand McNally College Publishing Company, 1978) for an analysis of the bond between compulsory schooling legislation, Americanization, the Play Movement, extracurricular activities, and vocational education, and public-school control of the individual.

　　　5. See Marsh's discussion in "Old Forms, New Visions," 23-24.

　　　6. Quoted in Stevens, *St. Louis, The Fourth City*, 2: 561.

　　　7. Lorenzo J. Greene, Gary R. Kremer, and Anthony F. Holland, *Missouri's Black Heritage* (Saint Louis: Forum Press, 1980), 9.

　　　8. The Missouri Compromise allowed for the extension of slavery into Louisiana Purchase lands south of the 36°30' north latitude. Missouri was

admitted to the Union as a slave state, in accordance with its state constitution, and Maine was admitted as a free state. See John Anthony Scott, *Hard Trials on My Way: Slavery and the Struggle Against It, 1800-1860* (New York: New American Library, 1974), 222-226. Mark Boatner describes the Missouri Compromise as the "First legislative compromise between the slavery and 'free' factions in a series of crises that led to the Civil War." See Mark M. Boatner III, *The Civil War Dictionary* (New York: David McKay Company, 1959), 556.

9. Stevens, *St. Louis*, 2: 668.

10. Greene, Kremer, and Holland, *Missouri's Black Heritage*, 10.

11. Ibid., 14-15.

12. Lewis F. Thomas, *The Localization of Business Activities in Metropolitan St. Louis*, Washington University Series, Social and Philosophical Sciences, no. 1 (Saint Louis: Washington University, 1927), 70.

13. Stevens, *St. Louis*, 2: 535.

14. Ibid., 455-456.

15. In 1857, the United States Supreme Court declared the Missouri Compromise unconstitutional in its prohibition of slavery in some territories and ruled that enslaved persons were not citizens of the United States, and therefore were not entitled to protection under the law. The Dred Scott decision was the first U.S. Supreme Court decision to declare an act of Congress unconstitutional since *Marbury v. Madison* (1803). It clarified the United States government's acceptance of slavery as a national institution by opening all U.S. territories to slavery. In its written opinions, the Court reinforced the notion that African Americans were not considered as persons, but as property. Paula Giddings writes that the Dred Scott decision prompted even the most sanguine activists to call for the violent overthrow of the slave system. See Paula Giddings, *When and Where I Enter: The Impact of Black Women on Race and Sex in America* (New York: Bantam Books, 1984), 60; Boatner, *Civil War Dictionary*, 247; Scott, *Hard Trials on My Way*, 230-242. There are few current works on the history of slavery in Missouri and St. Louis. The foremost study still seems to be Harrison A. Trexler, *Slavery in Missouri 1804-1865* (Baltimore: The Johns Hopkins Press, 1914). Other references include Donnie D. Bellamy, "Slavery, Emancipation, and Racism in Missouri, 1850-1865," Ph.D. diss., University of Missouri, 1970; Lloyd A. Hunter, "Slavery in St. Louis 1804-1860," *The Bulletin Missouri Historical Society* 30 (1974): 233-265; Benjamin G. Merkel, "The Abolition Aspects of Missouri's Antislavery Controversy 1819-1865," *Missouri Historical Review* 44 (April 1950): 232-253; and Earl J. Nelson, "Missouri Slavery, 1861-1865," *Missouri Historical*

Review 28 (July 1934): 260-274. See also Greene, Kremer, and Holland, *Missouri's Black Heritage.*

16. Greene, Kremer, and Holland, *Missouri's Black Heritage*, 31, 43.

17. Stevens, *St. Louis*, 2: 721.

18. Quoted in Douglas C. Stange, "Abolitionism as Treason: The Unitarian Elite Defends Law, Order, and the Union," *Harvard Library Bulletin* 28 (1980): 170; Merkel, "Abolitionist Aspects of Missouri's Antislavery Controversy," 234, 253.

19. Stevens, *St. Louis*, 2: 720-721.

20. Greene, Kremer, and Holland, *Missouri's Black Heritage*, 56-58.

21. Ibid., 48.

22. Ibid., 48, 49, 55.

23. Ibid., 54.

24. Ibid., 76-79.

25. The body of literature on immigration to the United States during the nineteenth and early-twentieth century is enormous. Readers may supplement personal accounts of the immigrant experience such as Mary Antin, *The Promised Land* (Boston: Houghton Mifflin, 1912) with the following government publications: *Abstracts of Reports of the Immigration Commission*, 2 vols., (Washington, DC: Government Printing Office, 1911); *The Children of Immigrants in Schools*, 5 vols., (Washington, DC: Government Printing Office, 1911); *Education of the Immigrant* (Washington, DC: Government Printing Office, 1913); and Caroline Manning, *The Immigrant Woman and Her Job* (Washington, DC: Government Printing Office, 1930). The *National Education Association Journal of Proceedings and Addresses* contained papers on immigrant education throughout the period under examination. Secondary sources to consult are John Bodnar, *The Transplanted: A History of Immigrants in Urban America* (Bloomington: Indiana University Press, 1985); Leonard Dinnerstein and David M. Reimers, *Ethnic Americans: A History of Immigration*, 3d ed. (New York: Harper and Row, 1988); Timothy J. Meagher, ed., *From Paddy to Studs: Irish American Communities in the Turn of the Century Era, 1880-1920* (Westport, CT: Greenwood Press, 1986); and Timothy Walch, ed., *Immigrant America: European Ethnicity in the United States* (New York: Garland Publishing, 1994). Work on immigrants in St. Louis includes Jay Corzine and Irene Dobrowski, "The Czechs in Soulard and South St. Louis," *Bulletin of the Missouri Historical Society* (January 1977); David Detjen, *The Germans in Missouri, 1900-1918: Prohibition, Neutrality, and Assimilation* (Columbia: University of Missouri Press, 1985); Mormino, *Immigrants on the Hill* (Urbana: University of Illinois Press, 1986); Timothy O'Leary and Sandra Schoenberg, "Ethnicity and Social Class Convergence in a Italian Community,

The Hill in St. Louis," *Bulletin of the Missouri Historical Society* (January 1977); and Margaret Lo Piccolo Sullivan, *Hyphenism in St. Louis, 1900-1921* (New York: Garland Publishing, 1990). On immigrants in St. Louis schools, see Michael R. Olneck and Marvin Lazerson, "The School Achievement of Immigrant Children: 1900-1930," in *The Social History of American Education*, B. Edward McClellan and William J. Reese, eds. (Urbana: University of Illinois Press, 1988): 257-286; and Selwyn K. Troen, *The Public and the Schools: Shaping the St. Louis System, 1838-1920* (Columbia: University of Missouri Press, 1975). Other secondary sources on immigrant education include Robert A. Carlson, *The Quest for Conformity: Americanization through Education* (New York: John Wiley & Sons, 1975); David K. Cohen, "Immigrants and the Schools," *Review of Educational Research* 40 (February 1970): 13-28; Marvin Lazerson, *Origins of the Urban School: Public Education in Massachusetts, 1870-1915* (Cambridge, MA: Harvard University Press, 1971); Michael Olneck and Marvin Lazerson, "Education," in *Harvard Encyclopedia of American Ethnic Groups*, Stephan Thernstrom et al., eds. (Cambridge, MA: Belknap Press of Harvard University, 1980); Joel Perlmann, *Ethnic Differences: Schooling and Social Structure among the Irish, Italians, Jews, and Blacks in an American City, 1880-1935* (New York: Cambridge University Press, 1988); John Rury, "Urban Structure and School Participation: Immigrant Women in 1900," *Social Science History* 8 (Summer 1984): 219-241; George F. Sanchez, "'Go after the Women': Americanization and the Mexican Immigrant Women, 1915-1929," in *Unequal Sisters: A Multi-Cultural Reader in U.S. Women's History*, Ellen Carol DuBois and Vicki Ruiz, eds. (New York: Routledge, 1990): 250-263; James W. Sanders, *The Education of an Urban Minority: Catholics in Chicago, 1833-1965* (New York: Oxford University Press, 1977); Maxine Seller, "The Education of the Immigrant Women, 1900-1935," *Journal of Urban History* 7 (May 1978): 307-330; Timothy L. Smith, "Immigrant Social Aspirations and American Education, 1880-1930," *American Quarterly* 21 (Fall 1969): 523-543; David B. Tyack, *The One Best System: A History of American Urban Education* (Cambridge: Harvard University Press, 1974); Violas, *Training of the Urban Working Class* (Chicago: Rand McNally College Publishing Company, 1978); and Bernard J. Weiss, *American Education and the European Immigrant, 1840-1940* (Urbana: 1982).

    26. Stevens, *St. Louis*, 2: 687.
    27. Detjen, *Germans in Missouri*, 7, 15.
    28. Ibid., 11.
    29. Ibid., 16.

30. The Know-Nothing Party peaked in popularity during the 1850s, capturing 6 governorships and 75 congressional seats between 1854 and 1856. The Know-Nothings flaunted an anti-Catholic, anti-immigrant platform. Originating in the Order of the Star-Spangled Banner, the Know-Nothings established a foothold in states that had been dominated by the Whig vote. The Know-Nothing power base receded with the rise of the Republican Party. See Donald M. Jacobs and Raymond H. Robinson, *America's Testing Time: 1848-1877* (Boston: Allyn and Bacon, 1973), 28-29; 204-206.

31. Detjen, *Germans in Missouri*, 8.

32. Stevens, *St. Louis*, 2: 745-746.

33. David T. Burbank, *Reign of the Rabble: The St. Louis General Strike of 1877* (New York: Augustus M. Kelley Publishers, 1966), 2.

34. Stevens, *St. Louis*, 2: 688, 691.

35. Dacus and Buel, *A Tour of St. Louis*, (St. Louis: Western Publishing, Jones & Griffin, 1878), 21.

36. Ibid., 201.

37. L.U. Reavis, *Saint Louis: The Future Great City of the World*, 3d ed. (St. Louis: Missouri Democrat Print, 1871), 111.

38. Dacus and Buel, *A Tour of St. Louis*, 125.

39. Burbank, *Reign of the Rabble,* 2-3.

40. Stevens, *St. Louis*, 2: 455-456.

41. Ibid., 2: 459.

42. Dacus and Buel, *A Tour of St. Louis*, 375-376.

43. Ibid., 44.

44. Ibid., 275.

45. Burbank, *Reign of the Rabble*, 3-4.

46. Quoted in Burbank, 11.

47. Ibid., 55.

48. Greene, Kremer, and Holland, *Missouri's Black Heritage*, 93.

49. The development of African-American schooling in St. Louis is addressed in the following works: J.W. Evans, "A Brief Sketch of the Development of Negro Education in St. Louis, Missouri," *The Journal of Negro Education* 7 (1938): 548-552; Elinor Mondale Gersman, "The Development of Public Education for Blacks in Nineteenth-Century St. Louis, Missouri," *The Journal of Negro Education* 41 (Winter 1972): 35-47; and Kurt F. Leidecker, "The Education of Negroes in St. Louis, Missouri, During William Torrey Harris' Administration," *The Journal of Negro Education* 10 (October 1941): 643-649. Aspects of nineteenth-century African-American education in Missouri are treated in Donnie D. Bellamy, "The Education of Blacks in Missouri Prior to 1861," *The Journal of Negro History* 59 (April 1974): 143-

157; Lawrence O. Christensen, "Schools for Blacks: J. Milton Turner in Reconstruction Missouri," *Missouri Historical Review* 76 (1982): 121-135; W. Sherman Savage, "The Legal Provisions for Negro Schools in Missouri from 1865 to 1890," *The Journal of Negro History* 16 (July 1931): 309-321; and Henry S. Williams, "The Development of the Negro Public School System in Missouri," *The Journal of Negro History* 5 (April 1920): 137-165. Philippe Bourgois offers a strong analysis of ethnic relations in St. Louis in "If You're Not Black You're White: A History of Ethnic Relations in St. Louis," *City & Society: Journal of the Society for Urban Anthropology* 3 (1989): 106-131. Other articles on ethnic relations in St. Louis during the 1870-1930 period include Lawrence O. Christensen, "Race Relations in St. Louis 1865-1916," *Missouri Historical Review* 78 (1983): 123-136; Katharine T. Corbett, "Missouri's Black History: From Colonial Times to 1970," *Gateway Heritage: Quarterly Journal of the Missouri Historical Society* 4 (1983): 16-25; Katharine T. Corbett and Mary E. Seematter, "Black St. Louis at the Turn of the Century," *Gateway Heritage: Quarterly Journal of the Missouri Historical Society* 7 (1986): 40-48; and Judy Day and M. James Kedro, "Free Blacks in St. Louis: Antebellum Conditions, Emancipation, and the Postwar Era," *The Bulletin: Missouri Historical Society* 30 (1974): 117-135. Research on African American schools in other cities is presented in D. L. Angus and E.K. Enomoto, "African American School Attendance in the 19th Century: Education in a Rural Northern Community, 1850-1880," *Journal of Negro Education* 64 (Winter 1995): 42-51; David L. Green, "Vocational Education and Race in the Chicago Public Schools: Three Historical Case Studies and Implications for Current Reform," *The Urban Review* 24 (1992): 39-54; Judy Jolley Mohraz, *The Separate Problem: Case Studies of Black Education in the North, 1900-1930* (Westport, CT: Greenwood Press, 1979); and David N. Plank and Marcia E. Turner, "Contrasting Patterns in Black School Politics: Atlanta and Memphis, 1865-1985," *Journal of Negro Education* 60 (1991): 203-218. Most literature on African-American education focuses on schooling in the South. Foundational primary sources are Horace Mann Bond, *Education of the Negro in the American Social Order* (New York: Prentice Hall, 1934); Bond, *Negro Education in Alabama: A Study in Cotton and Steel* (New York: Atheneum, 1939); W.E. Burghardt DuBois, *The Education of Black People*, Herbert Aptheker, ed. (Amherst: University of Massachusetts Press, 1973); DuBois, "Of Mr. Booker T. Washington and Others," in *The Souls of Black Folk* (New York: Vintage Books, 1990): 36-48; Booker T. Washington, "The Atlanta Exposition Address," in *Up from Slavery: An Autobiography* (New York: A.L. Burt Company, Publishers, 1900), 218-225; Carter G. Woodson, *The Education of the Negro Prior to 1861* (New York: Arno Press, 1968); and Woodson, *The*

Mis-Education of the Negro (New York: AMS Press, 1977). The best recent work on African-American education is that of James Anderson. See James D. Anderson, *The Education of Blacks in the South, 1860-1935* (Chapel Hill: University of North Carolina Press, 1988); Anderson, "Black Rural Communities and the Struggle for Education during the Age of Booker T. Washington, 1877-1915," *Peabody Journal of Education* 67 (Summer 1990): 46-62; Anderson, "The Historical Development of Black Vocational Education," in *Work, Youth, and Schooling: Historical Perspectives on Vocationalism in American Education*, Harvey Kantor and David B. Tyack, eds. (Stanford: Stanford University Press, 1982): 180-222; and Anderson, "Education as a Vehicle for the Manipulation of Black Workers," in *Work, Technology, and Education: Dissenting Essays in the Intellectual Foundations of American Education*, Walter Feinberg and Henry Rosemont, Jr., eds. (Urbana: University of Illinois Press, 1975): 15-40. Ronald E. Butchart's historiographical essay, "'Outthinking and Outflanking the Owners of the World': A Historiography of the African American Struggle for Education," *History of Education Quarterly* 28 (Fall 1988): 333-366, is excellent. Other recent works to consult are James L. Leloudis, *Schooling the New South: Pedagogy, Self, and Society in North Carolina, 1880-1920* (Chapel Hill: University of North Carolina Press, 1996); Theodore R. Mitchell, "From Black to White: The Transformation of Educational Reform in the New South, 1890-1910," *Educational Theory* 39 (Fall 1989): 337-350; and Harry Morgan, *Historical Perspectives on the Education of Black Children* (Westport, CT: Praeger, 1995).

50. Greene, Kremer, and Holland, *Missouri's Black Heritage*, (St. Louis: Forum Press, 1980), 95.

51. Detjen, *Germans in Missouri*, (Columbia: University of Missouri Press, 1985), 6; Stevens, *St. Louis* (St. Louis: S.J. Clarke, 1911), 2: 688, 692.

52. Mormino, *Immigrants on the Hill*, (Urbana: University of Illinois Press, 1986), 52, 67.

53. Ibid., 61, 113.

54. Ibid., 111.

55. Stevens, *St. Louis*, 2: 443, 487.

56. Greene, Kremer, and Holland, *Missouri's Black Heritage*, 96-97.

57. Ibid., 102, 111.

58. Mormino, *Immigrants on the Hill*, 19; Greene, Kremer, and Holland, *Missouri's Black Heritage*, 105. The United States Supreme Court ruled against a similar segregation ordinance in Louisville, Kentucky. Lawrence Christensen writes that this ruling, coupled with delays by Republican city officials, kept the

St. Louis act from going into effect. See Christensen, "Race Relations in St. Louis," 129-130.

59. "Better Housing: The New Tenement-House Law and Further Proposed Legislation," *Public Affairs* 1 (May 1913): 2.

60. Quoted in Stevens, *St. Louis*, 2: 521.

61. Charlotte Rumbold, *Housing Conditions in St. Louis: Report of the Housing Committee of the Civic League of St. Louis* (St. Louis: The Civic League of St. Louis, 1908), 31.

62. Ibid., 20. Charlotte Rumbold was a leader in the national public-recreation movement and an associate of Jane Addams. With Mary McCall, Rumbold founded the St. Louis Civic League. See George Lipsitz, *Sidewalks of St. Louis*, (Columbia: University of Missouri Press, 1991), 106-107.

63. Ibid., 34-36.

64. Ibid., 54.

65. Historical evidence in St. Louis supports Robert Wiebe's thesis that values of "continuity and regularity, functionality and rationality, administration and management," girded middle-class professionals' attempts to respond to the challenges of urbanization, industrialization, and immigration during the Progressive Era. See David H. Donald's introduction and Robert H. Wiebe, *The Search for Order 1877-1920* (New York: Hill and Wang, 1967), vii-viii. Edward C. Rafferty charges that progressive reformers' efforts in St. Louis for civic unity, urban planning, and governmental reform were built on the desire for middle-class control over the city. He argues that successful initiatives (the 1906 bond issue and the 1914 city charter are the most prominent) were few due to opposition from the working class. See Edward C. Rafferty, "Orderly City, Orderly Lives: The City Beautiful Movement in St. Louis," *Gateway Heritage: Quarterly Journal of the Missouri Historical Society* 11 (Spring 1991): 41. As a leader in the Progressive Movement in St. Louis, Charlotte Rumbold worked to curtail a lack of unity among citizens. Campaigns for playgrounds, public baths, parks, and adult education centers shared the theme of civic responsibility, as defined by the Progressives. After a new city charter that featured "efficiency, neutrality, and expertise" was defeated in 1911, Rumbold led Civic League members in a massive propaganda campaign in the form of the St. Louis Pageant and Masque of 1914. Lipsitz explains how the Pageant, held less than a month before the 1914 referendum vote on the new city charter, paved the way for voter approval. Yet discriminatory treatment of recent immigrants and total disregard of the 44,000 African-American citizens in St. Louis mocked the Pageant's motto, "If we play together, we will work together." See Lipsitz, *Sidewalks of St. Louis*, 108-112.

66. Detjen, *Germans in Missouri*, 179.

67. Ibid., 113-114.

68. Ibid., 1, 184-185.

69. H. Paul Douglass, *The St. Louis Church Survey: A Religious Investigation with a Social Background* (New York: George H. Doran Company, 1924), 37-38.

70. Ibid., 45.

71. Ibid., 43-44.

72. Ibid., 48-49.

73. Ibid., 46.

74. *Information about St. Louis Combined with Standard Market Data*, 16th ed. (St. Louis: *St. Louis Post-Dispatch*, 1936), 4-5.

75. Ibid., 4.

76. Ralph Carr Fletcher, Harry L. Hornback, and Stuart A. Queen, *Social Statistics of St. Louis by Census Tracts* (St. Louis: Washington University, 1935), 33.

77. Ibid., 20.

78. Greene, Kremer, and Holland, *Missouri's Black Heritage*, (St. Louis: Forum Press, 1980), 119.

79. Ibid., 124.

80. Quoted in "St. Louis School System Unequaled," *St. Louis Post-Dispatch*, 5 December 1903.

81. Journalist J.M. Rice conducted a five-month study of public schools in the United States for *The Forum*. The journal articles were reprinted in Rice's 1893 text, *The Public-School System of the United States*. In it, Rice charged that the schools of St. Louis were "the most barbarous schools in the country." A lengthy quote captures the essence of Rice's criticism:

During several daily recitation periods, each of which is from twenty to twenty-five minutes in duration, the children are obliged to stand on the line, perfectly motionless, their bodies erect, their knees and feet together, the tips of their shoes touching the edge of a board in the floor. The slightest movement on the part of the child attracts the attention of the teacher. The recitation is repeatedly interrupted with cries of "Stand straight," "Don't bend the knees," "Don't lean against the wall," and so on. I heard one teacher ask a little boy, "How can you learn anything with your knees and toes out of order?" The toes appear to play a more important part than the reasoning faculties. The teacher never forgets the toes; every few moments she casts her eyes "toe-ward."

That such a barbarous procedure should be tolerated in a civilized community to-day is surprising; and when we consider that it exists in a city which may be called the home of the kindergarten, it becomes truly marvellous. [J.M. Rice, *The Public-School System of the United States* (New York: The Century Co., 1893), 98-99; 220-221.]

82. Bourgois, "If You're Not Black You're White," *City & Society* 3 (1989): 108.

83. Ibid., 121, 124.

84. Visitors to St. Louis in the nineteenth and early twentieth centuries left accounts noting the dominant Southern element in St. Louis culture. Bourgois, 114.

85. Ibid., 112-113. Bourgois discusses the work of Wyatt W. Belcher, *The Economic Rivalry between St. Louis and Chicago 1850-1880* (New York: Columbia University Press, 1947); Primm, *Lion of the Valley*; (Boulder: Pruett, 1981); Julian S. Rammelkamp, "St. Louis in the Early 'Eighties," *Bulletin of the Missouri Historical Society* 19 (1963): 328-339; and Christopher Schnell, "Chicago versus St. Louis: A Reassessment of the Great Rivalry," *Missouri Historical Review* 71 (1977): 245-265.

86. Rafferty, "Orderly City, Orderly Lives," *Gateway Heritage* 11 (Spring 1991): 41.

87. George Mangold quoted in Bourgois, "If You're Not Black You're White," 120.

CHAPTER 2

St. Louis Women in United States History: Breaking the Silence

> In each field, the introduction of women changes the corpus of knowledge in major ways, and requires a wholesale reordering of priorities. [1]

> --Phyllis Stock Morton

Historian Gerda Lerner was part of a vanguard of scholars whose work broadened the body of knowledge deemed worthy by academicians to include the experiences, philosophies, and perspectives of women. As one who understood history as "an absolute lifeline to self-recognition and to giving our life meaning," Lerner directed her scholarship to the task of helping women come to self understanding.[2] With others, out of the fire of the feminist movement of the 1960s and 1970s, Lerner forged the subdiscipline of women's history and offered it to women as a primary tool for emancipation.[3] As women started to claim the power of history to give their lives meaning, historians influenced by feminist theory and research inched toward the realization that the inclusion of women leads to a reconstruction of the discipline. Peggy McIntosh charted a typology to mark the interactive phases in which scholars reexamine the assumptions and frameworks of their disciplines, a process that results in a more thorough understanding of the field.[4] William H. Chafe credits the development of labor history and African-American history along with women's history as significant levers in the transformation of the very meaning of history.[5]

A fundamental question that arises in women's history asks how gender serves to legitimate particular constructions of power and knowledge, and how this ideology is played out in a given political economy.[6] This book explores how educators used gender to legitimate changes in the public high-school curriculum at the close of the nineteenth century and how women's knowledge was restricted as a result of the curriculum transformation. Like the structure of women's history in general, this information may prove empowering to contemporary young women; in addition, an awareness of the impact of gender will enhance our understanding of curriculum history in the United States.

STAGES OF DEVELOPMENT IN WOMEN'S HISTORY

The McIntosh model of stages in curricular revision (stemming from the inclusion of women in the disciplines) parallels the stages Lerner predicted for the course of women's history (see table 1). McIntosh's term, "Womanless History," paints a fairly clear picture of the status of women in traditional historical texts prior to the 1960s. McIntosh's second phase, "Women in History," overlaps the first two stages forecast by Lerner: first scholars would seek evidence of women's historical existence and then they would recognize women's contributions to events in traditional, male-centered history. McIntosh gives explicit mention to "Women as a Problem, Anomaly, Absence or Victim in History," which, again, fits women into a male-centered history, but as the "other." Lerner's stage three and McIntosh's phase four mark the point at which historians began to recognize women's lives *as* history. Here women are recognized as active agents in history. Finally, both scholars point to a reconstructive phase. As gender analyses are introduced, Lerner predicted, they will radically unsettle traditional narratives. All standard topics in history will require reassessment.[7] So it is with curriculum history.

As Phyllis Stock-Morton notes in her essay, "Finding Our Own Ways," scholars in women's history have adopted many different methodologies. Historians have attempted to work with women's original sources, targeted issues that pertained to the "real lives" of women, and studied historical issues that remain relevant to contemporary women's lives. Within the last three decades, as Lerner predicted, historians have focused on women's oppression in the United States, chronicled the lives of prominent women, and documented the contributions of women to great historical movements led by men. Many now urge an approach to social history that acknowledges the complexities stemming from relationships between women and men *and* among women and from diverse discourses in society.[8]

Lerner	McIntosh
	1. Womanless History
1. Seek evidence of women's historical existence (biographical dictionaries, documentary collections)	2. Women in History
2. Recognize women's contributions to traditional, male-centered history	
	3. Women as a Problem, Anomaly, Absence or Victim in History
3. Appreciate enterprises women themselves shaped or reconfigured	4. Women's Lives *As* History
4. Recognize women's historical agency, restructure discipline	5. History Redefined and Reconstructed to Include Us All

Table 1. Stages of Development in Women's History

Sources: *U.S. History as Women's History: New Feminist Essays*, Linda K. Kerber, Alice Kessler-Harris, and Kathryn Kish Sklar, eds. (Chapel Hill: The University of North Carolina Press, 1995), 5-6; Gabriele Kaiser and Pat Rogers, "Introduction: Equity in Mathematics Education," in *Equity in Mathematics Education: Influences of Feminism and Culture*, Pat Rogers and Gabriele Kaiser, eds. (London: The Falmer Press, 1995), 2.

Rosalind Rosenberg has identified the major concepts in women's history with three distinct periods. In the 1960s, influenced by the civil-rights movement, women's historians emphasized women's sameness with men. Scholars wrote of a history that *happened to* women, featuring discrimination and sexist socialization themes.[9] Chafe agrees that the degree of difference between women and men, and the extent to which difference is the product of nature or imposed segregation and discrimination serve as dominant themes in women's history.[10] Chafe characterizes the emphasis on "sameness" in women's history as a liberal, natural-rights philosophy. Scholars produced evidence of separation and differential treatment of women in U.S. history that contradicted women's natural rights to self-determination and equal opportunity. Historians stressed women's efforts to reform social, political, and economic institutions in the effort to assimilate women as individuals into the existing society. The notion of a "women's culture" was dismissed as a by-product of separation and oppression. [11]

In the mid-1970s, however, historians began to underscore the importance of women's differences from men. Rosenberg writes that this was the period when scholars defined women as agents of change who openly criticized the dominant political system, nurtured by a separate culture. The objective for many was to identify ways in which women's distinctive values (interdependency and community, for example) had altered the course of history.[12] Chafe wrote that these scholars are often accused of being essentialists, those who believe that all women share values, temperament, and concerns that distinguish them from men. Historians in this camp celebrated "sisterhood" as a powerful, global phenomenon. The idea of separatism as a strategy for change dominated this period of historical analysis. [13]

Since the mid-1980s, historians have increasingly argued that gender has not always been the most powerful force in shaping women's lives. Rosenberg points out that differences between women and men have often been inconsequential when compared to differences among women of different social class, race, ethnicity, religious background, sexuality, or geography.[14] Ellen Carol DuBois and Vicki L. Ruiz, editors of *Unequal Sisters: A Multicultural Reader in U.S. Women's History*, assert that a more complex approach to women's history is needed to "illuminate the interconnections among the various systems of power that shape women's lives."[15] Following the period of women's history that assumed a universal female experience, some historians adopted a biracial approach for examining power among women. As DuBois and Ruiz point out, this paradigm was limited in that it compacted all nonwhite women into a single, "other" voice. Some scholars acknowledge the necessity of a multicultural approach to women's history that allows for overlapping narratives and recognizes multiple forms of power. The multicultural approach has already influenced the shape of women's history, just as women's history has influenced the shape of traditional, male-centered history.[16]

Nancy A. Hewitt's historiographical essay, "Beyond the Search for Sisterhood: American Women's History in the 1980s," illustrates the centrality of community in the shifting paradigms of women's history in that decade. As others have noted, women's history in the 1960s and early 1970s operated from the premise that gender was the primary source of oppression and that it served as a model for all other forms of oppression. Historians examined the restrictive bonds about women in education, medicine, the church, the state, and the family. Scholars acknowledge, however, that some gender oppression was double-edged: inclusion in an all-female enclave could be interpreted as supportive.[17] Hewitt contends that the "true woman/separate spheres/woman's culture triad" based on the scholarship of Barbara Welter, Nancy Cott, and Carroll Smith-Rosenberg, became the most widely used framework for interpreting women's history in the United States.[18] The community that formed inside the separate women's sphere was indeed a source of solidarity for the women encompassed within. Although the existence of a women's culture did not automatically translate into a solid public female sphere, Estelle Freedman's 1979 essay, "Separatism as Strategy: Female Institution Building and American Feminism, 1870-1930," attested to the strength of a separatist political strategy based in a women's culture.[19] In point of fact, from the mid-1970s into the 1980s, historians touted "separatism as strategy" as the leading paradigm in U.S. women's history. More recently, historians have studied the lives of women who were not welcomed into the women's sphere constructed by the middle-class; they offer another interpretation. The communities that served as secure, nurturing places for some women most often were spaces of exclusion for others. The incomplete "sisterhood" nursed prejudice as well as esprit de corps.[20] In different phases of U.S. women's history, then, community was perceived as restrictive, supportive, or exclusive.

The degree to which the metaphor of separate spheres has dominated the evolution of women's history in the United States is most clearly expressed by Linda Kerber in "Separate Spheres, Female Worlds, Woman's Place: The Rhetoric of Women's History." Historians' reliance on "separate spheres" in determining what to study regarding women, and how to report one's findings, can be traced to Alexis de Tocqueville, according to Kerber. Writing in *Democracy in America* that "the inexorable opinion of the public carefully circumscribes [married women] within the narrow circle of domestic interests and duties and forbids her to step beyond it," Tocqueville handed historians the trope used to describe women's part in United States culture.[21] The image of a circle as a limiting boundary on women's choices became a presupposition for historians of United

States history.[22] Kerber shows that the work of women's historians in the mid-1960s sprang from both Tocqueville's (positive) notion of separate spheres and Friedrich Engels' dichotomy between the public and private modes of life.[23] The period of women's history represented by scholars such as Barbara Welter, Aileen S. Kraditor, and Gerda Lerner equated separate spheres with subordination, deteriorating status, and the victimization of women.[24] Kerber focuses on the research of Carroll Smith-Rosenberg, Blanche Wiesen Cook, Kathryn Kish Sklar, Nancy F. Cott, and Carl N. Degler to characterize the period of women's history that turned the separate-spheres ideology on its head; throughout the 1970s, historians emphasized the supportive function of separate spheres for women. By the 1980s, the position from which scholars might survey the history of women in the United States was problematic. As Kerber notes, the separate-spheres metaphor, built almost exclusively around the experiences of white, middle-class women, allowed historians to avoid thinking about race. In addition, the metaphor itself was vulnerable to sloppy use; "separate spheres" often meant an ideology *imposed on* women, a culture *created by* women, and a set of boundaries *expected to be observed by* women.[25] In the latest phase of development in women's history, scholars address these problems. In unpacking the dominant metaphor in women's history, historians now ask how separate spheres have been socially constructed both for and by women.[26] The direction is toward a more complex analysis that moves beyond "the dualisms of the past, dichotomies which teach that women must be understood not in terms of relationship—with other women and with men—but of difference and apartness."[27] Finally, in Kerber's essay one is presented with a depiction of "separate spheres" as a strategy that has enabled historians to move the history of women out of the realm of the trivial and anecdotal and into the realm of analytic social history.[28]

Much of the richness of women's history as it is being written today emerges from the necessity to examine relationships *among* women and to contemplate the impact of the *intersection* of gender, ethnicity, class, sexuality, and other aspects of one's identity in understanding one's position in a given political-economic network. Audre Lorde's prose emphasizes the weakness inherent in a perspective that ignores issues of power other than gender.

> What woman here is so enamored of her own oppression that she cannot see her heelprint upon another woman's face. What woman's

terms of oppression have become precious and necessary to her as a ticket into the fold of the righteous, away from the cold winds of self-scrutiny.[29]

Until recently, African-American women have been virtually invisible in published research in women's history and women's studies.[30] Studies that address the intersection of ethnicity and gender are even less common. Beverly Guy-Sheftall notes that although the period from 1880 to 1920 represents a high point in women's history and a low point in African-American history, relatively little scholarly work on this period has the intersection of race and gender as a focus.[31] Many scholars agree that the tendency to assess the effect of race or gender independently of the other results in a simplistic analysis.[32]

Elsa Barkley Brown warns that the exclusion of African-American women from early histories has meant that the concepts, perspectives, methods, and pedagogies of women's history have developed without consideration of the considerable experiences of African-American women.[33] For instance, a popular methodology in women's history highlights the perspectives of exemplary individuals. This approach is inadequate to represent the experiences of African Americans who created a collective response to oppression in the United States, argues Barbara Omolade.[34] African-American scholars counter the intellectual perspective based on a division between racism and sexism with "a consciousness that incorporates racial, cultural, sexual, national, economic, and political considerations."[35] This is "womanist consciousness," as defined by Alice Walker and Chikwenye Okonjo Ogunyemi. Womanist consciousness leads not only to the sort of complex analyses that mark the current phase of women's history, but also to a "dynamism of wholeness and self-healing" for women and men.[36]

Methodological insights of multiple oppressions may be a recent addition to the literature of women's history, but these ideas are rooted in the work of scholars Anna Julia Cooper, Mary Church Terrell, Fannie Barrier Williams and others.[37] In 1893, Anna Julia Cooper addressed the World's Congress of Representative Women in Chicago, emphasizing the connecting links between racism and sexism.

Let woman's claim be as broad in the concrete as in the abstract. *We take our stand on the solidarity of humanity, the oneness of life,* and the unnaturalness and injustice of all special favoritisms, whether of sex, race, country, or condition. If one link of the chain be broken, the chain is broken. . . . The colored woman feels that woman's cause is one and universal; and that not till . . . race, color, sex, and condition are seen as the accidents, and not the substance of life; . . . not till then is woman's lesson taught and woman's cause won—not the white woman's, nor the black woman's, nor the red woman's, but the cause of every man and of every woman who has writhed silently under a mighty wrong. Woman's *wrongs are thus indissolubly linked with all undefended woe, and the acquirement of her "rights" will mean the final triumph of all right over might,* the supremacy of the moral forces of reason, and justice, and love in the government of the nations of the earth.[38]

Women's history needs to recapture the complexity of Cooper's vision if it is to adequately represent her struggle. The lifeline that gives our lives meaning is composed of many strands.

Scholars now recognize that differences among women are a "far more salient reality than the common bonds that unite them. "[39] As mentioned in the introduction, this text explores the impact of the differentiated curriculum on women high-school students in one particular school district, and therefore seeks an understanding of how decisions regarding secondary schooling have been influenced by perceptions of gender. The St. Louis case study, however, provides opportunity to weigh the effect of the intersection of gender, race, and class on girls' high-school experiences at the beginning of the twentieth century. The analytical framework employed here, a model of intersections, is in alignment with what one historian characterizes as the "most profound conclusion of feminist scholars in recent years."[40]

Although educational historians are now beginning to study secondary-school curriculum through a gender-sensitive lens, the amount of historical research on gender in primary and secondary schools is inadequate.[41] Studies that target the effect of gender *and* race on secondary schooling from a historical perspective are even more rare. Like other areas of women's history, then, conclusions regarding the impact of the differentiated curriculum on female high-school students have been reached without full consideration of the experiences of African-American students. To be sure, the path-breaking work of Millicent Rutherford, David Tyack and Elisabeth Hansot, Victoria Bissell Brown, John Rury, and Jane Bernard Powers has enhanced our understanding of the history of secondary schools in the United States by focusing their analyses on the schooling experiences of women and girls.[42] Some effort has been made to acknowledge the degree to which young women's high-school experiences differed according to race, but this work has, largely, been presented in general terms. The detail provided in this book allows one to contrast the force of the differentiated curriculum on African-American and European-American female students within similar, but segregated, school environments. Since the late 1960s, educational historians have argued that curriculum changes implemented in public high schools during the Progressive Era did not affect all students in the same ways; social class and ethnicity were key determinants in shaping one's schooling experiences. More recently scholars have written that these curriculum changes did not affect girls exactly as they affected boys. The latest work in women's history leads one to believe that the girls' schooling experiences were not monolithic. One of the objectives of this study is to discern significant differences among women students in St. Louis public high schools as they responded to the imposition of a differentiated curriculum.

One of the central questions posed by both educational historians and women's historians focuses on the power of ideology in bringing about social change. Having gone beyond the binary analytical model of women acting, or being acted upon, women's historians now engage in richer study as they try to determine how choices have been made both by and for women. This approach parallels the recognition by critical educational historians that, even within a hegemonic social institution, those with the least amounts of power still retain a degree of human agency.[43] The task for the historian is a delicate one: how to weigh the amorphous authority of ideology against the capacity of the individual to resist. In addressing this challenge in women's history, one cannot afford to neglect the force of dominant worldviews. "The subtle role of ideology and the nature of social expectation play significant roles in shaping what women want and how they perceive the world around them."[44]

Alice Kessler-Harris' "Reflections on a Field" suggests that historians understand gender as a process, one continually constructed and reconstructed both as a function of individual identity and also through community, family, religious institutions, and schools.[45] The watershed moment in the definition of the twentieth-century American high school offers a vantage point from which one might examine the construction of gender through school. A study of the impact of the differentiated curriculum on women high-school students provides a vehicle for addressing key questions in women's history as outlined by Kessler-Harris. In what ways did a gender system frame the choices of young women and men regarding selection of high-school curriculum? What economic and social reward systems helped to keep the gender system in place in schools? In what ways did students adapt to and resist the gender system sustained by the differentiated curriculum?[46] This is the theoretical ground upon which *From Female Scholar to Domesticated Citizen* rests. This study fits Kessler-Harris' description of the efforts of women's historians to comprehend gender as a salient factor in the social order, to find out how a larger gender system pulls together diffuse individual and social elements to regulate expectations and aspirations.[47]

WOMEN IN ST. LOUIS: 1870 TO 1930

Historian Linda Kerber posits that the decades from 1870 to 1920 may be the high-water mark of women's public influence in the United States, given women's level of activity in voluntary organizations, trade unions, political organizations, and the professions.[48] What was life like for the women of St. Louis during this period? Celebrated histories of the city are limited in addressing this question, for they contain, at best, scant references to women. For example, James Neal Primm's 1981 work, *Lion of the Valley: St. Louis, Missouri*, opens with a statement of omission: little here for students of women's history, although early founders Marie Therese Bourgeois Chouteau and Julia Soulard join Anne Lucas Hunt, Virginia Minor, Susan Blow, and Charlotte Rumbold who "appear as important figures."[49]

Limited access to primary sources and a lack of secondary sources have stood in the way of historians trying to recover the history of women in Missouri; until recently, information on African-American women has been nearly nonexistent.[50] Mary K. Dains' 1989 survey of historical work on Missouri women lists resources such as biographical dictionaries, biographies, and autobiographies representative of the early waves of women's history. Her examination of articles published in the *Missouri Historical Review,* the *Bulletin* of the Missouri Historical Society, and *Gateway Heritage,* uncovered sixty-nine articles about Missouri women and another eighty-nine that could be related to women.[51] This listing is useful, but the articles stretch over a historical period of about two hundred years and cover the entire state of

Missouri; thus, the number of articles relating to women in St. Louis from 1870 to 1930 is few. Access to more primary sources in women's history, however, is becoming available. Archives guides for women's historians may be obtained at the Missouri Historical Society and the Joint Collection, University of Missouri Western Historical Manuscript Collection and State Historical Society of Missouri Manuscripts.[52]

St. Louis women have not occupied extensive space in the histories of U.S. women written in the last three decades. Given the national prominence of St. Louis in the nineteenth century, and its relatively large African-American population, it is important that historians attempt to reclaim the voices of the women who lived there. In the attempt to piece together a picture of life for women in St. Louis from 1870 to 1930, a few stories are presented below. Each is connected to elements in U.S. women's history.

SOCIAL CONTROL AND VISIONS OF MORALITY

In 1870 a social control experiment targeting women began in St. Louis, which immediately evoked national attention. Ideologically, the issue at hand, the hygienic value of government-enforced medical inspection of prostitutes, emerged from a new conception of an individual's relationship to government.[53] Casting aside the classical liberal notion of freedom *from* government, St. Louis' "Social Evil Ordinance" rested on the argument that government should *increase* its involvement in the lives of individuals in the interest of public health. Citizens in conservative St. Louis who worked to overturn the measure (by an act of the Missouri State Legislature in 1874) did not hold up individual rights in their crusade. Rather, as John C. Burnham details in his study on nineteenth-century attempts at regulation of prostitution, "Americans in St. Louis and elsewhere seemed unable to keep moral arguments out of their public health campaigns."[54]

In January 1870, a St. Louis prosecutor accused Mary Ann Frost of being a "destroyer of innocence, a disgrace to the community, and a blot on her sex."[55] Frost was convicted of prostitution, fined one thousand dollars, and jailed as a result of being unable to pay the fine. The court sent her eight-year-old son to the city's House of Refuge. Up until 1870, crackdowns of this sort against prostitution fluctuated with periods of relative toleration.[56] For those who studied the effects of prostitution prior to the enactment of regulation ordinances, most considered the spread of venereal disease the primary concern.

Advocates of social control measures believed that prostitution itself was inevitable; to try to enforce morality was out of the question. Steps to protect public health, however, could be taken.[57] St. Louis' city health officer, Dr. William L. Barrett, reported in 1870 that prostitution was "destroying the health and vigor of a large portion of our inhabitants, and tainting their blood with an ineradicable poison. . . . "[58] Since prostitution could not be suppressed, he continued, it ought to be rendered as harmless to the community as possible.[59]

Although St. Louis became the first city in the United States to adopt a system for the public examination of prostitutes, reformers in New York City had pushed for this type of social control since the 1850s. Attempts at legislation in New York, however, were squelched by Susan B. Anthony's lobbying.[60] She associated the growth of prostitution with industrialization and poverty. Women's-rights leaders believed that purity reform, as part of the larger moral-reform movement, was important for the women's movement as well.[61] Anthony's perspective was that of the coalition of clergy persons, women, and politicians who brought an end to the social experiment in St. Louis. Opponents to the 1870 bill shared a belief that moral reform was indeed possible and argued that the Social Evil Ordinance operated as a legal sanction to sin.[62] These reformers became known as the "new abolitionists"; their mission was to abolish prostitution. Their efforts to eradicate prostitution stemmed from earlier action for the abolition of slavery and grew into a movement to purify all of society. Across the nation, emphases on temperance and "purity" formed the major pillars in the social-reform agenda.[63]

Proponents of the St. Louis regulatory system expected it to serve three purposes: to provide weekly inspections of all prostitutes in the city to prevent the spread of venereal disease; to isolate, treat, and care for infected women and offer them opportunity for reform; and to tighten control of prostitutes' residences and public behavior.[64] In fact, official toleration of prostitution stimulated investments in the business from which the city derived large amounts of revenue. Another, probably unexpected, result came in the form of a new sense of respectability and legitimacy for prostitutes, even though they found themselves under arrest as often as before the law had been adopted.[65] By 1873, opposition against the Social Evil Ordinance coalesced under the leadership of William Greenleaf Eliot, Unitarian minister and Chancellor of Washington University. Rebecca Hazard, a founder of the Women's Suffrage Association of Missouri, and Mrs. F. F. Holden, matron of the Women's Guardian Home in St. Louis, met with other women on 15 February 1873 to organize a petition campaign for an appeal to the legislature to rescind the Social Evil Ordinance.[66] Those who argued for the repeal of the ordinance pointed to the failure of the law regarding two key objectives: the incidence of disease had not declined and effective control of prostitution had not been achieved.[67] The law was repealed in 1874.

Advocates of social control continued to battle purity reformers on the St. Louis terrain for a number of years. Interestingly, the most successful attempt toward prostitution reform after 1874 came at the hands of the Evangelical Alliance, a coalition of Protestant ministers, in 1895. They proposed the establishment of a district in St. Louis where prostitution would be treated as a misdemeanor; in the rest of the city prostitution would be a felony. Such a measure would, it was hoped, contain the spread of the "social evil" while corralling those whom purity advocates wanted to reform.[68] The proposal ended up on the desk of Missouri Governor William J. Stone. His veto on 20 April 1895 brought an end to public scrutiny of the social experiment that began in St. Louis in 1870.[69]

The fact that the St. Louis experiment in social control spawned legislation against an entire class of women and was carried out in a blatantly discriminatory fashion was, generally, lost in the public debate over governmental regulation of prostitution.[70] Yet critique from a women's-rights perspective did surface. Some opponents of the St. Louis ordinance acknowledged that the law discriminated between female and male offenders with a double standard of morality, and an 1873 editorial in the *Missouri Republican* blamed prostitution on low wages paid to women workers.[71] Physicians who bemoaned the loss of social experimentation that followed the political defeat in St. Louis blamed women's-rights advocates along with other purity reformers. A practitioner from Georgia charged that a successful experiment had been cut off in its prime by "the ignorance and 'maudlin sentimentality' of preachers and 'whang-nosed' women's right women.'"[72] This, however, was an early skirmish in the battle for public policy. "Scientific expertise" would rally to exert its power in the days to come. And women would continue to join their efforts to all sides of the battle.

Mary E. Odem explores the policies of intervention and control by the state that arose in response to public anxiety over the sexuality of young women in the late nineteenth and early twentieth centuries in

Delinquent Daughters: Protecting and Policing Adolescent Female Sexuality in the United States, 1885-1920.[73] As in St. Louis during the 1870s, issues of morality took center stage in public-policy debate. Odem connects profound changes in the lives of working-class women and girls that led to increased opportunities for social and sexual autonomy to the broad trend toward greater control of sexual behavior in the United States during the late nineteenth century.[74] James R. McGovern points to "comprehensive efforts by civic officials and censorial citizens" to control morality as evidence that America was experiencing a major upheaval in morals during the Progressive Era, prior to 1920.[75]

Increased opportunities for women in the political economy corresponded to changing conceptions of the "ideal woman" in U.S. society. Although it is quite clear that the true womanhood paradigm of piety, purity, submissiveness, and domesticity did not reflect the realities of many women's lives in the United States, it was, nonetheless, a popular image during the nineteenth century.[76] In *Daughters of Sorrow: Attitudes Toward Black Women, 1880-1920*, Beverly Guy-Sheftall explained that European Americans combined notions of white supremacy with the cult of true womanhood in forging dominant attitudes toward African-American women. Most European Americans, writes Guy-Sheftall, maligned African-American women because of an assumed deviation in moral character. The traditional paradigm, however, was at its weakest when held up against the sexual abuse and exploitation African-American women had suffered at the hands of European-American men. African-American men reconstructed the philosophy of true womanhood in reaction to notions of white supremacy. African-American women expressed outrage over European-American attacks on their character and the refusal to recognize their womanhood.[77] "No other women on earth," wrote W.E.B. DuBois, "could have emerged from the hell of force and temptation which once engulfed and still surrounds black women in America with half the modesty and womanliness that they retain." DuBois expressed the rationale behind the reconceived sexual ideology.[78] Alongside support for suffrage and education for women, many African Americans held motherhood as the most essential function of women; but African-American women considered their work outside the home, for wages, improvement of society, and race uplift, as important functions as well. [79]

Frances B. Cogan has suggested that the ideal of real womanhood coexisted with true womanhood from 1840 to 1880. According to Cogan, real womanhood distinguished itself from true womanhood by stressing physical fitness and health, demanding education beyond the common school (to better prepare for the demands of womanhood and homelife), teaching "right" reasons for marriage (to improve the chances of obtaining a good mate), and by approving of employment for women (as long as it did not interfere with one's duties to family and home).[80] Real womanhood, perhaps because of the space of tension it occupied between true womanhood and nineteenth-century feminism, faded about 1880 just as "the new woman" was making her appearance.[81] The new woman was said to possess an independent spirit. She had an enhanced sense of self, gender, and mission—to purify, uplift, control, and reform. Vigorous and energetic, she was committed to a lifetime career, having been prepared in the college, club, and settlement house. She reached her stride during the Progressive Era, a product of industrialization, urbanization, and prosperity.[82] Nancy Cott notes that by the 1910s, the nineteenth-century woman movement had gained access to, but not transformed, many avenues of social, economic, and political power. The feminism that developed in the 1910s was broader in intent (arguing for revolution in all relations of the sexes) but narrower in its range of adherents than the nineteenth-century woman movement.[83] Feminists were opposed to a sex hierarchy, believed that women's condition was socially constructed rather than being predestined by God or nature, and maintained a consciousness of women as a social group able to effect change in the community.[84] Cott explains that feminists partook of the free-ranging spirit of rebellion in the 1910s as women severed ties their nineteenth-century predecessors attached to Christianity and conventional respectability. They abandoned their stance on the moral superiority of women and evoked women's sexuality.[85] Though not embraced by most women, feminism drew heavy fire for its positions on issues of morality in the 1910s. In 1918, the Missouri Anti-Suffrage League charged that "Feminism advocates non-motherhood, free love, easy divorce, economic independence for all women, and other demoralizing and destructive theories."[86]

James McGovern identifies urban living and the freedom it conferred as the cardinal condition of change that spurred the revolution in morals after the turn of the century. For women, the revolution took the form of a more permissive sexuality and a diminished femininity.[87] By 1910, social commentators were noticing a "Change in the Feminine Ideal" from the Gibson Girl of 1900. Novelist Margaret Deland wrote:

> This young person . . . with surprisingly bad manners—has gone to college, and when she graduates she is going to earn her own living . . . she won't go to church; she has views upon marriage and the birth-rate, and she utters them calmly, while her mother blushes with embarrassment; she occupies herself, passionately, with everything except the things that used to occupy the minds of girls. [88]

Mary Odem found that progressive women viewed sexual awakening as a normal part of women's adolescence, but they believed that girls' energy should be appropriately channeled through athletics or schooling until adulthood and marriage. [89] If one followed the advice of famed psychologist G. Stanley Hall, however, schooling for girls should avoid too much academic content. Volume two of his 1908 tome, *Adolescence*, contained the serious admonition:

> From the available data it seems, however, that the more scholastic the education of women, the fewer children and the harder, more dangerous, and more dreaded is parturition, and the less the ability to nurse children. Not intelligence but education by present man-made ways is inversely as fecundity.[90]

Public anxiety over shifting moral norms subsided by the end of the 1920s. As Odem indicates, middle-class women adopted the new sexual mores that had first been exhibited by working-class women, and a new sexual ideology endorsed heterosexual pleasure. [91] By 1924 a refashioned public image of women in St. Louis tolerated a headline in the Soldan High School newspaper, "Teachers Turn Flappers." The *Scrippage* reporter noted that nearly one-third of the women teachers at Soldan had bobbed their hair, creating a "bobbed office force and a bobbed faculty."[92] A comparison of two surveys of young women's goals, taken during the 1920s, highlighted a dilution of liberal attitudes across the country. In the early 1920s, Lorine Pruette conducted a survey of women ages fifteen to seventeen. She discovered that 35 percent were willing to give up marriage and a family in order to sustain a career. More wanted to combine career and marriage. A study by Blanchard and Manasses at the end of the decade found few women between the ages of eighteen and twenty-six willing to forego marriage for a career.[93]

"EVE HAD NO TYPEWRITER": ST. LOUIS WOMEN AT WORK

> St. Louis men have lost respect for St. Louis women because of the activities of the business girl. She ignores God's divine purpose. [94]

Mrs. Alvin W. Claxon, quoted above and wife of the pastor of the St. Louis Grand Avenue Baptist Church, delivered what the *St. Louis Post-Dispatch* described as a "bombshell" of a speech to those attending a 1903 Mother's Meeting. In the first portion of her presentation Mrs. Claxon derided the "new woman," arguing that competition in the workplace between women and men resulted in men's loss of respect for all women. The effect threatened the well-being of society, Claxon warned.

> If the business girl only lowered man's regard for herself, the social fester would not be so raw. But man, in ceasing to hold higher respect for the business girl, unconsciously loses some respect for wife, mother and daughter, for all womankind. [95]

Having labeled working women as a menace to the family, Claxon directed the balance of her remarks to "home women." Reminding her audience that Eve had no typewriter, the pastor's wife preached that "Woman's intellect was never intended to duplicate man's. . . . The full fruitage of a woman's life is attained in making the man she loves happy."[96] Claxon's "Ten Commandments for the 'Ideal Wife'" give evidence that the true woman had not yet made her exit from St. Louis:

1. Meet your husband with a smile.
2. If he is fretful, use good nature as a foil.
3. Treat him as your fiance [sic], not as a man secured.
4. Be as fascinatingly pretty as you can.
5. Dress for your husband as you dress for a beau.
6. Make him happy, he will reflect happiness to you.
7. Be a ladder for his ambition, not a rock to bar.
8. Don't be persuaded that marriage alone will make a man.
9. Regard your home as a throne, it gives you power.
10. Be not satisfied in ministering to his material needs alone.[97]

The same issue of the *St. Louis Post-Dispatch* that covered Claxon's explosive remarks also featured responses to the address by four stenographers, two telephone operators, two forewomen, three matrons, a lawyer, a florist, a saleswoman, a dry-goods buyer, a restaurant keeper, and an educator--seventeen in all. Many took Mrs. Claxon to task for not recognizing the fact that some women must work for the economic survival of their families. Seven claimed that women were respected in the business environment; writers also argued that if they were good women in the first place, working women were good wives and daughters. Some mixed responses suggest that, although women's increasing participation in the paid labor force was becoming an accepted practice, few had problems with the conservative philosophy exhibited in Claxon's statement. Mrs. M.W. Miller, a saleswoman, respected working women, but had no qualms about a segregated workplace.

> There is a place for women in the business world and these places must be filled by women—men could not fill them. A woman should avoid taking a man's place if she can, but no matter what place she fills she may still be the tender-hearted womanly woman and make any man a good wife. [98]

Three respondents worried that working outside the home was not natural for women. A depot matron expressed hope that the success women found in the business world would soon diminish so life could return to "normal." Matron Hunter's opinion was that

> this business craze on the part of women is but for a time. Women will go back to her own in time and things will become natural again. As it is now, girls have no desire to be married and to take up the cares of a home. Sometimes I dread to see many of them as successful as they are. It makes the time when they will be contented homekeepers so far away.[99]

Others agreed with Claxon that chivalry among men was on the decline, but charged mothers, rather than working women, with the blame. Police Matron Kintzing noted, "A man does not lose [politeness] if he has it. Men that have had good home training never forget to be polite." [100] Matron Hunter was more direct. "A boy or a man carries the impress of his mother about with him always. The mother and not the business woman is the one I would hold responsible [for the decline in manners.] "[101]

Not all opinions printed in the newspaper, however, adhered to Claxon's conservative ideology regarding the ideal woman. Lawyer Daisy Barbee objected to Claxon's description of the ideal wife, noting that the most unhappy homes Barbee encountered in her professional work were those in which "the wife's love followed very closely the rules for a model wife."[102] The only man to be featured in the *Post-Dispatch* article wrote forcefully in support of women in business. St. Louis educator Calvin M. Woodward asserted:

> If one regards a woman as a toy or a plaything, then the question has a different aspect than if she is looked upon as a sensible, rational being. The coming of woman into the business world has destroyed ideals. It has built up others, however, that are better.[103]

To be sure, many women considered the office a better working environment than other options open to them in the early decades of the twentieth century. The occupation of clerk recorded the highest increase in the number of women employed in the United States from 1910 to 1920.[104] The number of women employed as clerks, saleswomen, stenographers, typists, bookkeepers, cashiers, and accountants in 1870 (10,798) represented less than 1 percent of women employed in nonagricultural occupations. By 1900, the number of women in this classification increased by almost a factor of forty, to 394,747 workers, or 9.1 percent of the nonagricultural female workforce. In 1920, 1,910,695 women clerical workers constituted over one-fourth of the women engaged in nonagricultural employment.[105] In the 1910 census, 10,082 women in St. Louis registered as bookkeepers, cashiers, accountants, office clerks, messengers, stenographers, and typewriters. Of these, 9,688 (96 percent) were European-American women born in the United States; 356 (3.5 percent) were European-American immigrant women; and 38 (less than 1 percent) were African-American women.[106] Ten years later the number of female clerical workers had more than doubled. The 1920 St. Louis census noted 21,526 European-American native-born women employed in this category; 849 (3.7 percent) European-American immigrant women; and 180 (0.7 percent) African-American women obtained clerical positions.[107] Clearly, European-American women took the vast number of clerical positions. The office route to social mobility was open to very few African-American or immigrant women.

The occupation of domestic servant recorded the most significant decrease in the number of women employed in the United States from 1910 to 1920, from 1,234,758 to 981,557, a decrease of 20.5 percent.[108] As other job opportunities opened to them, women took jobs with more pay, regular and shorter hours, better work environments, and higher social standing. The number of women employed as servants, waitresses, charwomen, cleaners, porters, housekeepers, and stewardesses increased every year from 873,738 in 1870 to 1,430,692 in 1900, to 1,595,572 in 1910, before falling to 1,358,665 in 1920. This classification of women workers, however, accounted for 60.7 percent of the female workforce in 1870, 33.0 percent in 1900, and 18.2 percent in 1920.[109] While the number of European-American women employed as servants fell from 1910 to 1920, the number of African-American women in this occupation increased from 388,659 to 389,276, representing an increase of less than 1 percent. In 1910 and 1920, African-American women constituted the largest proportion of domestic workers.[110] In 1910, 27,775 St. Louis women reported their occupation as domestic or personal service: 51.3 percent were native-born European-Americans; 16.6 percent were European-American immigrants; and 31.9 percent were African-American women. The number of women working in domestic and personal service rose only slightly in 1920 to a total of 28,218: 50.1 percent were native-born European-Americans; 11.1 percent were European-American immigrants; and 38.6 percent were African-American women. While the percentage of European-American women in this category decreased slightly, African-American women gained about seven percentage points.[111]

The declining percentage of European-American women willing to take positions as domestic servants was brought to the attention of St. Louis-area residents in a startling way in 1903; a *St. Louis Post-Dispatch* headline proclaimed "Want Less Education And More Servants: Belleville Women Want High School Abolished Because It Enables Girls to Obtain Positions in Offices and Stores."[112] Adam Gintz and Jacob Leiner were elected to the school board in Belleville, Illinois, just across the Mississippi River from St. Louis, with the support of a number of "society" women. The Gintz-Leiner platform centered on the promise to abolish the public high school. One spokeswoman quoted in the *Post-Dispatch* explained:

When poor girls are given a High School education they get too proud to work in a kitchen and secure employment in offices and stores. It is almost impossible to get a girl now, and the High School is to blame for it. Belleville could learn something from Germany. They don't educate the poor people over there like they do here, and the result is that the supply of servants is adequate there.[113]

The *Post-Dispatch* responded in the next day's edition with a stinging rebuke.

If poor girls were taught to cook and scrub they would make good servants for the upper classes and be content in that walk of life in which it had pleased Providence to place them. But when they are taught history and geography and arithmetic and literature, even imperfectly, they lose interest in scrubbing. Its [sic] the strangest thing in the world how education affects poor people! It makes them want to work for themselves. It fills their heads with notions of 'getting on' and 'rising in the world.' The next we know they proceed to rise and get on, and their usefulness to the upper classes is quite destroyed. . . . Let poor girls be taught only what will make them useful to these ladies. To teach them what will help them to be useful to themselves is to revolutionize domestic life and upset society itself.[114]

The paper's position is not surprising, for St. Louis was becoming a place where women were "getting on" and "rising in the world" through the professions. The St. Louis school system had attained a national reputation for academic quality, the city had established a Normal School in 1857, and women could enroll in Washington University. Women made up a significant proportion of the city's teachers, reflecting national trends. In 1910, women accounted for 84.4 percent of school teachers listed in the U.S. census; in 1920, women constituted 87 percent of teachers living in St. Louis.[115] Teaching has always been the leading profession for women, accounting for 5.8 percent of all women employed in nonagricultural occupations in the United States in 1870 and 8.7 percent in 1920.[116] Women had been members of the St. Louis Philosophical Society since its earliest days. High-school teachers and educational writers belonged to the group. In fact, many of the young men and women who were drawn to St. Louis through the Philosophical Society taught in the public schools.[117]

Women artists played an important role in making St. Louis a center of Midwestern culture.[118] Art competitions and exhibitions at the annual St. Louis fairs garnered a high level of participation from local artists and expanded the public interest in art. Lincoln Bunce Spiess writes that two factors stimulated cultural development in St. Louis: artists anxious to represent the American West, like other pioneers, began their journey in St. Louis; and the trade resulting from westward movement generated wealth for some citizens who could commission works, providing financial security for artists.[119] Although painter Sarah Miriam Peale and sculptor Harriet Goodhue Hosmer were the only two women with connections to St. Louis to find their way into standard art histories, the number of prizes won by local women artists suggests that their work was of high quality.[120] The St. Louis School of Fine Arts, recognized as one of the best institutions in the United States, brought new opportunities for women artists with its founding in 1879. As social attitudes toward gender became less rigid at the turn of the century, women found new self-expression through art. St. Louis artists gained local, national, and international recognition.[121] One St. Louis artist, Lillian Mason Brown, taught in the St. Louis high schools from 1897 until her death in 1924. Brown began her teaching career at Central High School, organized the Art Department at McKinley High School when it opened in 1904, and joined the faculty of Soldan High School in 1910. Her work in black and white, watercolor, and oil painting frequently appeared in the annual exhibitions of the St. Louis Artists' Guild and the St. Louis Art League. Daughter of U.S. Senator and Missouri Governor Benjamin Gratz Brown, Lillian Brown had the opportunity afforded to women of her social class to study art in Paris and she traveled in Europe, Africa, Mexico, and the Bermuda Islands. She kept a studio in Provincetown, Massachusetts, spending her summers there. Seemingly, art held the central position in Brown's life; she referred to her St. Louis-county home as "a studio with living appurtenances."[122] High-school students considered visits to Brown's home studio "a privilege rich with rewards of peculiar interest."[123]

On 26 March 1870, Lemma Barkeloo was admitted to the Missouri Bar, becoming the first woman to practice law in St. Louis. She studied law at Washington University with St. Louisan Phoebe Couzins, the first woman admitted to the Arkansas Bar and the first woman to serve as a U.S. marshal. Barkeloo and Couzins were in select company; U.S. Census reports listed five women as lawyers, judges, or justices in 1870. By 1920, 3,221 women were working in the law profession.[124]

Perhaps because women's work in medicine could be more easily justified in terms of a relationship to the domestic sphere, more women entered the medical profession in the late nineteenth century. The 1870 census recorded 527 women physicians. Ten years later the numbers had increased to 2,432 and by 1920 there were 16,784 women physicians in the United States.[125] Martha R. Clevenger outlines two periods when women physicians established practices in St. Louis, the first starting in 1870 and the second beginning in 1890.[126] Dr. Mary Hancock McLean's success in St. Louis may be attributed to her ability to reconcile the emerging twentieth-century professional role of physicians with nineteenth-century notions of women's place in society. Marion Hunt writes that a "careful balance between conformity to and challenge of woman's place" characterized McLean's career in medicine.[127] Dr. McLean became the first woman to work as assistant physician at the St. Louis Female Hospital and the first woman physician admitted to membership in the St. Louis Medical Society. She sustained a commitment to public health issues throughout her career, with special emphasis on the health needs of poor women. In 1908, Dr. McLean worked with younger women physicians to open a free clinic "run by women, for women."[128] In spite of the many precedents established by Dr. McLean, the medical profession did not welcome women in the years to follow, a period when "professionalization" pushed women to the margins in medicine. Without a doubt, however, Dr. McLean's success did secure a definite place for women physicians in the St. Louis medical community.[129]

In the United States, the number of women engaged in the professions increased every decade from 1870 to 1920. In 1870, 91,963 women professionals accounted for 6.4 percent of the nonagricultural workforce. By 1920, 13.3 percent (992,638) of the female labor force were employed in professional occupations.[130] The Progressive Era is known as a time when women's opportunities in many professions expanded; historians also recognize the years from 1870 to 1920 as a period of escalating industrialization. The number of women in the United States who worked in mills and factories grew from 252,702 in 1870 to 966,167 in 1900 to 1,777,022 by 1920. These workers represented 17.6 percent of the female nonagricultural labor force in 1870; 22.3 percent in 1900; and 23.8 percent in 1920.[131] Governmental officials recognized women's participation in the industrial workforce as significant. The *Fourth Annual Report of the Commissioner of Labor* issued a document on *Working Women in Large Cities* in 1889. The study focused on 17,427 women working in 343 industries in 22 cities across the United States.[132] The authors of the report discovered that, in St. Louis, there was work in abundance for all women who wanted it. Many of the interviewers' questions dealt with living conditions for working women. Researchers were left with the impression that relatively few St. Louis working women attended church, while dance houses claimed "the attendance of altogether too many."[133] Interviewers could locate no libraries, lecture courses, or clubs available to working women in St. Louis; illiteracy was widespread. Some industries, such as tobacco factories, stamping works, match factories, and bagging and cotton mills, were heavily populated with workers with very little education. Although researchers could point to some exceptions, they found moral conditions among the working class in St. Louis, generally, to be of a "lower standard" than in many other cities. Researchers were gratified, however, to know that better moral standards were spreading throughout the city.[134] The Women's Christian Association of St. Louis did its share to aid working women. Its protective committee pledged itself "to afford all necessary aid to industrial women, securing to and protecting them in all their legal rights. . . . "[135] No factory or mill workers, however, lived in the Women's Christian home for self-supporting working women. The boarding rates were too high for industrial workers; residents tended to be saleswomen, sewers, dressmakers, milliners, clerks, and teachers. The Women's Christian Association also managed the Women's Training School, an institution devoted to teaching cooking, dressmaking, stenography and typewriting, and general housework. The Women's Training School operated a lunchroom for industrial women, offering substantial lunches at from five cents to fifteen cents each. In addition to the Women's Christian Association, women in St. Louis might board at the Working Women's Home. "Respectable" women could seek refuge while unemployed, obtain help in finding jobs, and be cared for while recovering from disease.[136]

In 1880, 7,089 women in St. Louis worked in manufacturing, mechanical, or mining industries. In 1910, 19,677 women were employed in manufacturing or mechanical industries, and by 1920 the number grew to 29,044.[137] The Women's Bureau of the U.S. Department of Labor conducted a study of *Women in Missouri Industries,* which was published in 1924. Missouri's standard nine-hour day, fifty-four-hour work week placed it among moderately progressive states regarding labor legislation.[138] Data from Missouri disproved the commonly held beliefs that women worked in industry for only a few years and left their jobs upon marriage. Among women industrial workers in Missouri, 36.4 percent were or had been married.[139] St. Louis and Kansas City were, in many respects, more progressive than smaller towns in Missouri regarding working conditions for women. Women who worked in smaller towns in rural areas usually worked longer hours than women in the cities, and pay was higher for European-American women in St. Louis and Kansas City. African-American women, however, earned less in St. Louis than in other parts of the state, including Kansas City. St. Louis claimed the largest proportion of African-American women workers. Industries that employed a large number of African-American women and assigned specific jobs on the basis of race set wages for African-American women conspicuously lower than those of European-American women. European-American women who worked in St. Louis industries received a median weekly earning of $13.50 in April 1922. African-American women received substantially less, $5.50 per week. [140]

In *Women and the American Labor Movement,* Philip S. Foner details the strike activity of women industrial workers in St. Louis, which captured national attention in the spring of 1933. African-American women comprised over 85 percent of the labor force in the pecan industry. African American women usually worked from 6:45 A.M. to 4:45 P.M. (with a forty-five-minute lunch period) five and one-half days a week. European-American women workers, predominately Polish, worked from 7:00 A.M. to 4:30 P.M. with a one-hour lunch period. A few African-American and European-American men held jobs as foremen, weighers, crackers, dryers, packagers, and shippers.[141] Foner's description of the conditions of the women's work is illustrative.

> Seated at a table before a 25-pound bag of nuts, each women [sic] would use a knife to separate the meats from the shells. Unbroken halves were placed in one pile and broken pieces in another, and the shells were also kept so that upon completion everything could be weighed once more to make sure it all added up to 25 pounds. A cleaner operation, in which only white women were employed, was that of sorting. The dirty work was parceled out among the black women.

The women worked under sweatshop conditions. Bathroom facilities were primitive, and despite the fact that this was a food industry, there were no health standards. Shelling the nuts caused a great deal of dust, which produced continual coughing, while the nutmeats produced permanent stains, so that it was necessary to wear an apron to prevent damage to clothes. The cost of the aprons was deducted from the weekly wages. [142]

Between 1931 and 1933, women's wages at the R.E. Funsten Company were cut five times. One African-American woman who had worked at Funsten for eighteen years averaged eighteen dollars a week in pay in 1918; her top weekly pay in 1933 was four dollars. About 60 percent of the women workers were on relief rolls during the Depression. [143] Although a 1927 strike against the company had ended in failure, women organized again in 1933 with the help of William Sentner, a local Communist Party leader and organizer for the Food Workers Industrial Union. The women demanded an increase in wages to ten cents for halves, four cents for pieces; equal pay for African-American and European-American workers and an end to discriminatory practices against African-American workers; and union recognition. [144] When these demands were rejected, nine hundred workers walked out. On the second day, the strike spread to two additional Funsten shops and two other factories, the Liberty Nut Company and the Central Pecan Company. African-American and European-American women picketed together with their husbands and children. They were supported by other St. Louis workers, Communist Party members, and members of the Unemployed Councils. The St. Louis Social Justice Commission voted to support the strike after examining the contents of eight unopened pay envelopes of the striking workers covering four days' work: two contained $2 and the rest contained $1.50. [145] About a month later, the strikers voted unanimously to accept the company's offer of eight cents for halves, four cents for pieces. Within a few days the company met the demands of "ten and four," a uniform scale of wages for African-American and European-American workers, and recognition of elected shop committees. [146] Foner emphasized the significance of this action. In the midst of the Great Depression, before Section 7(a) of the National Recovery Act guaranteed workers' rights to unionize, and as one hundred women strikers were being arrested, fourteen hundred women workers in St. Louis challenged a powerful corporation and the city power structure by bringing an end to wage differences based on race. While European-American women were active in the strike, Foner concludes that the "pivotal role of the black women . . . was responsible for the final victory."[147] The women's efforts in St. Louis inspired African-American and European-American women in Chicago to protest similar work conditions of very low wages and segregation in the workplace and it stimulated strikes in St. Louis in the garment industries.[148] Some two thousand women workers in St. Louis went on strike in 1933 as the International Ladies' Garment Workers' Union began a nationwide campaign to organize dressmakers. Some strike activity lasted among these workers until 1935. Five decades later, interviews with these women indicated that, regardless of one's level of employment and degree of activity within the union, each participant gave evidence of a positive self-image of herself as a working woman.[149] Mrs. Claxon's clarion call of 1903, "St. Louis men have lost respect for St. Louis women," lost its cutting quality when placed up against the enlivening self-respect of working women.

Historian Alice Kessler-Harris delineated three phases of women's work in the United States in her essay, "Independence and Virtue in the Lives of Wage-Earning Women: The United States, 1870-1930." Although "real-life" constraints, organization of the household, number of children, rural or urban environment, ethnic and community approval, and income level have always played a part in the varied pattern of women's workforce participation, public rationalization for women's paid labor changed significantly in the period from 1860 to 1930.[150] From the time of the Civil War into the 1880s, women justified their wage work in the absence of men's support. In St. Louis this line of defense extended into the twentieth century as one can see from the responses to Mrs. Claxon's statements in the *Post-Dispatch*. Florist Teresa Badaracco explained, "Many women are compelled to work. [I]t is not a matter of choice with them."[151] Kessler-Harris describes the period from 1890 to 1910 as one in which women were free to take "proper" jobs. Self-imposed and labor-market restraints limited the areas in which women could find employment. The notion that a woman might work for individual satisfaction developed between 1910 and 1930. This analysis fits with Katharine T. Corbett's study of St. Louis garments workers who were proud of their achievements as working women.[152] Kessler-Harris concludes that the transformation of the family economy was essential in making women's position in the labor force an accepted factor in U.S. society. "Independent women, in short, lacked virtue in society's eyes until the twenties, when their roles as wage earners began to be seen as a more permanent part of the family economy."[153]

The numbers of employed women in the United States increased from 2,647,157 in 1880 to 8,549,511 in 1920, paralleling the relaxed attitudes toward working women that Kessler-Harris documents.[154] Women's historians note, however, that gender has sometimes been less important a factor in determining whether a woman would enter the labor force than ethnicity or class. In 1910, for example, 17.1 percent of European-American women with native parentage in the United States were employed, compared to 54.7 percent of African-American women. Of European-American women with foreign or mixed parentage, 24.6 percent were members of the paid labor force, while 21.7 percent of European-American immigrant women worked for pay.[155]

Most often, women's jobs in the labor force reflected their class and ethnic positions in a discriminatory, stratified society. In 1920, more European-American women with native parentage in the United States were employed in clerical occupations (21 percent) than in any other category. Manufacturing was the chief area of employment for both European-American women with foreign or mixed parentage (30.1 percent) and European-American immigrant women (37.1 percent). In 1920, 50.3 percent of the African-American female workforce worked in domestic service.[156] Many women saw white-collar work (clerical work and the professions) as a standard of occupational and social mobility.[157] Most often, these jobs went to European-American women. In 1920, 16.7 percent of all women employed in the United States worked in clerical occupations; 21 percent of European-American women with native parentage, and 25.8 percent of European-American women with foreign or mixed parentage held clerical positions. By contrast, only 8.2 percent of European-American immigrant women and 0.5 percent of African-American women worked as clerks. The pattern held steady regarding the professions as well. Of the women listing a professional occupation in 1920, 17.6 percent were European-American with native parentage, 11.9 percent of European American women with foreign or mixed parentage; 6.3 percent were European-American immigrants; and 2.5 percent were African-American.[158]

Kessler-Harris detected a growing sense after World War I that marriage and satisfying work could be combined in a woman's life; the number of married women in the workforce grew from 515,260 in 1890 to 1,920,281 by 1920.[159] Again, ethnicity and social class were dominant factors in determining whether a married woman worked for wages. In 1920, 19.4 percent of employed European-American women of native parentage were married, compared to 11.7 percent of European-American women of foreign or mixed parentage, 26.6 percent of European-American immigrant women, and 44.9 percent of African-American women.[160] Sharon Harley emphasized the significance of poverty in explaining the high proportion of married African-American women in the workforce in her essay, "When Your Work Is Not Who You Are: The Development of a Working-Class Consciousness among Afro-American Women." Acknowledging the limited opportunities available to African Americans for economic and social advancement without a formal education, mothers chose to join the labor force in place of their children, so the children could go to school.[161] In the 1870s, Frances Ellen Harper characterized African-American mothers as "the levers that move in education. The men talk about it, especially about election time . . . but the women work most for it."[162] Nancy Woloch notes that while African-American women worked in order to allow their children to remain in school, the immigrant woman in the labor force was more likely to be a daughter than a mother. While diverse in many ways, new immigrants from southeastern Europe, whether Poles, Jews, Slavs, or Italians, shared a common cultural tradition: the family served as both cultural center and economic hub. "Providing a bridge between Old World patterns and the new environment, the working daughter played a special role in family acculturation and in the economy."[163]

It is important to note that, while African-American families made education for their children a high priority, their efforts to educate daughters were even greater than those to educate sons. The primary explanation for this is that teaching provided opportunity for professional work for more African-American women than for men.[164] The feminization of teaching, then, played an important role in the history of education in the United States in many respects. By encouraging African-American and European-American girls to pursue secondary education as preparation for teaching, it influenced the composition of the high-school student population as it provided educated women with job opportunities.[165] In the late nineteenth and early twentieth centuries, teaching represented the "one true and honorable vocation" for women, as a woman who left her teaching position to pursue a career in business learned.[166] It was the consummate "proper" job for a woman, paradigmatic of the 1890-1910 phase of women's work outlined by Kessler-Harris. Patricia Carter argues that the changing image of the female teacher--from altruistic social servant to socially conscious and fiscally concerned worker-- marked the beginning of general acceptance for women within the permanent workforce.[167] Teaching remained the principal occupation of educated women, even as economic conditions changed to allow women other possibilities in the workforce. Yet support for teaching did dim in the second and third decades of the twentieth century.[168] Teaching required more preparation, but paid less than clerical work. In 1900, the average annual earning for public school teachers hovered around 75 percent of the salary paid to manufacturing workers. The feminization of teaching led to a two-tier system of employment, in which men tended to occupy supervisory positions.[169] Finally, as married women were constituting a larger proportion of the female workforce, the prohibition against married women teachers remained in effect in many school districts until World War II. Prejudice against the married woman teacher was held in place, first, by racist eugenic theory and then by high unemployment during the Depression. As late as 1931, *School Executives Magazine* expressed such prejudice:

> My chief objection to married women teaching is the fact that it leads almost necessarily to childless homes or to the restriction of children in homes that really should produce more children. Every time you elect a married teacher, you tacitly endorse and encourage such practices which are the most reprehensible sins of the upper and middle classes.[170]

Reprehension to family women in the workplace was not limited to the teaching profession. The American Federation of Labor opposed organizing women industrial workers and contended that the employment of women and children led to forced idleness among men. A resolution at the 1914 AFL convention targeted women in the workplace as "destructive of the individual, the family, and our race. . . ."[171] Once again, some perceived women's foray into the public arena as threatening the common good. AFL members proposed to "do our utmost to restore individual, social, and racial health by restoring woman to the home."[172]

In most cases, unions did not attempt to organize women workers. Union leaders concentrated their efforts on skilled workers, and women were generally barred from the skilled trades. Union members were willing to accept the disparity in wages paid to men and women, they believed women's work in industry was of a short duration, and they believed that women were not committed to unions.[173] Philip Foner argues that even with a lack of support from most male-dominated unions, the militancy and perseverance of women workers laid the foundations of trade unionism in many important industries, in the face of employer and public hostility.[174] The "Uprising of the Thirty Thousand," the 1909 Shirtwaist Strike, left its mark on a generation of women organizers who led in the fight for "bread and roses." Annelise Orleck writes that this hybrid vision of working-class activism encompassed campaigns for shorter hours, higher wages, safer working conditions, medical care, and decent, affordable housing and food, as well as demands for meaningful work, access to education and culture, and egalitarian relations in the workplace. Working-class women activists used four strategies to obtain their goals: trade unionism, worker education, community-organizing around tenant and consumer issues, and lobbying for regulations of wages, hours, factory safety, and food and housing costs.[175] The 1911 Triangle Shirtwaist Factory fire that killed 146 workers ignited a "common sense" approach to social change in working-class women. A combination of pragmatism and passion marked the lifelong work of activists, whom organizer Pauline Newman labeled as the "1909 vintage."[176]

Labor activists in St. Louis included women whose family members worked at skilled and unskilled jobs, as well as women in the paid labor force. St. Louis labor-union leader Mary Ryder mobilized efforts to establish the St. Louis Joint Council of Women's Auxiliaries, founded in 1926. Members of the Joint Council worked to support strike efforts, lobby for improved working conditions, and pioneered the organization of state and national auxiliary groups.[177] In addition, member groups such as the Meatcutters Ladies Auxiliary, Local 88; the International Association of Machinists Ladies Auxiliary, Local 84; and the Painters District Council Women's Auxiliary, Local 17 held informational pickets and voter registration drives, developed leadership training sessions, bought Liberty Bonds, Thrift Stamps, and U.S. Savings Bonds, supplied bandages and materials for soldiers during World War I, and sponsored rooms at the Mary Ryder Home for Women and Girls. Women in the auxiliaries also strengthened community cohesiveness through nonprofit events such as picnics and other social events. Ardent in their work, auxiliaries moved their meeting times from afternoon to evening as more women entered the paid labor force. Employed or not, working-class women made significant contributions to the St. Louis community. A slogan of the International Association of Machinists Ladies Auxiliary, Local 84 expressed the commitment shared by the women of the St. Louis Joint Council of Women's Auxiliaries: "Hats Off To The Past—Sleeves Rolled Up To The Future."[178]

SOCIAL REFORM IN ST. LOUIS

Anne Johnson edited and published *Notable Women of St. Louis, 1914,* to stake a claim for women in St. Louis history. Her intention was to honor the "great women" of the city and to create a companion volume for the chronicles of men's history. Johnson wrote in the foreword to her text, "Every city of any size has one or more books of its important and noted men, but so far none has been published as a tribute to the noteworthy and capable women."[179] Thus, armed with biographies of sixty-five St. Louis women, Johnson initiated an early foray into the phase of "Women in History." Although the volume is deficient in that it is a collection of celebratory profiles of an elite group of women, Johnson did provide access to the perspective of middle-class, European-American social reformers of the Progressive Era.

Johnson's book extolled the work of conservative suffrage women, those who argued for the ballot in order to reinforce their reform efforts. Perhaps the clearest connection between woman suffrage and reform activity was expressed in the biography of Thekla M. Bernays, political-social-economic essayist. Bernays argued:

> Women need suffrage for sanitation, for the suppression of adulterated and unhygienic food, to enforce cessation of the wholesale murder of innocents by bad milk, to reduce the harm to health and energy by the smoke nuisance, to abolish the white slave traffic—in short, to protect our homes.[180]

Bernays' platform for suffrage called for equal facilities in education, equal rights in guardianship of children, equal wages for equal work, a single standard of morality, regulation and restraint of child labor, the abolition of sweatshops, safe working conditions, suppression of industrial smoke (a major issue in St. Louis), "minimizing the drink evil without interfering with personal liberty," and the abolition of prostitution.[181] Social reformers in St. Louis addressed most of the issues on the progressive agenda. Johnson's "Notable Women" took leadership roles in a number of organizations, including the St. Louis Equal Suffrage League, the Business Woman's Equal Suffrage League of St. Louis, the Equal Suffrage Association of Missouri, the Wednesday Club, the Women's National College Club, the Woman's State Bar Association of Missouri, the St. Louis Teachers' Fellowship, the Missouri State Teachers' Association, the St. Louis Froebel Society, the Missouri Division of the International Sunshine Society (a charity organization devoted to helping blind children), State and City Anti-Tuberculosis Societies, the Pure Milk Commission, the Women's Christian Temperance Union, the Playgrounds Association, the Consumers' League, the St. Louis Symphony Society, the St. Louis Pageant and Masque Association, the St. Louis Artists' Guild, the Self-Culture Hall, the Women's Trade Union League, and the Young Women's Christian Association. European-American women dominated these clubs; African-American women, generally excluded from these groups, organized the Saint Louis Association of Colored Women's Clubs in 1904. The Association encompassed over twenty civic and social organizations by 1930, including Harpers Married Ladies (founded in 1886), Informal Dames (1901), Book Lovers (1907), Bachelor Girls (1910), Wellston Progressive (1913), Prudence Crandall Study (1915), Postal Employees Matrons (1915), Metropolitan Excelsior Art (1921), Jessie Swanson Ivy (1925), Thursday Study Club (1927), and Coterie (1928). Initially groups in the Saint Louis Association of Colored Women's Clubs formed to further friendship and interest in the arts, education, and social welfare. Women designed projects to offset some of the social inadequacies caused by segregation, such as providing bed linens for hospitals and children's homes.[182]

The Wednesday Club, described as a "literary club broad enough in its scope to serve as a center of thought for women and to promote their practical interests," was one of many organizations that served as a nexus between nineteenth-century literary societies and twentieth-century social-reform groups.[183] Johnson described how the national federation of women's clubs broadened the scope of local groups as they became a conduit for women's "special" contributions to the public during the Progressive Era.

Most of these [local clubs] originally had no other object in view than literary improvement and social recreation. But of late years a great change has taken place in the relation of woman's influence to questions of a public nature. New problems, vitally affecting the condition and welfare of the masses, have arisen, and many of them are of a character to especially appeal to the interest and support of women. There has never been an era where matters of this kind have been so prominently presented. Existing evils and the methods of modifying and eradicating them have called forth a wide and earnest discussion that has been taken up by nearly all of the local clubs.[184]

Believing that women "naturally stand for what is pure and good," St. Louis women targeted areas for reform in which women suffered disproportionate consequences: intemperance, domestic relations, abuses in the workplace.[185] A Wednesday Club committee, consisting of Mrs. Martha Fischel, Mrs. Charles Damon, Mrs. John Allen, Mrs. Robert Moore, Mrs. William Trelease, Mrs. E.C. Runge, and Charlotte Rumbold, investigated the condition of women and children employed in St. Louis factories and stores over a two-year period. During the second year, state and city factory inspectors joined the effort. Fischel's 1901 report to the Missouri Federation of Women's Clubs noted that official inspections led to improved conditions in the factories, but further legislation was still needed. The labor study brought the class-bound vision of members of the Wednesday Club and similar organizations to the fore. A *St. Louis Post-Dispatch* article, "Where Women Work," emphasized the point that statistics on women's employment would be used in the Federation of Women's Clubs' discussion on the "housework problem." The Wednesday Club committee reported that 11,403 women were employed in tobacco factories, shoe factories, dry-goods stores, laundries, printing houses, tailors' sweat shops, bagging factories, candy-making factories, bakeries, and paper box-making factories, rather than domestic service.[186] Reform efforts of the Missouri Federation of Women's Clubs reflected the worldview of its middle-class, European-American membership.

Women also joined their "natural" strengths to other reform crusades: prison reform, health measures, child labor, compulsory schooling, and settlement work. Reformers' efforts met with mixed results. The thirty-year war against St. Louis' industrial smoke smoldered in spite of legislation on smoke emissions and the official declaration that smoke was a public nuisance. The smoke-abatement movement drew support from diverse elements, each with ties to major developments in Progressive-Era society. Engineers, concerned with the scientific aspects of smoke abatement, reflected the trend toward professionalization; inspectors were bound by growing bureaucratization; Wednesday Club members protested that the smoke cloud "endangers the health of our families, especially those of weak lungs and delicate throats, impairs the eyesight of our children, and adds infinitely to our labors and expenses as housekeepers."[187] Socialists joined the smoke abatement crusade, pointing to the health hazards caused by industrial smoke, while members of the Civic League based their protests on financial grounds.[188] Robert Dale Grinder concludes that public protest against smoke was difficult to sustain in the face of industrial power; the common interest in smoke abatement did not prove strong enough to overcome fundamental differences among the protesters.[189]

Women reformers were more successful with the Missouri Children's Code of 1919, legislation that put Missouri in the vanguard of child welfare reform.[190] After two years of study the first Missouri Children's Code Commission brought forty-three recommendations to the General Assembly in 1917; the commission met disappointing failure when only eleven recommendations were written into law. A second Missouri Children's Code Commission was appointed and, like the first, prepared a code that won national acclaim. But this time reformers mobilized public opinion to support the proposed code. Women's groups such as the WCTU, the Missouri Federation of Women's Clubs, the Missouri Women's Committee of the National Defense Council, and the Equal Suffrage Club played a crucial role in building support for the code.[191]

In another area of social reform, settlement volunteers at the St. Louis Self-Culture Hall directed their energies to indoctrinating poor men, women, and children about city ordinances and laws, and municipal rights and privileges. In *Notable Women of St. Louis,* Johnson did not trace explosive social conditions to poverty or discrimination; rather, she wrote that conflicting ethnic values and ignorance of American ways of living were to blame, again brandishing the assumptions of her class.

> Poverty is not the worst condition in those districts; it is the crowding
> and misunderstanding of widely different nationalities grouped in

neighborhoods, or crowded in them, and the social difficulties that
arise out of such misunderstandings and their lack of knowledge of
American habits of life and institutions. The only value in social
work—in settlement work—is when people are taught the laws that
protect them and are not obliged to call on some subsidized
institution. [192]

Social reform involving immigrants, while it existed, did not occupy as
central a position in St. Louis as in many other cities in the United
States. Compared to other areas, and to its own situation in the mid-
nineteenth century, St. Louis had a relatively small immigrant
population in the twentieth century. Ruth Crawford wrote on *The
Immigrant in St. Louis* in 1916, although to a reading public that tended
to equate "immigrant" with "social problem," she had little to say.
Crawford acknowledged that "St. Louis has never been considered a
city in which the presence of the foreign-born constituted an acute
problem."[193] School policy was one measure of the minor impact that
immigration had in St. Louis. As Crawford explained, U.S. citizens
expected the public schools to take the chief responsibility for
socializing immigrants to American culture. Yet in St. Louis, Crawford
found that the steady increase in registration of immigrant children in
public schools over a ten-year period was not significant enough to
"disturb unduly the equipment or the methods employed" in the
schools.[194] Although citizens did not believe St. Louis suffered an
"immigrant problem," they were as prejudiced toward new immigrants
as other Americans. One of the women featured in *Notable Women of
St. Louis*, Mrs. Anita Calvert Bourgeoise, published a journal devoted
to promoting "the standard of American aristocracy of birth by bringing
to light many hundreds of pedigrees of prominent men and women in
the high places of America today."[195] *The Invincible Magazine of
History and Biography* aimed to be one of the first authoritative
publications of identified Anglo-American families. [196]

It appears as if Johnson's 1914 publication was an attempt to
promote the "respectable" side of the suffrage movement. Over half of
the *Notable Women* were married and articles emphasized women's
roles as mothers. For instance, Johnson described Mrs. Samuel R.
Burgess, U.S. chess champion, as a "plain, straightforward, sensible,
clear-headed woman, absolutely without any pretense or desire for
notoriety. She is a delightful companion and a devoted mother." [197] Mrs.
Edmund A. Garrett, a sculptor, concluded the description of her work

with a reference to her sons. "What is the happiness of modeling and creating a clay image to that greater happiness of a mother in her children?"[198] Johnson was careful to soften her descriptions of active, enterprising women with references to their "womanly" qualities. Mrs. Philip N. Moore, a woman of versatile ability, "guides and directs with a grace that is hard to define. Above all, she is very conservative—her demands are made with quiet dignity and grace."[199]

Women's activism, however, was not always met with dignity and grace. Another mother, Kate Richards O'Hare, found herself writing letters to her children in St. Louis from the Missouri State Penitentiary in 1919. O'Hare was a Socialist organizer who was imprisoned under the wartime Espionage Act for criticizing the U.S. government's role in World War I. She entered prison in 1919 to serve a five-year term; there she worked with Emma Goldman for the welfare of women prisoners. O'Hare was pardoned by President Coolidge in 1920. Her book, *In Prison*, was considered influential in bringing about prison reform.[200]

Mari Jo Buhle writes that the brewing industry in St. Louis, Milwaukee, Chicago, and New York City prompted one of the earliest industrial union movements in the United States. Much of the German culture in nineteenth-century St. Louis was based on socialist principles, so when Socialists began to form trade unions and party branches, an array of social clubs and sick-and-death benefit societies sprang up as well.[201] In 1875, women in St. Louis answered the call of New York Socialist women to form women's groups within the organization. *St. Louis Labor* converted pages of fashion and recipes to politically sophisticated women's departments as Socialists appealed to the sizable population of young working women in St. Louis.[202] Buhle describes the Socialist women in St. Louis and other industrial centers as women who understood the notion of a women's sphere (most were married), who probably felt the sting of paternalism and twinges of self-doubt when asked to participate in party activities. Differences among the substantial ethnic components of the party and English-speaking radicals, including municipal reformers, ex-Populists, college-educated or independently wealthy intellectuals, made the development of a culturally cohesive force difficult.[203] In addition, socialist women found it difficult to reconcile women's-rights issues with the class struggle. Although the 1901 platform for the Socialist Party of America demanded equal civil and political rights for men and women, many took for granted that the end of capitalism would bring about equality between the sexes. Foner maintains that the Socialist party put forward no significant theoretical position on the "woman question."[204]

Anne Firor Scott recounts that women built vital communities during the Progressive Era: asylums, libraries, schools, colleges, kindergartens, health clinics, museums, parks, playgrounds; in the process, they created professional careers and engaged in self-discovery and formed the very core of social and political development in the United States at the turn of the century. Organizations provided the vehicles through which women made their voices heard. One woman reflected "Suddenly [women] . . . realized that they possessed influence; that as organizations they could ask and gain, where as women they received no attention . . . ."[205] Early on, many argued that women should have an influence on society because of the ways in which they were assumed to differ from men. In 1900, William T. Harris, former St. Louis school superintendent and then current U.S. Commissioner of Education, gave a speech in which he emphasized this point.

> Man has a tendency to use the principle of justice, not only in dealing with his fellow men in their full maturity, but with children and the weaklings of society, who have not the full normal endowment of responsibility. Woman has the characteristic of graciousness and kindness, perhaps I should say tenderness. Justice and grace or graciousness are thus the two characteristics appertaining to sex, and the admission of women into all spheres of social influence will bring the principle of nurture into those provinces where the principle of justice has been found not sufficient for the best development of certain classes of society. . . . Just as the tenderness of the mother nurtures the child into a responsible will power . . . so this feminine element added to the State will make it able to provide for that very larger population which fills the slums of our cities and constantly menaces life and property.[206]

Janet Zollinger Giele explains that this ethic of compassion, which many attributed specifically to women, paralleled the argument that women's sameness with men called for an ethic of science. A central argument in support of home economics focused on the use of scientific method in domestic science, whether applied in the individual home or in society at large. Ellen Richards, also writing in 1900, maintained that the "secret of success in housekeeping, as well as in manufacturing, lies in the right use of *methods and machinery*. . . . It is not a profound knowledge of any one or a dozen sciences which women need, so much as an attitude of mind . . . which impels them to ask, 'Can I do better than I am doing?'. . . "[207] Carried into social-reform work by the "feminine" capacity to nurture, women honed the professional expertise necessary to maintain agency in the early years of the twentieth century.

Although middle-class European-American women generated much of the social-reform activity during the Progressive Era, others with fewer resources and additional challenges made significant contributions to the St. Louis community. The women associated with the Annie Malone Children's Home and the Mary Ryder Homes for Women and Girls left tremendous legacies. In 1888, Sarah W. Newton led several African-American community leaders to organize a home to care for neglected and indigent children. Newton, a graduate of Oberlin College, was among the first African-American teachers employed in the St. Louis public schools. In 1919, Annie M. Malone accepted the presidency of the St. Louis Colored Orphans Home, and remained in that office until 1943. In 1902, Malone founded the Poro College and System of Beauty Culture; it became the wealthiest African-American enterprise in St. Louis.[208] Regarded as the world's richest African-American woman, Malone was said to have earned the highest per-day income in the state of Missouri. She made generous contributions to the St. Louis Y.M.C.A., the St. Louis Y.W.C.A., the Saint James A.M.E. Church, and made down payments on homes for each of her St. Louis employees. The name of the St. Louis Colored Orphans Home was changed to the Annie Malone Children's Home after Malone financed the lot and construction of a new facility.[209]

St. Louis' "Grand Old Lady of Labor," Mary Ryder, learned the printing trade as a girl and was a member of the International Typographical Union for over forty years. When she was widowed with four children at age thirty-five, Ryder returned to her trade, eventually becoming active in politics as a labor union leader. At age thirty-seven she started attending high-school night classes to study law, English, spelling, and public speaking. The homes that bear Ryder's name stand out as the most celebrated accomplishments in her sixty years of community service. The first Mary Ryder Home for homeless women was established in 1930 during the Depression. After a St. Louis police sergeant notified Ryder, then president of the Women's Trade Union League, of the many women seeking shelter at the police station, she organized a free shelter for European-American women at 3517 Pine Street. One hundred women filled the twelve-room house the first night it was opened. In less than a week a second shelter was opened for African-American women at 3533 Lawton Avenue. The St. Louis Joint Council of Women's Auxiliaries helped to establish the Ryder Homes and continued to support them for many years.[210]

The decade from 1910 to 1920 saw progressivism, which had been incubating at the local level, break out across the nation. Anne Firor Scott identified the following characteristics of women's voluntary associations in her book, *Natural Allies: Women's Associations in American History.* The associations served several purposes and created effective communication networks. Bureaucratic organization appeared about 1900; national groups were generally designed in a hierarchical fashion while local chapters tended to operate on consensus. National policy was often not congruent with local policy. Money was hard to come by and was often earned in very labor-intensive ways. Leadership was of high caliber, especially in the years before women gained access to the professions and business. Many women experienced conflict between their public and home responsibilities. Although most operated within the prevailing social norms, their own activity helped to alter societal norms over time. Linda Gordon explores the contours of separate networks in her article, "Black and White Visions of Welfare: Women's Welfare Activism, 1890-1945." Almost without exception, African-American and European-American reformers worked on separate paths.[211] Networks were segregated because national women's organizations were segregated; European-American groups usually excluded African- American women. Gordon uncovered three major differences between African-American and European-American women welfare activists. African-American women worked for universal entitlement programs while European-Americans promoted supervised, means-tested programs. The two groups of women held different attitudes toward working mothers. And, the groups designed different strategies for protecting women from sexual exploitation.[212] European-American women perceived of welfare as an urban reform activity and created governmental programs to address the problems they identified. Disfranchised African-American women had to turn to other sources to ameliorate living conditions in their communities, rural as well as urban. Gordon writes that education became the single most important area of activism for African-American women.[213]

In 1915, seven teachers in the St. Louis public schools, all graduates of Sumner High School's Normal Department, formed the Prudence Crandall Club, an association devoted to study. The club was named in honor of Prudence Crandall, a Connecticut teacher who maintained a school for African-American girls in spite of intense public pressure. From its beginning, the Crandall Club incorporated social activism with study. During the winter of 1914-1915, homeless, jobless men, African-American migrants and European refugees, sought relief in St. Louis. The Crandalls engaged in welfare work instituted by African-American churches. In the same year, the Crandalls studied Carter G. Woodson's text *The Negro in History* and his other works that integrated African-American history into "traditional" U.S. and world history. Crandalls joined public protests of the East St. Louis race riots in 1917, and ten years later were delegates to the National Association for the Study of Negro Life and History Annual Conference, which was held in St. Louis. Crandalls were among those to request that local school districts adopt textbooks that included contributions of African Americans and to require the teaching of African-American history. [214]

Sumner High School graduate Ethel Hedgeman Lyle initiated a movement at Howard University that resulted in the establishment of Alpha Kappa Alpha, the first Greek-letter organization established by and for African-American women. The St. Louis chapter of Alpha Kappa Alpha was organized in 1920. Charter member Felicia Alexander recalled that the women at that meeting "were so elated the six of us got together and we felt pretty important, if you please, because in the early 1920's there were not too many Negro women graduates, especially in the city of St. Louis." [215] The women of Alpha Kappa Alpha hosted scholarship teas for high-school students to discuss college and career information, provided scholarships, and worked to improve health facilities in rural areas along the Mississippi River. [216]

African-American women's groups have been recognized for their strength, but as Deborah Gray White states, the strength had to be cultivated. "It came no more naturally to them than to anyone. . . . If they seemed exceptionally strong it was partly because they often functioned in groups and derived strength from numbers." [217] The Independent Order of Saint Luke was one of the most successful African-American mutual-benefit societies in the late-nineteenth and early-twentieth centuries. It combined insurance functions with economic development and social-political activities. Saint Luke women expanded their roles in the Richmond, Virginia, community through their leadership in a 1904 streetcar boycott and in their pronouncements against segregation, lynching, and lack of equal educational opportunity. Elsa Barkley Brown holds up the Independent Order of Saint Luke as an example of the strength women claimed through organizations that recognized the value of interdependence between public and domestic spheres, community and family, male and female, and the race and sex struggles.[218] Similar organizations in St. Louis date to the 1863 founding of Heroines of Jericho, St. Mary's Court No. 1. The 1914 preamble to the constitution of the Queen Ester Court No. 6 provided a succinct explanation of the society: "We the wives, daughters, sisters and widows of master masons in the city of St. Louis, state of Missouri, do hereby agree to form a court for our mutual relief and protection in case of sickness or distress."[219] Records indicate that the Heroines of Jericho relied on male clergy for spiritual guidance but conducted business affairs on their own. By the turn of the century, St. Louis Heroines of Jericho had established a forty-year history of collective activity: "It has done much for the uplifting of the race by its pure and upright womanhood and its business like method in accumulating quite a goodly sum has stimulated other societies to do likewise."[220] The holistic nature of womanist history that Brown uncovered in Richmond, and that represented in St. Louis by the Heroines of Jericho, remains a promising model for social activism.

Arguing that 1920 is an inappropriate benchmark for women's history in the United States, Estelle B. Freedman believes that women's institution building did survive as a reform strategy after passage of the Nineteenth Amendment. Her essay "Separatism Revisited" advances the thesis that women developed new approaches to reform as their movement grew smaller, beleaguered, and more vulnerable. Grassroots women's institutions continued to nurture the U.S. women's reform tradition well into the twentieth century.[221]

A "SILENT" CRUSADE FOR SUFFRAGE

On 19 February 1869, the St. Louis City Council reportedly "broke up in hilarity" when councilman Jordan introduced a resolution urging the Missouri legislature to allow women the right to vote.[222] Two years earlier, U.S. Senator B. Gratz Brown (MO) spent his last days in Congress advocating for the franchise for women and African

Americans. "I stand for Universal Suffrage . . . and do not recognize the right of society to limit it on any grounds of race, color, or sex."[223] Brown's colleagues in the Senate considered his stand quixotic.[224] During the nineteenth century, however, the Missourian who challenged the forces of disfranchisement most significantly was Virginia Minor, president of the Missouri Woman Suffrage Association. On 15 October 1872, Minor attempted to register to vote in the St. Louis election district where she lived. When election registrar Reese Happersett refused to allow her to register, Minor and her husband, attorney Francis Minor, brought suit in the Circuit Court of St. Louis County.[225] Less than twenty years after the Dred Scott decision, St. Louis sent another momentous case to the U.S. Supreme Court.

The Minors first floated their ideas on the constitutional guarantee for woman suffrage at the 1869 national convention for women's rights, which activists held in St. Louis. Addressing the convention, Virginia Minor stated, "I believe that the Constitution of the United States gives me every right and privilege to which every other citizen is entitled."[226] Centering their argument around the Fourteenth Amendment to the U.S. Constitution, the Minors argued that American citizenship, which was national in character and therefore paramount to all State authority, extended to women the right to vote. The plaintiff's argument also addressed hardships to women related to disfranchisement and merits of woman suffrage. The Supreme Court's unanimous 1875 opinion in *Minor v. Happersett* stated that the U.S. Constitution did not confer the right of suffrage on citizens when it was adopted, thus suffrage was not coextensive with citizenship. States, having withheld the vote from certain classes of men, could prohibit woman suffrage. On this point, the Court contradicted its own language in the Slaughter-house cases of 1873: "[T]he negro having, by the Fourteenth Amendment, been declared a citizen of the United States, is thus made a voter in every State of the Union."[227] The Court did not address the other components of the Minor's argument. In spite of defeat in *Minor v. Happersett*, scholars note that Virginia and Francis Minor's efforts marked an early innovative attempt to secure votes for women. The ideas they presented at the St. Louis convention were taken up by other women in the long-term campaign for woman suffrage. Elizabeth Cady Stanton, for instance, relied on the St. Louis resolutions in her 1870 testimony before a congressional committee considering enfranchisement of women in Washington, D.C.[228]

Dina M. Young's characterization of the women's campaign for suffrage in St. Louis as "the silent search for a voice" accurately describes a movement that was sporadic in character, spasmodic in development, and poised between conflicting interests in a conservative city.[229] Monia Cook Morris' "History of Woman Suffrage in Missouri," and the collaborative piece, "History of Woman Suffrage in Missouri," written soon after passage of the Nineteenth Amendment, detailed the woman suffrage movement in Missouri. The growth of the woman suffrage movement was, it is well known, linked to the crusade for the abolition of slavery, but in Missouri the women's movement did not ignite until after the Civil War. St. Louis gave birth to the woman suffrage movement in Missouri with the founding of the Woman's Suffrage Association of Missouri on 8 May 1867.[230] Suffrage groups in Missouri focused their energy toward the state legislature. Women faithfully petitioned for school and municipal voting rights, presidential suffrage, and the general use of the ballot throughout the last half of the nineteenth century. But of the eighteen proposals introduced to the General Assembly in Jefferson City between 1867 and 1901, only eight came to a vote. These attempts to extend the right to vote to women were unsuccessful; presidential suffrage was the only woman suffrage request granted by the Missouri legislature in this period, and that came in 1919.[231]

The St. Louis Branch of the National Woman Suffrage Association formed in May 1879, but woman suffrage associations did not develop extensively in Missouri during the 1880s and 1890s. Temperance was uppermost in the minds of many reformers; since the Woman's Christian Temperance Union advocated woman suffrage, Morris surmised that many women felt membership in one society was sufficient. In 1892, the Missouri membership in the National American Woman Suffrage Association was only 1.2 per 100,000 population, the lowest rate in the midwest. By contrast, Missouri reported between 57 and 278 members per 100,000 population in the WCTU in 1890. The State Federation of Women's Clubs emerged in 1896 in Missouri, drawing women in yet another direction.[232]

A stillness settled over the suffrage movement in Missouri in the first years of the twentieth century. No petitions were made to the Missouri legislature from 1901 to 1911, and no woman suffrage conventions were held for several years. Florence Atkinson remembered that the "word 'Suffragette' was not even whispered in polite society at that time, and it was like throwing a bomb in conservative St. Louis to repeat the new slogan 'Votes for Women!'"[233] In 1910, when the St. Louis Equal Suffrage League was organized, its rationale reflected a cautious tone. The purpose of the club was entirely educational, to "bring together men and women who are *willing to consider* the question of Equal Suffrage and by earnest co-operation to secure its establishment."[234] Women in the Equal Suffrage League intended to steer clear of the radical image of women's-rights activists; they insisted to the press that they be referred to as "suffragists" rather than "suffragettes," to distance themselves from any hint of militant activity. The resulting headlines proclaimed "Society Women Organize, Repudiate Term Militant," and "Women to Seek Votes in Wholly Quiet Way Here."[235] The Equal Suffrage League brought prominent speakers to St. Louis to speak on the suffrage issue, issued press reports, organized street meetings, and established branch organizations in different parts of the city. By 1913, observers noted a change in public opinion toward woman suffrage with the Farmers' Alliance, the State Teachers' Association, Prohibitionists, Single Taxers, and leading papers lending their support to the cause.[236] Nonetheless, Missouri voters defeated a suffrage amendment in November 1914.[237]

When the National Democratic Convention came to St. Louis in June 1916, St. Louis suffragists drew upon their strength and created, perhaps, the most dramatic display of suffrage activity in St. Louis history. Seven thousand women dressed in white with yellow sashes, some carrying yellow parasols, lined the delegates' route to the convention site on the opening morning of the convention. It was a "walkless, talkless parade," pressing the case for woman suffrage. A poem evaluating the effect of the "moral gauntlet" appeared in the press the following day.

> Citizen and Democrat
> Marching down the Golden Lane,
> Marching out to nominate
> Wilson for a candidate.
> How the Democrats did hate
> Marching down the Golden Lane.
>
> Silence! My, but it did talk
> Marching down the Golden Lane.
> Fast the delegates did walk,
> Marching down the Golden Lane!

But they couldn't get away
From the "Women's Votes" display.

They'll all recall for many a day
Marching down the Golden Lane. [238]

Another appeal was staged on the steps of the old Art Museum, involving a number of women representing the states of the Union, arranged by their various degrees of suffrage for women. "Up to Liberty" and the "Golden Lane" converted some Missourians to the suffrage cause, according to press reports, but moved the convention delegates only to support a vague, noncommittal plank for suffrage. [239]

During World War I, St. Louis women combined their suffrage work with food conservation, War Savings Stamps sales, Red Cross work, and other wartime efforts. The civic work of the Equal Suffrage League included protesting against repeal of the Federal Child Labor Law, investigations into the high cost of milk, calls to reorganize the police-woman system, and appeals to increase appropriations for public health work. In 1917, St. Louis suffragists denounced White House picketing by members of the Congressional Union, maintaining their conservative approach in the suffrage battle. [240] In March 1919, the NAWSA convention was again held in St. Louis. That spring the 50th General Assembly passed the Presidential Suffrage bill, giving Missouri women the right to vote in presidential elections. In a special session in July, the Missouri legislature ratified the Susan B. Anthony Amendment to the U.S. Constitution. Missouri was the eleventh state to ratify the Nineteenth Amendment. [241]

In her insightful article "The Silent Search for a Voice," Dina M. Young drew important connections between women's positions on progressive reform and the trademark silence of the suffrage movement in St. Louis. The founding of the St. Louis Equal Suffrage League, which ended a dormant period of suffrage work in Missouri, stood also as a watershed, marking a change in the dominant ideology supporting woman suffrage. During the nineteenth century, St. Louis activists such as Virginia Minor argued that women deserved the vote based on their equality with men. Leading St. Louis suffragists in the twentieth century highlighted the argument that women's differences from men qualified them for suffrage. Society needed women's input, and to reform society effectively women needed the vote. English suffragist Ethel Arnold presented a lecture in St. Louis at the invitation of the St.

Louis Equal Suffrage League, just three days after its formation. Her nonthreatening challenge could not have been better suited for St. Louis.

> What are municipal, state and national governments but housekeeping on a large scale? And who should be more qualified to conduct them than the sex whose life has for centuries been devoted to housekeeping? Everyone knows that women are naturally more economical than men.[242]

Nancy Cott's research clarified that nineteenth-century women's-rights activists based their arguments on both women's sameness with men and women's unique sexual character. This theoretical framework embraced functional ambiguity. In the twentieth century the vote harmonized the two strands; suffrage--a just end in itself--became an expedient means to other worthy goals.[243] In St. Louis, however, the appeal for the vote as a means to an end dominated public discussion.

Women's reform activity in organizations such as the Civic Improvement League and the Wednesday Club provided practical experience in politics that carried over into the battle for suffrage. This class of women wanted the vote to add legitimacy to their other reform efforts. Reform efforts, however, were not popular throughout the city and the close ties that developed between suffragists and city reformers did not help the suffragist movement. In fact, some observers regarded St. Louis as the most hostile region in Missouri on the suffrage issue; the 1914 suffrage amendment failed by nearly a three-to-one margin there. [244] Immigrant groups, laborers, and socialists from the south and east sections of St. Louis associated city reform measures with the Big Cinch, Anglo-Saxon business elites from the affluent Central West End. The proposed city charter of 1911 (which also failed by a three-to-one margin), as well as city transportation, recreation, and beautification proposals, reflected the perspectives of the Big Cinch. As newsman William Marion Reedy noted in 1908, in the course of time the Big Cinch saw their interests as the public interest.[245] The St. Louis Equal Suffrage League did eventually establish branch organizations in northern and southern parts of the city and groups such as the Jewish Alliance League and the Wage-Earners' Suffrage League joined in the suffrage movement, but the locus of power remained in the Central West End. Equal Suffrage League members were slow to reach out to voters with backgrounds different than their own. Young contends that city politics between constituents in the Central West End and other sections of St. Louis caught the suffrage movement in its crossfire, keeping suffragists silent on issues of public concern.[246]

The conservative climate was not, of course, limited to St. Louis. The August 1920 issue of the *Ladies' Home Journal* contained the following creed:

> I believe in woman's rights; but I believe in woman's sacrifices also.
> I believe in woman's freedom; but I believe it should be within the
>   restrictions of the Ten Commandments.
> I believe in woman's suffrage; but I believe many things are vastly more
>   important.
> I believe in woman's brains; but I believe still more in her emotions.[247]

Those who believed that the Nineteenth Amendment would dramatically transform women's status in U.S. society were destined for disappointment. As the above quote from the popular women's magazine suggests, for many women the extension of suffrage did not rank among leading concerns. A certain continuity characterized the pre- and postsuffrage decades for African-American women, given the Jim Crow grip on voting rights.[248] Indeed, as Paula Baker discovered, woman suffrage had little impact on women; in addition, it failed to exert much influence on politics in the United States. In her article, "The Domestication of Politics: Women and American Political Society, 1780-1920," Baker argues that men granted women the right to vote just as the importance of traditional political culture, and the meaning of the vote itself, changed. Government moved farther away from voter accountability as appointed officials claimed more power. Interest groups began to chip away at the effectiveness of political parties.[249] Yet interest groups formed around women's issues drew heavy criticism. Once women gained the vote, and with it ostensible entry into the political process, women's political solidarity was perceived by men as a threat .[250]

Nancy Cott warns students of women's history not to confuse the end of the suffrage movement with the demise of feminism. The early struggle of modern feminism is rooted in the political shifts of the 1920s. In point of fact, the only time suffrage commanded a mass movement in the United States—involving working-class, middle-class, upper-class, African-American, European-American, radical, liberal, conservative, socialist, and capitalist women—was the decade between

1910 and 1920.[251] Elinor Lerner makes the convincing argument that passage of the Nineteenth Amendment required substantial support from a wide constituency, including immigrants and workers. As the suffragists in St. Louis were slow to realize, their ambition to get men to share the power of the vote depended upon strong support of women at the local, neighborhood level. The factors that Lerner found to be critical regarding community attitudes toward suffrage were the economic and social position of women within a specific ethnic group, the extent of suffrage organizing in the community, and the degree of interest in woman suffrage expressed by community organizations such as religious institutions, labor groups, and political parties. She discovered that interconnections between family structure and work patterns were more important than race and class in determining opinions on woman suffrage.[252]

Historians now understand that feminism was not confined to European-American women of the upper and middle classes. Orleck writes that many women struggled to forge a personal politics that balanced the conflicting pulls of gender, class, ethnicity, and family. Mildred Moore coined the term "industrial feminism" in 1915 to refer to feminism imbued with class consciousness and a vivid understanding of the harsh realities of industrial work.[253] African-American women developed a womanist perspective that wove together elements of gender, race, and class. Organizations of European-American women's-rights activists, however, separated issues of racism and sexism in the name of expediency. As history unfolded, narratives of expediency marred the work of the National American Woman Suffrage Association. In 1894, "expediency" meant that Susan B. Anthony asked Frederick Douglass, the only man who had spoken in favor of woman suffrage at Seneca Falls in 1848, not to attend the NAWSA convention in Atlanta. In 1899, "expediency" meant that the NAWSA formally recognized woman suffrage and African-American civil rights as separate causes. In 1913, "expediency" meant that suffrage marches were racially segregated. While European-American feminists constructed arguments for woman suffrage that deliberately omitted mention of racial oppression, African-American women articulated a social critique that embraced a commitment to universal human rights.[254]

"Justice, simple justice," drove the agenda of African-American women's coalitions against racism and sexism.[255] Gertrude E.H. Bustill Mossell, author of *The Work of the Afro-American Woman*, embedded feminist thought in her work for racial uplift. "To hold one's self in harmony with one's race while working out one's personal gift with freedom and conviction is to combine the highest results of inheritance and personal endeavor."[256] No one offered a more powerful insight into the multiple oppressions of women's lives in the nineteenth century than Ida B. Wells. Wells used her pen to deconstruct the white, southern cultures of lynching and chivalry as manifestations of patriarchal power, exposing pervasive constellations of race, gender, economics, and violence.[257] Caraway describes Wells' literature on lynching not as a construct of victimization, but as a discourse of empowerment for African-American women, African-American men, and European-American women.[258] As womanist history demonstrates, finding our way to justice requires an appreciation of the many elements that constitute our lives.

CONCLUSION

Since the 1960s, women's historians have worked to break the silence of women in United States history. In the earliest phase of this work scholars examined women's lives within what many perceived as restrictive communities. Driven by the liberal ideology nurtured during the civil rights and feminist movements in the second half of the twentieth century, historians were drawn to earlier women's efforts to claim their rights as persons. The underlying concept was women's equality with men. By the end of the 1970s, historians were finding that the separate spheres that encompassed women were quite often supportive and nurturing communities. Scholars began to explore the strength of a sisterhood built on the special qualities possessed by women and to wonder about its promise for society. The fundamental assumption that women differed from men in significant ways framed this historical analysis. Recent work on the history of African-American, Latina, Native-American, Asian-American, working-class, and other women has exposed the inherent weakness of a theory that ignores the diverse life experiences of women. Separate female communities that provided solidarity for some women quite often excluded others. Historians now begin their study with the axiom that women differ from each other; gender, ethnicity, class, sexuality, geographic location all influence women's lives and women's history. The relationships women forge with each other, the relationships women construct with men, the degree to which gender directs the impact of social structures on people, and the force with which women determine the dynamics of the political economy are issues that add to the richness and complexity of women's history.

More studies are needed to break the silence of St. Louis women's history. Much of the scholarly work on women's history in St. Louis is representative of the early "Women in History" stage of development. Susan Blow is hailed as an innovator in American education for her work establishing the first public-school kindergarten in the United States; people recall that Josephine Baker performed on the sidewalks outside the St. Louis Booker T. Washington Theater as a child; many have read of the hornet's nest that Kate Chopin stirred up with her 1899 publication of *The Awakening*; fewer are familiar with Fannie Cook's work in race relations and workers' rights.[259] The material presented in this chapter plots an outline of women's history in St. Louis from 1870 to 1930.

Public anxiety over morality paralleled women's increasing participation in the public sphere in the latter part of the nineteenth century and reached a peak in the 1920s. St. Louis found itself in a national spotlight in 1870 when the city enacted the Social Evil Ordinance, regulating prostitution. Purity reformers lost the initial battle in St. Louis but they rebounded with a repeal of the ordinance in 1874. Although the controversial ordinance was in effect for only four years, it appeared as a harbinger of social policy to come. As the United States moved into the twentieth century, government became increasingly involved in citizens' lives. Public attention to issues of morality accelerated when the "new woman" appeared on the scene. Psychologists turned to the new study of adolescence and suggested that young women channel their energies through school, but not through academic study. Public distress subsided during the 1920s; by the end of the decade girls once again preferred marriage to career goals.

The increase in the number and percentage of women working for wages at the turn of the century prompted a St. Louis minister's wife to speak out against the "new woman." Competition in the workplace between men and women would lead to an erosion in male-female relations, Mrs. Alvin W. Claxon prophesied, putting the well-being of society at risk. Although a number of people countered Claxon's position on women in the workforce, most based their argument on the fact that many women *had* to work. The time when women could work for personal satisfaction was still some years away. Gender, class, and ethnicity were all key factors in determining whether or not a woman would enter the paid labor force. Clerical work was the fastest growing occupation for women between 1910 and 1920, but this opportunity was almost exclusively reserved for European-American women. Domestic service registered the sharpest decline among women workers in this period. In St. Louis, however, the percentage of African-American women working in domestic service increased from 1910 to 1920. During the first decades of the twentieth century, women entered the professions and industrial work in increasing numbers. Women began to be accepted as permanent workers in the U.S. economy during the 1920s and expressed self-respect for their roles as working women.

Social reform in St. Louis emanated through suffrage organizations, civic groups, and professional associations. Women brought their "special" qualities to bear on the major social ills of the day, taking their place as the housekeepers of society. Their efforts were, no doubt, motivated by genuine concern (winning support for the Missouri Children's Code, for example) as well as personal interest. (Fischel's 1901 report to the Missouri Federation of Women's Clubs on factory conditions was to be used in a discussion on the "housework problem.") During the 1910s, women in the Wednesday Club and the Civic Improvement League pressed for the ballot in order to more effectively execute their social housekeeping duties. After all, Virginia Minor's attempts for suffrage on the basis of social equality had long since failed. "Silence" characterized the woman suffrage movement that developed in St. Louis.

The status of women in St. Louis at the turn of the twentieth century, then, was unsettled. Moral values were in flux, expectations for the "ideal" woman were in transition, increasing numbers of women were seeking employment, social problems appeared to be spinning out of control, and women were disenfranchised. For those who agree with Alice Kessler-Harris, that gender is a process continually reshaped from within the individual and by one's environment, the Progressive Era is an exciting period to study. [260] The school has long been a major force in the construction of gender. With the introduction of the differentiated curriculum in the Progressive Era, educators changed the U.S. high school in a way that altered its function for the rest of the twentieth century. *From Female Scholar to Domesticated Citizen* is a study of the impact of the differentiated curriculum on girls' education in St. Louis high schools. It offers a perspective from which one can assess the effect of gender on the most significant curriculum development in U.S. high schools during the twentieth century, and it provides a framework for analyzing the power of schooling in shaping gender during one of the most volatile periods of women's history.

NOTES

1. Phyllis Stock-Morton, "Finding Our Own Ways: Different Paths to Women's History in the United States" in *Writing Women's History: International Perspectives*, Karen Offen, Ruth Roach Pierson, and Jane Rendall, eds. (Bloomington: Indiana University Press, 1991), 70.

2. Quoted in *U.S. History as Women's History: New Feminist Essays*, Linda K. Kerber, Alice Kessler-Harris, and Kathryn Kish Sklar, eds. (Chapel Hill: The University of North Carolina Press, 1995), 4.

3. Ibid., 5. For an outline of steps to emancipation through women's history, see Gerda Lerner, *The Female Experience: An American Documentary* (New York: Oxford University Press, 1992), xxi-xxii.

4. Gabriele Kaiser and Pat Rogers, "Introduction: Equity in Mathematics Education," in *Equity in Mathematics Education: Influences of Feminism and Culture*, Pat Rogers and Gabriele Kaiser, eds. (London: The Falmer Press, 1995), 2. See also, Peggy McIntosh, *Phase Theory of Curriculum Reform* (Wellesley, MA: Center for Research on Women, 1983).

5. William H. Chafe, *The Paradox of Change: American Women in the 20th Century* (New York: Oxford University Press, 1991), vii.

6. Kerber, Kessler-Harris, and Sklar, *U.S. History as Women's History,* 7.

7. Ibid., 5-6; Kaiser and Rogers, "Introduction," 2.

8. Stock-Morton, "Finding Our Own Ways," 59-60, 69.

9. Rosalind Rosenberg, *Divided Lives: American Women in the Twentieth Century* (New York: Hill and Wang, 1992), x.

10. Chafe, *Paradox of Change*, viii.

11. Ibid., x-xi.

12. Rosenberg, *Divided Lives*, x.

13. Chafe, *Paradox of Change*, ix-x.

14. Rosenberg, *Divided Lives*, x.

15. *Unequal Sisters: A Multicultural Reader in U.S. Women's History*, Ellen Carol DuBois and Vicki L. Ruiz, eds. (New York: Routledge, 1990), xi.

16. Ibid., xi-xiii. See pages xiii-xv for notes on how the multicultural approach to women's history influences the way one interprets the histories of family, work, politics, sexuality, and women's relationships.

17. Nancy A. Hewitt, "Beyond the Search for Sisterhood: American Women's History in the 1980s," in *Unequal Sisters: A Multicultural Reader in U.S. Women's History*, 1.

18. Ibid., 2; See Nancy F. Cott, *The Bonds of Womanhood: "Women's Sphere in New England, 1780-1835* (New Haven: Yale University Press, 1977); Carroll Smith Rosenberg, "The Female World of Love and Ritual: Relations between Women in Nineteenth-Century America," *Signs: Journal of Women in Culture and Society* 1 (Autumn 1975): 1-29; and Barbara Welter, "The Cult of True Womanhood: 1820-1860," *American Quarterly* 18 (1966): 151-174.

19. Estelle Freedman, "Separatism as Strategy: Female Institution Building and American Feminism, 1870-1930," *Feminist Studies* 5 (Fall 1979): 513.

20. Hewitt, "Beyond the Search," 1.

21. Linda K. Kerber, "Separate Spheres, Female Worlds, Woman's Place: The Rhetoric of Women's History," *The Journal of American History* 75 (June 1988): 10.

22. Ibid., 10-11.

23. Kerber, "Separate Spheres," 9-13.

24. Ibid., 12-14. Kerber notes that Welter's work supported the premise that separation denigrated women and kept them subordinate; Kraditor contrasted autonomy with women's "proper" sphere; and Lerner pointed to the fact that, as class distinctions in U.S. society sharpened, social attitudes toward women became increasingly polarized.

25. Ibid., 14-17.

26. Ibid., 17-18.

27. Michelle Zimbalist Rosaldo quoted in Kerber, "Separate Spheres," 38.

28. Kerber, "Separate Spheres," 37.

29. Audre Lorde, quoted in Nancie Caraway, *Segregated Sisterhood: Racism and the Politics of American Feminism* (Knoxville: University of Tennessee Press, 1991), 13.

30. Elsa Barkley Brown, "Womanist Consciousness: Maggie Lena Walker and the Independent Order of Saint Luke," *Signs: Journal of Women in Culture and Society* 14 (Spring 1989): 610. The same is true for Native-American women, Asian-American women, Mexican-American women, and other "women of color" in the United States. The focus on African-American women here corresponds to my study of African-American and European-American young women in St. Louis schools.

31. Beverly Guy-Sheftall, *Daughters of Sorrow: Attitudes toward Black Women, 1880-1920*, vol. 11 in *Black Women in United States History*, Darlene Clark Hine, ed. (Brooklyn: Carlson Publishing, 1990), 11: 2.

32. Donna Gabaccia, *From the Other Side: Women, Gender, and Immigrant Life in the U.S., 1820-1990* (Bloomington: Indiana University Press, 1994), 130-131; Brown, "Womanist Consciousness," 611.

33. Brown, "Womanist Consciousness," 610-611.

34. Caraway, *Segregated Sisterhood*, 125.

35. Brown, "Womanist Consciousness," 613.

36. Chikwenye Okonjo Ogunyemi, quoted in Brown, "Womanist Consciousness," 614.

37. Caraway, *Segregated Sisterhood*, 166-167; Brown, "Womanist Consciousness," 614.

38. Anna Julia Cooper, quoted in Brown, "Womanist Consciousness," 614. Emphasis added by Brown.

39. Chafe, *Paradox of Change*, (New York: Oxford University Press, 1991), xii.

40. Ibid., xi.

41. Victoria Bissell Brown, "The Fear of Feminization: Los Angeles High Schools in the Progressive Era," *Feminist Studies* 16 (Fall 1990): 494; Helen Lefkowitz Horowitz, "Women and Education," in *Reclaiming the Past: Landmarks of Women's History*, Page Putnam Miller, ed. (Bloomington: Indiana University Press, 1992), 119.

42. Millicent Rutherford, "Feminism and the Secondary School Curriculum, 1890-1920." Ph.D. dissertation, Stanford University, 1977; David Tyack and Elisabeth Hansot, *Learning Together: A History of Coeducation in American Public Schools* (New Haven: Yale University Press, 1990); Brown, "Fear of Feminization;" John L. Rury, *Education and Women's Work: Female Schooling and the Division of Labor in Urban America, 1870-1930* (Albany: State University of New York Press, 1991); Jane Bernard Powers, *The "Girl Question" in Education: Vocational Education for Young Women in the Progressive Era* (London: The Falmer Press, 1992).

43. See, for instance, James D. Anderson, *The Education of Blacks in the South, 1860-1935* (Chapel Hill: The University of North Carolina Press, 1988); Powers, *The "Girl Question," in Education*; Joel Spring, *Deculturalization and the Struggle for Equality: A Brief History of the Education of Dominated Cultures in the United States*, (New York: McGraw-Hill, 1994); William J. Reese, *The Origins of the American High School* (New Haven: Yale University Press, 1995); Vanessa Siddle Walker, *Their Highest Potential: An African American School Community in the Segregated South* (Chapel Hill: The University of North Carolina Press, 1996); and, Howard Zinn, "The Question Period in Kalamazoo," *Z Magazine* V (December 1994): 33-38.

44. Judith Friedlander, Blanche Wiesen Cook, Alice Kessler-Harris, and Carroll Smith-Rosenberg, eds., *Women in Culture and Politics: A Century of Change* (Bloomington: Indiana University Press, 1986), 1.

45. Alice Kessler-Harris, "Reflections on a Field," in *New Viewpoints in Women's History: Working Papers from the Schlesinger Library 50th Anniversary Conference, March 4-5, 1994* (Cambridge, MA: The Arthur and Elizabeth Schlesinger Library on the History of Women in America, 1994), 24.

46. Ibid.

47. Ibid., 23.

48. Kerber, "Separate Spheres," *Journal of American History* 75 (June 1988): 27.

49. James Neal Primm, *Lion of the Valley: St. Louis, Missouri* (Boulder: Pruett Publishing, 1981), preface.

50. Mary K. Dains, "Missouri Women in Historical Writing," *Missouri Historical Review* 83 (1989): 427.

51. Ibid., 418-419.

52. See Beverly D. Bishop and Deborah W. Bolas, eds., *In Her Own Write: Women's History Resources in the Library and Archives of the Missouri Historical Society* (St. Louis: Missouri Historical Society, 1983) and "Collection Guide: Women" at the Joint Collection, University of Missouri Western Historical Manuscript Collection and State Historical Society of Missouri Manuscripts. Dains, 427-428.

53. John C. Burnham, "Medical Inspection of Prostitutes in America in the Nineteenth Century: The St. Louis Experiment and Its Sequel," *Bulletin of the History of Medicine* 45 (1971): 209.

54. Ibid., 218.

55. Quoted in Duane R. Sneddeker, "Regulating Vice: Prostitution and the St. Louis Social Evil Ordinance, 1870-1874," *Gateway Heritage: Quarterly Journal of the Missouri Historical Society* 11 (1990): 20.

56. Ibid.

57. Ibid., 21; John C. Burnham, "The Social Evil Ordinance—A Social Experiment in Nineteenth-Century St. Louis," *The Bulletin: Missouri Historical Society* 27 (1971): 211; Burnham, "Medical Inspection of Prostitutes," 217.

58. Quoted in Burnham, "Medical Inspection of Prostitutes," 206.

59. Ibid.

60. Burnham, "Social Evil Ordinance," 205; Sneddeker, "Regulating Vice," 21.

61. David J. Pivar, *Purity Crusade Sexual Morality and Social Control, 1868-1900* (Westport, CT: Greenwood Press, 1973), 31-32, 50-51.

62. Sneddeker, "Regulating Vice," 21; Burnham, "Social Evil Ordinance," 205, 211; Burnham, "Medical Inspection of Prostitutes," 208.

63. Sneddeker, "Regulating Vice," 21, 31; Burnham, "Medical Inspection of Prostitutes," 217.

64. Sneddeker, "Regulating Vice," 24-25.

65. Ibid., 27, 29.

66. Ibid., 31.

67. Ibid., 41-42.

68. Ibid., 43.

69. Ibid., 44.

70. Ibid., 42.

71. Burnham, "Social Evil Ordinance," 211.

72. Quoted in Burnham, 216.

73. Mary E. Odem, *Delinquent Daughters: Protecting and Policing Adolescent Female Sexuality in the United States, 1885-1920* (Chapel Hill: University of North Carolina Press, 1995), 1.

74. Ibid., 1-2.

75. James R. McGovern, "The American Woman's Pre-World War I Freedom in Manners and Morals," *Journal of American History* 55 (September 1986): 330-331.

76. See the seminal work by Welter, "Cult of True Womanhood, 1820-1860," *American Quarterly* 18 (1966).

77. Guy-Sheftall, *Daughters of Sorrow,* vol. 11 in *Black Women in U.S. History* (Brooklyn: Carlson, 1990), *11*: 12-13.

78. W.E.B. DuBois, "The Damnation of Women," in *The Seventh Son: The Thoughts and Writings of W.E.B. DuBois*, Julius Lester, ed., vol. 1 (New York: Vintage Books, 1971), 1: 526.

79. Guy-Sheftall, *Daughters of Sorrow*, 1: 12; 161-163.

80. Frances B. Cogan, *All-American Girl: The Ideal of Real Womanhood in Mid-Nineteenth Century America* (Athens: University of Georgia Press, 1989), 26, 65.

81. Ibid., 100, 257-258.

82. Ibid., 258; Nancy Woloch, *Women and the American Experience* (New York: Alfred A. Knopf, 1984), 269-271.

83. Nancy F. Cott, *The Grounding of Modern Feminism* (New Haven: Yale University Press, 1987), 3, 7.

84. Ibid., 3-4. See Cott's distinction between the nineteenth-century woman movement and twentieth-century feminism in chapter 1: 11-50.

85. Ibid., 35, 36, 42.

86. Quoted in Cott, 13.

87. McGovern, "American Woman's Freedom," 333.

88. Quoted in McGovern, 323.

89. Odem, *Delinquent Daughters*, 187.

90. Quoted in Dorothy Schneider and Carl J. Schneider, *American Women in the Progressive Era, 1900-1920* (New York: Facts on File, 1993), 153.

91. Odem, *Delinquent Daughters*, 188-189.

92. "Teachers Turn Flappers," *Scrippage*, 19 Sept. 1924. Soldan High School Collection, Western Historical Manuscript Collection, University of Missouri-St. Louis.

93. Woloch, *Women and the American Experience*, 406-407.

94. Mrs. Alvin W. Claxon, quoted in "Business Girl's Activity Robs Men of Respect for Womankind," *St. Louis Post-Dispatch*, 27 Feb. 1903.

95. Ibid.

96. Ibid.

97. Ibid.

98. Mrs. M.W. Miller quoted in "Indignant Business Women Reply to Mrs. Claxon," *St. Louis Post-Dispatch*, 27 Feb. 1903.

99. Matron Hunter quoted in "Business Women Reply."

100. Matron Kintzing quoted in "Business Women Reply."

101. Matron Hunter quoted in "Business Women Reply."

102. Daisy Barbee quoted in "Business Women Reply."

103. Calvin M. Woodward quoted in "Business Women Reply."

104. Joseph A. Hill, *Women in Gainful Occupations 1870 to 1920: A Study of the Trend of Recent Changes in the Numbers, Occupational Distribution, and Family Relationship of Women Reported in the Census as Following a Gainful Occupation* (Washington, DC: U.S. Government Printing Office, 1929): 32.

105. Ibid., 39-40.

106. *Thirteenth Census of the United States Taken in the Year 1910*, Vol. 4, *Population 1910 Occupation Statistics* (Washington, DC: U.S. Government Printing Office, 1914), 4: 599.

107. *Fourteenth Census of the United States Taken in the Year 1920*, Vol. 4, *Population 1920 Occupations* (Washington, DC: U.S. Government Printing Office, 1923), 4: 1218.

108. Hill, *Women in Gainful Occupations*, 33.

109. Ibid., 35-36.

110. Ibid., 38.

111. *Thirteenth Census of the United States* (1910), 4:599; *Fourteenth Census of the United States* (1920), 4: 1218.

112. "Want Less Education And More Servants: Belleville Women Want High School Abolished Because It Enables Girls to Obtain Positions in Offices and Stores," *St. Louis Post-Dispatch*, 22 May 1903.

113. Quoted in "Want Less Education..."

114. "Education and Servant Girls," *St. Louis Post-Dispatch*, 23 May 1903.

115. *Thirteenth Census of the United States* (1910), 4:598-599; *Fourteenth Census of the United States* (1920), 4: 1217-1218.

116. Hill, *Women in Gainful Occupations*, 41.

117. Primm, *Lion of the Valley*, (Boulder: Pruett, 1981), 338-339.

118. Karen McCoskey Goering, "St. Louis Women Artists 1818-1945: An Exhibition," *Gateway Heritage: Quarterly Journal of the Missouri Historical Society* 3 (1982): 15.

119. Lincoln Bunce Spiess, "St. Louis Women Artists in the Mid-19th Century," *Gateway Heritage: Quarterly Journal of the Missouri Historical Society* 3 (1983): 11.

120. Ibid.

121. Goering, "St. Louis Women Artists," 15.

122. "Funeral Services For Miss Brown To Be Held At Her Residence Today," *Scrippage*, 24 Oct. 1924. Soldan High School Collection, Western Historical Manuscript Collection, University of Missouri-St. Louis.

123. Ibid.

124. Frances Hurd Stadler, *St. Louis Day by Day* (St. Louis: The Patrice Press, 1989), 57; Hill, *Women in Gainful Occupations*, 42.

125. Marion Hunt, "Woman's Place in Medicine: The Career of Dr. Mary Hancock McLean," *The Bulletin: Missouri Historical Society* 36 (1980): 255; Hill, *Women in Gainful Occupations*, 42.

126. Martha R. Clevenger, "From Lay Practitioner to Doctor of Medicine: Woman Physicians in St. Louis, 1860-1920," *Gateway Heritage: Quarterly Journal of the Missouri Historical Society* 8 (1987/88): 17-20.

127. Hunt, "Woman's Place in Medicine," 255, 259.

128. Ibid., 257-263.

129. Ibid., 261-263; Marion Hunt, "Women and Childsaving: St. Louis Children's Hospital 1879-1979," *The Bulletin: Missouri Historical Society* 36 (1980): 79.

130. Hill, *Women in Gainful Occupations*, 41. This data set includes actresses, architects, artists, clergy, dentists, editors, lawyers, literary and scientific persons, musicians, photographers, physicians, teachers, and nurses as professional workers.

131. Ibid., 40.

132. *Fourth Annual Report of the Commissioner of Labor, 1888: Working Women in Large Cities* (Washington, DC: U.S. Government Printing Office, 1889), 9-10.

133. Ibid., 24-25.

134. Ibid., 25.

135. Quoted in ibid., 55.

136. Ibid., 54-55.

137. *Statistics of the Population of the United States at the Tenth Census,* vol. 1 (Washington: Government Printing Office, 1883), 1:900; *Thirteenth Census of the United States* 4:598; *Fourteenth Census of the United States,* 4: 1217.

138. *Women in Missouri Industries: A Study of Hours and Wages,* Bulletin of the Women's Bureau, No. 35 (Washington, DC: U.S. Government Printing Office, 1924), 45.

139. Ibid., 58-60.

140. Ibid., 8-10, 39-40.

141. Philip S. Foner, *Women and the American Labor Movement: From World War I to the Present* (New York: The Free Press, 1980), 270-271.

142. Ibid., 271.

143. Ibid.

144. Ibid., 271-272.

145. Ibid., 272-273.

146. Ibid., 274.

147. Ibid.

148. Ibid., 274-275.

149. Katharine T. Corbett, "St. Louis Women Garment Workers: Photographs and Memories," *Gateway Heritage: Quarterly Journal of the Missouri Historical Society* 7 (Summer 1981): 19-20, 24.

150. Alice Kessler-Harris, "Independence and Virtue in the Lives of Wage-Earning Women: The United States, 1870-1930," in *Women in Culture and Politics: A Century of Change,* Judith Friedlander, Blanche Wiesen Cook, Alice Kessler-Harris, and Carroll Smith-Rosenberg, eds. (Bloomington: Indiana University Press, 1986), 3.

151. Quoted in "Business Women Reply"; Kessler-Harris, "Independence and Virtue," 5.

152. Kessler-Harris, "Independence and Virtue," 5; Corbett, "St. Louis Women Garment Workers," 18-25.

153. Kessler-Harris, "Independence and Virtue," 5.

154. *Facts about Working Women: A Graphic Presentation Based on Census Statistics and Studies of the Women's Bureau*, Bulletin of the Women's Bureau, No. 46 (Washington, DC: U.S. Government Printing Office, 1925), 12.

155. Kessler-Harris, "Independence and Virtue," 9; *Facts about Working Women*, 12-13. Government documents referred to groups of persons in the United States using the following terms: "native-white—native parentage; native white—foreign or mixed parentage; foreign-born white; negro; and Indian, Chinese, Japanese, and all other."

156. Kessler-Harris, "Independence and Virtue," 10; *Facts about Working Women*, 16.

157. Winifred D. Wandersee, *Women's Work and Family Values 1920-1940* (Cambridge, MA: Harvard University Press, 1981), 89.

158. *Facts about Working Women*, 16.

159. Kessler-Harris, "Independence and Virtue," 12; *Facts about Working Women*, 34.

160. *Facts about Working Women*, 42.

161. Sharon Harley, "When Your Work Is Not Who You Are: The Development of a Working-Class Consciousness among Afro-American Women," in *Gender, Class, Race, and Reform in the Progressive Era*, Noralee Frankel and Nancy S. Dye, eds. (Lexington: University Press of Kentucky, 1991), 45-46.

162. Frances Ellen Harper, quoted in Woloch, *Women and the American Experience*, 230.

163. Woloch, *Women and the American Experience*, 230-231.

164. Ibid., 248.

165. John L. Rury, "Who Became Teachers?: The Social Characteristics of Teachers in American History," in *American Teachers: Histories of a Profession at Work*, Donald Warren, ed. (New York: Macmillan, 1989), 28.

166. Patricia Carter, "The Social Status of Women Teachers in the Early Twentieth Century," in *The Teacher's Voice: A Social History of Teaching in Twentieth-Century America*, Richard J. Altenbaugh, ed. (London: The Falmer Press, 1992), 127.

167. Ibid., 138.

168. Ibid., 129; Susan B. Carter, "Incentives and Rewards to Teaching," in *American Teachers: Histories of a Profession at Work*, Donald Warren, ed. (New York: Macmillan, 1989), 57.

169. Carter, "Social Status of Women Teachers," 132; Carter, "Incentives and Rewards," 49; Rury, "Who Became Teachers?" 29.

170. Quoted in Geraldine Jonçich Clifford, "Man/Woman/Teacher: Gender, Family, and Career in American Educational History," in *American Teachers:*

Histories of a Profession at Work, Donald Warren, ed. (New York: Macmillan, 1989), 305.

171. Quoted in Philip S. Foner, *Women and the American Labor Movement: From Colonial Times to the Eve of World War I* (New York: The Free Press, 1979), 487-488.

172. Quoted in ibid., 488.

173. Ibid., 294.

174. Ibid., x.

175. Annelise Orleck, *Common Sense and a Little Fire: Women and Working-Class Politics in the United States, 1900-1965* (Chapel Hill: University of North Carolina Press, 1995), 5-7.

176. Ibid., 5-6.

177. St. Louis Joint Council of Women's Auxiliaries scrapbook, Western Historical Manuscript Collection, University of Missouri-St. Louis.

178. Ibid.

179. Anne Johnson, ed., *Notable Women of St. Louis, 1914* (St. Louis: Woodward, 1914), foreword.

180. Thekla M. Bernays, quoted in Johnson, 22.

181. Johnson, *Notable Women of St. Louis*, 22.

182. "Club's 75 Years of Doing," *St. Louis Post-Dispatch*, 1976, news article in St. Louis Association of Colored Women's Clubs papers, Western Historical Manuscript Collection, University of Missouri-St. Louis.

183. Ibid., 72.

184. Ibid., 160.

185. Ibid., 116.

186. "Where Women Work," *St. Louis Post-Dispatch*, 21 Oct. 1901.

187. Robert Dale Grinder, "The War against St. Louis's Smoke 1891-1924," *Missouri Historical Review* 69 (January 1975): 201, 204.

188. Ibid., 205.

189. Ibid.

190. Peter Romanofsky, "'The Public Is Aroused': The Missouri Children's Code Commission 1915-1919," *Missouri Historical Review* 68 (January 1974): 205.

191. Ibid., 208-220.

192. Johnson, *Notable Women of St. Louis*, 86.

193. Ruth Crawford, *The Immigrant in St. Louis: A Survey* (St. Louis: 1916), 17-18.

194. Ibid., 50-52.

195. Johnson, *Notable Women of St. Louis*, 32.

196. Ibid.

197. Ibid., 42.

198. Mrs. Edmund A. Garrett quoted in Johnson, 78.

299. Ibid., 161.

200. Stadler, *St. Louis Day by Day*, 222-223.

201. Mari Jo Buhle, *Women and American Socialism, 1870-1920* (Urbana: University of Illinois Press, 1981), 6.

202. Ibid., 17; Joseph A. Hill, *Women in Gainful Occupations, 1870-1920* (Washington, DC: 1929), 147, 185.

203. Buhle, *Women and American Socialism*, 121.

204. Glenna Matthews, *The Rise of Public Woman: Woman's Power and Woman's Place in the United States, 1630-1970* (New York: Oxford University Press, 1992), 202-203; Foner, *Women and the American Labor Movement: to World War I*, 270.

205. Anne Firor Scott, *Natural Allies: Women's Associations in American History* (Urbana: University of Illinois Press, 1991), 2-3.

206. William T. Harris, quoted in Janet Zollinger Giele, *Two Paths to Women's Equality: Temperance, Suffrage, and the Origins of Modern Feminism* (New York: Twayne Publishers, 1995), 23-24.

207. Ellen Richards quoted in Giele, 24.

208. "Our Heritage," Annie Malone Children's Home Folder, Afro-Americans in St. Louis, Collection, 1920-1980, Western Historical Manuscript Collection, University of Missouri-St. Louis; "Contributions of Blacks from A to Z," Afro-Americans in St. Louis, Collection, 1920-1980, Western Historical Manuscript Collection, University of Missouri-St. Louis; Herman H. Dreer, "Highlights of Negro History," *St. Louis Argus*, 9 May 1974. UMSL Black History Project Collection, 1911-1983, Western Historical Manuscript Collection, University of Missouri-St. Louis.

209. "Our Heritage," Annie Malone Children's Home Folder, Afro-Americans in St. Louis, Collection, 1920-1980, Western Historical Manuscript Collection, University of Missouri-St. Louis; Herman H. Dreer, "Highlights of Negro History," *St. Louis Argus*, 9 May, 1974. UMSL Black History Project Collection, 1911-1983, Western Historical Manuscript Collection, University of Missouri-St. Louis.

210. Mary Ryder obituary, St. Louis Joint Council of Women's Auxiliaries scrapbook, Western Historical Manuscript Collection, University of Missouri-St. Louis.

211. Firor Scott, *Natural Allies*, 179-181.

212. Linda Gordon, "Black and White Visions of Welfare: Women's Welfare Activism, 1890-1945," *Journal of American History* 78 (September 1991): 559-564.

213. Ibid., 560-565.

214. Julia Davis, "1915-75 Historical Review," Prudence Crandall Club folder, St. Louis Association of Colored Women's Clubs papers, Western Historical Manuscript Collection, University of Missouri-St. Louis.

215. Alpha Kappa Alpha, Gamma Omega Chapter, St. Louis, Scrapbook, Western Historical Manuscript Collection, University of Missouri-St. Louis.

216. Ibid.

217. Deborah Gray White, quoted in Elsa Barkley Brown, "Womanist Consciousness: Maggie Lena Walker and the Independent Order of Saint Luke," *Signs: Journal of Women in Culture and Society* 14 (1989): 617.

218. Brown, "Womanist Consciousness," 616-618; 632.

219. Heroines of Jericho, St. Louis, Missouri History and Proceedings, 1891, 1903, Western Historical Manuscript Collection, University of Missouri-St. Louis.

220. Ibid.

221. Estelle B. Freedman, "Separatism Revisited: Women's Institutions, Social Reform, and the Career of Miriam Van Waters," in *U.S. History as Women's History: New Feminist Essays*, Linda K. Kerber, Alice Kessler-Harris, and Kathryn Kish Sklar, eds. (Chapel Hill: University of North Carolina Press, 1995), 173, 187-188.

222. Stadler, *St. Louis Day by Day*, 35.

223. B. Gratz Brown , quoted in Primm, *Lion of the Valley*, 283-284.

224. Primm, *Lion of the Valley*, (Boulder: Pruett, 1981), 284.

225. Laura Staley, "Suffrage Movement in St. Louis During the 1870s," *Gateway Heritage: Quarterly Journal of the Missouri Historical Society* 3 (Spring 1983): 39.

226. Virginia Minor quoted in Staley, 38.

227. Ibid., 38-41; Eleanor Flexner, *Century of Struggle: The Woman's Rights Movement in the United States* (Cambridge, MA: The Belknap Press, 1959), 168-169.

228. Staley, "Suffrage Movement in St. Louis," 34, 38.

229. Dina M. Young, "The Silent Search for a Voice: The St. Louis Equal Suffrage League and the Dilemma of Elite Reform, 1910-1920," *Gateway Heritage: Quarterly Journal of the Missouri Historical Society* 8 (Spring 1988): 2-19; Monia Cook Morris, "The History of Woman Suffrage in Missouri, 1867-1901," *Missouri Historical Review* 25 (October 1930): 67.

230. Young, "Silent Search for a Voice," 3; Morris, "History of Woman Suffrage in Missouri," 67-69; Mrs. Emily Newell Blair, Christine Orrick Fordyce, Florence Atkinson, Althea Somerville Grossman, Mrs. Thomas McBride, Helen Guthrie Miller, Marie B. Ames, Agnes I. Leighty, Edna

Fischel Gellhorn, Madeleine Liggett Clarke, Bertha K. Passmore, Mary Semple Scott, Mrs. Henry N. Ess, Laura L. Runyon, and Rosa Russell Ingels, "History of Woman Suffrage in Missouri," *Missouri Historical Review* 14 (April/July 1920): 284-383.

231. Morris, "History of Woman Suffrage in Missouri," 74, 81-82.

232. Ibid., 73-76; Giele, *Two Paths to Women's Equality*, 91, 140.

233. Morris, "History of Woman Suffrage in Missouri," 79; Florence Atkinson, "'Middle Ages' of Equal Suffrage in Missouri," *Missouri Historical Review* 14(April/July 1920): 300.

234. Quoted in Atkinson, "Middle Ages," 299-301. Emphasis added.

235. Young, "Silent Search for a Voice," 6.

236. Atkinson, "Middle Ages," 301-304.

237. Althea Somerville Grossman, "The Part of the St. Louis Equal Suffrage League in the Campaign for Equal Suffrage," *Missouri Historical Review* 14(April/July 1920): 310-311.

238. Young, "Silent Search for a Voice," 14-15; Grossman, "Campaign for Equal Suffrage," 312-313.

239. Young, "Silent Search for a Voice," 15; Grossman, "Campaign for Equal Suffrage," 313.

240. Grossman, "Campaign for Equal Suffrage," 315-317.

241. Ibid., 317-319; Emily Newell Blair, "Foreword: History of Woman Suffrage in Missouri," *Missouri Historical Review* 14 (April/July 1920): 285-286.

242. Quoted in Young, "Silent Search for a Voice," 4-6.

243. Cott, *Grounding of Modern Feminism*, (New Haven: Yale University Press, 1987), 19-20, 29-30.

244. Young, "Silent Search for a Voice," 4-11.

245. Ibid., 4-5.

246. Young, "Silent Search for a Voice," 9, 17-18.

247. Quoted in Schneider and Schneider, *American Women in the Progressive Era*, 18.

248. Estelle B. Freedman, "Separatism Revisited," 173.

249. Paula Baker, "The Domestication of Politics: Women and American Political Society, 1780-1920," *American Historical Review* 89 (June 1984): 643-645. See also Chafe, *Paradox of Change*, (New York: Oxford University Press, 1991), 232.

250. Cott, *Grounding of Modern Feminism*, 279.

251. Ibid., 10, 30.

252. Elinor Lerner, "Family Structure, Occupational Patterns, and Support for Women's Suffrage," in *Women in Culture and Politics: A Century Of*

Change, Judith Friedlander, Blanche Wiesen Cook, Alice Kessler-Harris, and Carroll Smith-Rosenberg, eds. (Bloomington: Indiana University Press, 1986), 223-224, 234.

253. Orleck, *Common Sense and a Little Fire*, (Chapel Hill: University of North Carolina Press, 1995), 6.

254. Paula Giddings, *When and Where I Enter: The Impact of Black Women on Race and Sex in America* (New York: William Morrow and Co., 1984), 126-127; Caraway, *Segregated Sisterhood*, (Knoxville: University of Tennessee Press, 1991), 148-149.

255. Frances Ellen Watkins Harper, quoted in Nancie Caraway, *Segregated Sisterhood*, 119-122; 144.

256. Mrs. N.F. Mossell, *The Work of the Afro-American Woman*, introduction by Joanne Braxton (New York: Oxford University Press, 1988); see also Braxton's introduction, pp. xxvii-xxix.

257. Caraway, *Segregated Sisterhood*, 160-161.

258. Ibid., 161.

259. *Show Me Missouri Women: Selected Biographies*, Mary K. Dains, ed. (Kirksville, MO: Thomas Jefferson University Press, 1989), 27-28; 104-105; 117-118; 227-228.

260. Kessler-Harris, "Reflections on a Field," *New Viewpoints in Women's History* (Cambridge, MA: The Arthur and Elizabeth Schlesinger Library of the History of Women in America, 1994), 24.

CHAPTER 3

The Decline of an Academic System

> Those who have an intelligent interest in education will not expect
> these same pupils to be turned out at the end of four years as
> linguists, chemists, practical mechanics, architects, historians and
> authors. What may be reasonably demanded is, that they shall have
> learned how to study,. . . [1]
>
> *St. Louis Annual Report*, 1872

The curriculum transformation that occurred in St. Louis public high
schools with the introduction of the differentiated curriculum resulted
in academic decline. [2] Academic decline may be measured in a number
of ways. The argument presented here rests on an analysis of the
educational philosophies of the St. Louis public-school system from
1870 to 1930 and on an examination of the curriculum transformation
in those years.

During the nineteenth century, school officials defined the primary
purpose of schooling as intellectual and moral development for the
individual. At the onset of the twentieth century, preparation for work
and citizenship training took command as the fundamental rationale for
schooling. The shift in philosophy was significant and brought
extensive curriculum changes in its wake. As a result, graduation
requirements were reduced, the content of academic classes was altered
to bring them into line with a "social efficiency" standard, vocational
courses of study claimed a portion of the school curriculum, and
educational "experts" designed new programs of study to meet the

presumed needs of a large majority of students whom they considered less academically able.

There were three major phases of curriculum development in the public high schools of St. Louis. In the first phase a General Course of study and a Classical Course of study were offered in the nineteenth-century tradition. This existed at Central High School from 1858 to 1898.[3] The second phase of curriculum development in the St. Louis secondary schools is distinguished by multiple course offerings. Between 1898 and 1930 all students except those attending schools for African Americans could choose from seven courses: General, Classical, Scientific, Commercial, Art, Domestic Art and Science, and Manual Training.[4] Although the requirements for each course of study changed during this period, the name of a course signified its focus. Latin and Greek formed the core of the Classical Course, while the Scientific Course included advanced classes in science and mathematics. The Commercial Course required students to devote a portion of each year's study to classes in penmanship, typing, bookkeeping, commercial law, and economics. The Art, Domestic Art and Science, and Manual Training Courses incorporated classes in drawing, home economics, and vocational education, respectively. The structure of the General Course changed considerably from 1870 to 1930, however, it represented the basic high-school education throughout. After 1930, students no longer committed to a specific course of study, marking the third phase of curriculum development in St. Louis high schools.

The same three-phase curricula pattern developed in St. Louis' high schools for African Americans. The dominant ideology that demanded segregated schools, however, delayed expanded course offerings at Sumner High School. Thus, a general curriculum was the only offering at Sumner High School (aside from the Normal Course) from 1885 to 1911.[5] Sumner, and later Vashon High School, the St. Louis high schools for African Americans during this period, offered the General, Classical, Scientific, Commercial, Art, Domestic Art and Science, and Manual Training curricula from 1911 to 1930. All of the St. Louis high schools abandoned distinct courses of study in 1930.

These are the curricula, then, on which this study is focused. In addition, students in the St. Louis public-school system during the nineteenth and twentieth centuries had the option to enroll in one- and two-year commercial and manual-training/domestic-science courses, continuation schools, vocational schools, and normal courses of study.

These may enter the discussion peripherally, but the exposition is grounded in research on the four-year programs that constituted the St. Louis high-school curriculum from 1870 to 1930. The normal course will not be incorporated into the mainstream of this chapter due to the oscillatory nature of its official status. A Normal School was established in St. Louis in 1869 to supply the district schools with teachers. European-American women age sixteen and over were admitted.[6] Recommendations were made for a Normal Department at Sumner High School in 1890. In 1893, the Normal School was consolidated as a department at Central High School. Shortly after, in 1895, the Normal School became a separate professional school, to be discontinued just two years later. In 1905, the Harris Teachers College opened for European-American students and African-American students gained access to the Sumner Teachers College in 1921.

The pattern of curriculum development that occurred in St. Louis public high schools in the nineteenth and early twentieth centuries represented changes taking place across the nation. A significant exception is that few public high schools comparable to Sumner High School were established for African-American students during this period. In this regard the St. Louis public-school system positioned itself in more select company.[7] Nonetheless, most nineteenth-century high schools offered both classical and nonclassical studies. The Classical Course of study consisted primarily of Latin, Greek, and mathematics classes; the English (or General) Course of study focused on the modern subjects, which also comprised much of the course work in the academies. Just as in St. Louis, most public high schools in the United States up until the close of the nineteenth century offered classes in classical studies, modern languages, science, mathematics, history, English, and bookkeeping. The next phase of high-school curriculum development, the adoption of the differentiated curriculum, was national in scope as well. Near the turn of the century, new courses of study appeared with discernible variation in content and method.[8] After some debate, the comprehensive high school with its multitrack course design triumphed as the model for twentieth-century secondary schooling in the United States. Although extreme course differentiation, such as that found in St. Louis, occurred mainly in larger cities, the differentiated curriculum had taken hold in city, town, and rural high schools by the second decade of the twentieth century.[9]

This study of curriculum development in St. Louis public high schools from 1870 to 1930 finds much common ground with Selwyn

Troen's 1975 history of the St. Louis school system. Troen writes that 1904 marked the beginning of the transformation of the St. Louis high school that would make it into a "fundamentally different institution."[10] Troen accents the degree of change induced by the differentiated curriculum, noting that it took "little more than a decade to destroy the uniformity of the classical curriculum that had characterized [the school's] program in the nineteenth century."[11] This study goes beyond Troen's work on curriculum development by expanding the analysis of the impact of gender, race, and social class on students' course selection in St. Louis. The data presented in the chapters to follow, however, lead to an interpretation that differs from Troen's traditional conclusions.

Like many books on the nineteenth-century public high school, this study does not focus on the origins of the high school prior to 1870. It does offer an analysis of a stage of development of the public high school that had been underrepresented in case-study histories, that of the post-Civil War surge in high-school growth in the midwest. This research, then, supplements the discussion on the origins of antebellum public high schools in the East, most notably that canvassed by Michael Katz and Maris Vinovskis.[12]

David F. Labaree's work is among the best recent additions to the field of curriculum history. *The Making of an American High School* is a case study of curricular transformation in Philadelphia's Central High School; it is the story of a school's acquiescence to public demand in a market-driven pursuit of credentials.[13] Many of Labaree's findings concur with my research on St. Louis high schools. For instance, Labaree writes that the earliest U.S. high schools emerged from a middle-class ideology that fostered the common school movement. Proponents of this ideology struggled in support of public high schools, basing their arguments on the utility of the high school, its positive effect on other schools, notions of meritocracy, and by highlighting the "modest" origins of high-school students.[14] Also, Labaree notes that social class was a significant factor in predicting which boys would attend Central High School in Philadelphia in the early years. This was true of many early high schools, as Labaree demonstrates by citing Troen's study of St. Louis, Katz's work on Somerville, Massachusetts, Perlmann's research on Providence, and George Counts' 1920 study of four cities (including St. Louis.)[15] Perhaps most importantly, research on St. Louis is aligned with Labaree's analysis of the differentiated curriculum. Labaree describes the differentiated curriculum as a structure that assigned a different kind of value to each course of study. He presents evidence that shows that, when the uniform course of study was abandoned, students became partly differentiated by social class. As I will argue in the case of St. Louis, Labaree notes that in the period from 1900 to 1920 academic content in the curriculum was significantly diluted as the differentiated curriculum took root.[16] In evaluating the impact of the differentiated curriculum, Labaree is correct in asserting that the characteristic form of the twentieth-century high school is a peculiar combination of comprehensiveness and stratification.[17] My work on St. Louis provides additional evidence for this claim. Aside from geographic diversity, the St. Louis case study is distinguished from Labaree's study in the following aspects. Philadelphia Central High School differs from high schools in St. Louis (and most other early high schools) due to its extended period of curricular uniformity. From 1856 to 1889, Central High School offered only one course of study; the characteristic choice between the Classical and the English curriculum was not an option for students.[18] The more prominent distinction, however, is that Philadelphia Central High School did not admit girls until late in the twentieth century. Therefore, the opportunity to assess the impact of the intersection of gender, race, and social-class factors on students' experiences in St. Louis promises to supplement Labaree's history of high school curriculum development in important ways.

EDUCATIONAL PHILOSOPHY IN ST. LOUIS SCHOOLS

> There is nothing that the Board has done for many years that has had a tendency to popularize the Public Schools so much and make them the schools of the city as the organization of this High School, and the erection of the splendid High School edifice now in progress. . . . A great point has therefore been gained, that of uniting all classes and conditions in the support of the Public School system. . . . Great reliance must be placed upon the High School for the purpose of sustaining the reputation of the schools and infusing still greater uniformity of system and method of instruction and discipline into their administration. This it can only do by remaining as it is now, the head of the system, in which the last and full development to the mental training is given, commenced in the Primary School, and by furnishing, as it must, to a great degree, . . . the annual supply of teachers needed for the other schools.[19]

In the first annual school report of the St. Louis public schools, the high school was thus christened in 1854 as the great organizer, protector, and supplier of teachers for the city's common school system. These responsibilities would remain with the high school throughout the century. The St. Louis public high school was organized in 1852 and accepted pupils for the first time in February 1853.

The high school was a relatively new institution in 1853. Boston established the first high school in the United States, the English Classical School, in 1821. Three years later it was renamed "the English High School." Boston was also the site of the first high school to admit girls. The Boston High School for Girls opened in 1826 but, citing its overwhelming popularity, school officials closed the school in 1828. Boston major Josiah Quincy argued that providing secondary schooling for all the girls who wanted it would bankrupt the city. [20]

In an early history of public education in the United States, Ellwood Cubberley wrote that the Massachusetts Law of 1827 marked the "real beginning of the American high school as a distinct institution."[21] The law mandated that every town with 500 or more households provide a high school. While noting that the law was suspended and reinvoked until permanent legislation was passed in 1859, Michael Katz concurs that the Massachusetts Law of 1827 was the "legal origin of the American high school."[22] By 1840, twenty-six high schools sprang up in Massachusetts as a result of the 1827 law.[23] In addressing Massachusett's strong influence in the development of the high school, Alexander Inglis (one of the first to write on the history of the institution) asserted that, with only a few exceptions, high schools in the United States owed "the basis of their aim, theory, and practice to the high school first created and earliest developed in Massachusetts."[24] State authorization for high schools followed in Pennsylvania in 1836 and in New York in 1853.[25] Other New England states, Maine, Vermont, and New Hampshire, followed Massachusett's lead in establishing high schools, however, many of the schools that emerged in the early stages were discontinued. Maintenance costs, public opposition to taxation for the support of high schools, and (Massachusetts notwithstanding) a general pattern of permissive, rather than mandatory legislation for the formation of schools, threatened the viability of high schools prior to the Civil War.[26] In the West, cities established high schools in a pattern that reflected urban development.[27] St. Louis, the first city west of the Mississippi River to support a public high school, was in the vanguard of a movement that witnessed the establishment of the first high school in Wisconsin in 1849 and the opening of a high school in San Francisco in 1856.[28] Cubberley counted only five high schools west of the Mississippi River by 1860.[29] Public high schools emerged later in the South, near the end of the nineteenth century, and then only for European Americans.[30]

Just as the Massachusetts Law of 1827 appeared to be the catalyst that ignited high-school development in the early period, the Kalamazoo court decision of 1874 spurred the rapid development of the high school in the 1880s. In that case the Supreme Court of Michigan determined that public funds could be used for the support of high schools. As Edward Krug has explained, the court decision, while not legally binding in other states, was effective in establishing a national climate of support for public high schools.[31] As many historians have noted, it was during the 1880s that the public high school overtook the academy as the dominant institution of secondary education in the United States. Historians also agree that for most of the nineteenth century, it is difficult to determine with precision the number of high schools in the United States. Complete and reliable records were not kept, and conflicts exist in the data that are available. Furthermore, "high school" was an ambiguous term in the nineteenth century. Given this admission, it is clear that an explosion in high-school development occurred just after 1900. Records indicate that there were 2,526 public high schools in the United States in 1890, 6,005 in 1900, and 14,326 by 1920.[32] Missouri claimed 386 of the 10,213 U.S. public high schools enumerated in 1910.[33]

The founding of Central High School in 1853, then, places St. Louis among the leaders in the West in high-school development, and in the initial phase of the history of the high school in the United States. The founding of Sumner High School for African-American students in 1875 clarifies the significance of St. Louis in the development of the U.S. public high school. Public high schools for African Americans were virtually nonexistent in the South until well into the twentieth century.[34] St. Louis was one of few cities in the nation to include a substantial African-American population in public high-school development during the nineteenth century.

In 1858, St. Louis Superintendent Ira Divoll expanded upon objectives of the high school in the *Fourth Annual Report*. The high school was justified economically; it allowed capable pupils from the district's eighteen grammar schools to join together in one class for the purposes of instruction. Divoll reminded readers that the high school, at the head of the school system, imposed a structural uniformity on the district schools. Further, it was declared a matter of public policy to afford the "children of the people an opportunity of acquiring a full and complete English Education, as well as a knowledge of the German and French languages." Finally, there was the matter of justice in extending the opportunity for literacy education to all, regardless of individual circumstances.[35] Troen has pointed out an interesting alteration in this guiding principle. In 1862, Divoll stated the doctrine on public instruction: "The public schools shall be made good enough for the rich, and ample and free for all."[36] Three years later, after the destruction of the Civil War had wrecked havoc with the public-school system and the economy, his statement read that "the schools should be free and ample for all who wish to attend them."[37] Perhaps this was an unintentional transposition. Or perhaps the notion of common schools was safely cemented in the public mind so that Divoll no longer felt the need to court the upper class. It could be that in the economic struggle for survival, the schools could no longer offer a system "good enough for the rich." At any rate, the school still had a very important function to perform, that of moral education.

Moral education was the main connection between State support and public schools as was indicated in the *Fourth Annual Report*. "The primary object of the State in encouraging and supporting public instruction, is to secure its own safety, prosperity, and perpetuity; and regarding the purposes of education in this light, it is evident that moral culture is far more important than intellectual training . . . "[38] The author went on to declare that, based on statistical proof, most crimes and illnesses were traceable to illiterate and uneducated persons while education and intelligence tended to promote virtue and honesty. This connection surfaced repeatedly in the annual reports in statements such as "the people must build school houses or prisons."[39] In the 1868 report teachers were instructed "on all proper occasions to impress upon the minds of their pupils the principles of morality and virtue, a sacred regard for truth, love to God, love to man, sobriety, industry and frugality."[40]

It would be a mistake to emphasize the attention given to moral education to the neglect of what was considered an equal factor in the educational equation, development of the intellect. William Torrey Harris, superintendent of the St. Louis public school system from 1868 to 1880, wrote that the pillars on which public education rests are *behavior* and *scholarship*.[41] Principal of Central High School, H.H.

Morgan, wrote in 1875 that "if our expectations are realized, the graduates of the school will be qualified to enter our colleges and scientific schools . . . or to begin the work of every-day life with abilities and habits of thought so trained as to be impelled towards all that is high and useful, and feel an unconquerable repugnance to the baseness of ignorance."[42] During the nineteenth century, and especially during Harris' administration, the annual reports contained philosophical essays dealing with educational issues. It is helpful to refer to two of these essays, one written by Harris, the other written by Morgan, to clarify their perceptions of the moral-intellectual basis of education.

Historian David B. Tyack has described William Torrey Harris as "the outstanding intellectual leader in American education in the years between the death of Horace Mann in 1859 and the emergence of John Dewey as a spokesman for the new education at the turn of the twentieth century."[43] An insatiable learner, Harris' study of education and philosophy propelled him to national attention during his years in St. Louis. Through speeches and articles that were widely read, leadership in a prominent school system, the National Education Association, and the U.S. Bureau of Education, and active membership in philosophical societies, Harris made an indelible mark on educational development in the United States. The force of his life's work prompted Harris' colleague, Nicholas Murray Butler, to comment, "The history of American education and of our American contributions to philosophical thought cannot be understood or estimated without knowledge of the life work of Dr. William Torrey Harris."[44]

Harris left Yale College and moved to St. Louis in 1857. His tenure with the St. Louis school system began in 1858 when he accepted a teaching position at Franklin School. From 1859 to 1867, Harris served as principal at Clay School before working for one and a half years as St. Louis' first assistant superintendent. It was during Harris' years as superintendent, 1868 to 1880, that his influence outside of St. Louis grew. In point of fact, the thirteen annual reports that Superintendent Harris penned captured international acclaim and remain today as a paradigm of the philosophical work educators produced in the nineteenth century.

Although Harris contributed no major philosophical texts, he was the consummate philosophy student and was recognized in his time as the leading Hegelian scholar in the United States.[45] Harris was a key figure in originating the Philosophical Society of St. Louis in 1866.

This led to the founding of the *Journal of Speculative Philosophy*, a significant vehicle for the study of German philosophy in the United States. The journal, in publishing some of the first writings of Charles Peirce, William James, and John Dewey, indicated again that Harris' most influential work was as student-teacher-scholar rather than philosopher. From 1880 to 1889, Harris was a driving force in the Concord School of Philosophy. After his return to Massachusetts, Harris served as superintendent of the Concord schools, from 1882 to 1885.

Harris held the position of United States Commissioner of Education from 1889 to 1906, communicating his educational philosophy through a plethora of reports, lectures, and articles. Throughout the latter part of the nineteenth century, and until his death in 1909, Harris navigated debate in the National Education Association (he was an influential member of the Committee of Ten), the National Association of School Superintendents, the American Social Science Association, and the American Philosophical Association. Over the course of his life, Harris produced 479 titles; the writing he generated in St. Louis marked the early articulation of his educational philosophy.

In 1871 Harris wrote on the nature and importance of moral education. The essay was prompted by criticisms that the public school system was immoral due to its lack of special religious instruction. Harris advocated the teaching of a secular morality stating that "the relation of the Human to the Divine cannot form a subject of legislation in a free state nor a topic of instruction in public schools . . ."[46] This did not mean, however, that a system of education could be maintained without morality. Harris wrote of the duties of the individual to self. These included the preservation of one's physical organism; the pursuit of a rational end, that is, some avocation in life; the control of natural desires through proper limits; and the struggle for self-culture. Due to the inevitable contact one has with the human race, there were also duties toward others, family, civil society, and the state. Harris argued that school discipline, based on punctuality, regularity, silence, truth, justice, and kindness, was necessary in order for one to secure moral education. He gave much attention to punctuality and regularity; the impact of industrialization was apparent. Harris emphasized an end result in schooling that he expected to allow for growth in cultural activities.

The necessity of conformity to the time of the train, to the starting of work in the manufactory, fixes the times for the minor affairs of life with absolute precision. Only by obedience to these abstract external laws of time and place may we achieve that social combination necessary to free us from degrading slavery to our physical wants and necessities. But the school makes these duties the ground and means of higher duties. . . . They render possible, higher spiritual culture. [47]

Harris based his philosophy on Hegelian theory which emphasized orderly systematic change in a rationally ordered universe. According to Harris, the school was to be used as an agent for preserving the values of the past and adjusting the individual to society.[48]

Morgan's essay justifying the public high school was written in 1877 in response to complaints regarding the provision of free high schools at public cost. He stated that, undoubtedly, the purpose of education was the full, complete, and harmonious development of every human faculty.[49] This was a concern of the State, he argued, because educated citizens would contribute most to the common good. Defining the limit to public education according to the means and will of the community, Morgan suggested that for most communities this limit would be the public high school. He directed his argument to specific perspectives of those against public high schools. Morgan relied on arguments of economy, improvements for the lower grades, the assertion that a thriving republic requires that independence and self-help be developed in all persons, the notion of reciprocal duties of the citizens and community, and the political necessity that equated lack of education with crime.

Since the inception of the St. Louis High School, educators were steadily called upon to justify its existence. Time and again the responses supported the notion of the high school as a preparatory institution *and* a finishing school. The *Forty-First Annual Report* listed the following as aims of high-school education.

1. The high school should communicate to its pupils the elements of the highest culture of the race.
2. It should bring the pupil into close contact with the spiritual life of his country and his time.
3. It should awaken and widen the civic and higher human interests in the pupil, and arouse and stimulate the desire for an active life in their service.[50]

Whether St. Louis high-school students were among the few preparing for college or the majority preparing for other avenues in life, they were expected to achieve intellectual and moral development. Direct vocational preparation was not a concern except as young women were influenced to prepare for a teaching career. The themes of intellectual and moral development are clear in Thomas Richeson's 1876 statement as president of the Board of Directors of the St. Louis Public Schools.

> I am not in favor of the so-called "practical" ideas which would change the course of study in the District and High Schools, and make them teach the arts and trades instead of the rudiments of liberal culture. The period from six or seven years to sixteen or eighteen years ought to be devoted in school to the gain of theoretical culture and moral insight.[51]

Superintendent Long drew upon the nineteenth-century philosophy of the public high school in his report for the 1882 *St. Louis Annual Report*. Responding to criticisms that the schools lacked practical emphasis, Long stated

> that preparation which gives strength of mind to comprehend things, and strength of character to resist temptation, is as necessary as any other preparation for special trades or occupations. . . . While we look to that which better enables man to earn a livelihood, we must not lose sight of that which alone enables him to continue his own culture through life, and to perform the high moral, social, and political duties that devolve on every true citizen living under a free government.[52]

Soon after the turn of the century, educators in St. Louis altered their schooling philosophy in ways that reflected a nationwide shift in educational thought. In the United States, a wealth of information on manual training, one of the emerging innovations in schooling, materialized beginning in the 1880s. The U.S. Bureau of Labor produced a report on industrial education in 1892. This preceded the 1893 report of a Massachusetts committee that investigated existing systems of manual training. In 1889, the National Council of Education issued a publication on *The Educational Value of Manual Training*. The National Association of Manufacturers released documents in 1905 and 1912 issued by its Committee on Industrial Education. The

Education Report of 1910 contained an article on "Manual and Industrial Training," and the *Biennial Survey of Education*, published in 1923, dealt with manual training in its treatment of "Public High Schools." In addition to governmental and other committee reports, educational journals proved to be fertile ground for manual training literature. During the four decades from 1880 to 1920, *Education, Educational Review, Journal of Education, Manual Training Magazine, Proceedings of the National Education Association,* and *School Review* yielded space to the treatment of manual training or industrial training. Many school officials wrote on the manual-training movement; William Torrey Harris and Albert P. Marble offered notable opposition while St. Louisan Calvin Woodward became a leading voice among the supporters of manual training.[53]

Woodward had been promoting the cause of manual training since the last two decades of the nineteenth century. That he saw it as a complementary study to intellectual education was evidenced in his motto for the St. Louis Manual Training School: "The cultured mind, the skillful hand." Admitting that his idea seemed paradoxical to many, Woodward explained that manual training as he envisioned it would aim concurrently at intellectual culture, moral worth, and practical power and efficiency.[54] Historian Paul Violas delineated distinctions among manual training, industrial training, and vocational education in *Training of the Urban Working Class*. Manual training, as Woodward designed it, required educators to add manual activities to the traditional curriculum. *All* students were expected to benefit from this study, supporters argued, because manual training helped one to develop a practical understanding of the world. Industrial training, on the other hand, was occupationally specific. It was intended to *replace* the traditional curriculum. Violas explains that the vocational-education movement was a complex development, constructed to create a wide range of personnel for the corporate industrial structure. Vocational educators were committed to developing workers at all levels of the industrial hierarchy.[55] By the time he became president of the St. Louis Board of Education, Woodward was convinced that by bringing more practical studies into the high-school curriculum, educators could stem the tide of student withdrawals from school. In the *Forty-Sixth Annual Report*, for the school year 1899-1900, Woodward argued for the establishment of manual-training and domestic-science courses in the St. Louis high schools. He advocated manual training for boys and domestic science for girls because he considered these courses "suited to their tastes."[56] The industrial-education movement soon exploded, gaining widespread acceptance under the leadership of those who strayed from Woodward's original conception. It led to the establishment of a differentiated curriculum with a strong vocational emphasis. In St. Louis one of the final attempts to uphold the high-school curriculum of the nineteenth century was made by F. Louis Soldan, superintendent from 1895 to 1908. Arguing that it was inefficient and unwise to offer practical courses because no one could determine the future of children, Soldan warned of "the danger that education, instead of being purely a preparation for life, will encroach on the time and functions of life itself."[57] His warning went unheeded. By 1920 the philosophy of secondary education in St. Louis had gone through a major transformation.

St. Louis high schools began the new century with a commitment to manual training. The annual report for the year 1900-1901, in anticipation of the need for new high-school buildings due to growing enrollments, stated that "they should be made Manual Training High Schools in which the student can find not only the education which fits him for college, but also the more recent educational appliances which train the hand and eye."[58] The same report contained the words of confidence of Oscar Waring, principal of Sumner High School. "The success which has attended the introduction of Manual Training and Domestic Science, has undoubtedly given these branches a permanent place in our schools."[59]

While supporters of the differentiated curriculum stressed its "democratic" nature—allowing students to chose the educational plan best suited to their interests—the incorporation of manual-training and domestic-science courses in the high-school curriculum served to separate students among gender, race, and social class lines.[60] The *Forty-Eighth Annual Report* described the nature of the manual-training and domestic-science programs for the new McKinley and Yeatman High Schools.

> It is contemplated to teach the boys woodwork, including bench work, the use of the turning lathe, and metal work, including forge work and the use of the machine lathe. . . . For the girls a course of training in Domestic Science, in artistic and ordinary needlework, and in the household arts, including the care of the sick and rendering first assistance in accidents, together with suitable branches of manual training, will be provided.[61]

Gender distinctions such as those drawn in this example would be reconstructed over and over again in the next two decades. The statement was made quite clear in 1903: "The course for the training of girls in Domestic Science and Art runs parallel with the manual training course for boys."[62]

As Jeffrey Hirsh explained, Superintendent Long and the St. Louis Board of Education at first refused to institute manual training in the St. Louis school system, despite Calvin Woodward's influence. They did, however, allow Obadiah M. Wood to introduce manual-training classes to African-American students at L'Ouverture Elementary School. By 1903, St. Louis administrators reported that all students at Sumner High School had attended classes in manual training or domestic science during the previous year.[63] In "Manual Training and the Negro in St. Louis, 1880-1898," Hirsh shows that the general educational value of manual training demanded by Calvin Woodward evaporated when applied to African Americans. The St. Louis Board of Education understood manual training for African Americans as a form of industrial education.[64]

Soldan's report as superintendent in the *Forty-Ninth Annual Report* illustrated the necessity in 1903 to accommodate the St. Louis school philosophy to the emerging vocational-education movement. He began by stating that the general purpose of a high-school education was to develop strength of character and trained intelligence. Reminiscent of Harris, Soldan noted that education transmitted the great cultural achievements of the race in the arts and sciences to young men and women. He continued that, while the high school did prepare some students for college, it was mainly a finishing school; however, it did not train for any vocation in particular.[65] In the last portion of his report, that concerning manual training, Soldan was careful to emphasize the educational value of manual training. In fact, the first sentence in two consecutive paragraphs on one page virtually say the same thing: the purpose of manual training was strictly educational. The point is difficult to miss. The remainder of the report was spent detailing the intricate relationship of intelligence, character, culture, and work.

> Intelligent labor not only trains the hand but influences the mind and character. . . . Man's character and intelligence find embodiment in the work of his hands. . . . The history of the race establishes fully the claim of manual labor as an element of culture.[66]

Soldan then went on to discuss three practical aims of manual training: the adaptation of work to purpose, the perfection of its workmanship, and the beauty of its shape. The essay concluded with some words on freedom, mind, and spirit, but the overall tone was that of a man trying to convince himself of the educational worth of manual training.[67]

The 1914 report of the superintendent gave no evidence of any qualms on the part of Soldan's successor, Ben Blewett, in articulating the school's philosophy. His report reflected the influence of the New Liberal ideology, which emphasized, among other concepts, individual action for the larger social unit, a government very much in control of social progress, and a "positive freedom," that is, freedom to act in accord with society. The school, as an arm of the state, had a powerful role to play, which was recognized by many, including Professor Ernest R. Groves of New Hampshire State College.

> Any definition of education in terms of the individual begins with a fallacy. . . . Society can largely determine individual characteristics, and for its future well-being it needs more and more to demand that the public schools contribute significantly and not incidentally to its pressing needs by a social use of the influence that the schools have over the individual in his sensitive period of immaturity.[68]

This theme was echoed by Blewett.

> In any stage of civilization the social whole or state, however loose or closely knit the bonds of union may be, never assumes responsibility and authority in the education of its youth except for the purpose of making its youth of most value to the common welfare.[69]

Arguing that the school's guiding conscience was to be the purpose of the state in its establishment, Blewett stated that the work of the school must change with the changing needs of the state. In a statement that bolstered industrial education, Blewett claimed that the nearer the school can approach the healthy situations of actual life in organizing the experiences to which it subjects its pupils, the more successful it will be in fixing habits, producing skill, training judgment, and creating ideals that shall make the individual efficient in the new situations that will confront her or him.[70] It was probably no accident that "fixing habits" headed the list. Blewett went on to present the conclusions of a school committee that was concerned with educational aims. The committee reported that the "primary purpose of education, from the social or public point of view, is the determination or control of behavior; knowledge and other organizational forms of mental life are only of secondary importance, and even of no importance at all unless they actually or conceivably influence behavior in some desirable way."[71] Of course, it would be difficult for the school to influence the behavior of youth if they were not attending classes. Public officials addressed this problem, however, with the passage of the Missouri compulsory education law in 1905. William Landes and Lewis Solmon contend that compulsory-schooling laws did not cause the observed increase in school attendance in the late-nineteenth and early-twentieth centuries. Rather, relatively high levels of schooling preceded the passage of compulsory-schooling legislation. States passed more effective compulsory-attendance laws, however, after 1900.[72] Cities such as St. Louis established truancy departments within the school systems to deal with students who failed to comply with the laws. The information regarding the truancy department commanded a lion's share of the St. Louis annual reports in the years to follow. This response probably gave little pause to the citizens of St. Louis; as Tyack, James, and Benavot establish in *Law and the Shaping of Public Education, 1785-1954*, reformers began to equate education with compulsory schooling during the Progressive Era.[73] Compulsory-attendance laws provided yet another vehicle for state control of individual lives.[74] Forest Ensign recognized this aspect of New Liberal ideology in his renowned 1921 text on compulsory schooling. In his analysis of compulsory-schooling legislation, Ensign wrote "yet there remains constant the principle that the welfare of the state demands a citizenship with established habits of industry and thrift; that it is the duty of the state to require the formation of such habits; and that to secure these ends a certain degree of public control of young children in regard to their labor and training is essential."[75] It is no surprise that the school officials who forged these ideas also devoted a good deal of space in the annual reports to the problems connected with compulsory schooling. Compulsory schooling was, indeed, considered as the "prime reform of the day in education," beginning in the nineteenth century.[76] Articles addressing the issue of compulsory schooling appeared in educational journals and in the proceedings of the National Education Association well into the twentieth century. Calvin Woodward wrote in support of a compulsory-schooling law for Missouri in the *1904 St. Louis Annual Report* and St. Louis

Superintendent Ben Blewett raised the issue of compulsory schooling in his 1909 address before the National Education Association. The U.S. Bureau of Education published documents pertaining to compulsory schooling and truancy during the 1910s.[77]

Troen argues that Missouri's 1905 compulsory-attendance legislation was quite effective in increasing school attendance. From 1880 to 1910 the percentage of all children attending school jumped from 52.3 percent to 74.1 percent for fourteen-year-olds, 36.9 percent to 49.0 percent for fifteen-year-olds, and 20.3 percent to 31.1 percent for sixteen-year-olds.[78] Not all of these students would have attended the high school, however, enrollment grew there as well. In 1880, 1,096 students were enrolled at the high school; in 1910 the high-school enrollment of 5,147 represented a 369-percent increase. Paralleling this increase in high-school attendance, citizenship and vocational training began to take center stage in the annual reports. In 1911, the report proclaimed "the aim of the public schools is to aid in the production of efficient citizenship." An efficient citizen was defined as one "who can and does use his natural powers skilfully in his own work to his own profit and happiness and to the comfort and welfare of his fellow men."[79] The primacy of industrial education was given credence in the same volume by the use of a quote from Dr. Georg Kerchensteiner's *Grundfragender Schul-Organization.* "The first task upon the road to training for the individual is for him to know his work and to know how to exercise his power, intelligence and will upon it, and appreciation of the vocations must stand at the gateway of all education."[80] The rhetoric was followed by action. The *Sixtieth Annual Report* announced the organization of a card catalogue in the office of the Superintendent of Instruction to aid graduates in finding employment, and the report described an early form of a cooperative work program between various printers' shops and the school. While the placement service was intended for both male and female graduates, references to the printing program included only male students. It is not clear whether these programs were also offered to African-American students. One might suspect that students at Sumner High School were not included, given that the job-placement information appeared under a section labeled "High Schools" in the Report of the Superintendent. A separate section, which addressed all schools for African-American students, made no mention of the placement program.

Although drastic changes were occurring in St. Louis high schools, progress was not being made quickly enough for some. In the mid-

1910s, the St. Louis school system was in need of a bond referendum to meet economic necessities for the schools. Prior to the vote, school officials arranged for a survey of the system in order to convince the public that the schools were being managed effectively. Charles H. Judd of the University of Chicago headed a fourteen-member research team whose findings were published in 1918. (After the favorable report was released, the bond referendum passed easily.) The report suggested that stricter differentiation of courses was necessary, along with the provision of closer guidance to help students select a curriculum best suited to their individual needs.[81] Further, the survey members were concerned that the social-studies program was deficient in its duty to "assist in the training of young people for effective citizenship."[82] Also, the report recommended that the schools make an industrial survey of the city in order to "closer relate the work of the school shops to the fundamental industries of the city."[83] School officials evidently took these comments seriously. In the *Sixty-Fifth Annual Report*, for the 1918-1919 school year, President of the Board of Education, Henry L. Wolfner, wrote that "the city will require of its citizens in the years to come,

1. Better and more varied vocational preparation.
2. More knowledge of our nation outside of St. Louis and of other new world nations.
3. A more intelligent social conscience for cooperation in the economic and social relations of the city's life.
4. A firmer foundation in the principles of American life and the development of stronger personal character."[84]

This was the agenda for the St. Louis high schools in the twentieth century.

In 1924, the St. Louis Superintendent of Instruction recommended that a Division of Vocational Counseling be established to facilitate bringing the relatively recent objective of vocational preparation into the purview of the public high school. The functions of the Division of Vocational Counseling as approved by the Board of Education in 1925 included counseling students toward "appropriate" high-school courses, issuing certificate permits to students ages fourteen to sixteen who left school to work, vocational placement, and investigating industrial employment. Although the report failed to establish clearly whether the Division of Vocational Counseling worked with students of all races, there is reason to suspect it did. Information in the *Seventy-Third*

Annual Report referred to plans for vocational counseling in all St. Louis schools. The *Seventy-Second Annual Report* noted that counselors were expected to stress to their students the importance of character, appearance, personality, skill, and a willingness to work.[85] In order to "direct the child's efforts along [the] most promising and profitable lines," that is, to advise students into appropriate channels of study, counselors relied on data from intelligence tests, accomplishment tests, and elementary-school records.[86] As the curriculum moved closer to vocational concerns, school administrators were careful to emphasize their distinction between vocational education—that designed for "preparing people to get a job, to assist employed people in getting a better job, or in improving their work on the job" and general education—schooling that included "pre-vocational exploratory courses in shop work, work in industrial arts and manual training, and other forms of shop work. . . ."[87]

As the emphasis on vocational preparation increased, so too did the importance of character and citizenship training. The weight of these agenda converged on the high-school curriculum in St. Louis throughout the 1920s and 1930s, and effectively squeezed out the greater part of what had been left of the core of the academic curriculum. This was made blatantly clear in repeated instances, but perhaps no more discernibly than in the *Seventy-Seventh Annual Report* of 1931. "The major aim of the Saint Louis Public Schools is to develop in children a high type of citizenship. The entire curriculum is designed to contribute to this end."[88] The report went on to list seven areas of concentration for all courses of instruction, echoes of the 1918 *Cardinal Principles of Secondary Education*: Health and Physical Development; Discovery, Communication, and Expression; Worthy Home Membership; Vocation; Worthy Citizenship; Worthy Use of Leisure; Ethical Character.[89]

The twin themes of schooling for citizenship and preparation for work continued to permeate the St. Louis annual reports through 1945 and, not surprisingly, intensified during World War II. Yet, even prior to 7 December 1941, the *St. Louis Public School Approved Recommendations of the St. Louis School Survey*, released in September of 1941, reported that the "ultimate objectives of education are effective citizenship and good character. . . . " Further, it proclaimed that "General education and education for work are the two major aspects of an adequate educational offering."[90] The philosophy of the

St. Louis public high schools had changed drastically from its nineteenth-century notions of moral and intellectual education.

CURRICULUM TRANSFORMATION IN ST. LOUIS

The first curriculum in St. Louis public high schools was published in the *First Annual Report* of the St. Louis school system, a publication that coincided with the first full year of classes at Central High School. There was but one program of study, strictly defined for all students. The curriculum reflected elements of the academy, with practical courses in surveying, navigation, and bookkeeping, as well as the Latin grammar school, with an emphasis on the classics. Yet, the major purpose of the high school at this early date in St. Louis was to support the common school system. This was to be accomplished by providing an organized opportunity for higher learning to elementary-school graduates. Thus, the high-school curriculum included courses in higher mathematics, mental philosophy, logic, and political economy. In addition, the high school was looked upon to supply teachers for the St. Louis common schools. Toward this end, the high-school curriculum provided for study in analytical grammar, history, and penmanship. In its beginning stages, then, it appeared as if Central High School had designed a curriculum to meet a diverse set of needs (see table 2).

By the 1870s, public high-school attendance had increased in St. Louis, however, conflict concerning the institution had intensified as well. While some members of the community were questioning the right to draw on public funds for financial support of the high school, others (for instance, educators embroiled in the battle over the set curriculum or those questioning the educational value of the classics) were demanding more practical courses in lieu of the traditional disciplinary course. Requests for more science and less Latin were coupled with calls for an extension of the elective system.[91] This debate encompassed far more than the citizens of St. Louis; it was seething in cities throughout the United States. The public high school, from its conception, had been an institution of the American city while the academy was better suited for rural areas. As Clarence Karier noted, the predominance of the high school over the academy gained strength with the rise in urbanization in the latter nineteenth century.[92]

GRADE LEVEL			
9	10	11	12
Higher Algebra	Geometry	Trigonometry, Mensuration, Surveying, Navigation	Analytic Geometry, Calculus
Analytic Grammar	Latin	Caesar, Cicero, Virgil	Livy, Horace
Higher Arithmetic	Natural Philosophy	Chemistry, Bookkeeping	Geology, Astronomy
U.S. History	General History	U.S. Constitution, Political Economy	Rhetoric, Logic, Mental Philosophy
German (optional)	German (optional)	French (optional)	French (optional)

Penmanship, Vocal Music, Composition, Elocution, Sentential Analysis, Declamation throughout the Course.

Table 2: St. Louis High School Curriculum, 1854

Source: *St. Louis Annual Report* (1854), 1: 116.

Concerns over how best to develop this ascending secondary institution, the public high school, merged with an educational respect for the Prussian state school system. Prussia was building national strength on a two-tiered schooling system that directed the masses to a basic education for literacy and loyalty to the state, that is, citizenship, while the elite had access to an intellectual education based on the academic disciplines. While the children of the elite went from the *vorschule* to the *gymnasium*, and then perhaps on to military academies or universities, the children who attended the *volkschule* could only hope for admittance to technical or normal schools. This system was in the minds of the educators in the United States who were in the process of molding the nascent public high school. Its essence can be found at the root of the ensuing debates on the classical curriculum and the place of electives in high school and college study. The St. Louis public-school response to the Prussian style of schooling is key, given the city's strong German influence. For an insight on this development in the St. Louis high-school curriculum, one can again turn to Hegelian philosopher William T. Harris, superintendent of St. Louis schools during this period.

Noting political and industrial interest in nineteenth-century public education, Harris addressed the issue of whether there should be different courses of education adapted to the supposed destinies of students in the *Nineteenth Annual Report*. He rejected the schism that would train the masses for industrial work and educate the elite in the disciplines, in spite of its appeal to industrialists, on the grounds that such a system would shape the public schools into the institution of a caste system. Harris realized that public schools would become nothing more than schools "founded especially for the industrial class to the end that its children being born from 'hands' shall be 'hands' still and shall not mingle with the children of the wealthy nor with those of the liberally educated."[93] Further, he predicted that the public schools would degenerate to a point where reproduction of inferior status would be the primary result of schooling. "On the one hand those who have received higher education have been nurtured in an atmosphere of contempt for the free schools of the laboring classes; on the other hand the laboring classes themselves despise the symbol of their inferiority and the institution designed to make their inferiority hereditary."[94] Harris recognized, however, that students using the high school as a means of preparing for college required a different emphasis than those who were planning to complete their formal education with high-school study. His work throughout the century, including his contributions to the NEA report of the Committee of Ten, addressed the relationship between high-school and college courses of study. Harris suggested that the St. Louis public high school adopt two courses of study, General and Classical. Each offered a sound educational curriculum while individually meeting the needs of those preparing for "life" as well as those preparing for college. Central High School maintained the General and Classical Courses of study throughout most of the nineteenth century.

Both courses of study operated from the same basic foundation. The Classical Course was distinguished by a four-year study of Latin and Greek. Students in the General Course had the option of modern languages and were required to take more classes in mathematics and science (see table 3).

Unlike the Prussian system, regardless of which course of study that a student pursued in the St. Louis high school, the education was intellectually challenging. This was important in a democracy, for as Harris perceived, "to educate the ruling class (in a democracy) means to educate all the people."[95] Of course, only a small percentage of the total population were able to attend high school. Harris also differentiated the method of learning in the public high school, which he preferred, to that in operation at the American colleges of his day. He criticized the colleges for separating discipline and knowledge, likening college education to a palm tree that does not branch out in growth until the top of the system is reached. The public-school course that incorporated higher mathematics, sciences, history, and literature along with the classics, Harris argued, allowed the student to experience a full "flowering" of education from the beginning of his or her study. Using one of his favorite metaphors, Harris proclaimed that the "mind should grow with all its windows open from the beginning."[96] He continued that the more one could develop the learning process in school, the more adept one would be in translating knowledge into practice in everyday life. In the *Eighteenth Annual Report* Harris wrote that two directions of culture were essential for the education of citizens in the nineteenth century. The first was the power of combination, quantification, which allows some degree of control of the physical world. The important study in relation to this aspect was mathematics. The second power of combination was that which enabled individuals to combine with each other, to form a community and rationally profit by it. Thus, students were led to the importance of communication and those studies that engaged in reading and writing. Harris believed that the high-school study of these two "roads of culture" should be at the level of reflection or higher generalization.[97]

	GRADE LEVEL			
	9	10	11	12
CLASSICAL COURSE	Algebra	Geometry		Algebra/ Geometry Review
	Latin	Greek, Latin	Greek, Latin	Greek, Latin
	English Analysis	Physiology	Astronomy	Shakespeare, English Lit.
	Physical Geography	Ancient Geography	Universal History	U.S. Constitution
	Drawing	Drawing		
GENERAL COURSE	Algebra	Geometry	Trigonometry or Botany	Analytic Geometry, Calculus
	German or Latin	German or Latin	French and German or Latin	French and German or Latin
	English Analysis	Bookkeeping (optional)	Universal History	Shakespeare, English Lit.
	Physical Geography	Natural Philosophy, Chemistry	Zoology	U.S. Constitution
	Drawing	Drawing	Manual of Art	
		Physiology	Astronomy	Mental and Moral Philosophy

Music and Rhetoricals throughout both courses. Girls may consider the Calculus and Philosophy as optional.

Table 3. St. Louis High School Curriculum, 1870

Source: *St. Louis Annual Report* (1870), 16: lxxxix.

The following year, Harris wrote again on the controversy of the practical studies of the general course versus the traditional discipline of the classical course. He argued in favor of the course that united the disciplinary studies with collateral studies in pursuit of information and insight; the union of discipline and knowledge must begin in the primary school and continue through the high school.[98] The superintendent provided a powerful defense of the classics in his essay. He noted the results of classical study, discipline, culture, exactness of thought, and a refining influence. The power of his argument came, however, from his contention that immediate contact with the Greek and Latin languages was necessary to thoroughly claim the understandings of those civilizations for oneself. Harris encapsulated this notion in a quote by Schopenhauer: "A man who does not understand Latin is like one who walks through a beautiful region in a fog; his horizon is very close to him. He sees only the nearest things clearly, and a few steps away from him the outlines of everything become indistinct or wholly lost. But the horizon of the Latin scholar extends far and wide through the centuries of modern history, the middle ages and antiquity."[99]

Harris continued with a description of his ideal course of study. He argued that the intellectual view of the world, and thus the demands of education, are divided into two realms, the world of nature and the world of humanity. The natural world existed of inorganic and organic domains while the world of humanity contained the spheres of theoretical or thinking power, practical or will power, and aesthetic or art power. Each of these five domains corresponded to five essential branches of education, the five "windows of the soul." Data in table 4 illustrates the close connection between Harris' educational plan and the St. Louis high-school curriculum during the 1870s.

The St. Louis high school curriculum changed very little through the 1880s. The curriculum was presented later as one course of study with choices given between the classics and modern languages, higher mathematics, and sciences. One was, however, still able to discern the classical from the general preparation. Courses were offered which supported culture as the "journey on the road toward rational freedom."[100] Educators continued to seek a balance between the practical concerns of life and the development of the intellect and moral character. Evidently, school officials were pleased with their success. In the *Twenty-Eighth Annual Report* of 1882 it was noted that

> In our Course of Study we try to avoid the two extremes of teaching simply a handicraft, and of sacrificing every-day usefulness to the development of the spiritual nature. Human institutions are from

necessity imperfect, but the success met with by the pupils of the High School, proves the prescribed Course to be specially well adapted for developing our pupils into excellent and efficient men and women, whether these have followed humble occupations, or taken charge of our most weighty responsibilities. [101]

By 1891 school officials apparently believed the St. Louis high school course of study could use some improvement, for the *Thirty-Seventh Annual Report* noted that the high school curriculum had been revised to include Classical, Scientific, English, Normal, and Business Courses. Core classes were maintained across the curriculum, however, each course of study emphasized classes designed for its own particular discipline. These developments did not, however, occur in Sumner High School. Sumner was established as a secondary school for African Americans in 1875, but Missouri laws prohibiting education for African Americans had placed considerable barriers in the educational progress of many. It took a few years for African Americans in St. Louis to work through the segregated elementary-school system that was finally, and reluctantly, organized for African-American children. Commencement services were held for the first graduating class of Sumner High School in 1885. Sumner High School, which defined its objectives as preparing students for college and training teachers for elementary schools in St. Louis, soon became a national leader among segregated secondary schools. While Central High School was dividing its population into various courses of study, then, Sumner High School students continued to pursue a liberal education through one course of study. [102]

WINDOW	OBJECTIVE	VISTA	COURSES
Arithmetic	Quantify; Theoretical dominion over time and space	World of quantity	Algebra, Geometry, Trigonometry, Analytic Geometry, Natural Philosophy, Chemistry
Geography	Localize; Spatial relation to the rest of the world	Organic world	Physical Geography, Astronomy, Botany, Physiology, Zoology
Grammar	Fixes and defines speech; mastery over mind as an instrument	Spiritual world	Philology, Latin, Greek, French, German, Mental and Moral Philosophy
History	Learns of human progress and process; recognize existence as continued into the past	World of deeds and events	Universal History, U.S. Constitution
Reading	Mastery of literature	World of art	History of English Literature, Shakespeare, Rhetoricals, Drawing

Table 4. Harris' Educational Model: 1873

Source: *St. Louis Annual Report* (1873), 19: 73-78.

Manual-training and domestic-science courses emerged just before the turn of the century, in 1899. In that year Sumner High School added a Department of Domestic Science and sent male students for manual-training classes, which were held in the L'Ouverture Elementary School. Concurrently, arguments were advanced in favor of building a new manual-training high school for European-American students. In 1902, the *Forty-Eighth Annual Report* announced plans for building the new McKinley and Yeatman Manual Training High Schools, which were to give "complete opportunity to boys and girls for either a purely literary education or for manual training and domestic science combined, with the customary High School studies."[103] On 2 September 1902, the St. Louis high schools also adopted a new course of study. The new guidelines required at least twenty recitations per week in every course. One hundred recitations in a single study translated into one point. A minimum of thirty-two points was necessary for graduation, half of which had to be taken in English, literature, history, algebra, geometry, biology, and physics. The other sixteen points varied according to the student's course of study.[104] By 1903, the St. Louis school system was offering its European-American students nine courses of study at the secondary level. As a look at table 5 will indicate, the curriculum emphasized general courses in English, mathematics, history, and science, and included concentrated courses based on a student's particular study. This was the curriculum that was constructed to support the emerging St. Louis philosophy of 1903: "The general purpose of the High School education is to develop manhood and womanhood with strength of character and trained intelligence."[105] An astute observer might have detected an omen of the changes to come.

Table 5. St. Louis High School Curriculum, 1903

| | GRADE LEVEL | | | |
	9	10	11	12
ART COURSE	English	English	English	English, Shakespeare
	Drawing	Drawing	Drawing	Drawing
	Botany, Physiology	Physics	Laboratory Physics, Chemistry or Geometry and Algebra	Chemistry or Trigonometry and Ethics and Psychology
	Algebra	Geometry	History	History
			Latin or German or French or Spanish	Latin or German or French or Spanish
GENERAL COURSE	English	English	English	English, Shakespeare
	Latin or German or French or Spanish	Latin or German or French or Spanish	Latin or German or French or Spanish-2	Latin or German or French or Spanish-2
	Algebra	Geometry	History	History
	Botany, Physiology	Physics	Laboratory Physics, Chemistry or Geometry and Algebra	Chemistry or Trigonometry and Ethics and Psychology

SCIENTIFIC COURSE	English	English	English	English, Shakespeare
	Latin or German or French or Spanish	Latin or German or French or Spanish	Latin or German or French or Spanish-2	Latin or German or French or Spanish-2
	Botany, Physiology	Physics	Laboratory Physics, Chemistry	Chemistry
	Algebra	Geometry	Algebra, Geometry	Trigonometry
			History	History
COLLEGE SCIENTIFIC COURSE	English	English	English	English, Shakespeare
	Latin, German or French	Latin, German or French	Latin, German or French	Latin, German or French
	Botany, Physiology	Physics	Laboratory Physics, Chemistry	Chemistry
	Algebra	Geometry	Algebra, Geometry	Trigonometry Reviews in Algebra, Geometry, Latin
			History	History
CLASSICAL COURSE	English	English	English	English, Shakespeare
	Latin	Latin, Greek	Latin, Greek, German or French or Spanish	Latin, Greek, German or French or Spanish
	Botany, Physiology	History	History	Physics
	Algebra	Geometry		

COLLEGE CLASSICAL COURSE	English	English	English	English, Shakespeare
	Latin, German or French	Latin, Greek, German or French	Latin, Greek, German or French	Latin, Greek, German or French
	Botany, Physiology	History	History	Physics
	Algebra	Geometry	Algebra, Geometry	Reviews in Latin, Greek, Algebra, Geometry
COMM. COURSE	English	English	English	English, Shakespeare
	Drawing or Latin or German or French or Spanish	Drawing or Latin or German or French or Spanish	Latin or German or French or Spanish	Latin or German or French or Spanish
	Botany, Physiology	Physics	Laboratory Physics, Chemistry	Chemistry or Ethics and Psychology
	Algebra	Geometry	History	History, Civics
	Penmanship	Arithmetic, Bookkeeping	Bookkeeping, Phonography, Typing, Commercial Law	Economics, Commercial Geography, Phonography, Typing

MANUAL TRAINING	English	English	English	English, Shakespeare
	Manual Training	Manual Training	Manual Training	Manual Training
	Drawing	Drawing	Drawing	Drawing
	Latin or German or French or Spanish	Latin or German or French or Spanish	Latin or German or French or Spanish	Latin or German or French or Spanish
	Botany, Physiology	Physics	Laboratory Physics, Chemistry	Chemistry
	Algebra	Geometry	Algebra, Geometry	Trigonometry
			History	History

PREP. TEACHERS COURSE	English	English	English	English, Shakespeare
	Drawing	Drawing	Drawing	Drawing
	Music, Penmanship	Music, Penmanship	Music, Penmanship	Music, Penmanship, Physiography
	Latin	Latin	Latin, German or French or Spanish	Latin, German or French or Spanish
	Botany, Physiology	Physics	Laboratory Physics, Chemistry	History
	Algebra	Geometry	History	

Source: *St. Louis Annual Report* (1903), 49: 153-157.

In 1909 there were calls for a radical change in the single course of study at Sumner High School. The *Fifty-Fifth Annual Report* included a recommendation that the course of study available to African-American students in St. Louis be altered "as to give a suitable range of choice and to give a very much larger time to manual training work. . . . "[106] The emphasis on practicality extended in the 1910s beyond course structure and throughout all St. Louis high schools. The 1911 *Annual Report* suggested that the "school can increase its efficiency greatly by merely placing a greater stress upon the practical bearing of the subjects now in its course."[107] A new educational philosophy had definitely emerged with the implementation of the multi-course curriculum. After the NEA Committee of Ten Report was released in 1894, college entrance requirements became decreasingly influential in shaping high-school curricula. The corresponding change in the secondary school curriculum, however, went beyond replacing the classics with the more practical disciplines of higher mathematics and the sciences. The balanced curriculum that Harris had argued for was slipping away as well. Vocational concerns came to dominate the high-school curriculum. These observations were not reserved for historians alone; the shifting curriculum pattern was quite evident to St. Louis school officials in 1911.

> The last quarter of a century has seen a radical change in the determinants of the high school course of study. College entrance requirements, based on the foundations of thought necessary for the professions, have gradually become less of a factor in shaping the work and regard for a difference in interest and plans for the future created a variety of courses through a regrouping of the old elements or through the addition of new subjects. In this way commercial and manual training courses for both boys and girls have grown up, offering opportunity for High School study arranged with direct regard for the kind of work the pupil intends to pursue after leaving the High School; still there remains much to be done to arouse in the students the motives for their school work which will associate it vitally with the vocation to be followed.[108]

The St. Louis high-school curriculum that was adopted in 1917 made an even sharper contrast with the nineteenth-century course of study. The most recent graduation requirements called for sixteen units of subjects (a unit equaled one year's work consisting of five periods per week,) two periods per week of chorus work in music, and two periods per week of work in physical training. One or more subjects were required per semester; the rest were electives. Each student had to establish two majors of three years' study each, and two minors of two years' study each. All students were required to take three units of English, one unit of science, one unit of history, one-half unit of community civics, and one-half unit of vocational information. Credit in the languages was not given for less than two years of study of one language. [109] A comparison of table 6 with tables 2, 3, and 5 accents the changes that had occurred in the St. Louis curriculum by 1917.

Table 6. St. Louis High School Curriculum, 1917

	GRADE LEVEL			
	9	10	11	12
GENERAL COURSE	Chorus	Chorus	Chorus	Chorus
	Physical Training	Physical Training	Physical Training	Physical Training
	English	English	English	History
	Community Civics, Vocations, Elective— 2 units	Elective— 3 units	Elective— 3 units	Elective— 3 units
FINE ARTS COURSE	Chorus	Chorus	Chorus	Chorus
	Physical Training	Physical Training	Physical Training	Physical Training
	English	English	English	History
	Community Civics, Vocations, Elective— 1 unit	Elective— 2 units	Elective— 2 units	Elective— 2 units
	Art or Music— 2 units	Art or Music— 2 units	Art or Music— 2 units	Art or Music— 2 units

CLASSICAL COURSE	Chorus	Chorus	Chorus	Chorus
	Physical Training	Physical Training	Physical Training	Physical Training
	English	English	English	History
	Latin	Latin	Latin	Latin
	Community Civics, Vocations, Elective— 1 unit	Elective— 2 units	Elective— 2 units	Elective— 2 units
HOME EC. COURSE	Chorus	Chorus	Chorus	Chorus
	Physical Training	Physical Training	Physical Training	Physical Training
	English	English	English	History
	Household Arts—2 units	Household Arts—2 units	Household Arts—2 units	Household Arts—2 units
	Botany, Physiology	Physics	Chemistry	
	Community Civic, Vocations	Elective— 1 unit	Elective— 1 unit	Elective— 2 units

COMM. COURSE	Chorus	Chorus	Chorus	Chorus
	Physical Training	Physical Training	Physical Training	Physical Training
	English	English	English	Modern History, American History
	Bookkeeping, Arithmetic, Penmanship --2 units	Book-keeping, Arithmetic, Penmanship --2 units	Typing, Spelling— 2 units	Commercial Law, Salesman-ship, Advertising
	Community Civics, Vocations	Industrial History, Commercial Geography	Stenography	Stenography
	Elective— 1 unit	Elective— 1 unit	Elective— 1 unit	Typing, Dictation— 2 units

Source: *St. Louis Annual Report* (1917), 63: 119-121.

In addition to these courses of study, short courses were also available in the St. Louis high schools. Two-year courses were offered in manual training, home economics, and commercial subjects. One-year courses were offered in bookkeeping and stenography.

In 1926, the St. Louis Board of Education approved the establishment of a vocational school for students who had finished the eighth grade but did not expect to go to high school, those who had dropped out of high school, and those about to graduate from high school. Instruction was provided in mechanical drawing, commercial art and design, cabinet making, carpentry, pattern making, sheet-metal working, machine-shop practice, applied electricity, homemaking, millinery, dressmaking and design, and retail selling. The philosophy of the vocational school was clearly stated in the 1927 *Annual Report*. "The Vocational School opens the doors for Opportunity and cultivates right attitude toward the World's Work."[110] The vocational school operated in addition to the continuation schools, which had been established for fourteen- and fifteen-year-olds who had not completed eighth grade. These youth were required by law to attend classes four hours per week. Courses in woodworking, general metal work, electricity, printing and commercial work, cooking, and dressmaking dominated the program.[111]

Nineteen-thirty was the last year that students graduated from St. Louis high schools in a particular course of study. The school system had moved toward a single, multitracked curriculum in which a minimum of sixteen units was required for a high-school diploma. Table 7 provides data on the various tracks in the St. Louis system. Gradually, the distinctions between these tracks would merge into a three-track system that sorted students into distinct areas: college preparatory, general education, and vocational education.

	English	Social Studies	Math	Science	Track-Related Classes/ Elective Classes
Classical	4	3	2	1	6/2
Scientific	4	3	3	3	2/3
General	4	3	1	1	0/7
Comm.	4	3	1	1	3/4
Fine Arts	4	3	1	1	3/4
Home Ec.	4	3	1	1	3/4
Indust. Arts	4	3	2	2	3/2
Modified General	3	3	1	1	1/7

Table 7. St. Louis High School Curriculum, 1936 (units required)

Source: *St. Louis Annual Report* (1936), 82: 20.

In 1941, the St. Louis high schools took further steps toward the three-track curriculum by promoting greater flexibility in the choice of subjects and increasing the number of electives. In addition, courses were added in "American Problems," retail merchandising, and secretarial practice.[112] In 1944, the high schools entered a program of core-curriculum development "as a step in line with a policy of meeting the needs of all pupils of High School age."[113] Based on the curriculum contortions in St. Louis high schools, these "needs" did not include a rigorous, academic education.

ACADEMIC DECLINE

The evolution of the St. Louis high-school curriculum, which was based on underlying educational philosophies in flux, created an environment of academic deterioration from 1870 to 1930. Throughout much of the nineteenth century, the high school curriculum conformed to a philosophy that emphasized education for intellectual growth and the development of moral character. In 1882, school officials proclaimed the "scholarship of the High School claims to be both exact and liberal, and its teaching, both intellectual and ethical, is conducted with the ever-present aim of making industrious, capable, and upright men and women."[114] The same objectives were explicitly stated for Sumner High School students. "The Sumner High School must do its share to train the future leaders of the race, so that they may be men and women of good intelligence and pure character."[115] During the twentieth century, however, school officials in St. Louis cast and recast the secondary curriculum into a series of programs that reflected a much different philosophy. The twin pillars of the emerging curricula, schooling for citizenship and schooling for work, were both cemented in a new ideology that perceived the individual simply as a cell in the social organism. There was little doubt whose interests were to be served in preparing students for citizenship and for work. As stated in 1926 by a school committee formed for the purpose of establishing principles for the formulation of aims of public education, "Schools serve two interests: those of the individual and those of society; wherever the two come into conflict those of society take precedence."[116]

A new conception of the individual lay at the root of the distinction between this ideology and that of earlier times. Prominent twentieth-century sociologist Charles H. Cooley argued that the individual could only find expression as part of a social group. Cooley wrote that the social group produced "a certain fusion of individualities in a common whole, so that one's very self, for many purposes at least, is the common life and purpose of the group."[117] Thinking that welded the individual and the social group together in this way was evident in school statements that encouraged the promotion of the interests of society over the interest of the individual. The individual in this new ideology was not the unfettered individual of classical liberal thought; rather, the twentieth-century individual was tied to service in the social order, not necessarily service of one's choosing. Cooley outlined parameters for individual freedom by stating that individuals were to have freedom to serve society.[118] Intellectuals argued that society's need for social order underscored the necessity of compulsory schooling laws. Intellectuals argued, also, that the modern order required that individuals be trained for specific social roles, and thus, the differentiated curriculum was initiated. Individual interests—to attend school or not, what to study once there—were of little consequence when measured against the interests of the social order.

Proponents of the new ideology held up the public school as the institution charged with the responsibility of preparing individuals for their specific social roles. The function of the twentieth-century school (unlike its nineteenth-century counterpart) was to sort and train. During the Progressive Era, changes in the structure of work brought on by scientific management in the industrial sector created a climate of intense industrial conflict; many looked to the school to train the "right" kind of workers for the industrial workplace. At the same time, governmental reforms altered the process of political participation; many looked to the school to train the "right" kind of citizens.[119] The desire to train workers and citizens born of political-economic changes merged with the discovery of a new explanation for how people learn to undergird a massive shift in school curriculum. As behavioral psychology moved the emphasis on human learning from mind to body, from the rational to the nonrational, curricular objectives shifted from intellectual and moral education to schooling for citizenship and work. Sociologist Edward A. Ross captured much of the essence of the emerging ideology that supported these changes in schooling with his definition of schooling as a device to promote order. "To collect little plastic lumps of human dough from private households and shape them on the social kneadingboard, exhibits a faith in the power of suggestion which few peoples ever attain to. And so it happens that the role of the schoolmaster in the social economy is just beginning."[120] The role of the school in the new social economy was, indeed, in transition. In St.

Louis, three curricular trends marked this period of development. First, from 1870 to 1930 graduation requirements were reduced. Second, during this period there was a distinct alteration in the courses that were offered. Finally, alternative programs of study were devised for the new high-school students who educators believed to be less "academically inclined."

Graduation requirements in the St. Louis high schools declined from 1870 to 1930 regarding the number of courses needed to fulfill one's program. Comparing the number of classes taken to complete the General Course, twenty-one courses were required in 1870 and twenty were required in 1903. With Physical Training and Chorus excluded, sixteen courses constituted the General Course in 1917; eleven of these were electives. By 1936, a student enrolled in the general track in St. Louis high schools still needed only sixteen courses for graduation, and of these, seven units were electives.

Beginning around the turn of the century, St. Louis secondary schools began to add manual-training and domestic-science courses to the curriculum. Commercial studies had been included late in the nineteenth century, and by 1917 a course titled "The Vocations" was required for all students. In order to make room for these new additions, other courses, Greek and philosophy, for example, were gradually phased out. In *The Shaping of the American High School, 1880-1920*, Edward Krug detailed the battles that were joined by teachers of the traditional academic subjects in the effort to maintain their discipline's right to exist in American secondary schools during the age of "social efficiency." Practical subjects, such as manual training, domestic science, and commercial education, were acceptable to the efficiency experts by definition. The academic subjects that survived did so usually by "professing adherence to social efficiency as an aim, partly by recommending and effecting some modification in what was taught." [121] The transformation of history courses provides a good example.

By 1936, the St. Louis high-school curriculum had incorporated what was left of its political economy, geography, and history courses into the social studies. As if in answer to David Snedden's assertion, "The study of history . . . can no longer be regarded as an end in itself," the social-studies courses at St. Louis, as elsewhere, centered around citizenship training.[122] As Rolla M. Tryon noted in his comprehensive study entitled, *The Social Studies as School Subjects*, "Training for effective citizenship" emerged as a popular slogan in the 1910s. Tryon acknowledged that the efforts to translate such values into the everyday lives of students were nationwide from 1910 to 1925.[123] Historians concur that a national movement in the high-school course of study surfaced around the turn of the century.[124] In *Middletown*, the watershed sociological study of the 1920s, the authors suggested that program changes related to social studies rivaled the principal curricular transformation, the introduction of vocational courses: "[S]econd only in importance to the rise of these courses addressed to practical vocational activities is the new emphasis upon courses in history and civics."[125] Indeed, social studies claimed 16 percent of the total student hours in Middletown High School; the only areas to demand more student time were English and vocational education.[126] The authors of the study described the social studies as "yet another point at which Middletown is bending its schools to the immediate service of its institutions—in this case, bolstering community solidarity against sundry divisive tendencies."[127] Apparently, the ways in which the social-studies curriculum was called upon to support a new school philosophy, this "bending of the schools" to the twentieth-century social order, were clear. Marvin Lazerson has described the redefinition of citizenship that occurred in schools as a movement from "a faith in literacy and broad moral values to an explicit teaching of behavior and patriotism."[128] David Nasaw states that the transition to a socially efficient social studies was realized by the early 1920s.[129]

In Tryon's analysis of the twentieth-century evolution of the social-studies curriculum, he displayed that the articulated values of history from 1900 to 1920 "were made to *fit* the *time*."[130] That is, the structure of high-school history courses underwent "a terrific overhauling" in these years.[131] Joseph Roemer remarked in 1928 that "No subject, perhaps, in the whole secondary school program of studies has undergone a more thorough reorganization than the so-called 'history course' of the old days. . . . since the World War, there has been a growing demand for functional training in the social studies."[132] Tryon argued that the shift in the emphasis from history to social studies originated with the 1916 report of the Committee on the Social Studies in Secondary Education.[133]

The Committee on the Social Studies in Secondary Education developed as part of the Committee on the Reorganization of Secondary Education, headed by Clarence Kingsley and created under the auspices of the NEA in 1913. Edward Krug argues that some of the recommendations of the Committee on the Social Studies were adopted in schools, but he implies that a more important contribution was that the committee's work served as a point of reference in subsequent discussions of the social studies.[134] Krug characterized the committee's recommendations as one version of social control, aligned with the ideas of Lester Frank Ward.[135] Extreme positions on the issue of social control dominated the debate on the place of the social studies in the school curriculum. The height of the debate found expression in the question of whether history was to be included in the social studies or eliminated from the school curriculum. The Committee on Social Studies, which had conferred with the American Historical Association and the American Political Science Association, did not eliminate history from the social studies.[136] In contrast, C.H. Judd, Chair of the Committee on Social Science of the National Association of Secondary-School Principals, expressed the position of educationists and other social scientists: "Social studies, as the term is employed in this report, includes sociology, economics, ethics, vocational guidance, and civics, not history."[137] Tryon recognized the power held by social scientists in this struggle: "If one keeps in mind the emphasis on the teaching of current topics and the enthusiasm for courses in modern history, which was running riot during the early 1920s, one can account for the alarm among the historians."[138] The arguments in support of the social-studies curriculum did, indeed, offer cause for alarm.

David Snedden acknowledged in a 1917 article that history might be an appropriate study for a few; but, he continued, "the study of social sciences in the interests of democratic citizenship in a highly complex civilization must be directed chiefly towards pragmatic ends. . . ."[139] Snedden was willing to offer history to some, but the social sciences, which targeted a "quest for laws, principles, generalizations, and the means of social control to be derived therefrom," were of far greater importance to him.[140] This perspective placed Snedden and other supporters of the social studies transformation in the camp of progressive social philosophy as analyzed by Karier, Spring, and Violas in *Roots of Crisis*.[141] This was a philosophy that promoted the school as an institution for social control. Pragmatic concerns for social efficiency were paramount. Academic study (history, in this case) might be appropriate for an elite group, but most were to be schooled in the rudiments of "good citizenship."

Professor James E. Russell of Teachers College, Columbia University, commented on the changes taking place in the social-studies curriculum.

> Good citizenship as an aim in life is nothing new. . . . But good
> citizenship as a dominant aim of the American public school is
> something new. . . . For the first time in history, as I see it, a social
> democracy is attempting to shape the opinions and bias the judgment
> of oncoming generations. [142]

This element of "progressive" school reform belied the notion of democratic growth. The efforts to instill "good citizenship" through the social studies were, at root, attempts at social control.

Preparation for citizenship became the route through which other academic disciplines justified their presence in the school curriculum as well. The combined emphasis on citizenship flowed through individual courses and permeated the entire school system. Consider the *St. Louis Public School Approved Recommendations of the St. Louis School Survey of 1941*.

> While facts, knowledge, and skills are and always will be essential in
> the education of children, they do not represent the major purposes
> for which the schools are maintained. It is only as the schools
> inculcate worthy attitudes and ideals, develop powers of critical
> analysis, initiative, and resourcefulness, and encourage habits of
> conduct that are socially desirable that they adequately serve our
> society. . . . [The] ultimate objectives of education are effective
> citizenship and good character. . . .[143]

Curriculum changes in St. Louis, then, led to an academic drain. Academic courses that remained in the school curriculum had to undergo transformation in order to satisfy the cry for practicality. This action created courses that were lacking in academic rigor. And, traditional academic courses were replaced in students' programs by courses that were not academic. Some educators spoke against these changes. In Dr. William Henry Black's 1900 presidential address before the State Teachers' Association in Jefferson City, Missouri, he stated that the commercial course was "in the first place a diversion from genuine educational work, and secondly, a means of getting many a boy and girl to stop education in order to get a job. . . . "[144] Others, often in more powerful positions, encouraged the incorporation of the "practical studies" into the curriculum. The course of study for Missouri high schools published by the State Department of Education in 1919 suggested that

Courses should not be offered for the benefit of a very few pupils. It is poor management to maintain small classes in subjects such as advanced Latin and mathematics when the teaching force is limited and other classes are overcrowded. [145]

The report went on to encourage installation of domestic-science and manual-training courses in the curriculum. Although a limited teaching force was not a problem for the St. Louis school system as it was for rural districts, the overriding message of the official document was aimed at schools in all financial circumstances.

Significant curriculum changes do not occur in a vacuum; compulsory-schooling laws interlocked with child-labor legislation during the Progressive Era to create another force that induced academic drain of the high-school curriculum. State legislatures adopted compulsory school-attendance laws in the latter decades of the nineteenth century. Historians agree that the first wave of compulsory attendance legislation did not prove to be very effective in increasing school attendance. In point of fact, they probably served as a confirmation of already established attendance levels. A second phase of compulsory-attendance legislation swept the nation after 1900, which did lead to students attending schools for longer periods of time and an overall increase in student enrollment. [146]

While some believe that compulsory-attendance laws and child-labor laws were "logically interwoven," so that the advance of one was connected to the advance of the other, a stronger argument suggests that child-labor laws had an indirect effect on schooling by limiting employment opportunities for school-age children.[147] In a 1921 text that is still recognized as a foremost source on compulsory-attendance and child-labor legislation, Forest Ensign argued that laws relating to child labor were not in harmony with laws relating to compulsory attendance. The legislation was written to reflect different interests and administration of the laws was meted out to different levels of government. (State agents normally supervised the enforcement of child-labor laws while compulsory attendance laws often fell under local control.)[148] Nonetheless, as Stanford Professor of Education Ellwood Cubberley noted in 1919, the general revision of compulsory-attendance laws after 1900 combined with child-labor laws to produce the following results: labor of children was restricted; children were prohibited from working in some industries; compulsory-schooling laws were extended to cover the full school year; poverty and physical or mental "defects" were no longer accepted as exemptions from school attendance in many states; the school census was altered to help locate children of attendance age; and, truant officers were authorized to enforce compulsory-attendance and child-labor laws.[149]

Although school officials could claim only an "inconspicuous place" in the development of public sentiment in support of compulsory-attendance laws, their response to the changes in schools brought on by the laws was reactionary and substantial.[150] One clear message articulated by prominent educators in the wake of compulsory-attendance and child-labor legislation pointed to a presumed lack of intellectual ability in the children who were forced by law into the nation's schools. According to the educational experts, such children required "specialized" education that included schooling to train them for the workplace. Cubberley expressed the reactionary character of the school people's response to compulsory-attendance laws in his treatment of the topic. Cubberley stated that compulsory-attendance laws placed

> an entirely new burden on the schools. . . . our schools have come to contain many children who, having no natural aptitude for study, would at once, unless specially handled, become a nuisance in the school and tend to demoralize schoolroom procedure. . . . a compulsory-education law cannot create capacity to profit from education.[151]

In a text published one year later, Cubberley drew a connection between child-labor laws and the vocational emphasis in public schools, an emphasis that helped to displace academic content in the school curriculum. Cubberley wrote, "Shown to be economically unprofitable, and for long morally indefensible, child labor is now rapidly being superseded by suitable education and the vocational training and guidance of youth in all progressive nations."[152]

Those who supported the state in its action to enforce school attendance rested their argument on notions of positive freedom. Scholars described a benevolent state that relied upon coercive measures to protect the interests of children. The list of benefits for children, however, rarely included academic study beyond basic educational skills. Toward the end of his book on compulsory schooling and child-labor laws, Ensign concluded

> It is now a kindly state that safe-guards the child, secures his physical and moral health, insists that he acquire the fundamentals of a literary education, puts him in possession of some industrial skill and seeks to advance him to intelligent, useful citizenship. [153]

The mission to mold industrial workers and intelligent citizens was exactly the charge taken up in the St. Louis high-school curriculum of the twentieth century.

The point man behind the passage of Missouri's compulsory-attendance law in 1905 was Calvin Woodward. His concern for the lack of school attendance in St. Louis had driven his campaign for changes in the course of study at the close of the nineteenth century. Woodward tapped into the national movement for compulsory-attendance legislation in the twentieth century, hoping for better results. [154] Woodward presented an argument in favor of a compulsory-schooling law in the 1904 *St. Louis Annual Report*. Woodward's report emphasized inconsistencies in legislation noted by historians for other areas in the Unites States. The Missouri child-labor law did not attend to the concerns of those advocating compulsory attendance laws. That is, the child-labor law did not secure school attendance; it merely "turns the children from the factory into the street." [155] Woodward's critique of the child-labor law embodied the concept of positive freedom, contrasting it to the "freedom" of children to choose a life in the streets. Woodward wrote that the child-labor law

> leaves the child at liberty to spend his time in idleness, and it leaves the parent at liberty to bring up his children in ignorance and laziness. When we consider the public weal, and the work that a system of schools supported by taxation ought to do, we cannot afford to omit all provision for those unfortunate children who from poverty, neglect, or cruelty are practically deprived of an elementary education. [156]

Woodward's appeal was successful. The Missouri legislature passed a law the next year that required children from the age of six to the age of fourteen to attend school for at least half of the school year. Exemptions were granted for children ages fourteen to sixteen if they were gainfully employed, or to any child if his or her earnings were necessary for financial support of the family. Developmentally disabled or physically challenged children and those classified as juvenile delinquents might be compelled to attend special schools. In 1907, further legislation extended mandatory school attendance to a full year, closed the loopholes for children aged fourteen to sixteen, ended the poverty exemptions for children under the age of fourteen, and made provisions for truant officers.[157]

Troen offers convincing evidence for his position that compulsory-attendance laws were effective in St. Louis. According to census reports, by 1910 the vast majority of children between the ages of six and fourteen were attending school. Noticeable increases were also evident in the percentage of persons aged fourteen to twenty who attended school.[158] The increase in school attendance paralleled a decrease in the percentage of high-school students taking the Classical and Scientific courses of study in St. Louis. Among high-school seniors in 1910, most girls selected the General (34.6 percent), Art (20.6 percent), Normal (15. 8 percent), or Domestic Arts and Science (14.6 percent) courses of study. Most boys selected the General (31.8 percent), Manual Training (27.7 percent), Commercial (15.9 percent), or Scientific (12.3 percent) courses of study. In 1900, 10.2 percent of the girls and 14.5 percent of the boys graduated from the Classical Course while 38.8 percent of the girls and 67.7 percent of the boys graduated from the Scientific Course.[159] Certainly, there was a correlation between the increased numbers of students attending school as a result of compulsory-attendance and child-labor laws, and the curricular changes noted in St. Louis high schools at the turn of the century.

If any doubts remain as to the academic chasm between the study of the traditional subjects, which were on the wane in the twentieth-century St. Louis curriculum, and the newer additions to the high-school program of study, one might consult the *Fifty-Fourth Annual Report.* This volume contains a detailed outline of the courses in the school curriculum for the 1907-1908 school year. The stated ultimate purpose of the study of Latin was

> to train the mind through the acquisition of a knowledge of language structure in general; to lay a broad foundation for the study of other languages . . . ; to acquire the mental discipline which Latin is peculiarly fitted to impart; and to gain the measure of culture the study of ancient masterpieces in the original gives.[160]

Over the course of four years, students read Caesar, Cicero, and Aeneid, did translations, wrote compositions, and studied historical, mythological, geographical, and archaeological references. In contrast, the established ultimate purpose in the commercial studies was "the purpose common to all high school training, discipline and culture along general lines and preparation for citizenship, to which is added the specific purpose of preparing the student for actual business life."[161] Over the course of four years, these students engaged in activities such as the application of movement to formation of letters and figures, the fundamental processes of addition, subtraction, multiplication, and division, taking inventories, transcription, care and mechanism of the typewriter, and general office practice.

Another curricular change that marked the shift from an intellectual and moral education to one focused on citizenship and work was the notion that, first, schools were to prepare students specifically for their predicted futures, and second, different futures required different high-school educations. As students were separated into various courses of study, some experienced a more drastic separation from the academic realm than others. By 1917, the only classes all students in St. Louis high schools had in common were chorus, physical training, community civics, vocations, English, and history. As the following statement indicates, expected occupations and social status were key elements in support of a differentiated educational system.

> In addition to recognizing the need for a common body of knowledge, ideals, and habits, the schools recognize also a wide variation in the abilities and interests of individuals and also in their occupational aptitudes and social companionships. Since no two individuals will occupy identical places in life, meet identical problems, or solve their problems by identical methods, it is illogical to assume that identical training by a uniform standard is practicable.[162]

Superintendent Henry J. Gerling, in 1936, confirmed that the twentieth-century curriculum changes in St. Louis resulted, one way or another, in a less rigorous academic program.

> Increased enrollment in the high schools brings with it a further problem in the field of education, the problem of curriculum adjustment. Many of the students now entering high school are not

inherently academic minded. . . . It is necessary either to simplify the content of the high school courses for such pupils to a degree that will make success possible for them or to provide entirely different courses for their election.[163]

Clearly, steps were to be taken that would lower academic expectations for the student population as a whole, or new courses would be created that would adhere to lower academic standards. Ironically, although the school system had been concerned since the turn of the century that new students could not handle the academic courses, and had, consequently, provided them with other channels of less demanding study in order to preserve academic standards, by 1939 the majority of St. Louis high-school students had met only the lowest level of expectations. In that year, 95 percent of St. Louis high-school students were enrolled in the general track of the curriculum. Only 5 percent continued in the college-preparatory track. (Vocational students were enrolled in separate schools.) These statistics prompted a Columbia University survey committee to conclude

> It is absolutely indefensible . . . to pattern the program for the 95 per cent on the requirements laid down by colleges for the 5 per cent. General education in the high school curriculum must be evaluated in terms of the development in all youth of high school age of understandings, abilities, and attitudes needed for effective participation in the social and civic life of St. Louis and the nation.[164]

In other words, results of an earlier abandonment of academic education led to the rationale for further shredding of the tattered academic remnant in St. Louis high schools.

The shift to education for citizenship and work was so secure by 1941 that it was no longer considered necessary to disguise the lack of intellectual stimulation in the work for which many were being trained. Further, it seems that the relationship between schooling and work was not questioned. Yet traces of democratic rhetoric were apparently still required in the St. Louis school system's fundamental philosophy of 1941.

> The democratic ideal demands, therefore, that every educated person should possess a keen appreciation of the social worth and dignity of all varieties of labor which contribute to the common good. . . . It

demands further that where, owing to technological inventions, the intellectual range of the individual's specialized vocation has become so narrow as to require little more of him than sheer mechanical physical movement, special provisions should be made to see that he appreciates the social value of the work he is doing. . . . [165]

Educational philosophy in St. Louis had strayed far from the commitments to intellectual growth and moral development that had dominated the high-school curriculum seven decades before. The focus on citizenship and work had eclipsed the traditional academic curriculum.

Throughout the nineteenth century, the St. Louis high-school curriculum was devoted to academic study. The course of study and its underlying educational philosophy gave evidence of this fact. As the curriculum shifted early in the twentieth century, the academic status of the high school occupied less sure ground. Nonacademic courses of study made inroads into the curriculum, the structure of the curriculum moved toward a general course of study from which academic content was seeping, the number of academic classes overlapping various courses of study decreased, and the academic requirements for general study in the high school receded. School officials reversed an earlier stand and embraced vocational education as a primary goal of schooling.

These changes were not peculiar to St. Louis; the curriculum transformation that followed the introduction of the differentiated curriculum brought academic decline throughout the United States. Decades later, Americans would wonder how an inadequate public-educational system had developed. Historian Arthur Bestor pointed to the displacement of an educational philosophy. "The basic trouble is that the persons running our public-school system lost sight of the main purpose of education—namely, intellectual training."[166] During the early years of the twentieth century, the persons running the public-school system in St. Louis readjusted their educational sights. The curricular target was rearranged, and academic study moved to the periphery.

NOTES

1. *Seventeenth Annual Report of the Board of Directors of the St. Louis Public Schools, for the Year Ending August 1, 1871* (St. Louis: Plate, Olshausen & Co., Printers and Binders, 1872), 17: 62-63.

2. Here I define academic studies as those studies that sustain liberal or classical education, with particular attention to intellectual development. Academic education targets the refining of critical-thinking skills as a major schooling objective and promotes the notion of gaining knowledge simply for the sake of learning. Under this definition, vocational studies are not considered academic; however, that is not to say that vocational subjects do not belong in the high-school curriculum.

3. The dates used in this study regarding curriculum enrollments are those responding to graduating classes. For example, even though classes opened at Central High School in February 1853, the first graduating class was that of 1858, thus 1858 is the first date used in the discussion above.

4. The General Course was not offered from 1898 to 1902 at Central High School.

5. I found no evidence in the *St. Louis Annual Reports that* course of study differed among the St. Louis high schools for African-American and European-American students.

6. In this text I use the term "European American" to refer to Americans of European ancestry, native-born as well as immigrant.

7. See James D. Anderson, *The Education of Blacks in the South, 1860-1935* (Chapel Hill: University of North Carolina Press, 1988) for an analysis of public secondary schooling for African Americans during the first decades of the twentieth century.

8. Clarence J. Karier, *The Individual, Society, and Education: A History of American Educational Ideas*, 2d ed. (Urbana: University of Illinois Press, 1986), 73-74.

9. Edward A. Krug, *The Shaping of the American High School: 1880-1920*, Vol. 1 (Madison: University of Wisconsin Press, 1969), 319-320. See also Karier, *Individual, Society, and Education*; Michael B. Katz, *Class, Bureaucracy, and Schools: The Illusion of Educational Change in America* (New York: Praeger Publishers, 1975); David F. Labaree, *The Making of an American High School: The Credentials Market and the Central High School of Philadelphia, 1838-1939* (New Haven: Yale University Press, 1988); Robert S. Lynd and Helen Merrell Lynd, *Middletown: A Study in American Culture* (New York: Harcourt, Brace and Co., 1929); and David Nasaw, *Schooled to Order: A Social History of Public Schooling in the United States* (Oxford: Oxford

University Press, 1979) on curriculum development in U.S. high schools during the nineteenth and early twentieth centuries.

10. Selwyn K. Troen, *The Public and the Schools: Shaping the St. Louis System, 1838-1920* (Columbia: University of Missouri Press, 1975), 185.

11. Ibid., 187.

12. For information on the antebellum high school in New England, see Emit Duncan Grizzell, *Origin and Development of the High School in New England before 1865* (New York: Macmillan, 1923); Alexander James Inglis, *The Rise of the High School in Massachusetts* (New York: Teachers College, 1911); Michael B. Katz, *The Irony of Early School Reform: Educational Innovation in Mid-Nineteenth Century Massachusetts* (Cambridge: Harvard University Press, 1968); and Maris A. Vinovskis, *The Origins of Public High School: A Reexamination of the Beverly High School Controversy* (Madison: University of Wisconsin Press, 1985).

13. Labaree, *Making of an American High School*, 137.

14. Ibid., 9, 35.

15. Ibid., 41-45.

16. Ibid., 157, 161-163.

17. Ibid., 8.

18. Ibid., 16.

19. *First Annual Report of the General Superintendent of the St. Louis Public Schools, for the Year Ending July 1, 1854* (St. Louis: Republican Office, 1854), 1:34.

20. David Tyack and Elisabeth Hansot, *Learning Together: A History of Coeducation in American Public Schools* (New Haven: Yale University Press, 1990), 126-128; William J. Reese, *The Origins of the American High School* (New Haven: Yale University Press, 1995), 170-171.

21. Ellwood P. Cubberley, *Public Education in the United States: A Study and Interpretation of American Educational History* (Boston: Houghton Mifflin Company, 1919), 193.

22. Katz, *Irony of Early School Reform*, 228, 231.

23. Joel Spring, *The American School 1642-1993*, 3d ed. (New York: McGraw-Hill, 1994), 215.

24. Cubberley, *Public Education*, 194.

25. Spring, *American School*, 215.

26. Cubberley, *Public Education*, 196-197.

27. Ibid., 197; Katz, *Irony of Early School Reform*, 34.

28. Katz, *Irony of Early School Reform*, 34.

29. Cubberley, *Public Education*, 198.

30. Patricia Albjerg Graham, *Community and Class in American Education, 1865-1918* (New York: Wiley, 1974), 18.

31. Edward A. Krug, *Salient Dates in American Education, 1635-1964* (New York: Harper & Row, 1966), 91-94.

32. Krug, *Shaping of the American High School*, 169, 439; Spring, *American School*, 214.

33. *Statistical Abstract of the United States 1910*, Thirty-Third Number (Washington, DC: U.S. Government Printing Office, 1911), 102.

34. Anderson, *Education of Blacks in the South*, 186-237.

35. *Fourth Annual Report of the President, Superintendent and Secretary to the Board of St. Louis Public Schools, for the Year Ending July 1st, 1858* (St. Louis: R.P. Studley, Printer and Binder, 1858), 4:23-24.

36. *Seventh and Eighth Annual Reports of the Superintendent and Secretary to the Board of St. Louis Public Schools, for the Years Ending August 1, 1860-61, and 1861-62* (St. Louis: R.P. Studley Printers, Binders and Lithographers, 1862), 7: 64.

37. *Eleventh Annual Report of the Board of Directors of the St. Louis Public Schools, for the Year Ending August 1, 1865* (St. Louis: R.P. Studley, Printers, 1865), 11: 30.

38. *St. Louis Annual Report*, 4: 47.

39. *St. Louis Annual Report*, 11: 36.

40. *Fourteenth Annual Report of the Board of Directors of the St. Louis Public Schools, for the Year Ending August 1, 1868* (St. Louis: George Knapp & Co., Printers and Binders, 1869), 14: 74.

41. *Seventeenth Annual Report of the Board of Directors of the St. Louis Public Schools, for the Year Ending August 1, 1871* (St. Louis: Plate, Olshausen & Co., Printers and Binders, 1872), 17: 31.

42. *Twenty-First Annual Report of the Board of Directors of the St. Louis Public Schools, for the Year Ending August 1, 1875* (St. Louis, 1876), 21: 67.

43. David B. Tyack, *The One Best System: A History of American Urban Education* (Cambridge: Harvard University Press, 1974), 43. Historian Lawrence Cremin referred to Harris as "the commanding figure of his pedagogical era." Lawrence A. Cremin, *The Transformation of the School: Progressivism in American Education, 1876-1957* (New York: Alfred A. Knopf, 1961), 14.

44. Quoted in Kurt F. Leidecker, *Yankee Teacher: The Life of William Torrey Harris* (New York: Philosophical Library, 1946), foreword.

45. See Denys P. Leighton, "William Torrey Harris, 'The St. Louis Hegelians,' and the Meaning of the Civil War," *Gateway Heritage: Quarterly*

Journal of the Missouri Historical Society 10 (1989): 32-45 for a discussion of Harris' interpretation of Hegelian philosophy.

46. Quoted in *St. Louis Annual Report* 17: 37.

47. Quoted in *St. Louis Annual Report 17*: 32.

48. Karier, *Individual, Society, and Education*, (Urbana: University of Illinois Press, 1986), 99-100.

49. *Twenty-Third Annual Report of the Board of Directors of the St. Louis Public Schools, for the Year Ending August 1, 1877* (St. Louis: John J. Daly & Co. Printers, 1878), 23: 55.

50. *Forty-First Annual Report of the Board of President and Directors of the St. Louis Public Schools, for the Year Ending June 30, 1895* (St. Louis: Buxton & Skinner Stationery Co., 1897), 41: 107.

51. Quoted in *Twenty-Second Annual Report of the Board of Directors of the St. Louis Public Schools, for the Year Ending August 1, 1876* (St. Louis, 1877), 22: 12.

52. Quoted in *Twenty-Eighth Annual Report of the Board of President and Directors of the St. Louis Public Schools, for the Year Ending August 1, 1882* (St. Louis: Slawson & Co., Printers, 1883), 28: 105-106.

53. Early histories on the manual-training movement include Charles A. Bennett, *History of Manual and Industrial Education up to 1870* (Peoria: Manual Arts Press, 1926) and *History of Manual and Industrial Education, 1870-1917* (Peoria: Manual Arts Press, 1937). Charles Penney Coates, *History of the Manual Training School of Washington University*, Bureau of Education, Bulletin, 1923, provides an early account of the institutional origins of manual training in St. Louis. Other key primary sources include Isaac E. Clarke, *Art and Industry* (46th Congress, 2d session, U.S. Senate, Executive Documents, 1897), VII, No. 209, pts. 1-4; Paul H. Douglas, *American Apprenticeship and Industrial Education*, Columbia University Studies in Economics, History and Law, 95, No. 2 (New York: Longman, Green and Co., 1921); and Ray Stombaugh, *A Survey of the Movements Culminating in Industrial Arts Education*, 1936. Troen, *The Public and the Schools*, (Columbia: University of Missouri Press, 1975) addresses the manual-training movement in St. Louis. Classic histories that address the manual-training movement in the United States are Krug, *Shaping of the American High School*, Vol. 1; Marvin Lazerson, *Origins of the Urban School: Public Education in Massachusetts, 1870-1915* (Cambridge: Harvard University Press, 1971); Marvin Lazerson and W. Norton Grubb, eds. *American Education and Vocationalism: A Documentary History, 1870-1970* (New York: Teachers College Press, 1974); and Paul C. Violas, *The Training of the Urban Working Class: A History of Twentieth-Century American Education* (Chicago: Rand McNally College

Publishing Co., 1978). Donald Spivey, *Schooling for the New Slavery: Black Industrial Education, 1868-1915* (Westport, CT: Greenwood Press, 1978), and Anderson, *Education of Blacks in the South* address the effects of the manual-training movement on the schooling experiences of African-American students.

54. C.M. Woodward, *Manual Training in Education* (London: Charles Scribner's Sons, 1892), 263.

55. Violas, *Training of the Urban Working Class*, 124-137.

56. Troen, *Public and the Schools*, 174.

57. Quoted in Ibid., 184.

58. *Forty-Seventh Annual Report of the Board of Education of the City of St. Louis, Mo., for the Year Ending June 30, 1901* (St. Louis: Nixon-Jones Printing Co., 1902), 47: 57.

59. Quoted in *Forty-Seventh Annual Report*, 47: 84.

60. Krug, *Shaping of the American High School*, 1: 321; Rury, *Education and Women's Work*, 134.

61. *Forty-Eighth Annual Report of the Board of Education of the City of St. Louis, Mo., for the Year Ending June 30, 1902* (St. Louis: Nixon-Jones Printing Co., 1903), 48: 81.

62. *Forty-Ninth Annual Report of the Board of Education of the City of St. Louis, Mo., for the Year Ending June 30, 1903* (St. Louis: Nixon-Jones Printing Co., 1904), 49: 253.

63. Jeffrey Hirsh, "Manual Training and the Negro in St. Louis, 1880-1898," unpublished paper, Missouri Historical Society, 1974, 11. *St. Louis Annual Report* 49: 160-161.

64. Hirsh, "Manual Training and the Negro," 11-18.

65. *St. Louis Annual Report* 49: 239-241.

66. Quoted in *St. Louis Annual Report, 49*: 254-255.

67. Ibid.

68. Quoted in Krug, *Shaping of the American High School*, (Madison: University of Wisconsin Press, 1969), 1: 254.

69. Quoted in *Sixtieth Annual Report of the Board of Education of the City of St. Louis, Missouri for the Year Ending June 30, 1914* (N.p., n.d.), 60: 307.

70. Ibid., 307-311.

71. Ibid., 317.

72. William Landes and Lewis Solmon, "Compulsory Schooling Legislation: An Economic Analysis of Law and Social Change in the Nineteenth Century," *Journal of Economic History* 32 (March 1972): 86; David Tyack, Thomas James, and Aaron Benavot, *Law and the Shaping of Public Education, 1785-1954* (Madison: University of Wisconsin Press, 1987), 124; Moses Stambler, "The Effect of Compulsory Education and Child Labor Laws

on High School Attendance in New York City, 1898-1917," *History of Education Quarterly* 8 (Summer 1968): 205.

73. Tyack, James, and Benavot, *Law and the Shaping of Public Education*, 125.

74. Ibid., 96.

75. Forest Chester Ensign, *Compulsory School Attendance and Child Labor* (New York: Arno Press and The New York Times, 1969), 258.

76. Tyack, James, and Benavot, *Law and the Shaping of Public Education*, 96.

77. Three important early texts in the literature of compulsory schooling are John W. Perrin, *The History of Compulsory Education in New England*, (Meadville, PA: 1896); Edith Abbott and Sophonisba Breckenridge, *Truancy and Non-Attendance in the Chicago Schools* (Chicago: University of Chicago Press, 1917); and Ensign, *Compulsory School Attendance*. Helpful secondary sources that deal with compulsory schooling and truancy include Krug, *Shaping of the American High School*; Lazerson, *Origins of the Urban School*, Cambridge: Harvard University Press, 1971); Anthony M. Platt, *The Child-Savers: The Invention of Delinquency* (Chicago: University of Chicago Press, 1969); David B. Tyack, "Ways of Seeing: An Essay on the History of Compulsory Schooling," *Harvard Educational Review* 46 (August 1976): 355-389; Tyack, James, and Benavot, *Law and the Shaping of Public Education*; and, Violas, *Training of the Urban Working Class*.

78. Troen, *The Public and the Schools,* (Columbia: University of Missouri Press, 1975), 201-202.

79. *Fifty-Seventh Annual Report of the Board of Education of the City of St. Louis, Mo., for the Year Ending June 30, 1911* (N.p., n.d.), 57:170.

80. Quoted in *Fifty-Seventh Annual Report*, 57:186.

81. Charles H. Judd, *Survey of the St. Louis Public Schools* (Yonkers-on-Hudson, NY: World Book Company, 1918), 2: 300.

82. Ibid., 328.

83. Ibid., 355.

84. Quoted in *Sixty-Fifth Annual Report of the Board of Education of the City of St. Louis, Missouri for the Year Ending June 30, 1919* (N.p., n.d.), 65: 18.

85. *Seventy-Second Annual Report of the Board of Education of the City of St. Louis, Missouri for the Year Ending June 30, 1926* (N.p., n.d.), 72: 50-51.

86. *Seventy-Fourth Annual Report of the Board of Education of the City of St. Louis, Missouri for the Year Ending June 30, 1928* (N.p., n.d.), 74: 28.

87. Ibid., 526.

88. *Seventy-Seventh Annual Report of the Board of Education of the City of St. Louis, Missouri for the Year Ending June 30, 1931* (N.p., n.d.), 77: 28.

89. Ibid.

90. *St. Louis Public Schools Approved Recommendations of the St. Louis School Survey* (St. Louis, 1941), 9, 14-15.

91. *Nineteenth Annual Report of the Board of Directors of the St. Louis Public Schools, for the Year Ending August 1, 1873* (St. Louis: Democrat Litho. and Printing Co., 1874), 19: 54.

92. Karier, *Individual, Society, and Education*, 70-71. See Theodore R. Sizer, ed., *The Age of the Academies*, Classics in Education, No. 22 (New York: Bureau of Publications, Teachers College, Columbia University, 1964).

93. *St. Louis Annual Report* 19: 55-56.

94. Ibid., 56.

95. Ibid., 62.

96. Ibid., 58-64.

97. *Eighteenth Annual Report of the Board of Directors of the St. Louis Public Schools, for the Year Ending August 1, 1872* (St. Louis: Democrat Litho. and Printing Co., 1873), 18: 44-46.

98. *St. Louis Annual Report* 19: 58.

99. Quoted in *St. Louis Annual Report*, 19: 67.

100. *Twenty-Sixth Annual Report of the Board of Directors of the St. Louis Public Schools, for the Year Ending August 1, 1880* (St. Louis: Slawson & Co., Printers, 1881), 26: 78.

101. *St. Louis Annual Report* 28: 106.

102. *St. Louis Annual Report* 41: 132.

103. *St. Louis Annual Report* 48: 81.

104. Ibid., 288.

105. *St. Louis Annual Report* 49: 239.

106. *Fifty-Fifth Annual Report of the Board of Education of the City of St. Louis, Mo. for the Year Ending June 30, 1909* (St. Louis: Nixon-Jones Printing Co., 1910), 55: 46.

107. *St. Louis Annual Report* 57: 172.

108. Ibid., 171.

109. *Sixty-Third Annual Report of the Board of Education of the City of St. Louis, Missouri for the Year Ending June 30, 1917* (N.p., n.d.), 63: 117-118.

110. *Seventy-Third Annual Report of the Board of Education of the City of St. Louis, Missouri for the Year Ending June 30, 1927* (N.p., n.d.), 73: 45-46.

111. *St. Louis Annual Report* 74: 17.

112. *Eighty-Seventh Annual Report Board of Education of the City of St. Louis, Missouri for the Year Ending June thirty, Nineteen forty-one* (N.p., n.d.), 87: 10.

113. *Ninetieth Annual Report Board of Education of the City of St. Louis, Missouri for the Year Ending June Thirty, Nineteen Forty-Four* (N.p., n.d.), 90: 15.

114. *St. Louis Annual Report* 28: 109.

115. *St. Louis Annual Report* 49: 159.

116. *St. Louis Board of Education Curriculum Bulletin* no. 1 (St. Louis, 1926), 1-7.

117. Quoted in Paul C. Violas, "Progressive Social Philosophy: Charles Horton Cooley and Edward Alsworth Ross," in *Roots of Crisis: American Education in the Twentieth Century*, Clarence J. Karier, Paul Violas, and Joel Spring (Chicago: Rand McNally College Publishing Company, 1973), 44.

118. Ibid., 50.

119. See Violas, *Training of Urban Working Class* and Robert Wiebe, *The Search for Order* (New York: Hill and Wang, 1967).

120. Quoted in Violas, "Progressive Social Philosophy," 63.

121. Krug, *Shaping of the American High School*, (Madison: University of Wisconsin Press, 1969), 1: 336-377.

122. Ibid., 336.

123. Rolla M. Tryon, *The Social Studies as School Subjects*, Part XI: Report of the Commission on the Social Studies American Historical Association (New York: Charles Scribner's Sons, 1935), 247.

124. See Graham, *Community and Class in American Education*, (New York: Wiley, 1974), 80; Lazerson, *Origins of the Urban School*; (Cambridge: Harvard University Press, 1971); Nasaw, *Schooled to Order* (Oxford: Oxford University Press, 1979); Krug, *Shaping of the American High School*.

125. Lynd and Lynd, *Middletown*, (New York: Hartcourt, Brace and Co., 1929), 196.

126. Ibid., 197.

127. Ibid., 196.

128. Lazerson, *Origins of the Urban School*, (Cambridge: Harvard University Press, 1971), 204.

129. Nasaw, *Schooled to Order*, 144.

130. Tryon, *Social Studies*, 87.

131. Ibid., 208.

132. Quoted in Tryon, 210-211.

133. Tryon, 216.

134. Krug, *Shaping of the American High School*, 353-355.

135. Ibid., 354.

136. Ibid., 355-358.

137. Quoted in Krug, 360.

138. Tryon, *Social Studies*, 93.

139. David Snedden, "History and Other Social Sciences in the Education of Youths Twelve to Eighteen Years of Age," *School and Society* 115 (10 March 1917 and 17 March 1917): 308-309.

140. Ibid., 276.

141. Traditional historians refer to intellectuals and reformers in the early twentieth century as "progressives." Critical historians distinguish their analysis of this period, in one way, by adopting the term "New Liberals" to describe the same group. Karier, Violas, and Spring led in the formation of critical educational history. See Karier, Violas, and Spring, *Roots of Crisis,* for a thorough analysis of this period in U.S. educational history.

142. Quoted in Lynd and Lynd, *Middletown*, 197.

143. St. Louis Public Schools, *Approved Recommendations of the St. Louis School Survey*, (N.p., 1941), 9.

144. William Henry Black, "Present Educational Problems in Missouri" (President's Address delivered at the Meeting of the State Teachers' Association, Jefferson City, Missouri, December 1900), 6.

145. State Department of Education, *Course of Study Missouri High Schools, 1919* (N.p., n.d.), 10.

146. Troen, *The Public and the Schools*, (Columbia: University of Missouri Press, 1975), 201; Tyack, James, and Benavot, *Law and the Shaping of Public Education*, (Madison: University of Wisconsin Press, 1987), 124; Stambler, "Effect of Compulsory Education," 210.

147. Stambler, "Effect of Compulsory Education," *History of Education Quarterly* 8 (Summer 1968): 195; Landes and Solmon, "Compulsory Schooling Legislation," *Journal of Economic History* 32 (March 1972): 55.

148. Ensign, *Compulsory School Attendance*, (New York: Arno Press and The New York Times, 1969), 234-246.

149. Cubberley, *Public Education*, (Boston: Houghton Mifflin Co., 1919), 380.

150. Ensign, *Compulsory School Attendance, 234*.

151. Cubberley, *Public Education*, 381.

152. Ellwood P. Cubberley, *History of Education; Educational Practice and Progress Considered as a Phase of the Development and Spread of Western Civilization* (Boston: Houghton Mifflin, 1920), 815. Note the primary position given to decline in profits as one of the causes leading to the abolition of child labor.

153. Ensign, *Compulsory School Attendance*, 234.

154. Troen, *The Public and the Schools*, 200-202.

155. Quoted in *Fiftieth Annual Report of the Board of Education of the City of St. Louis, Mo., for the Year Ending June 30, 1904* (St. Louis: Nixon-Jones Printing Co., 1905), 50: 20.

156. Quoted in *Fiftieth Annual Report*, 50: 20.

157. Troen, *The Public and the Schools*, 202.

158. Ibid., 201.

159. Ibid., 189.

160. *Fifty-Fourth Annual Report of the Board of Education of the City of St. Louis, Mo., for the Year Ending June 30, 1908* (St. Louis: Buxton & Skinner Stationery Co., 1909), 54: 135.

161. Ibid., 180.

162. *St. Louis Annual Report* 77: 28.

163. Quoted in *Eighty-Second Annual Report of the Board of Education of the City of St. Louis, Missouri, for the Year Ending June 30, 1936* (N.p., n.d.), 18.

164. George D. Strayer, *A Report of a Survey of the Public Schools of St. Louis, Missouri* (New York: Bureau of Publications, Teachers' College, Columbia University, 1939), 24-25.

165. St. Louis Public Schools, *The Purposes of Education in the Public Schools of St. Louis* (N.p., 1941), 32.

166. Arthur Bestor, "What Went Wrong with U.S. Schools," in *Experts Warn: Our Schools, Colleges, Laboratories Are Turning Out Second-Rate Brains* Kermit Lansner, ed. (N.p., 1958), 55.

CHAPTER 4

The Changing Composition
of the Student Population

" . . . the education of any period is a pretty faithful mirror of its social life. "[1]

—Willystine Goodsell, 1923

The 1870 public-high-school enrollment in St. Louis stood at 391 students. By the turn of the century, enrollment increased by more than five times the 1870 figure; in 1900, school reports listed 2,243 high-school students. In 1930, St. Louis public-high-school officials counted 14,647 pupils enrolled in high school. The sheer increase in numbers of students between 1870 and 1930 marked a primary change in secondary schooling in St. Louis. Another major alteration within the composition of the student population paralleled momentous changes in educational philosophy and curriculum in St. Louis high schools during this period. In 1870, the typical St. Louis high-school student was likely to be a middle-class, native-born, European-American girl. Notwithstanding increases in the enrollment of working-class, immigrant, and African-American high-school students, the typical St. Louis high-school student of 1930 was likely to be from the middle class, native born, and European American. The chance that the student representative was a boy, however, was fifty percent. Girls comprised 58 percent of the St. Louis high-school student enrollment in 1870; this percentage maximized at 77 percent in 1893 before registering a gradual decline. Girls constituted 65 percent of the student population in 1900, 59 percent in 1910, and 54 percent in 1920. The purpose of this chapter is to examine changes in the St. Louis high-school population from 1870 to 1930 in terms of gender, race, ethnicity, and social class.[2] Of the differences to be discerned between the composition of the nineteenth- and early twentieth-century student bodies, gender is the most significant.

Year	St. Louis	Percent of increase over 1890	Percent St. Louis youth ages 14-17	U.S.	Percent of increase over 1890	Percent U.S. youth ages 14-17
1890	1445	—	03.0	203,000	—	03.7
1900	2243	55	05.2	519,000	156	08.4
1910	5147	256	10.2	915,000	351	12.6
1920	3823	165	07.9	2,200,000	984	28.4
1930	14,647	914	29.1	4,399,000	2067	47.0

*1890 percentage is based on the St. Louis population ages 15-20.

Table 8. Public High School Enrollment in St. Louis and the United States: 1890-1930

Sources: *St. Louis Annual Reports; Foundations of Educational Policy in the United States,* 4th ed., revised, Alicia Rodriguez, Jay Bennett, Jean Bettridge, Robert Carson, Todd Dinkelman, Chieko Fons, José Solís-Jordán, Kirk Masden, Bert Powers, John Schmitz, Anne Sikwibele, Paul Theobald, Audrey Thompson, Steve Tozer, Marlene Wentworth , eds. (USA: Ginn Press, 1990), 110; *The Miscellaneous Documents of the House of Representatives for the First Session of the Fifty-Second Congress 1891-92* 50, part 18 (Washington, DC: U.S. Government Printing Office, 1896), 50: 358; U.S. Bureau of the Census, *Thirteenth Census of the United States Taken in the Year 1910* 1 (Washington, DC: U.S. Government Printing Office, 1913), 1: 449; U.S. Bureau of the Census, *Fourteenth Census of the United States Taken in the Year 1920* 3 (Washington, DC: U.S. Government Printing Office, 1922), 3: 569; U.S. Bureau of the Census, *Fifteenth Census of the United States: 1930* 2 (Washington, DC: U. S. Government Printing Office, 1933), 2: 1146.

High-school enrollment data revealed two key phenomena in the 1870 to 1930 period. Rates of increase in student enrollment were large enough to effect an overwhelming challenge to organizers of the secondary institution. Yet the increases were not massive enough to encompass even half of the school-age population. Neither of these factors need diminish the import of the other. The trends that characterized the situation in St. Louis were national in scope (table 8).

In the 1870s and 1880s only a small minority of the St. Louis population attended high school. Selwyn K. Troen explained that most of these students were girls preparing to teach, boys preparing for other professions, and others whose families could afford the luxury of advanced formal education.[3] The major period of growth in high-school enrollment occurred in St. Louis after 1900. (There was a drop in enrollment during the years surrounding World War I, from 1916 to 1920. Enrollment increased sharply during the 1920s.) These increases, however, did not bring the majority of school-age persons into the high school. Even after the Missouri compulsory-school-attendance law was passed in 1905, a small proportion of elementary-school students continued their study at the high-school level. Continuation schools with a vocational emphasis were established for students who had not completed the eighth grade and the law allowed children to leave school at age fourteen if they obtained work permits. George Counts included St. Louis in his 1920 study of four U.S. school systems, *The Selective Character of American Secondary Education*. Using data from 1918, Counts reported that only 17.8 percent of high-school-age children in St. Louis were enrolled in the public high schools.[4] Counts' research led him to a conclusion that highlighted the two key factors of the high-school enrollment phenomenon of the early twentieth century. Counts wrote that "High school students, even today and in spite of the amazing growth of the high-school enrolment since 1880, are a highly selected group."[5] Even after a decade of substantial growth, the 1930 high-school enrollment of 14,647 represented only 29.1 percent of youth ages fourteen to seventeen in St. Louis. Yet by virtue of size alone, the 14,647 high-school students of 1930 constituted a much different body than that created by the 391 students in 1870.

GENDER

One prominent characteristic of the St. Louis public-high-school population became the subject of much comment by school officials. President of the St. Louis Board of Education, Gist Blair, was one of many to acknowledge the high proportion of female students. In 1893, when girls constituted 77 percent of the St. Louis high-school enrollment (the highest percentage recorded), Blair pointed to

> the increase in the number of women who are seeking the advantages of a higher education. The records show that for a number of years their number has constantly increased, and proportionately they far exceed those of the other sex who attend the High School.[6]

In 1888, administrators had concluded that the large percentage of girls in the high schools was due to three factors: high-school graduation was required for entrance to the Normal School (which enrolled only women students); a growing appreciation in the community for the importance of a good education for girls; and, boys were more likely to withdraw from school at an earlier age than girls to go to work.[7] Data from a collective biography used by Troen in *The Public and the Schools: Shaping the St. Louis System, 1838-1920* supports these conclusions. The collective biography draws on data from a sample of 15,314 children from twenty-six election precincts from the 1880 St. Louis census. Troen observes that 1880 serves as a midpoint for a condition that spanned several decades, a consistent pattern of school attendance for a few years during the preteen period. Thus, the 1880 study serves as a reliable indicator of nineteenth-century conditions.[8] The largest gaps between the percentages of European-American male and female children attending school (not necessarily high school) occur at ages twelve, fourteen, and sixteen. At age fourteen, 46 percent of the European-American boys were in school while 43.2 percent were engaged in various forms of labor. By age sixteen, only 14.8 percent of the European-American boys were in school and 73.7 percent were working at jobs ranging from unskilled labor (26.1 percent) to what Troen defines as the higher occupations (2.8 percent). In contrast, 51.7 percent of the European-American girls at age fourteen remained in school, while 23.3 percent were engaged in various forms of labor. At age sixteen, 23.6 percent of the girls were still in school, and 46.9 percent were in the workforce. Interestingly, the percentage of European-American females working at jobs classified as unskilled increased with age, from 0.3 percent at age ten, to 5.7 percent at age twelve, to 20.7 percent at age fourteen, to 39.4 percent at age sixteen, to 47.5 percent at age eighteen, to 55.8 percent at age twenty. This occurred in spite of the fact that women tended to stay in school longer than men. The percentages of European-American men engaged in unskilled labor increased until age sixteen, and then stabilized in the mid-twenty-percent range. These data support the widely held notion that schooling was not a direct connection to work in nineteenth-century America.[9]

The number of African-American boys attending school declined with age, but at age fourteen, 50 percent of African American males were still in school. The number of African-American girls attending school fluctuated more than did the number of European-American girls, however, as in the case of European-American children, African-American girls maintained higher attendance percentages than African-American boys at ages fourteen and sixteen. The striking difference in the data for African-American children as compared to European-American children concerned the type of occupation. The paucity of African-American workers in the skilled, white-collar, and higher occupations reflected the tremendous discrimination that existed toward African Americans, and it helps to explain the desire to stay in school for those whose families could afford it. Faced with the probability that the job one could obtain was classified as unskilled, students, no doubt, preferred the intellectually stimulating and social environment of the high school. Further, the high school represented an important route to the future that African-American parents hoped for their children. Historian Sharon Harley explained that African-American mothers sacrificed for their children's education in spite of the obstacles that African Americans faced in the job market. Harley cites the work of sociologist Bonnie Thornton Dill who found that African-American families perceived education as a "means of equipping oneself for whatever breaks might occur in the nation's pattern of racial exclusion."[10] This theme surfaced in African-American literature as well. In Ann Petry's novel, *The Street*, the character Lutie sorted through her thoughts to find a way to explain to her son, Bub, why he should not leave school for an unskilled job.

> It's also that you're afraid that if he's shining shoes at eight, he will be washing windows at sixteen and running an elevator at twenty-one and go on doing that for the rest of his life. And you're afraid that this street will keep him from finishing high school. . . . [11]

In St. Louis, African-American men were engaged in semiskilled work increasingly with age, hitting a peak of 39 percent at age twenty. This paralleled an increase in the unskilled category, which reached 51.2

percent at age twenty. Most African-American women were engaged in unskilled labor, growing from 8.1 percent at age ten, 19.1 percent at age twelve, 4.8 percent at age fourteen, 42.9 percent at age sixteen, 69.1 percent at age eighteen, and 70.6 percent at age twenty. [12]

These data indicate that while most European-American and African-American women who entered the labor force were relegated to positions classified as "unskilled" (domestic work, servants, seamstresses, etc.), a higher percentage of African-American women worked than did European-American women. At age twenty, 3 percent of European-American women and 3.4 percent of African-American women in this sample were engaged in the higher occupations; probably the majority of these were teachers. [13] Thus, whether to prepare for a career in education, or to prolong the period before engaging in unskilled labor, it is not surprising that women in the nineteenth century elected to remain in school for as long as possible. Young men, seeing no direct connection between school and work, often chose to give up school as soon as possible in order to work their way into the skilled and white-collar occupations. [14] These two situations, when melded together, produced a student population consisting of a high proportion of girls.

During the six decades from 1870 to 1930, girls' enrollment in St. Louis high schools fell below 50 percent of total high-school enrollment only once, to 40 percent in 1877. (The school year that ended in 1877 preceded the general strike in St. Louis during the summer. The depressed economy leading up to the strike probably accounted for a higher percentage of boys staying in school.) It is important to note that after hitting the peak percentage in 1893, girls' proportion of high-school enrollment began a slow and steady decline. During the first three decades of the twentieth century, years that witnessed drastic changes in the high-school curriculum, the St. Louis high-school population shifted from a group dominated by girls to a body approaching gender equilibrium. Girls, who had constituted 64 percent of the high-school population in 1900, made up 50 percent of the high-school enrollment in 1930 (see table 9).

Data for both African-American and European-American students show a decline in the percentage of girls enrolled in St. Louis high schools. African-American girls, however, composed a significant majority of African-American high-school enrollment up to 1930. After 1896, percentages of African-American females were consistently higher than were the percentages of European-American females. In

1900, African-American girls constituted 72 percent of the total African-American high-school enrollment while European-American girls constituted 63 percent of the total European-American high-school enrollment; in 1910 the percentages were 71 and 58 percent; in 1930, African-American girls still made up 57 percent of the African-American high-school population but European-American girls had dropped to 49 percent (see table 9).

Year	Total	Total: Girls	Girls' Percent of Total	AA Girls	AA Girls (Percent of AA)	EA Girls	EA Girls (Percent of EA)
1900	2243	1451	64	182	72	1269	63
1905	4394	2849	64	272	73	2577	64
1910	5147	3046	59	279	71	2767	58
1915	7019	3902	55	461	67	3441	54
1920	3823	2070	54	—	—	—	—
1922	12,078	6301	52	702	62	5599	51
1925	11,871	6280	52	849	64	5431	51
1930	14,647	7390	50	1107	57	6283	49

Table 9. Enrollment in St. Louis Public High Schools, by Sex: 1870 to 1930

Source: *St. Louis Annual Reports.*

Not surprisingly, but worthy of comment, those who accounted for the majority of students enrolled in St. Louis high schools constituted the majority of graduates. Every year from 1870 to 1930, girls earned more than half of the high-school diplomas. Among African-American students, girls comprised 70 percent or more of the graduating classes thirty times between 1889 and 1930. Ninety-four percent of African-American graduates were girls in 1890. European-American girls earned 70 percent or more of the high-school diplomas given to European-American graduates twenty-five times between 1872 and 1917. In 1889, girls constituted 93 percent of the European-American high-school graduates.

The fact that girls accounted for the majority of high-school students, and graduates, in the late-nineteenth and early-twentieth centuries was not unique to St. Louis; this was a national trend. Although the gender disparity in enrollment was most acute in urban schools, girls constituted 57 percent of all public-high-school students in the United States in 1890, 58 percent in 1900, 56 percent in 1910, and 56 percent in 1920. Nationally, girls took 65 percent of all public-high-school diplomas in 1890, 63 percent in 1900, and 61 percent in 1910 and 1920. St. Louis reflected national high-school enrollment patterns in another aspect; the proportion of girls among African-American students remained higher than the proportion of girls among European-American students in the first decades of the twentieth century. In 1898, girls comprised 68.1 percent of the African-American high-school population in the United States, compared to 57.8 percent of the U.S. European-American high-school population. In 1908, the percentages were 66 and 57.4 percent; in 1918, 67.9 and 57 percent; and in 1928, 62 and 51.6 percent. [15]

Two pertinent factors emerge from the data regarding the gender composition of St. Louis public high schools. The preponderance of the nineteenth-century high-school population was female. By 1930, student enrollment had reached an equilibrium; girls and boys each made up half of the high-school enrollment. The "feminized" institution of the high school disappeared along with the academic curriculum in the early decades of the twentieth century. The overall picture, however, obscured the different enrollment pattern at African-American high schools in St. Louis. Although percentages of girls' enrollment dropped there as well, girls constituted a significant majority of African-American high-school students as late as 1930.

RACE

Throughout the period of this study, race was a major determinant in the schooling available to students in St. Louis. After the Civil War, Missouri's new state constitution included the establishment of separate schools for children of African descent and required that school funds be distributed equally without regard for race. [16] St. Louis, however, responded slowly to the law. Sumner High School was not established until 1875. Further, the school system's reticence in providing decent elementary schools for African-American children, in spite of the great demand for education by the African-American community, delayed

Sumner's first graduating class until 1885. St. Louis public schools remained segregated until the second half of the twentieth century. A significant increase in high-school enrollment of African Americans was recorded between 1870 and 1930. Yet its general impact on the total high-school population was slight.

Enrollment figures for Sumner High School students are difficult to obtain for the early years of the school because at the beginning high-school classes were held at one of the elementary schools and statistics for all students in the building were combined. The size of the first graduating classes, however, indicates that enrollment at Sumner High School was small in the early years. In 1885 the first graduating class consisted of two people. The numbers of graduates remained less than ten through 1888 and then ranged from seventeen to thirty-nine for the period from 1889 through 1900. The number of graduates of Sumner High School rose steadily during the first three decades of the twentieth century, hitting a high of 305 in 1930.

Year	Enrollment	Percent of Total Enrollment	Percent of AA in St. Louis Population (all ages)
1900	250	11	6
1910	391	8	6
1925*	1324	11	—
1930	1919	13	11

* Information for 1920 was not available.

Table 10. African-American Enrollment in St. Louis Public High Schools: 1900 to 1930

Source: *St. Louis Annual Reports.*

Enrollment at Sumner High School also rose markedly after 1900 (see table 10). Throughout the period of intense curriculum adjustment (1900 to 1930), African-American high-school students comprised a stable proportion of the student population, in numbers exceeding the African-American percentage of the St. Louis population. In 1900, African-American students accounted for 11 percent of the total high-school enrollment in St. Louis, a year in which African Americans constituted 6 percent of the city population. In 1930, 13 percent of St. Louis high-school enrollment and 11 percent of the city's population were African American.

While these figures compare school-enrollment percentages to the city population of all ages, federal census data provide more detailed information. In 1930, St. Louis ranked eleventh among United States cities having an African-American population of 50,000 or more in the number of African-American children, ages seven to fifteen, attending school (10,692). St. Louis placed seventh in percentage of seven- to fifteen-year old African Americans attending school (94.2 percent).[17] The percentages of St. Louis African Americans attending school exceeded national proportions in both the fourteen to fifteen and the sixteen to seventeen age groups in 1930. Eighty-six percent of fourteen- to fifteen-year olds attended school in St. Louis compared to 78.1 percent nationally; 48.1 percent of St. Louis sixteen- to seventeen-year olds attended school in contrast to 46.3 percent across the United States.[18] High-school enrollment figures are more difficult to obtain, however, based on information from a compilation of sources, 39.5 percent of African Americans, fourteen to seventeen years old, were enrolled in St. Louis public high schools in 1930. This is lower than the national percentage for all high-school students in the fourteen to seventeen age range (51.4 percent.)[19] Nonetheless, the numbers of African-American students enrolled in St. Louis high schools increased considerably from 1870 to 1930.

The rate of increase in the African-American student population at St. Louis high schools was notably higher than the rate of increase in the European-American student population (see table 11). During the quarter century stretching from 1905 to 1930, the African-American student population grew by 420 percent, nearly twice the rate of growth in the European-American population. Again, two facts emerged that fill in important details concerning the St. Louis high-school population. The expansion of the African-American student population was a development of great consequence. Its importance during an age of struggle over the definition of African-American education in the United States cannot be overlooked.[20] Yet, the African-American percentage of the total St. Louis high-school enrollment stayed within a range between 8 and 13 percent in the years from 1900 to 1930 (table 10). Thus, in terms of the general high-school population, little had changed. The St. Louis high-school student body, which, overwhelmingly, was composed of European Americans in 1870, remained so in 1930.

ETHNICITY

One element of the changing public-school population in the United States ignited a profuse body of commentary beginning about 1890. Massive numbers of southeastern Europeans immigrated to the United States in the 1890s, 1900s, and 1910s.

Year	African-American Enrollment	Percent Increase over 1905	European-American Enrollment	Percent Increase over 1905
1905	369	—	4025	—
1915	688	86	6331	57
1925	1324	258	10,547	162
1930	1919	420	12,728	216

Table 11. Increases in Enrollment of St. Louis Public High School Students, by Race: 1905 to 1930

Source: *St. Louis Annual Reports.*

By 1900, almost half of the total United States population were first- or second-generation immigrants; immigrants composed an even greater percentage in some cities.[21] Stanford Professor of Education Ellwood P. Cubberley captured the response of many "native" Americans in his 1919 work, *Public Education in the United States*.

As large numbers of the foreign-born have come to our shores, and particularly from countries where general education is not common and where the Anglo-Saxon conception of law, order, government, and public and private decency do not prevail, a new and still greater burden has been placed on all the educative forces of society to try to impart to these new peoples, and their children, something of the method and the meaning of our democratic life. As the children of these new classes have crowded into our public schools, our school systems have been compelled to pay more attention to the needs of these new elements in our population, and to direct their attention less exclusively to satisfying the needs of the well-to-do classes of society. [22]

Cubberley's statement is an example of the nativist sentiment issued by prominent intellectuals.[23] Fearful that new immigrants would disrupt the American social order and threaten democracy, an intellectual elite prescribed the public school as a panacea for the "immigrant problem." Cubberley's rhetoric described immigrant children as a burden that crowded schools were compelled to accept. In order to attend to this newly appointed task, he implied, educators needed to shift attention away from the group traditionally served by the public schools, the "well-to-do classes of society." Presumably, schooling for immigrant and working-class children was not to be the same as schooling designed for the well-to-do.

In their essay on school achievement of immigrant children from 1900 to 1930, Michael R. Olneck and Marvin Lazerson underscore the point that the immigrant experience in United States schools was complex and varied. Although there was no single immigrant experience, during the first decades of the twentieth century, younger children of immigrants were as likely to be in school as children of native-born European Americans. At the point of high-school entry, however, substantial disparities in attendance and completion developed.[24] There was a disparity, too, regarding the proportion of immigrants in the school population among cities. In 1911 the federal government published what it described as one of the most extensive studies carried out by the Immigration Commission.[25] *The Children of Immigrants in Schools* is a report based on data obtained from public schools in thirty cities in the United States during midwinter of the 1908-1909 school year. In this survey, St. Louis ranked among cities with the lowest proportion of students who were children of foreign-born fathers. St. Louis placed sixth on this list at 31.9 percent.[26]

From 1870 through the first two decades of the twentieth century, St. Louis, in contrast to other urban school districts, maintained relatively low percentages of students who were immigrants or children of immigrants. Also, first- and second-generation immigrants from southeastern Europe constituted a very small percentage of the St. Louis school population. The numbers of immigrants in St. Louis schools did increase, particularly during the period from 1912 to 1920. The largest percentage of immigrants enrolled in St. Louis high schools during the twentieth century, however, was 10 percent, recorded in 1905.

The *St. Louis Annual Reports* contained information on the birthplaces of students from 1859 through 1920.[27] During these years, most St. Louis public-high-school students were born in the United States. From 1859 to 1900 the percentages ranged from 88 to 98 percent and most immigrants came from countries in northwestern Europe. Few immigrants attended Sumner High School from 1876 to 1900. For most years, over half of the Sumner students were born in St. Louis, and the number born in Missouri ranged from 65 to 90 percent. The *Annual Reports* did not include statistics regarding second-generation immigrants although this was, perhaps, a considerable number. In 1880, 74.1 percent of the fathers of children ages six to sixteen in all St. Louis public schools were foreign-born. In the same year, only 6.1 percent of the children themselves were immigrants. Of the 74.1 percent of the fathers who were immigrants, 46.2 percent came from Germany, 16 percent came from Ireland, and the rest came from other European countries.[28]

The *Annual Reports* showed an increase in the enrollment of immigrants in St. Louis high schools from 1900 to 1920, including those from southeastern Europe. Percentage gains, however, were meager. Immigrant enrollment stood at 2 percent or less every year between 1900 and 1912, except for 1905 when 10 percent of the student population was composed of immigrants. Following 1912, these percentages increased slightly, reaching a high point of 4 percent for the years from 1918 to 1920. As in the nineteenth century, immigrant enrollment was nearly nonexistent at Sumner High School from 1900 to 1920. The majority of African-American students were born in Missouri; until 1917 more than half of the Sumner High School population were born in St. Louis.

The Immigration Commission study provides some insight into the number of second-generation immigrants enrolled in St. Louis schools in 1908. Out of the 4,105 pupils counted in St. Louis high schools, 1,028 (25 percent) listed foreign-born fathers. The five largest ethnic groups represented were: German (557), English (122), Irish (81), Russian Hebrew (55), and Scotch (40). Southeastern-European countries (including Russia) accounted for only 79 of the 1,028 students with foreign parentage, 7.6 percent. These students made up only 1.9 percent of the high-school population in St. Louis.[29] Even though a strong Italian-American community was forming in St. Louis, only eight second-generation Italian immigrants were enrolled in high school in 1908.[30] This is consistent with Gary Mormino's research published in *Immigrants on the Hill: Italian-Americans in St. Louis, 1882-1982.* Mormino found that in the 1940s only 17 of 1,600 men and 22 of 1,600 women over the age of twenty-five who lived on the Hill were high-school graduates. Not only did most Italians in St. Louis not graduate from high school, few even attended.[31] On this point, St. Louis did reflect a national pattern. As Olneck and Lazerson demonstrate, differences among ethnic groups regarding school attendance became more pronounced at the secondary level. Italians and Poles tended to enroll in high school in small numbers compared to students of other ethnic groups.[32]

Although St. Louis recorded a lower percentage of second-generation immigrant students than most cities in the Immigration Commission study, high-school persistence slightly favored children of immigrants there. In St. Louis in 1908, 56 percent of eighth graders who were children of native-born European Americans reached high school while 41 percent of eighth graders with foreign parentage did so. However, 32 percent of the second-generation immigrants in ninth grade reached the twelfth grade compared to only 24 percent of the children of native-born European Americans.[33]

Counts wrote in 1922 that the tendency for girls to attend high school in greater numbers than boys was not characteristic of all ethnic groups. In "Urban School Enrollment at the Turn of the Century: Gender as an Intervening Variable," John Rury supported the argument that children from lower-class and immigrant families attended school at lower rates than those from native-born or middle- and upper-class families.[34] He argued that school participation was consistently higher among immigrant boys than among immigrant girls during the early twentieth century. Rury suggested that some ethnic groups may have wanted to protect young women from alien or potentially compromising influences. American schools did not teach respect for traditional cultural values or languages of many immigrant groups. Other immigrant parents may have considered female education to be superfluous. In addition, the widespread employment of young immigrant women in factories and as servants kept most from attending school.[35] It is interesting, then, to note that in St. Louis in 1908, the number of second-generation immigrant girls exceeded the number of second-generation immigrant boys in each grade of the high school (table 12). The likely explanation here is rooted in diversity of the immigrant experience, as explained by Olneck and Lazerson. For some groups, including immigrants from northwestern Europe, girls did outnumber boys in high-school enrollment. But for others, Russian Jews, Poles, and southern Italians, for example, boys outnumbered girls in high-school enrollment, as Rury noted.[36] In St. Louis, most second-generation immigrants came from northwestern Europe, representing ethnic groups in which girls did tend to attend high school more than boys. On the other hand, Russian Jews, Poles, and southern Italians accounted for only 56 of the 1,028 high-school students with foreign parentage. These groups' influence on the gender balance in high-school enrollment, then, was negligible.

Like other urban school districts, St. Louis experienced an increased enrollment of immigrant students in the early twentieth century. The increase in numbers, however, did not translate into significant percentages of the high-school student population. Even in the midst of an intense period of immigration, St. Louis ranked near the bottom of major United States cities in a comparison of immigrant population in the schools. Of the immigrants who did attend St. Louis high schools, few came from southeastern Europe. It appears as if the "floods of new immigrants" that were of great concern for educators across the country were little cause for nativist alarm in St. Louis.

GIRLS				
Parentage	9th Grade	10th Grade	11th Grade	12th Grade
Native European American	744 (69%)	485 (68%)	267 (62%)	192 (56%)
Native African American	81 (7%)	62 (8%)	40 (9%)	42 (12%)
Foreign	240 (22%)	166 (23%)	120 (28%)	103 (30%)
Total Girls Enrollment	1065	713	427	337

BOYS				
Parentage	9th Grade	10th Grade	11th Grade	12th Grade
Native European American	508 (70%)	280 (68%)	184 (67%)	111 (69%)
Native African American	34 (4%)	13 (3%)	20 (7%)	14 (8%)
Foreign	180 (24%)	116 (28%)	69 (25%)	34 (21%)
Total Boys Enrollment	722	409	273	159

Table 12. Enrollment in St. Louis Public High Schools, by Grade, Sex, and Ethnicity: 1908
(Percentage of total enrollment for each grade and sex in parentheses.)

Source: Calculated from U.S. Immigration Commission, *The Children of Immigrants in Schools*, 5: 255-261.

SOCIAL CLASS

The perceived threat to social and political harmony in the United States during the early twentieth century did not arise out of the "immigrant problem" alone. The transformation of industry spurred on by Taylorization of the workforce led to heightened class conflict. Again, the intellectual establishment argued that the public school was to serve as the vehicle for uniformity.[37] Cubberley documented this development in 1919.

> As our industrial life had become more diversified, its parts narrower, and its processes more concealed, new and more extended training had been called for to prepare the worker for his task, to reveal to him something of the intricacy and interdependence of our modern and social and industrial life, and to point out to him the necessity of each man's part in the social and industrial whole. With the ever-increasing subdivision and specialization of labor, the danger from class subdivision has been constantly increasing, and more and more has been thrown upon the school the task of instilling into all a social and political consciousness that will lead to unity amid our great diversity, and to united action for the preservation and improvement of our democratic institutions.[38]

Indeed, educational policy makers and social reformers were motivated to expand schooling for working-class children. The work of educational historians over the past two decades has shown, however, that efforts to expand schooling did not bring about equal opportunity for education.[39] Nor did such efforts need result in major increases in high-school enrollment for working-class children. For instance, requirements for school attendance mandated by compulsory-attendance laws could be satisfied by attendance at continuation schools, evening schools, or special vocational schools.[40] As a result of his study of St. Louis; Seattle; Bridgeport, Connecticut; and Mount Vernon, New York; Counts concluded that

> While the establishment of the free public high school marked an extraordinary educational advance, it did not by any means equalize educational opportunity; for the cost of tuition is not the entire cost of education, or even the larger part of it. Education means leisure, and leisure is an expensive luxury.[41]

In spite of tremendous growth in enrollment during the early decades of the twentieth century, the public high school in St. Louis remained primarily a middle-class institution.

Until 1898 the St. Louis *Annual Reports* contained information on the occupations of parents of children in the public-school system. For Central High School during these years, the majority of the students came from middle-class families. In 1870, 1880, and 1890, 60 percent of the student population had fathers who worked as clerks, minor white-collar workers, businessmen, managers, or professionals. The percentages of students whose fathers were skilled or unskilled workers were 23 percent in 1870, 20 percent in 1880, and 21 percent in 1890. (A number of students were listed as unclassified in each of the years.) It is interesting to examine the skilled and unskilled category further. In 1870, only 5 percent of the Central High School students had fathers who were unskilled laborers. Two percent of the student population listed unskilled labor as their father's occupation in 1880, and 3 percent in 1890. Clearly, St. Louis Central High School was not utilized equally by all social classes during this period.

The situation is different for students at Sumner High School. Discrimination against African Americans allowed only a small percentage to obtain jobs as clerks, minor white-collar workers, businessmen, managers, or professionals. Thus, most of the parents of children at Sumner High School worked as skilled and unskilled laborers. In 1880, 93 percent of the Sumner students had parents engaged in working-class jobs; 86 percent of the total were in the category of unskilled labor. Only 7 percent were classified in middle-class occupations. By 1890 the situation had changed very little. Eighty-one percent of the children had parents who worked at skilled or unskilled jobs. Seventy-six percent were classified as unskilled workers and 10 percent were engaged in white-collar work, business, or the professions.

The information in the yearly reports for this period does not distinguish between Sumner's secondary and elementary students; therefore, comparisons between the data for Sumner High School and Central High School are offered with the following caveat: Very few students went to Sumner High School during this period, so if they were the children of professionals or other middle-class workers as were most of their colleagues at Central High School, these small numbers would be translated into a minute percentage of the total student body. If the statistics of the elementary schools serving European-American children are included with the data on Central High School, the result is closer to the pattern at Sumner High School: a larger percentage of parents were classified as unskilled or skilled laborers. For instance in 1880, a year when 3 percent of the Central High School students had fathers who worked as unskilled laborers, 18 percent were skilled workers, and 59 percent were middle-class workers, the statistics for the total number of European-American children in the public schools translated to 27 percent unskilled, 26 percent skilled, and 39 percent middle-class occupations. A comparison to the Sumner data for 1880, however, indicates that the pattern of racial discrimination in occupations was still apparent.

These data, then, point to two conclusions. First, discrimination in St. Louis meant that greater numbers of Sumner students were the children of skilled and unskilled laborers than was the case at Central High School. Second, very few European-American children of skilled or unskilled laborers continued study at the secondary level. The public high school in St. Louis during the nineteenth century was primarily an institution for middle-class European Americans.

When George Counts conducted his study of the secondary school system in 1920, he found that "the public high school is still a class institution in a very real sense . . . "[42] Seventy-one percent of the European-American students in the St. Louis high schools had fathers whose occupations were defined as middle-class jobs: proprietors, professionals, managers, commerce, clerks, artisans, public service. Only 26 percent of the students had fathers with working-class occupations: agriculture, building, machine, printing, and miscellaneous trades, transportation, personal service, miners, lumber-workers, fishers, and common laborers.[43] Counts' data for Sumner High School specifically dealt with secondary students, unlike the information provided in the *St. Louis Annual Reports* during the nineteenth century. In 1920, 61 percent of the students at Sumner High School had parents who performed working-class jobs. Only 29 percent had middle-class occupations.[44]

Not only did the majority of European-American students in St. Louis high schools come from a middle-class background, but the chances that one would complete the secondary course of study were class-bound as well. Counts found that, among all of the cities in his survey, the chances that the child of a professional would reach the senior year were sixty-nine times as great as the chances of a common laborer's child doing so. This reality did not go unnoticed by the students. While 20 percent of the children of laborers did not expect to finish high school, only 3.3 percent of the children of professionals did not expect to finish.[45]

Counts was convinced in 1920 that the high school was, "in the main, serving the occupational groups representative of the upper social strata."[46] He concluded that

> In a very large measure participation in the privileges of a secondary education is contingent on social and economic status. . . .this ideal of equality of educational opportunity does not mean sameness of opportunity nor does it mean necessarily equality in years of educational experience.[47]

Counts' work indicated that the middle-class high school of 1870 remained an institution that served the middle class throughout the first decades of the twentieth century.

CONCLUSION

The St. Louis public high school underwent far-reaching transformations in the principal elements of the institution's structure between 1870 and 1930. During this period, school officials reshaped their philosophy of education; schooling designed to nurture intellectual and moral development was pushed aside in order to maintain an agenda favoring work and citizenship training. The traditional academic curriculum could not advance the new program, many believed, and so a massive curriculum reconstruction followed. Significant changes in the student population paralleled the revisions of philosophy and curriculum. The most striking difference in the St. Louis high-school population over the six decades from 1870 to 1930 was size. High-school enrollment multiplied itself by a factor of thirty-seven during these years. Although the high school did not reach universal status, increased numbers of students, girls and boys, African American and European American, immigrant and native-born, working class and middle class, enrolled. All segments of the student population were growing, in terms of numbers. Proportionally, enrollment gains were recorded by working-class youth, immigrants, and African Americans, but these were slight and did not lead to displacement in the general student population. The crucial shift in student population that occurred as the St. Louis high school entered the twentieth century revolved around gender.

Alterations in student enrollment involving working-class youth, immigrants, and African Americans were not substantial enough to reconfigure the St. Louis student body. Working-class youth, who had constituted 21 percent of the European-American high-school population in 1890, made up only 26 percent of the European-American high-school enrollment in 1920. Well over half of the high-school student population were middle-class youth in both periods. The percentages of working-class African-American students declined between 1890 and 1920, from 81 percent to 61 percent of the total African-American high-school population. Between 1900 and 1912, the immigrant population in St. Louis high schools stayed at 2 percent or less, with the exception of 1905 when 10 percent of the student body was composed of immigrants. From 1913 until 1920, immigrant students accounted for, at most, 4 percent of the total high-school enrollment. This increase of two percentage points proved to be a modification of little consequence. Although African-American high-school enrollment increased at a faster rate than European-American high-school enrollment in the first three decades of the twentieth century, the expansion of the African-American proportion of the total high-school enrollment amounted to a 2-percent growth. African Americans made up 11 percent of the St. Louis high-school enrollment in 1900, 13 percent in 1930.

The fourteen-point decline in the percentages of girls as a proportion of St. Louis high-school students stands in sharp relief to the 2 and 5 percent increases recorded by European-American working-class youth, immigrants, and African Americans. Especially given that educators' expressed concern over the "feminized" high school at the turn of the century, the steady decline in the percentage of girls in high-school enrollment marks a trend of critical importance. As educators erected the differentiated curriculum in St. Louis high schools, the girls' percentage of enrollment dropped from 64 percent in 1900, to 59 percent in 1910, to 54 percent in 1920, to 50 percent in 1930. Although the high-school population registered some changes in its composition in terms of social class, ethnicity, and race, only the gender imbalance was overturned.

NOTES

1. Willystine Goodsell, *The Education of Women: Its Social Background and Its Problems* (New York: The Macmillan Company, 1923), 336.

2. Race is a socially constructed term that has been used to oppress members of nondominant cultures in the United States. I use it here to gather

information about the period from 1870 to 1930 when "race" was a very real determinant in the type of schooling one might obtain.

3. Selwyn K. Troen, *The Public and the Schools: Shaping the St. Louis System, 1838-1920* (Columbia: University of Missouri Press, 1975), 140.

4. Ibid., 188; George Sylvester Counts, *The Selective Character of American Secondary Education* (Chicago: University of Chicago, 1922), 20.

5. Ibid., 141.

6. *Thirty-Ninth Annual Report of the Board of President and Directors of the St. Louis Public Schools, for the Year Ending June 30, 1893* (St. Louis: Nixon-Jones Printing Co., 1894), 39:31.

7. *Thirty-Fourth Annual Report of the Board of President and Directors of the St. Louis Public Schools, for the Year Ending June 30, 1888* (St. Louis: Nixon-Jones Printing Co., 1888), 34:76-77.

8. Troen, *The Public and the Schools*, 130-131.

9. Ibid., 122-124.

10. Dill quoted in Sharon Harley, "When Your Work Is Not Who You Are: The Development of a Working-Class Consciousness among Afro-American Women," in *Gender, Class, Race, and Reform in the Progressive Era*, Noralee Frankel and Nancy S. Dye, eds. (Lexington: University Press of Kentucky, 1991), 53. See Bonnie Thornton Dill, "The Means to Put My Children Through: Child-Rearing Goals and Strategies among Black Female Domestic Servants," in *The Black Woman*, LaFrances Rodgers-Rose, ed. (Beverly Hills: Sage, 1980).

11. Ann Petry, "From *The Street*," in *Afro-American Literature Fiction*, William Adams, Peter Conn, and Barry Slepian, eds. (Boston: Houghton Mifflin Company, 1970), 8-9.

12. Troen, *The Public and the Schools*, 236.

13. Ibid., 123, 236.

14. Many who continued their study in the high school, no doubt, remained because they enjoyed the pursuit of education. While this rationale should not be overlooked, it cannot be extended into an explanation for the reason others dropped out. For the children of the poor and working class, even a free education was too costly when it interfered with the necessity of working to help support one's family.

15. David Tyack and Elisabeth Hansot, *Learning Together: A History of Coeducation in American Public Schools,* (New Haven: Yale University Press, 1990), 164, 173.

16. Elinor Mondale Gersman, "The Development of Public Education for Blacks in Nineteenth-Century St. Louis, Missouri," *The Journal of Negro Education* 41 (Winter 1972): 35. The Missouri State Constitution of 1865

provided for the establishment and the maintenance of free public schools for all persons between the ages of five and twenty-one. Segregated schools were allowed by law, but all funds were to be appropriated in proportion to the number of children without regard to color. A constitutional convention in 1875 altered this provision by mandating segregated schools. See also, W. Sherman Savage, "The Legal Provisions for Negro Schools in Missouri from 1865 to 1890," *The Journal of Negro History* 16 (July 1931) and Henry Sullivan Williams, "The Development of the Negro Public School System in Missouri," *The Journal of Negro History* 5 (April 1920).

17. Charles E. Hall, *Negroes in the United States 1920-32* (Washington, DC: U.S. Government Printing Office, 1935), 210.

18. Ibid., 209, 221.

19. Ibid., 224; *St. Louis Annual Reports*; Carl F. Hansen, *The Four-Track Curriculum in Today's High Schools*, (Englewood Cliffs, NJ: Prentice-Hall, 1964), 19.

20. The best secondary source on the development of African-American education in the United States after the Civil War is James D. Anderson, *The Education of Blacks in the South, 1860-1935* (Chapel Hill: University of North Carolina Press, 1988). See also, J.M. Stephen Peeps, "Northern Philanthropy and the Emergence of Black Higher Education—Do-Gooders, Compromisers, or Co-conspirators?" *Journal of Negro Education* 50 (Summer 1981): 251-269 and Donald Spivey, *Schooling for the New Slavery: Black Industrial Education, 1868-1915* (Westport, CT: 1978). Classic primary sources are Horace Mann Bond, *Negro Education in Alabama: A Study in Cotton and Steel* (New York: Atheneum, 1939); Bond, *Education of the Negro in the American Social Order* (New York: Prentice Hall, 1934); and W.E.B. DuBois, "Of Mr. Booker T. Washington and Others," in *The Souls of Black Folk* (New York: Vintage Books, 1990): 36-48.

21. Paul C. Violas, *The Training of the Urban Working Class: A History of Twentieth-Century American Education* (Chicago: Rand McNally College Publishing Co., 1978), 8.

22. Ellwood P. Cubberley, *Public Education in the United States: A Study and Interpretation of American Educational History* (Boston: Houghton Mifflin, 1919), 357. See also Helen Horvath, "The Plea of an Immigrant— Abstract" *National Education Association Addresses and Proceedings* (1923): 680-682; Herbert Adolphus Miller, *The School and the Immigrant* (Cleveland: Survey Committee of the Cleveland Foundation, 1916); Julia Richman, "The Immigrant Child," *National Education Association Addresses and Proceedings* (1905): 113-21; Frank Thompson, *The Schooling of the Immigrant* (New York: Harper & Row, 1920); U.S. Bureau of Education, *Education of the Immigrant*,

Bulletin no. 51 (Washington, DC: U.S. Government Printing Office, 1913); U.S. Immigration Commission, *The Children of Immigrants in Schools* 5 vols. (Washington, DC: U.S. Government Printing Office, 1911); and U.S. Senate, *Abstracts of Reports of the Immigration Commission*, II, 1-86. Senate Document 747, 61st Cong., 3d sess., 1910.

    23. See Violas, *Training of the Urban Working Class*; Clarence J. Karier, Paul Violas, and Joel Spring, *Roots of Crisis: American Education in the Twentieth Century* (Chicago: Rand McNally College Publishing Company, 1973); and Edward A Krug., *Shaping of the American High School 1880-1920* vol. 1 (Madison: University of Wisconsin Press, 1969) for discussion of the intellectual response to immigration during the Progressive Era.

    24. Michael R. Olneck and Marvin Lazerson, "The School Achievement of Immigrant Children: 1900-1930," in *The Social History of American Education*, B. Edward McClellan and William J. Reese, eds. (Urbana: University of Illinois Press, 1988), 257-264. For other secondary sources on immigrants and schools, see Ezri Atzmon, "The Educational Programs for Immigrants in the United States," *History of Education Journal* 9 (September 1958): 75-80; Robert A. Carlson, *The Quest for Conformity: Americanization through Education* (New York: John Wiley & Sons, 1975); David K. Cohen, "Immigrants and the Schools," *Review of Educational Research* 40 (February 1970): 13-28; D. Harrington-Lueker, "Demography or Destiny: Immigration and Schools," *Education Digest* 56 (January 1991): 3-6; Joel Perlmann, *Ethnic Differences: Schooling and Social Structure among the Irish, Italians, Jews, and Blacks in an American City, 1880-1935* (New York: Cambridge University Press, 1988); John Rury, "Urban Structure and School Participation: Immigrant Women in 1900," *Social Science History* 8 (Summer 1984): 219-241; Timothy L. Smith, "Immigrant Social Aspirations and American Education, 1880-1930," *American Quarterly* 21 (Fall 1969): 523-543; David B. Tyack, *The One Best System: A History of American Urban Education* (Cambridge: Harvard University Press, 1974); and Violas, *Training of the Urban Working Class*.

    25. U.S. Immigration Commission, *Children of Immigrants in Schools*, 1:3.

    26. Ibid., 2:17.

    27. The years 1860-1864, 1875-1876, 1882-1883, 1885-1886 are unaccounted for regarding Central High School. The years 1882-1883, 1885-1886 are unaccounted for regarding Sumner High School.

    28. Troen, *The Public and the Schools*, (Columbia: University of Missouri Press, 1975), 58.

    29. U.S. Immigration Commission, *Children of Immigrants,* 5:217.

    30. Ibid.

31. Gary Ross Mormino, *Immigrants on the Hill: Italian-Americans in St. Louis, 1882-1982* (Urbana: University of Illinois Press, 1986), 108.

32. Olneck and Lazerson, "School Achievement of Immigrant Children," 264-266.

33. Ibid., 262.

34. John L. Rury, "Urban School Enrollment at the Turn of the Century: Gender as an Intervening Variable," *Urban Education* 23 (April 1988): 69.

35. Ibid., 73-83.

36. Olneck and Lazerson, "School Achievement of Immigrant Children," 267.

37. See Norman Pollack, *The Populist Response to Industrial America* (Cambridge: Harvard University Press, 1962); James Weinstein, *The Corporate Ideal in the Liberal State 1900-1918* (Boston: Beacon Press, 1968); and Robert Wiebe, *The Search for Order* (New York: Hill and Wang, 1967) on changes in the U.S. political economy during this period. For the industrial impact on school policy, see Raymond E. Callahan, *Education and the Cult of Efficiency* (Chicago: University of Chicago Press, 1962); Karier, Violas, and Spring, *Roots of Crisis*; and Violas, *Training of the Urban Working Class*.

38. Cubberley, *Public Education in the United States*, 356-357.

39. See, for example, Anderson, *Education of Blacks in the South*; Samuel Bowles and Herbert Gintis, *Schooling in Capitalist America: Educational Reform and the Contradiction of Economic Life* (New York: Basic Books, 1976); Harvey A. Kantor, *Learning to Earn: School, Work, and Vocational Reform in California, 1880-1930* (Madison: The University of Wisconsin Press, 1988); Harvey Kantor and David B. Tyack, eds., *Work, Youth, and Schooling: Historical Perspectives on Vocationalism in American Education* (Stanford: Stanford University Press, 1982); Clarence J. Karier, *The Individual, Society, and Education: A History of American Educational Ideas*, 2d ed., (Urbana: University of Illinois Press, 1986); Michael B. Katz, *Class, Bureaucracy, and Schools: The Illusion of Educational Change in America* (New York: Praeger Publishers, 1975); Joel Spring, *The Sorting Machine Revisited: National Educational Policy Since 1945* (New York: Longman, 1989); Joseph L. Tropea, "Bureaucratic Order and Special Children: Urban Schools, 1890s-1940s," *History of Education Quarterly* 27 (Spring 1987): 29-53; and Violas, *Training of the Urban Working Class*.

40. Cubberley, *Public Education in the United States*, 355-356.

41. Counts, *Selective Character of American Secondary Education*, 148.

42. Ibid., 140.

43. Ibid., 26.

44. Ibid., 116.

45. Ibid., 43, 85.

46. Ibid., 87.

47. Ibid., 149. As Paul Violas explains in *The Training of the Urban Working Class*, the phrase "equality of educational opportunity" did not enter the educator's lexicon until 1900. It accompanied the advent of the differentiated curriculum.

CHAPTER 5

The Eclipse of the Female Scholar

> The older classical and academic courses do not fit the girl of average ability.... It requires intellectual tastes and aptitudes which the average person does not possess.[1]
>
> Winifred Richmond, *The Adolescent Girl*, 1925

As the function of secondary schooling deviated from its nineteenth-century prescription, educators voiced uncertainties regarding the academic curriculum for girls. In 1907, H.J. Wightman explained " . . . we are beginning to recognize that the highest function of woman is as queen of the home, and we are beginning to weigh in her educational balance Latin vs. Cooking, Solid Geometry vs. Dress-making, and Algebra vs. Household Duties."[2] Wightman's reference to the "beginning" of deliberations between Latin and mathematics and domestic art and science subjects for girls underscored the fact that, in spite of long-held convictions that girls' schooling should be directed toward preparing women as wives and mothers, the inclusion of domestic art and science topics in the high-school curriculum was a development of the Progressive Era. The introduction of the differentiated curriculum, however, involved more than the inauguration of domestic studies; it launched an ideology that would govern secondary schooling for the greater part of the twentieth century in the United States. The differentiated curriculum developed in response to and reinforced the notion that schooling, in order to prepare individuals for specific societal roles as worker and citizen, should differ according to gender, ethnicity, and social class.[3]

The differentiated curriculum effected girls' high-school experiences to an astounding degree. A belief that gender was a prominent factor in determining appropriate education for students, and, consequently, that girls' schooling should differ from boys' schooling, permeated educational treatises published in the early decades of the twentieth century.[4] The contrast with nineteenth-century advocates of equal education for women and men was stark, as was illustrated by St. Louis school officials. In 1874 Superintendent William Torrey Harris wrote that

> The demand of woman for equal advantages in education with men is not a mere temporary demand arising out of the sentimentalism incident to the epoch, but only an index of the social movement that underlies our civilization. . . .The demand for the same course of study is paramount, . . .[5]

Forty years later those involved in a time-management study recorded statistics for girls and boys separately so that assertions regarding "natural differences of the sexes in their aptitudes and in their responses to various subjects offered in the schools" might be confirmed or refuted.[6]

St. Louis is a useful locale for measuring not only the impact of the differentiated curriculum on girls' secondary education, but also the effect of gender on students' course selection. As noted in the previous chapter, immigrants did not account for a significant proportion of the St. Louis high-school enrollment at the time of the implementation of the differentiated curriculum. Thus, curricular choice was less likely to have been determined on the basis of one's status as immigrant versus native-born than in other cities. The influence of ethnicity, however, was still significant, given St. Louis' African-American population. As a case study, St. Louis offers the opportunity to explore the impact of the differentiated curriculum on course selection by African-American and European-American female students.

The conjunction of new curricular orbits and a declining female-student percentage created a force in St. Louis high schools that led to the eclipse of the female scholar. "Female scholar" personified the nineteenth-century high-school student, most likely a girl, most assuredly engaged in an academic course of study. As presented in chapter 3, the academic curriculum had reached its zenith early in the twentieth century. By 1930, the academic core of the general course of study had collapsed, leaving many academic classes as electives. The eclipse of the female scholar was also accomplished by the ebb of the female proportion of the student population.[7] The recession of the female scholar will be charted in this chapter by an analysis of course selection during the period from 1900 to 1930.

David F. Labaree includes an analysis of the changing curriculum of Philadelphia's Central High School in *The Making of an American High School*. He concludes that changes in courses of study resulted in "different courses for different people" but since throughout the period of his study, Central High School remained a school for boys only, the impact of these changes on female students is, of course, not offered.[8] In Jane Bernard Powers' excellent book on vocational education for girls during the Progressive Era, she provides a thorough study of this development in girls' schooling. Focusing the three parts of *The "Girl Question" in Education* on prescription, politics, and practice, Powers examines the national debate on vocational education for women and the results of its implementation.[9] Millicent Rutherford explores the impact of curriculum evolution on girls at San Jose High School from 1890 to 1920 in chapter 6 of her 1977 dissertation, "Feminism and the Secondary School Curriculum, 1890-1920."[10] This St. Louis case study complements these works: by tracing the changing enrollments of girls in the various courses of study in St. Louis high schools from 1900 to 1930, data from the midwest are added to existing knowledge of curriculum development in the east and west. The St. Louis analysis is more detailed than Rutherford's treatment of San Jose High School, and while it targets different questions than Labaree's study, it provides a contrast to the pattern of course development for boys in Philadelphia's Central High School.[11] This chapter allows the reader to gauge the impact of the development of vocational education which Powers describes in one city, within the context of the total school curriculum.

With the advent of the differentiated curriculum in St. Louis high schools, the pattern of girls' course selection changed in such a way that the image of the female scholar was overshadowed. Although girls and boys still sat in many of the same classes together (because some classes overlapped different courses of study), the notion that particular courses of study were better suited for one sex or the other flourished. The pattern of course selection that developed in St. Louis bolstered the belief in separate functions of schooling based on sex.

THE SCIENTIFIC COURSE

A section of the 1905 *St. Louis Annual Report*, directed to parents and students, provided an explanation of the structure of the high-school curriculum, amended in 1894 to include new courses of study. The description offered insight into the educators' appraisal of the value of each of the courses of study as well. Listed under the heading of "The Best General Education" and "recommended in the order in which they are here given" were the Scientific, Classical, General, and Art Courses. The College Classical and College Scientific Courses constituted the second tier of courses.[12] The third tier of the curricular hierarchy consisted of the "Special Course[s] of Training": Commercial, Manual Training, and Normal.[13] The pattern of girls' enrollment in the Scientific Course, hailed as "The Best General Education" offered in St. Louis High Schools, evinced the decline of the female scholar brought on by the differentiated curriculum.

Over one-third of all European-American female graduates completed the scientific course of study in 1900. After 1908, the percentage of European-American girls graduating from the Scientific Course did not exceed 6 percent. By 1928, less than 1 percent of European-American girls graduated from the Scientific Course (see table 13). With the implementation of the differentiated curriculum, girls' participation in the scientific course of study diminished significantly. The "best general education" in St. Louis high schools was not offered at Sumner High School until the 1907-1908 school term, the year the differentiated curriculum was implemented in schools for African-American students. As a result, the highest percentage of African-American female graduates completing the Scientific Course was 4.5 percent in 1915.

European-American girls' completion of the scientific course of study dropped in terms of numbers as well as percentages during the first two decades of the twentieth century (table 15). In the early years of the implementation of the differentiated curriculum, the number of female graduates from the Scientific Course rose from fifty-seven in 1900 to ninety-eight in 1903. In 1907, one year after the publication of the *Fifty-First Annual Report* in which school officials declared the Scientific Course the best general education in the St. Louis High School, only five girls graduated from this course of study. The trend marking the girls' defection from the Scientific Course, beginning in 1904, did not reverse itself.

Data suggest that gender was a significant factor in course selection. An increase in the number of male graduates from the scientific course of study accompanied the decline in the numbers of girls. The number of European-American boys who graduated from the Scientific Course climbed from forty-two in 1900 to sixty-five in 1928; during the same years the number of European-American girl graduates went from fifty-seven to two. After 1906, boys dominated the scientific course of study, claiming 92.8 percent of the graduating class in 1916, 83 percent in 1924, and 80.2 percent in 1928. The male appropriation of the scientific course occurred among African-American students as well, although the later application of the differentiated curriculum yielded fewer graduates from this course of study. By the time girls had the option of taking the Scientific Course at Sumner High School, all but a few European-American girls had vacated the program at other St. Louis high schools. African-American female graduates selected the scientific course of study in numbers exceeding 1 percent only three times between 1914 and 1930. Although the number of African-American boys who graduated from the Scientific Course was small, the numbers increased from 1916 to 1928, and boys constituted two-thirds or more of the scientific-course graduates among African Americans in these years.

Within ten years of the introduction of the differentiated curriculum, girls' participation in the course of study at the top of the curricular hierarchy had waned considerably. After 1904, less than 5 percent of the total number of St. Louis high-school female graduates completed the Scientific Course, which, after 1906, was overwhelmingly populated by male students. This pattern held regardless of race. The female scholar, if she were to pursue the scientific course of study, had become a rarity in St. Louis.

Year	Scient.	Class.	General	Art	Comm.	Dom. Art & Science	Normal
1900	38.7	10.2	—	—	04.7	—	46.2
1904	20.2	16.0	44.0	11.3	07.7	—	00.5
1908	04.9	04.9	33.5	17.7	11.3	04.5	23.0
1912	03.2	01.8	36.0	24.8	08.2	13.6	12.2
1916	00.2	02.0	39.0	22.4	13.2	22.1	00.8
1920	02.9	06.9	61.7	03.4	13.1	11.8	—
1924	00.5	02.6	59.0	05.9	23.8	07.8	—
1928	00.2	02.2	69.5	04.9	18.0	04.9	—

Table 13. Percentages of European-American Female Graduates in Various Courses of Study in St. Louis High Schools: 1900-1928

Source: Calculated from *St. Louis Annual Reports*.

Year	Scient.	Class.	General	Art	Comm.	Dom. Art & Science	Normal
1900	—	—	60.7	—	—	—	39.2
1904	—	—	52.7	—	—	—	47.2
1908*	—	—	—	—	—	—	—
1912	—	—	—	—	—	62.1	37.8
1916	02.7	—	75.0	—	02.7	19.4	—
1920	—	02.2	46.6	—	06.6	44.4	—
1924	00.8	—	51.2	—	26.0	21.9	—
1928	01.4	—	73.3	—	03.7	21.4	—

* Information not available for 1908.

Table 14. Percentages of African-American Female Graduates in Various Courses of Study in St. Louis High Schools: 1900-1928

Source: Calculated from *St. Louis Annual Reports*.

Year	European-American Girls	European-American Boys	African-American Girls	African-American Boys
1900	57 (57.5%)	42 (42.4%)	—	—
1901	59 (61.4%)	37 (38.5%)	—	—
1902	75 (70.0%)	32 (29.9%)	—	—
1903	98 (71.5%)	39 (28.4%)	—	—
1904	34 (82.9%)	7 (17.0%)	—	—
1905	38 (74.5%)	13 (25.4%)	—	—
1906	23 (52.2%)	21 (47.7%)	—	—
1907	05 (16.1%)	26 (83.8%)	—	—
1908	13 (34.2%)	25 (65.7%)	—	—
1912	12 (22.2%)	42 (77.7%)	—	—
1916	01 (01.7%)	52 (92.8%)	01 (01.7%)	02 (03.5%)
1920	16 (14.9%)	87 (81.3%)	—	04 (03.7%)
1924	04 (06.1%)	54 (83.0%)	01 (01.5%)	06 (09.2%)
1928	02 (02.4%)	65 (80.2%)	02 (02.4%)	12 (14.8%)

Table 15. Graduates in Scientific Course of Study, by Sex and Race: 1900-1928
(percentages of the total number of graduates of the Scientific Course in all St. Louis high schools in parentheses)

Source: Calculated from *St. Louis Annual Reports*.

THE GENERAL COURSE

Few girls selected the scientific course of study after the differentiated curriculum was established in St. Louis high schools. Instead, most graduated from the General Course, third on the 1905 list of preferred options.[14] Perceptions involving degree of rigor distinguished the General Course from the Scientific and Classical Courses. In 1904, a writer for the *St. Louis Post-Dispatch* explained that the "general course is not considered as difficult as the scientific or classical course, as it gives students more freedom in selecting branches of study."[15] In 1904, the composition of the courses of study did not vary from each other as much as they later would; however, the fact that girls most often ended up in the course of study characterized as less difficult offers an indication concerning the changing perception of the female scholar.

More girls graduated from the General Course than from any other course of study from 1900 to 1930 (tables 13 and 14). From 1904 to 1928, between 33.5 and 69.5 percent of European-American female graduates selected the General Course. The noticeable boost in percentages between 1916 and 1920 probably reflected the discontinuation of the Normal Course, a declining interest in the Domestic Art and Science Course, and the impending transition away from distinct courses of study to a cursory program interspersed with electives.

As mentioned above, the differentiated curriculum was not adopted at Sumner High School until 1911; therefore, the General and Normal Courses claimed all of the graduates until 1912. Even after other courses were made available, the majority of African-American female graduates completed the General Course. Between 1916 and 1930, the number of African-American girls graduating from the General Course dropped below 50 percent only three times.[16] These high percentages suggest that the legacy of education for "race uplift" continued to influence young women in their schooling decisions. The General Course, while recognized as less rigorous than the Scientific or Classical Courses (which never established a foothold at Sumner High School), placed more emphasis on academic subjects than did the Domestic Art and Science or Commercial courses of study. Thus, the General Course was better able to satisfy the "great desire for education" that Paula Giddings discusses in *When and Where I Enter*. Giddings shows that many women looked to an academic education to escape the limitations imposed by a racist society.[17]

Not only did most girls graduate from the General Course of study in the first three decades of the twentieth century, but girls constituted the majority of graduates from this "weaker" academic curriculum as well. From 1900 to 1928, girls composed at least half of those graduating from the General Course (tables 16 and 17). European-American girls accounted for 70.3 percent of the General Course graduates in 1912; African-American girls accounted for 87 percent of the General Course graduates in 1916. African-American girls maintained a strong influence in the General Course of study up until 1930, with percentages of 72.4 percent in 1920, 81.8 percent in 1924, and 81.1 percent in 1928. European-American girls, on the other hand, recorded slimmer majorities: 61.7 percent in 1920, 50.7 percent in 1924, and 58.8 percent in 1928. This difference in likely explained by the fact that a higher percentage of African-American males than European-American males graduated from the Manual Training Course in this period.[18] Nonetheless, for all St. Louis students, the General Course evolved as a course of study that graduated a higher percentage of girls than boys.

The evolving general course of study helped to obscure the image of the female scholar in St. Louis schools in two ways. First, as part of the process of establishing the hierarchy of courses in the differentiated curriculum, educators sent out the message that the General Course was less academically challenging than the Scientific and Classical Courses. Yet the General Course became the "girl's choice." More girls graduated from the general course of study than from any other curriculum, and each year the General Course graduating class was composed primarily of girls. Second, as the differentiated curriculum developed in the twentieth century, much of the academic content of the General Course drained away. By 1930, the general course of study in St. Louis high schools was quite unlike its nineteenth-century predecessor, which had included advanced mathematics, languages, and the sciences. In 1916, the St. Louis Board of Education approved the superintendent's recommendation that students in the General Course be permitted to substitute work in subjects from other courses of study for advanced work in languages, mathematics, and science.[19] For students taking the General Course in 1917, electives claimed eleven of twenty-four classes over a four-year period. Nine of the twenty-four spaces were reserved for chorus, physical training, community civics, and vocations. Many of the electives were specifically vocational in nature: Industrial History, Commercial Geography, Manual Training, Mechanical Drawing, Household Arts, Bookkeeping, Stenography, Typewriting, Commercial Law, Salesmanship, and Advertising. Thus, while it was still possible for a student to graduate from the General Course of study and take most classes in academic subjects, such a program was no longer guaranteed. The academic content of the General Course was further weakened by 1927. Although an academic strand remained in the school curriculum, few students completed a course of study comparable to that taken by all graduates in 1870.[20]

Year	Scientific	Classical	General	Art	Comm.
1900	57.5	62.5	—	—	38.8
1904	82.9	75.0	62.7	61.2	54.1
1908	34.2	54.1	67.4	90.3	63.8
1912	22.2	36.8	70.3	97.8	51.6
1916	01.8	63.6	61.8	98.7	51.6
1920	15.5	86.3	61.7	95.0	67.9
1924	06.8	80.7	50.7	79.6	70.1
1928	02.9	61.2	58.8	74.1	70.5

Table 16. Female Percentages of Graduating European-American Classes in St. Louis High Schools, by Course of Study: 1900-1928

Source: Calculated from *St. Louis Annual Reports*.

Year	Scientific	Classical	General	Art	Comm.
1900	—	—	73.9	—	—
1904	—	—	73.0	—	—
1908*	—	—	—	—	—
1912*	—	—	—	—	—
1916	33.3	—	87.0	—	33.3
1920	—	100	72.4	—	50.0
1924	14.2	—	81.8	—	76.1
1928	14.2	—	81.1	—	35.7

* Information for 1908 was not available. All girl graduates in 1912 graduated from the Domestic Art and Science and Normal Courses.

Table 17. Female Percentages of Graduating African-American Classes in St. Louis High Schools, by Course of Study: 1900-1928

Source: Calculated from *St. Louis Annual Reports*.

THE CLASSICAL AND ART COURSES

Although educators gave the Classical Course a high recommendation in 1906, few St. Louis high-school graduates selected it from that point on. Proponents of the classical curriculum were losing the battle for its existence on a national stage; there were no major efforts in St. Louis to turn the tide. Six percent of all students in the United States took the classical curriculum in 1900. By 1910, this figure dropped to 3.08 percent.[21] The female scholar's access to academic study through the classical curriculum was a declining probability in St. Louis after 1904.

During the early years of the differentiated curriculum, the Classical Course maintained respectable percentages of girls in the European-American graduating classes. In 1900, 10.2 percent of all European-American female graduates in St. Louis finished the Classical Course, 16 percent in 1904 (table 13). The declining interest in the classical curriculum was evident by 1908, however, and in 1912 only 1.8 percent of all European-American girls graduated from the Classical Course.

Examination of percentages alone, however, conceals an interesting pattern concerning numbers of graduates. The number of female European-American graduates from the Classical Course was at its lowest during the 1910 decade, the "social efficiency" period when much attention was given to incorporating the "practical" studies into the high-school curriculum (table 18). In 1912 and 1916, only seven girls graduated from the Classical Course. The thirty-eight graduates of 1920 represented a revival of interest in the classical curriculum. The nineteen graduates of 1928, while only 2.2 percent of the total female class, did exceed the number of girls who graduated from the Classical Course in 1900.

Year	European-American Girls	European-American Boys
1900	15 (62.5%)	09 (37.5%)
1904	27 (75.0%)	09 (25.0%)
1908	13 (54.1%)	11 (45.8%)
1912	07 (36.8%)	12 (63.1%)
1916	07 (63.6%)	04 (36.3%)
1920	38 (86.3%)	06 (13.6%)
1924	21 (80.7%)	05 (19.2%)
1928	19 (61.2%)	12 (38.7%)

Table 18. European-American Graduates in Classical Course of Study, by Sex: 1900-1928
(percentages of total graduates of Classical Course in parentheses)

Source: Calculated from *St. Louis Annual Reports*.

Another important observation is that girls composed a considerable part of the Classical Course graduating classes. With the exception of 1911 and 1912, girls constituted the majority of the Classical Course graduates among European-American students (table 16). Among European-American students, girls accounted for three-fourths or more of the classes in 1904 (75 percent), 1920 (86.3 percent), and 1924 (80.7 percent). While boys' names dominated the rosters of Scientific Course graduates, the Classical Course lists were filled predominately by girls. Both courses of study were considered academically challenging, but it was the Classical Course that was criticized as being "too academic." The death knell for the classics came at the hands of early-twentieth century liberals who came to define "good" education based on an efficiency quotient. Abraham Flexner, a former teacher of the classics turned efficiency expert, wrote in 1916

> Learning to read Virgil is, of course, just as valid a purpose as learning to play a symphony, or to bake a pumpkin pie . . . and because people rarely care to read Virgil, because almost none of the thousands who study Virgil ever can or do read Virgil, therefore, in so far as they are concerned, Latin has no purpose.[22]

The academic course of study "belonging to girls" in St. Louis schools was one abandoned by most educators as inappropriate study during the 1910s.

The Art Course ranked fourth on St. Louis educators' recommendation list for general-education programs. Like the Classical and General Courses, it was taken primarily by girls. The Art Course was a popular course of study for European-American female graduates from 1904 to 1916 (Table 13). Almost one-quarter of all girls graduated from the Art Course in 1912. By 1920, the percentages declined considerably. By 1928, less than 5 percent of the graduates completed the Art Course. Throughout the period from 1904 to 1928, however, the Art Course evolved as the most sex-segregated course of study. Over 90 percent of Art Course graduates were girls in 1908, 1912, 1916, and 1920--98.7 percent in 1916. With the introduction of the differentiated curriculum near the turn of the century, the St. Louis high-school curriculum was dispersed: four courses of study made up the general-education program. Each of these produced classes of graduates marked by gender disparity. The course of study most highly recommended by school officials, the Scientific Course, became the preserve of boys. All of the others, the Classical Course, the General Course, and the Art Course, were characterized by large percentages of female graduates.

Gender was a significant factor regarding graduation from the Scientific and General Courses. As discussed above, neither African-American nor European-American girls tended to complete the Scientific Course after 1906; most African-American and European-American girls graduated from the General Course. Race, however, was the predominant factor concerning graduation from the Classical and Art Courses. Although most of the African-American high-school graduates from the Classical Course were girls, they selected this option only five times: 1913, 1920, 1925, 1926, and 1929. In most years the Classical Course accounted for 2 percent or less of all African-American female graduates, but in 1913 32.1 percent of African-American girls completed the Classical Course. The Art Course never claimed more than 5 percent of African American female graduates.

The low graduation rates in the Classical and Art Courses among African-American girls may be partially explained by the fact that the differentiated curriculum was adopted at Sumner High School thirteen years after new courses of study were introduced at Central High School. The crest in European-American girls' graduation rates from the Classical Course occurred in 1904, before the course was offered at Sumner High School. The peak of graduation rates from the Art Course was reached in 1912, when the differentiated curriculum at Sumner had only been in place for a few years (table 13). If the shift to distinct courses of study involved any degree of adjustment regarding gender course-taking patterns, the period of stabilization may have occurred before the Classical and Art Courses were offered at Sumner High School.

Differences between African-American and European-American high-school curricula that developed in the wake of the differentiated curriculum should not overshadow the excellent quality of secondary education provided at Sumner High School in the nineteenth century. School officials indicated that the course of study at Sumner was as academically challenging as that offered at Central High School in the *1892 Annual Report.* Reflecting upon the first Sumner High School classes, educators wrote that the Sumner diploma represented "a degree of scholarship and attainments equal to that required for graduation from the Central High School."[23] In the 1901 *Annual Report,* Principal Oscar Waring noted that Sumner High School graduates had continued their studies in almost every college that accepted African-American students. He also reported that through the "liberal appropriations of the Board for the extension of our department of science, and for the purchase of scientific apparatus, we have to-day probably as well appointed a chemical laboratory as any High School in the State."[24] Such claims from St. Louis educators have been substantiated by additional sources. Horace Mann Bond listed Sumner High School along with Dunbar High School in Washington, D.C. as examples of superior high schools in large, segregated city school systems.[25] Yet one must not lose sight of the fact that the educational excellence achieved by students and faculty at Sumner High School occurred *in spite* of its place in an unjust system. A statement in the *Seventy-Fourth Annual Report* (1928) exposed the racist ideology of school officials.

> . . . the law requires that both white and negro [sic] children must be afforded equal educational opportunities. It should be noted that equal educational opportunity does not necessarily imply the *same* educational opportunity.[26]

This type of thinking underpinned the reoccurring lag in extending schooling to African Americans in St. Louis.

The delay in introducing the differentiated curriculum at Sumner High School was not unlike other acts of procrastination regarding African-American students. Public schools for African Americans were not established in St. Louis until the state constitution of 1865 required it. After voting to provide for elementary schools for African-American children in February 1866, the St. Louis Board of Education did not secure space for the schools until December of that year. The schools were identified by number rather than name until repeated requests by the Colored Educational Association were heeded. The process took twelve years. The Board of Education did not employ African-American teachers until 1877, again after repeated petitions by the Colored Educational Association.[27] Sumner High School was not firmly established until 1885, thirty-two years after Central High School opened for European-American children. The school district opened a Normal School for European Americans in 1869; recommendations for a Normal Department at Sumner High School followed much later, in 1890. As part of the irregular progression of normal schools and departments in St. Louis, Harris Teachers College opened for European Americans in 1905. Sumner Teachers College, for African Americans, was not established until 1921. Parents and community members found themselves arguing for similar schooling opportunities for African-American children again in 1928, this time for access to vocational schools. In 1928 and 1929 members of parent-teachers associations and the Urban League of St. Louis sent representatives to the St. Louis Board of Education asking for vocational training for African-American students to parallel a program for European Americans.[28]

Another explanation for African-American girls' low rates of participation in the Classical and Art Courses is suggested by the tenor of the educational philosophy that emerged in the early twentieth century connecting schooling to work. Students, parents, and school counselors made school decisions with an eye toward job opportunities. George Counts discovered that student expectations concerning future occupations correlated highly with selected courses of study. Children of working-class parents tended to end up in the "practical" courses designed to prepare students for wage-earning jobs while children of middle- and upper-class parents constituted the majority of students in academic courses. Counts wrote that the lower the parents' occupational status, the stronger this tendency was manifested.[29] Recalling the social-class differences among African-American and European-American high-school students in St. Louis, then, it is reasonable to project that fewer African-American girls were in a position to enroll in the classical or art curricula, courses of study that were probably perceived as a luxury. Few jobs open to African-American women required knowledge of the classics or art. Teaching, a key avenue for women's leadership in nineteenth-century efforts for "race uplift," remained an important vehicle for women's contributions to the twentieth-century civil-rights struggle.[30] But teaching did not require completion of the Classical or Art Courses. After the Normal Course was discontinued at Sumner High School, the General Course provided the most direct path to teaching; it claimed the majority of female graduates.

Although young women who had graduated from any course of study in St. Louis high schools might enter Harris Teachers College or Stowe Teachers College, the majority of women who matriculated at Stowe Teachers College from 1922 to 1930 were graduates of Sumner High School's General Course. From 1908 to 1915, most European-American women enrolling at Harris Teachers College had completed the Normal Course in St. Louis high schools; after 1915 most first-year students at Harris Teachers College had taken the General Course of study in high school.[31] For fourteen of the twenty-three years between 1908 and 1930, 20 percent or more of the European-American female graduates from St. Louis high schools entered Harris Teachers College (table 19). Although percentages dropped below 20 percent beginning in 1919, the actual number of students remained stable, and actually increased to 307 in 1926. Significantly, over 70 percent of African-American female graduates from St. Louis high schools entered Stowe Teachers College three of the nine years from 1922 to 1930. The lowest percentage, 17 percent, occurred in 1929; every other year in this period at least 37 percent of the African-American women high-school graduates matriculated at Stowe Teachers College. In terms of numbers, the high points of enrollment were attained in 1922 and 1930 when 100 and 163 women entered in the college to continue their preparation as teachers.

Year	Harris Teachers College	Percentage of Female EA High-School Graduates	Stowe Teachers College	Percentage of Female AA High-School Graduates
1908	054	20	—	—
1909	118	44	—	—
1910	109	32	—	—
1911	116	30	—	—
1912	131	34	—	—
1913	104	30	—	—
1914	101	25	—	—
1915	126	31	—	—
1916	095	27	—	—
1917	107	27	—	—
1918	113	23	—	—
1919	094	17	—	—
1920	108	19	—	—
1921	089	10	—	—
1922	144	16	100	71
1923	133	13	078	76
1924	129	12	047	37
1925	141	13	067	45
1926	307	28	061	47
1927	289	29	066	39
1928	238	22	061	44
1929	182	18	032	17
1930	113	11	163	76

Table 19. Number and Percentage of Female St. Louis High-School Graduates Entering Harris and Stowe Teachers Colleges: 1908-1930

Source: *Seventieth Annual Report of the Board of Education of the City of St. Louis, Missouri, for the Year Ending June 30, 1924* (St. Louis: 1924), 70:

150; *Seventy-Sixth Annual Report of the Board of Education of the City of St. Louis, Missouri , for the Year Ending June 30, 1930* (St. Louis, 1930), 76: 110, 118.

1905 marked the end of European-American girls' graduation from the Classical Course in double-digit percentages. The Art Course flourished as a popular choice among European-American female graduates through 1916. Neither course of study attracted a significant number of African-American female graduates. In an age infatuated with social efficiency, the study of the classics and art was reserved for an elite group. If young women were to have legitimate ties to scholarship, they needed to attach their study to some socially sanctioned function. For many, teaching provided such justification. Girls' high rates of graduation from the General Course (followed by matriculation at St. Louis' teacher colleges) attested to the power of the new educational philosophy that linked schooling with work.[32] The strength of such thinking materialized again in girls' graduation patterns from the Commercial and Domestic Art and Science Courses. The ideology that welcomed these courses of study further diminished the image of the female scholar in St. Louis high schools.

THE COMMERCIAL AND DOMESTIC ART AND SCIENCE COURSES

I want to get married some time. If I'm a teacher I'll never meet any men and so what is there to do except be a stenographer.[33]

This young woman's response to an interview question posed in the late 1920s illustrated the narrow range of life choices women perceived for themselves. It also helps to explain the surge of interest in commercial education in United States high schools during the first decades of the twentieth century, years that witnessed the solidification of the notion that schooling should be directly related to job preparation. One historian labeled commercial education as a vocational groundswell, with good reason. Between 1890 and 1920 public-school enrollment in commercial classes grew from less than 15,000 to almost 300,000. The percentage of public-high-school students enrolled in commercial classes went from 21.7 percent in 1900 to 57.7 percent in 1934. George Counts reported in his 1924 survey of fifteen United States high schools that "commercial subjects have come to occupy a place in the program of studies second only to English based on the amount of time devoted to the coursework."[34] Although commercial courses of study were not designed originally as a curriculum for women, the feminization of clerical work was a principal stimulus for the sex-typed curriculum that resulted. Powers acknowledges the potency of the school-to-work ideology in girls' course selection in The *"Girl Question" in Education*, stating simply, "Young women flocked to commercial classes because they provided skills that converted to jobs."[35]

In St. Louis, European-American girls graduated from the Commercial Course in increasing numbers from 1900 to 1928. The percentage of girls graduating from the Commercial Course ranked second to the General Course in 1920, with 13.1 percent; in 1924 with 23.8 percent; and in 1928 with 18 percent (table 13). Between 1898 and 1915, boys accounted for the majority of graduates from the Commercial Course; from 1916 to 1930, however, the female percentage of European-American Commercial Course graduates ranged from 51 to 75 percent.[36] The inverted ratio of female to male graduates in the Commercial Course reflected changes in the workplace. The ascendancy of scientific management in the industrial sector found its complement in secretarial pools that sprang up in corporate bureaucracies. The feminization of clerical work paralleled its conversion to a lower-skill, lower-pay, lower-status position. By 1920, office work emerged as the leading employer of women, accounting for 25.6 percent of women in the United States labor force.[37] In his 1920 study of high schools in St. Louis, Bridgeport, Mount Vernon, and Seattle, Counts found that boys who did take commercial subjects in high school were motivated by different goals than girls: boys tended to take commercial classes as a prelude to college business courses while girls most often expected to apply their knowledge to clerical work after high school.[38]

The racial discrimination that kept African-American women out of clerical positions in the workforce translated to relatively low enrollments in commercial courses of study for African-American high-school students. Although African-American women had the highest rate of workforce participation among women workers, they were underrepresented in clerical work. In 1920, African Americans held less than 1 percent of clerical positions in the United States.[39] Undoubtedly, the experience of Addie W. Hunter, a graduate of the Cambridge Latin and High School, characterized employment frustrations for many.

Writing in 1916 on her unsuccessful lawsuit to gain a clerical position for which she was qualified, Hunter commented,

> For the way things stand at present, it is useless to have the requirements. Color—the reason nobody will give, the reason nobody is required to give, will always be in the way. [40]

Evidently, African-American girls in St. Louis had learned that "it is useless to have the requirements" as well, for few graduated from the Commercial Course. With the exception of the years between 1922 and 1925, when 10 to 25 percent of African-American female graduates completed the commercial course of study, less than 10 percent of African-American girls graduated from the Commercial Course. Employment figures for St. Louis support the conclusion that women's options in the labor force made an impact on course selection. In 1910, 99 percent of women employed in clerical occupations in St. Louis were European American. Only thirty-eight African-American women were hired for the 10,082 clerical positions reported in the census. In contrast, 92 percent of all African-American women workers were hired as domestic laborers. [41] Not surprisingly, the Domestic Art and Science Course claimed rather high percentages of African-American female graduates in St. Louis.

In 1912, just one year after graduates of Sumner High School were distinguished by various courses of study, 62.1 percent of all African-American girls completed the Domestic Art and Science Course (table 14). This percentage may have reflected the appeal of a new curriculum, for it was the highest recorded during the existence of the Domestic Art and Science Course. Nevertheless, the Domestic Art and Science Course accounted for a significant number of African-American female graduates from 1912 to 1929. The percentages were in double digits for seventeen of the nineteen years from 1912 to 1930, peaking again at 52 percent in 1919 and 44.4 percent in 1920. While secondary schooling in St. Louis public high schools did not reflect the Booker T. Washington philosophy of education, which spread through the South after his Atlanta Exposition Address in 1895, pragmatic elements regarding the economic value of schooling filtered in some way to most schools. Giddings' point that "Funds for Black schools were easier to come by if one's curricular 'buckets' were cast in the Washingtonian mold" is well taken. [42] In addition to the advocates of home economics who preached thrift and morality lessons, were the voices of those such as Mary Church Terrell who looked to the professionalization of domestic work as one solution to the labor problem encountered by African Americans early in the twentieth century.[43]

The pattern of European-American girls' graduation from the Domestic Art and Science Course contrasted that of African-American girls. European American girls graduated from the Domestic Art and Science Course in double-digit percentages only in the eleven years between 1910 and 1920. The highest percentage ever recorded was 26 percent in 1917, the year Congress passed the Smith-Hughes legislation on vocational education. The peak of interest in the Domestic Art and Science Course occurred from 1915 to 1919, the only years when 20 percent or more of European-American female graduates completed the course.[44] As was true across the nation, girls showed little interest in home-economics education after 1920. By 1928, only 4.9 percent of European-American girls graduated from the Domestic Art and Science Course in St. Louis (table 13). Yet the force with which advocates of home economics pushed for its place in the differentiated curriculum affected girls' secondary education in a manner that is difficult to measure. As Powers states, "Home economics in the curriculum reminded students of women's place in the economic and social order."[45]

The idea that gender delineated a particular "place" for women was apparent in St. Louis, where school administrators expected all girls to take some classes in home economics. This presumption encompassed the entire (female) high-school population, African American, European American, upper-, middle-, and working-class. Educators declared no parallel assumption concerning male students and the Manual Training Course (or any other). The following declaration appeared in the *Sixty-Seventh Annual Report* :

> There is so much vital subject matter in the Household Arts Course, that all high school girl students should be required to take at least one year of this subject. We know that 80 % of all girls will sooner or later have some care of a home. But whether or not, all girls should know how to preserve their health by means of proper food, and how to purchase garments and keep them in repair. To the regular four year course in household arts should be added a one-year course for all girls in the high school.[46]

It is important to note that this mandate was issued in 1921, a year in which the percentages of European-American girls graduating from the Domestic Art and Science Course fell to single digits for the first time since 1909. Educators were likely concerned by students' attitudes toward home economics, one exposed by Counts in his 1920 study and made public in 1922. Few girls in St. Louis listed domestic life as their major goal after high school. "Home" appeared seventh on a list of eleven responses to a question involving future expectations. Only 64 of 3,978 girls made that selection. Most named college (1,340) and clerical service (1,208) as their primary plans. [47]

There is no record of protest in St. Louis against this educational philosophy that assigned studies on the basis of one's gender. Indeed, critique of the differentiated curriculum such as the one raised by Latin teacher Mary Leal Harkness in 1914 was rare. As if in response to the St. Louis declaration of 1921, Harkness wrote

> I cannot see that girls were created essentially to be "home-keepers" any more than boys. Men and women, so far as they choose to marry, are to make a home together, and any system of education which so plans the division of labor between them that the woman shall "make" and stay in a place for which the man pays and to which he returns once in twenty-four hours, is wrong for at least two good reasons.[48]

Harkness' first objection to schooling that inculcated different responsibilities for girls and boys was that such an arrangement led to the defeat of true companionship and community of interest between women and men. Her second objection called attention to the fact that such schooling sacrificed true education for the girl. ". . . and it so magnifies a specialized manual training for the woman that it places her at the end in the artisan class, and not in the educated."[49]

St. Louis school officials emphasized the importance of work in their school philosophy by publishing "A Creed of Work for Women" in the *Sixty-Sixth Annual Report*. The creed was written by Laura Drake Gill, an educator and leader in vocational education for women. The author of Gill's biography in *The National Cyclopaedia of American Biography* described her as committed to the educational and social advancement of women, but not involved in "controversial issues bearing upon the so-called 'rights' of women."[50] "A Creed of Work for

Women" reflected the conservative perspective of its author, and was well-matched to the conservative population of St. Louis.

A Creed of Work for Women

I believe that every woman needs a skilled occupation developed to the degree of possible support. She needs it commercially, for an insurance against reverses. She needs it socially, for a comprehending sympathy with the world's workers. She needs it intellectually, for a constructive habit of mind which makes knowledge usable. She needs it ethically, for a courageous willingness to do her share of the world's work. She needs it aesthetically, for an understanding of harmony relationships as determining factors in conduct and work. I believe that every young woman should practice this skilled occupation up to the time of her marriage for gainful ends with deliberate intent to acquire therefrom the widest possible professional and financial experience. I believe that every woman should expect marriage to interrupt for some years the pursuit of any regular gainful occupation, that she should pre-arrange with her husband some equitable division of the family income such as will insure a genuine partnership, rather than a position of dependence (on either side) and that she should focus her chief thought during the early youth of her children upon the science and art of wise family life. I believe that every woman should hope to return in the second leisure of middle age to some of her early skilled occupations,—either as an unsalaried worker in some one of its social phases, or, if income be an object, as a salaried worker in a phase of it requiring maturity and social experience. I believe that this general policy of economic service for American women would yield generous by-products of intelligence, responsibility, and contentment.[51]

Gill's creed implied important differences between women's work and men's work. She expected women's public work to be interrupted by the work of establishing a family. Women, then, were to be generally excluded from occupations that required long-term commitments or development over time. The implication, during an age when the prevailing educational philosophy was one that equated schooling with work preparation, was that girls and boys should have different educational experiences: boys should prepare for careers and girls should prepare for short-term employment and domestic service.

Gender differences assumed in the economic sphere were to be parlayed into schooling disparities between the sexes. The traditional academic curriculum was not adaptable to such notions. Its replacement, the differentiated curriculum, was designed for them. The fact that there was no "Creed of Work" for men was itself enlightening. Had educators held no distinctions between women's and men's work, there would have been little reason to elaborate on one but not the other.

"A Creed of Work for Women" exhibited an ignorance of the realities of life for most working-class women as well, few of whom could afford to leave work during child-rearing years. It is curious, then, that the creed was directed to adolescent working girls.[52] St. Louis school officials may have included Gill's creed in their 1920 *Annual Report* as a means to bolster support for the Domestic Art and Science Course where the percentage of graduates was dropping. The conviction that a woman should "focus her chief thought during the early youth of her children upon the science and art of wise family life" was central to the creed.

Part of the struggle over the public-school curriculum during the decade beginning in 1910 was due to different conceptions of the role of women in United States society. In the area of vocational schooling for girls, home economics, industrial education, and commercial education were the key players. By 1920, home economics had achieved the official blessing of the federal government as the primary representative of vocational education for women; however, commercial education experienced the greatest degree of success in the schools.[53] The introduction to "A Creed of Work for Women" provides insight into the way people perceived the changing role of women in 1920. The creed was acclaimed as a "working principle for the reconciliation of the home and wage earning occupations under present day conditions."[54] Perhaps what educators sought were ways to reconcile elements of the Commercial and Domestic Art and Science Courses of study. But whether to prepare workers for the burgeoning bureaucracies of industrial society or as caregivers for the home, the primary task of the school was not to nurture the female scholar.

CONCLUSION

The academic tradition carried on by girls in the nineteenth-century high school ran counter to educational philosophy adopted in the twentieth century. The female scholar became an anachronism in the shadow of the differentiated curriculum. Nationally, educators discussed ways to reconcile "cross-purposes in the education of women." In her 1908 address to the National Education Association, Sarah Louise Arnold argued that schools had given too much attention to scholastic pursuits by women.

> In our efforts to secure a generous education for women have we not come to overemphasize and overestimate scholastic ability? to see it out of proportion to its advantage? to magnify schooling, and to minimize the value of the qualities and of the knowledge which are essential to fullest development—and particularly that knowledge and those qualities upon which her success in her home administration will depend?[55]

One way to measure the impact of such rhetoric on high-school girls' images of themselves as learners is to examine changes in their selections of courses of study. In St. Louis, graduation rates from the Scientific, Classical, General, Art, Normal, Commercial, and Domestic Art and Science Courses from 1900 to 1928 suggest that girls pulled away from courses that would designate them as "scholars" and diverted their efforts to job-related courses of study. Given a sex-stratified labor market, job-related courses of study translated to a sex-stratified curriculum. The notion that schooling should serve "gender-appropriate" functions led to the demise of the female scholar. Academic proficiency was not consistent with the prevailing image of women in society.

The eclipse of the female scholar was marked by plummeting percentages of girls graduating from the most highly recommended course of study, concentrated numbers of female graduates completing an academically diluted curriculum, and significant percentages of girls graduating from the "Special Courses of Training." All of this paralleled a steady decline in the percentage of female students in St. Louis high schools. Importantly, differentiation of courses itself did not lead to girls' immediate exit from the Scientific Course. As late as 1904, 20.2 percent of European-American girls graduated from the Scientific Course of study (table 13). The exodus began after St. Louis school officials promoted the Scientific Course as the most rigorous course of study in the curriculum. Most girl graduates after 1904 completed the courses of study ranked third (General) and fourth (Art) on the educators' recommendation list. The timing of the drop in female graduation from the Scientific Course suggests that educators' rhetoric was influential in the way girls perceived their academic status. As science came to represent the pinnacle of scholarship in the twentieth century, intellectuals drew sharp distinctions between female and male capacities in the field. A professor of education from the University of Wisconsin wrote the following in a chapter on girls' education in 1912: "The boy is better suited to deal with the laws of nature on the mathematical and physical side, for which the girl is not so well adapted."[56] The not-so-hidden curriculum that girls were unsuited for study in mathematics and science did not enhance the perception of the female scholar.

Commentators described the General Course as less challenging than the Scientific or Classical Courses in 1904. Curricular changes through 1930 sapped the academic content of the General Course of study further.[57] Yet this was the course of study that claimed the highest percentage of female graduates from 1904 to 1928, with generally increasing percentages (tables 13 and 14). Other top choices for female graduates came from the "training" tier of the curriculum hierarchy. Educators praised the Commercial and Domestic Art and Science Courses for their "practical" focus; girls would not have been drawn to them to enhance their standing as scholars. The three courses of study graduating the most girls from 1900 to 1928 are charted in table 20. The Scientific and Classical Courses appear only in 1900 and 1904. (In 1916, one girl graduated from the Scientific Course at Sumner High School, and one graduated from the Commercial Course. These two courses shared third place that year.) If one allows that the General Course was perceived as a route to teacher preparation, then the list took on a decidedly vocational bent, particularly after 1904. With a drop in graduation rates from the Scientific Course, and increasing participation in the General, Commercial, and Domestic Art and Science Courses, young women in St. Louis high schools reconstructed the academic legacy left to them by their nineteenth-century predecessors.

Year	European American	African American
1900	Normal Scientific Classical	General Normal
1904	General Scientific Classical	General Normal
1908	General Normal Art	—
1912	General Art Domestic Art and Science	Domestic Art and Science Normal
1916	General Art Domestic Art and Science	General Domestic Art and Science (1 Each In Commercial and Scientific)
1920	General Commercial Domestic Art and Science	General Domestic Art and Science Commercial
1924	General Commercial Domestic Art and Science	General Commercial Domestic Art and Science
1928	General Commercial Art/Domestic Art and Science	General Domestic Art and Science Commercial

Table 20. Top Three Courses of Study Selected by St. Louis High-School Girl Graduates, by Race: 1900-1928

Source: Calculated from *St. Louis Annual Reports*.

Although the academic decline that attended the push for practicality and social efficiency affected boys as well as girls, educators made distinctions based on gender that were particularly harmful to girls. At a time when schooling decisions were reduced to work-related applications of knowledge, Professor M.V. O'Shea complained of the requirements in mathematics for girls in a text for teachers:

> . . . not more than one girl in a hundred thousand in the public schools will need algebra for engineering or mechanics. The majority of boys, perhaps, will have need for algebra as a tool; and people go on requiring of the girl what will possibly be of service to the boy, but what is practically certain not to be of value to herself.[58]

Science and mathematics were intended, clearly, to be the domain of boys. Thus, an estrangement did not develop between the Scientific Course and boys, as it did for girls in St. Louis. In point of fact, boys' graduation rates from the Scientific Course remained in double digits for most of the years between 1898 and 1930; more boys graduated from the Scientific Course in 1928 than in 1900.

Counts provided another indication that gender played a role in students' course selection and future expectations. Data from Counts' 1920 study demonstrated that girls' future expectations were more closely tied to social class than were boys'. In addition, the percentages of boys in St. Louis high schools who expected to go to college were significantly higher than the ratios for girls. Differences in future expectations carried over into course selection. According to Counts, boys were less influenced in their choice of courses of study by the social groups they came from, than were girls.[59]

The impact of the differentiated curriculum affected girls, as a group, in yet another way. By encouraging all girls to take some classes in home economics, regardless of skills, desires, or future expectations, educators reinforced the notion of "a woman's place" in society. The educational climate in 1920 was much different than it had been in the 1870s. The academic curriculum required that all students be splintered into "role-appropriate" courses of study. Social-role expectations, still demarcated by gender, now were influential in determining a students' course of study. Although Mary Leal Harkness pointed out, ". . . it is no more essential to the progress of the universe that every woman should be taught to cook than that every man should be taught to milk a cow," gender-specific courses were not prescribed for all boys as they were for girls.[60]

Similarities in course-taking patterns for African-American and European-American girls in St. Louis illuminate ways in which gender appeared as the determining factor in one's schooling experience.

Neither African-American nor European-American girls graduated from the Scientific Course in substantial percentages after 1904; they gravitated to the "less difficult" General Course. In addition, vocational courses of study claimed increasing numbers of graduates.

Differences between African-American and European-American students concerning the Commercial and Domestic Art and Science Courses at once confirm and challenge theories in women's educational history. Rury's conclusion, that the differentiated curriculum reproduced the social division of labor within the female workforce, is supported by the St. Louis data.[61] Hiring patterns in St. Louis funneled most African-American women into domestic service and reserved clerical work for European-American women. Only 0.3 percent of the female clerical workers reported in the 1910 St. Louis census were African American. Course-taking patterns in St. Louis high schools reflected this economic reality as more African-American girls graduated from the Domestic Art and Science Course than the Commercial Course, while the reverse held for European-American girls. The data from St. Louis do challenge the trend regarding commercial subjects in one way. Powers reports that only 2 percent of all African-American high school students were enrolled in commercial courses in 1925.[62] In St. Louis, however, 1925 capped off a four-year period in which African-American girls graduated from the Commercial Course in double-digit percentages. The interest in the Commercial Course between 1922 and 1925 may reflect the increase in the number of clerical positions held by African-American women in St. Louis from 1910 to 1920. In 1910, 38 African-American women listed their occupation in the clerical category of the U.S. Census; by 1920 that number had increased to 180. Nonetheless, the 180 clerical workers represented only 1.3 percent of all African-American women workers in St. Louis and less than 1 percent of all St. Louis women identified as clerical workers.[63]

Histories of girls' experiences with the differentiated curriculum have stressed the prominent place of home economics in African-American women's education. To be sure, this point is upheld by the St. Louis data. Domestic Art and Science did account for a substantial percentage of African-American female graduates. An equally vital point, however, is that more girls graduated from the General Course, rejecting the Domestic Art and Science Course. It is probable that the impact of the differentiated curriculum on African-American women's secondary education varied by geographic region and the histories of institutions. Anderson's study of African-American education in the South documents that as African Americans lost political and economic power in the post-Reconstruction years, they lost substantial control of public schools. A second-class education emanated from a social ideology designed to foster conformity to racist forms of political and economic subordination.[64] It is logical to suspect that the differentiated curriculum in southern high schools for African Americans, where they existed in the early years of the twentieth century, channeled girls into Domestic Art and Science courses. Thus, high school for many African-American girls became training for domestic work. Rury states that this is the pattern that developed in Memphis.[65] Evidence from St. Louis, however, suggests that the differentiated curriculum did not affect all African Americans in the same way, nor did it affect African-American students exactly as it affected European-American students. The differentiated curriculum wielded a different impact on African-American girls in schools such as Sumner High School in St. Louis or M Street High School in Washington, D.C., schools that offered liberal education prior to the shift to a new curriculum. Studies of other high schools are needed to fully understand the influence the differentiated curriculum brought to bear on girls' secondary education.[66]

This analysis of high-school curriculum choices in St. Louis shows that gender was a significant factor in determining a student's course of study. Historians disagree on the importance of this phenomenon. Tyack and Hansot admit that the public high school of the 1920s evinced more sex differentiation than its nineteenth-century counterpart; however, they claim that segregation by gender occurred only on the periphery of the curriculum.[67] Their argument discounts the hidden messages embedded in a gender-segregated curriculum. Powers' interpretation aligns with graduation patterns in which courses of study were dominated by one sex or the other. Her theory stresses the strength of dominant ideology in forming one's educational experiences and life opportunities.[68] By simply differentiating courses of study and advertising some as gender-appropriate, school officials passed on clearly articulated ideals concerning schooling. Powers writes that although home-economics courses never measured up to the social-efficiency ideal promoted by reformers in the first decades of the twentieth century, it did become a standard offering in most junior and senior high schools in the United States.[69] Indeed, school reform seldom attains the vision extended by its proponents; yet educators' efforts, generally, are built upon an elemental faith in the power of schools to influence how people think and behave. The fact that girls constituted the majority of high-school graduates from the Classical, General, Art, Commercial, and Domestic Art and Science Courses, while boys predominated in the Scientific Course, is one indication that educators' beliefs in a sex-typed curriculum "took" in St. Louis. A legacy of gender segregation in the high schools was established with the differentiated curriculum, fueling the notion that the school's function was to prepare girls and boys for different social roles.[70]

NOTES

1. Quoted in James W. Lichtenberg, "The Adolescent Girl—1925," *Journal of Counseling and Development* 63 (February 1985): 342.

2. H.J. Wightman, "Technical Courses in High Schools," *The Pennsylvania School Journal* 55 (March 1907): 400.

3. James D. Anderson, *The Education of Blacks in the South, 1860-1935* (Chapel Hill: University of North Carolina Press, 1988); Samuel Bowles and Herbert Gintis, *Schooling in Capitalist America* (New York: Basic Books, 1976); Michael B. Katz, *Class, Bureaucracy, and Schools: The Illusion of Educational Change in America* (New York: Praeger Publishers, 1975); Edward A. Krug, *The Shaping of the American High School: 1880-1920* 1 (Madison: University of Wisconsin Press, 1969); David F. Labaree, *The Making of an American High School: The Credentials Market and the Central High School of Philadelphia, 1838-1939* (New Haven: Yale University Press, 1988; David Nasaw, *Schooled to Order: A Social History of Public Schooling in the United States* (Oxford: Oxford University Press, 1979); John L. Rury, *Education and Women's Work: Female Schooling and the Division of Labor in Urban America, 1870-1930* (Albany: State University of New York Press, 1991); Joel Spring, *The American School 1642-1993*, 3d ed. (New York: McGraw-Hill, 1994); Paul C. Violas, *The Training of the Urban Working Class: A History of Twentieth-Century American Education* (Chicago: Rand McNally College Publishing Company, 1978).

4. See Karen L. Graves, "Women and 'Democracy's High School,'" *Journal of the Midwest History of Education Society* 23 (1996): 49-54.

5. *Nineteenth Annual Report of the Board of Directors of the St. Louis Public Schools, for the Year Ending August 1, 1873* (St. Louis: Democrat Litho. and Printing Co., 1874), 19:120.

6. *Sixtieth Annual Report of the Board of Education of the City of St. Louis, Missouri for the Year Ending June 30, 1914* (N.p., n.d.), 60:109.

7. As noted in chapter 4, the decline in the female percentage of the St. Louis high-school population did not occur at the same rate for African-American and European-American students.

8. Labaree, *The Making of an American High School*, 171. See chapter 6, "Courses and Credentials: The Impact of the Market on the Curriculum," pp. 134-172.

9. Jane Bernard Powers, *The "Girl Question" in Education: Vocational Education for Young Women in the Progressive Era* (London: The Falmer Press, 1992).

10. Millicent A. Rutherford, "Feminism and the Secondary School Curriculum, 1890-1920," Ph.D. diss., Stanford University, 1977.

11. In this study, I examine the course selection of St. Louis High School graduates from the class of 1898 (the first year students graduated in courses of study other than the Classical, General, or Normal Courses) through the class of 1930 (the last year in which graduates were distinguished in the *St. Louis Annual Reports* by various courses of study). Limiting data to information concerning only graduates does not account for the experiences of the majority of high-school students during this period. This is important information that should be addressed in future studies to enhance understanding of secondary school curriculum development.

12. *Fifty-First Annual Report of the Board of Education of the City of St. Louis, Mo., for the Year Ending June 30, 1905* (St. Louis: Nixon-Jones Printing Co., 1906), 51: 201-202. Since the College Classical and College Scientific courses of study involved so few students and were phased out after a few years, they are not included in this analysis.

13. Ibid. At this time, the Manual Training Course included shopwork in wood and metal for boys and instruction in needlework, cooking, and household arts for girls.

14. *Fifty-First Annual Report*, 51: 201-202.

15. "Three Courses for Teachers," *St. Louis Post-Dispatch*, 13 January 1904.

16. Karen L. Graves, "The Impact of the Differentiated Curriculum on African American Women High School Students: The Case in St. Louis," *Mid-Western Educational Researcher* 8 (Fall 1995): 6.

17. Ibid., 5; Paula Giddings, *When and Where I Enter: The Impact of Black Women on Race and Sex in America* (New York: William Morrow and Co., 1984), 101.

18. Karen L. Graves, "Curriculum Changes in St. Louis Public High Schools, 1870-1930: The Transformation from Female Scholar to Domesticated Citizen," Ph.D. diss., University of Illinois at Urbana-Champaign, 1993, 182.

19. *Sixty-Third Annual Report of the Board of Education of the City of St. Louis, Missouri for the Year Ending June 30, 1917* (N.p., n.d.), 63: 117.

20. Karen L. Graves, "A Matter of Course: Curriculum Transformation and Academic Decline in St. Louis," *Journal of the Midwest History of Education Society* 22 (1995): 167-168.

21. *Report of the Commissioner of Education for the Year 1899-1900*, 2 vols., (Washington, DC: U.S. Government Printing Office, 1901), 2:2122; *Report of the Commissioner of Education for the Year Ended June 30, 1910*, 2 vols., (Washington, DC: Government Printing Office, 1910), 2: 1135. See Clarence J. Karier, *The Individual, Society, and Education: A History of American Educational Ideas*, 2d ed (Urbana: University of Illinois Press, 1986) and Krug, *Shaping of the American High School*, (Madison: University of Wisconsin Press, 1969) for analyses of the decline of the classical curriculum in the United States.

22. Quoted in Krug, *Shaping of the American High School*, 1: 343.

23. *Thirty-Eighth Annual Report of the Board of President and Directors of the St. Louis Public Schools for the Year Ending June 30, 1892* (St. Louis: The Mekeel Press, 1893), 38: 58.

24. *Forty-Seventh Annual Report of the Board of Education of the City of St. Louis, Mo., for the Year Ending June 30, 1901* (St. Louis: Nixon-Jones Printing Co., 1902), 47: 85.

25. Horace Mann Bond, *Black American Scholars: A Study of Their Beginnings* (Detroit: Balamp Publishing, 1972), 114.

26. *Seventy-Fourth Annual Report of the Board of Education of the City of St. Louis, Missouri, for the Year Ending June 30, 1928* (N.p., n.d.), 74: 546.

27. For information on the development of public schools for African-American children in St. Louis see chapter 4, "The Consequences of Racial Prejudice," pp. 79-98 in Selwyn K. Troen, *The Public and the Schools: Shaping the St. Louis System, 1838-1920* (Columbia: University of Missouri Press, 1975); Elinor M. Gersman, "The Development of Public Education for Blacks in Nineteenth-Century St. Louis," *Journal of Negro Education* 41 (Winter 1972): 35-47; J.W. Evans, "A Brief Sketch of the Development of Negro Education in St. Louis, Missouri," *The Journal of Negro History* 7 (October 1938): 548-552; and Kurt F. Leidecker, "The Education of Negroes in St. Louis, Missouri, during William Torrey Harris' Administration," *Journal of Negro Education* 10 (October 1941): 643-649.

28. *Printed Record of the Board of Education of the City of St. Louis* 33 (July 1st, 1926 to June 30th, 1927), 33: 810; *Printed Record of the Board of Education of the City of St. Louis* 34 (July 1st, 1927 to June 30th, 1928), 34:

981; *Printed Record of the Board of Education of the City of St. Louis* 35 (July 1st, 1928 to June 30th, 1929), 35: 587, 987.

29. George Sylvester Counts, *The Selective Character of American Secondary Education* (Chicago: University of Chicago, 1922), 73. John Rury confirms that girls from high-status backgrounds dominated the academic courses in the schools in Counts' study. See Rury, chapter 5, "Varieties of Adaptation: Local Patterns of Women's Education and Work," pp. 175-210 in *Education and Women's Work*.

30. See Linda M. Perkins, "The Education of Black Women in the Nineteenth Century," in *Women and Higher Education in American History*, John M. Faraher and Florence Howe, eds. (New York: W.W. Norton & Company, 1988), 64-86; Perkins, "The Impact of the 'Cult of True Womanhood' on the Education of Black Women," *Journal of Social Issues* 39 (1983): 17-28; Perkins, "The History of Blacks in Teaching: Growth and Decline within the Profession," in *American Teachers: Histories of a Profession at Work*, Donald Warren, ed. (New York: Macmillan, 1989): 344-369.

31. *Seventieth Annual Report of the Board of Education of the City of St. Louis, Missouri for the Year Ending June 30, 1924* (N.p., n.d.), 70: 149; *Seventy-Sixth Annual Report of the Board of Education of the City of St. Louis, Missouri for the Year Ending June 30, 1930* (N.p., n.d.), 76: 110, 118. The William T. Harris Teachers College, for European-American students only, was founded in 1905. The Harriet Beecher Stowe Teachers College was established in 1921 to prepare African-American teachers. The two colleges merged in 1954.

32. Preparation for teaching was, evidently, one of the major reasons girls attended St. Louis high schools in the nineteenth century. In 1874, the Central High School Alumni Association compiled statistics on occupations of St. Louis high-school graduates. Slightly under half of the women reporting were or had been teachers. The president of the St. Louis Board of Education wrote in 1882: "the advanced general education of the teachers of our schools is itself a work, which, in my opinion, justifies the existence of a high school as part of our public school system, irrespective of other questions." [Quoted in Rury, *Education and Women's Work*, (Albany: State University of New York Press, 1991), 22.] 177 (63.4 percent) Sumner High School graduates between 1895 and 1905 became teachers or had enrolled in normal school. Although this information did not distinguish women from men, 82.7 percent of Sumner High School graduates in this period were women. 55 of the 179 Sumner High School graduates from 1906 to 1909 (30.7 percent) became teachers or enrolled in normal school. See *Twentieth Annual Report of the Board of Directors of the*

St. Louis Public Schools, for the Year Ending August 1,1874 (St. Louis: Democrat Litho. and Printing Co., 1875), 20: 88; *Fifty-First Annual Report of the Board of Education of the City of St. Louis, Mo., for the Year Ending June 30, 1905* (St. Louis: Nixon-Jones Printing Co., 1906), 51: 234-235; *Fifty-Fifth Annual Report of the Board of Education of the City of St. Louis, Mo. for the Year Ending June 30, 1909* (St. Louis: Nixon-Jones Printing Co., 1910), 55: 71. The distinction I wish to emphasize between female high-school graduates becoming teachers in the nineteenth and twentieth centuries is that, in the nineteenth century the high-school education taken by girls who wished to teach did not differ substantially from boys' high-school study. With the distinction in courses of study implemented at the turn of the century, the curriculum leading to a career in teaching did deviate from curricula with more academic status. The girls taking the General Course of study were set apart, by distinctions in course of study and, especially later, by academic content, from the boys in the Scientific Course. See also Rury, *Education and Women's Work*, 14-16, 21-23.

33. Quoted in Powers, *The "Girl Question,"* 119.

34. Quoted in Powers, 114; Rury, *Education and Women's Work*, 147-149; Powers, *The "Girl Question'*,*"* 113. On the development of commercial education in United States high schools, see Powers, *The "Girl Question," especially* chapter 10, "The Success of Commercial Education," pp. 113-124; Rury, *Education and Women's Work*, especially chapter 4, "Vocationalism Ascendant: Women and the High School Curriculum, 1890-1930," pp. 131-174; and David Tyack and Elisabeth Hansot, *Learning Together: A History of Coeducation in American Public Schools* (New Haven: Yale University Press, 1990), especially chapter 8, "Differentiating the High School: The 'Woman Question,'" pp. 201-242.

35. Rury, *Education and Women's Work*, 132, 147-149; Powers, *The "Girl Question,"* 114.

36. Graves, "Curriculum Changes in St. Louis Schools," 197-198.

37. Steven E. Tozer, Paul C. Violas, and Guy Senese, *School and Society: Educational Practice as Social Expression*, 1st ed (New York: McGraw-Hill, 1993), 126.

38. Counts, *Selective Character of American Secondary Education*, (Chicago: University of Chicago, 1922), 67.

39. Rury, *Education and Women's Work*, 122-129; Powers, *The "Girl Question,"* 117.

40. Quoted in Jacqueline Jones, *Labor of Love, Labor of Sorrow: Black Women, Work and the Family, from Slavery to the Present* (New York: Vintage Books, 1985), 179.

41. U.S. Bureau of the Census, *Thirteenth Census of the United States Taken in the year 1910* 4 (Washington, DC: U.S. Government Printing Office, 1914), 4: 598-599.

42. Giddings, *When and Where I Enter*, (New York: Wm. Morrow and Co., 1984),101.

43. Graves, "African American Women High School Students," 5. See Anderson, *The Education of Blacks in the South* (Chapel Hill: University of North Carolina Press, 1988) and Giddings, *When and Where I Enter*. The literature on the development of home economics is vast. (The term "domestic art and science" is used in this text to correlate with the label applied to the home-economics curriculum in St. Louis high schools.) Important secondary texts on the history of home economics at the high-school level include Geraldine Jonçich Clifford, "'Marry, Stitch, Die, or Do Worse': Educating Women for Work," in *Work, Youth, and Schooling: Historical Perspectives on Vocationalism in American Education*, Harvey Kantor and David B. Tyack, eds. (Stanford: Stanford University Press, 1982): 223-268; Powers, *The "Girl Question"*; Rury, *Education and Women's Work*; Tyack and Hansot, *Learning Together*; and Emma Seifrit Weifley, "It Might Have Been Euthenics: The Lake Placid Conferences and the Home Economics Movement," *American Quarterly* 27 (Spring 1975): 79-86. Catharine Beecher's 1843 text, *Treatise on Domestic Economy for the Use of Young Ladies at Home and at School* (Boston: T.H. Webb & Co.) in Kathryn Kish Sklar, *Catharine Beecher: A Study in American Domesticity* (New Haven: Yale University Press, 1973) is a foundational work in the early history of home-economic schooling. P.I. Ellis, *Americanization through Homemaking* (Los Angeles: Wetzel Publishing Co., 1929) and Albert H. Leake, *The Vocational Education of Girls and Women* (New York: MacMillan, 1918) are useful primary sources as is Mary Leal Harkness, "The Education of the Girl," *Atlantic Monthly* 113 (March 1914): 324-330, a rare critique of home economics in the differentiated curriculum. Articles by Ellen Richards provide the perspective of a recognized leader in the home-economics movement. See, for instance, "The Present Status and Future Development of Domestic Science Courses in High School," in the *Fourth Yearbook of the National Society for the Scientific Study of Education* (Bloomington: Pantagraph Printing and Stationery Company, 1903): 39-52. The *Journal of Home Economics* is a major source for articles on home-economics education as is the *National Education Association Journal of Addresses and Proceedings*. Publications of governmental and other organizations promoting vocational education offer additional primary sources. See A. Hoodless, "The Education of Girls," *National Society for the Promotion of Industrial Education Bulletin No. 10, Proceedings, Third Annual Meeting* (March 1910); E. White,

"The Place of Homemaking in Industrial Education for Girls," *National Society for the Promotion of Industrial Education Bulletin No. 18, Proceedings Seventh Annual Meeting* (Peoria: Manual Arts Press, 1914); L. H. Weir, "Housing and Homemaking," *National Society for the Promotion of Industrial Education Bulletin* 24 (1917); Federal Board for Vocational Education, *Home Economics Education Organization and Administration*, Bulletin No. 28, Home Economics Series No. 2, (Washington, DC: U.S. Government Printing Office, 1919); Federal Board for Vocational Education, *Vocational Education in Home Economics* (Washington, DC: U.S. Government Printing Office, 1930); *Annual Report of the Commissioner of Education, 1909* 1; "Manual Arts and Homemaking Subjects," in the *Annual Report of the Commissioner of Education, 1920* (Washington, DC: U.S. Government Printing Office, 1921); *Education of the Home*, Bulletin No. 18, Bureau of Education (1911); and "Homemaking as a Vocation for Girls," in *Cooking in the Vocational School*, Bulletin No. 1, U.S. Bureau of Education, (1915).

44. Graves, "Curriculum Changes in St. Louis High Schools," 182.

45. Powers, *The "Girl Question,"* 97. See Powers, chapter 8, "Home Economics: A 'Definitely Womanly Curriculum'," pp. 86-100, for an analysis of the impact of home economics in the public-high-school curriculum.

46. Quoted in *Sixty-Seventh Annual Report of the Board of Education of the City of St. Louis, Missouri for the Year Ending June 30 1921* (N.p., n.d.), 67:150.

47. Counts, *Selective Character of American Secondary Education*, (Chicago: University of Chicago, 1922), 64, 76.

48. Harkness, "Education of the Girl," *Atlantic Monthly* 113 (March 1914): 328.

49. Ibid.

50. *The National Cyclopaedia of American Biography* 24 (New York: James T. White and Co., 1935), 24: 236-237.

51. Quoted in *Sixty-Sixth Annual Report of the Board of Education of the City of St. Louis, Missouri for the Year Ending June 30, 1920* (N.p., n.d.), 66:114.

52. Troen, *The Public and the Schools*, 192.

53. See Powers, *The "Girl Question,"* on vocational education for girls during this decade.

54. *Sixty-Sixth Annual Report*, 66: 114.

55. Sarah Louise Arnold, "The Reconcilement of Cross-Purposes in the Education of Women," *National Education Association Journal of Proceedings and Addresses* 46 (1908): 97.

56. M.V. O'Shea, *Everyday Problems in Teaching* (Indianapolis: The Bobbs-Merrill Co., 1912), 335. See Graves, "Women and 'Democracy's High School,'" for an extended discussion on the impact of New Liberal ideology on girls' secondary schooling.

57. See Graves, "A Matter of Course," *Journal of the Midwest History of Education Society* 22 (1995).

58. O'Shea, *Everyday Problems in Teaching*, 326-327.

59. Counts, *Selective Character of American Secondary Education*, 65, 66, 82, 84.

60. Harkness, "Education of the Girl," 325.

61. Rury, *Education and Women's Work*, 7.

62. Powers, *The "Girl Question,"* 123.

63. *Fourteenth Census of the United States Taken in the Year 1920* 4 (Washington, DC: U.S. Government Printing Office, 1923): 4: 1217-1218.

64. Anderson, *Education of Blacks in the South*, (Chapel Hill: University of North Carolina Press, 1988), 3.

65. Rury, *Education and Women's Work*, 191-192.

66. Graves, "Impact of the Differentiated Curriculum on African American Women High School Students," *Mid-Western Educational Research* 8 (Fall 1995): 7-8.

67. Tyack and Hansot, *Learning Together*, (New Haven: Yale University Press, 1990), 231.

68. Powers, *The "Girl Question,"* 9-11; 128-132; See also Myra Sadker and David Sadker, *Failing at Fairness: How America's Schools Cheat Girls* (New York: Charles Scribner's Sons, 1994).

69. Powers, *The "Girl Question,"* 128-132.

70. Ibid.

CHAPTER 6

The Ascent of
Domesticated Citizen

> In the education of every high-school girl, the household arts should
> have a prominent place because of their importance to the girl herself
> and to others whose welfare will be directly in her keeping. . . . our
> traditional ideals of preparation for higher institutions are particularly
> incongruous with the actual needs and future responsibilities of girls.[1]
> —*Cardinal Principles of Secondary Education,* 1918

Women's historians are interested in how gender ideology has led to
particular constructions of power and knowledge. In St. Louis, gender
ideology legitimated change in the public-high-school curriculum
during the first decades of the twentieth century, just as high-school
attendance was on the rise. This institutional change established a
gender system in the schools that altered girls' experience in the high
school; the gender system that paralleled the introduction of the
differentiated curriculum would define secondary schooling in the
United States for much of the twentieth century.[2] The evidence from St.
Louis correlates with Victoria Bissell Brown's research on Los Angeles
high schools at the turn of the century. Brown found that gender
ideology spurred institutional changes that increased the significance of
gender in high-school students' lives in the twentieth century.[3]

New Liberal ideology, vocational education, the "boy problem,"
and domestic feminism coalesced to reshape the contours of the St.
Louis high-school curriculum during the Progressive Era. Each of these
forces infused an ideology based on sex differences into the high-
school curriculum. Although the curriculum conversion transformed

girls' (and boys') high-school experiences considerably, the ascent of the domesticated citizen in St. Louis schools provoked little in the way of protest in the conservative community.

NEW LIBERAL IDEOLOGY

In this text, the term "New Liberalism" refers to the dominant ideology in the United States that started to break away from Classical Liberalism in the latter part of the nineteenth century, as characterized by Clarence Karier and Paul Violas.[4] Elements that constitute New Liberal ideology were articulated by middle-class, Progressive-Era reformers: educators and scholars, governmental officials, social workers, industrialists, and others. A helpful outline of the foundational tenets of New Liberal ideology is presented in *School and Society: Historical and Contemporary Perspectives*. In brief, New Liberals (who grounded their understanding of natural law in Darwinian biology) perceive truth as relative. Given the plasticity of truth, New Liberals connect reason with scientific method and profess a strong faith in the rational knowledge of an elite few. Progress is considered possible, but only as a result of scientific planning and management; the rugged individual is an anachronism. New Liberals seek government regulation to create conditions for "positive" freedom, the situation created when those in power order society for the good of all.[5]

Karier contrasted Classical Liberals' philosophic justification of a competitive economy, private property, individualism, and freedom from state interference with New Liberals' support of a controlled economy, state planning, group thought, and managed change.[6] Violas explained that New Liberal intellectual, social, and political leaders wrote public policy aimed at strengthening the compulsory corporate state and visioning the individual as part of a greater collective unity. He argued that a key concern of New Liberals is finding a more effective means of social control to eliminate conflict and establish a harmonious organic community.[7] Two aspects of the New Liberal agenda, the desire for social change without conflict and the faith in science and technology as creators of human values, converged on the mass system of schooling in the United States. Education for citizenship and work came to the fore as major objectives of schooling with the introduction of compulsory schooling, vocational education, and extra-curricular activities organized by school officials.[8] Karier and Violas charge that twentieth-century schooling in the United States has failed to enhance democracy; following the New Liberal philosophy of schooling, students have been trained to seek security and comfort rather than educated to be critical citizens. They concur that mere cultural participation in a greater collective unity is a pale substitute for political and economic power.[9]

New Liberalism as defined by Karier and Violas contradicted the interpretations of progress, social melioration, and meritocracy advanced by liberal historians Merle Curti, Henry Steele Commager, Richard Hofstader, and Lawrence Cremin, work that dominated the "vital center of American social, intellectual, and political life for half a century."[10] The critical historians' understanding of New Liberalism aligned more closely with social-control theory. The basic belief supported by scholars such as Michael Apple, Samuel Bowles and Herbert Gintis, Michael Katz, Edward Krug, and Joel Spring is that school systems have reflected the structure of the society in which they operate. Rather than allow for social mobility, schools have served as a vehicle for social control.[11]

NEW LIBERALISM: INTERDEPENDENCE AND ROLE SPECIALIZATION

Sparked by Charles Darwin's 1859 publication of *On the Origin of Species by Means of Natural Selection, or, The Preservation of Favoured Races in the Struggle for Life*, and in the face of tremendous change in the United States political economy, many in the U.S. intellectual community began to perceive society as a social organism, growing and evolving.[12] Sociologists Charles H. Cooley and Edward A. Ross suggested that the self found definition only in relationship to society.[13] A popular metaphor emerged, that of the individual as a single cell in the social body. Each "cell" was to perform specific functions to insure the health of the body; at the same time, an interdependence among the cells would develop. For New Liberals, the complexity of U.S. society demanded role specialization. For progress to occur, individuals had to be trained to perform distinct functions. In contrast to the nineteenth-century conception of schooling for full human development, the differentiated curriculum became the means by which schools prepared students for specific tasks in society. An emphasis was placed on subjects with "practical" applications to better prepare for the transfer of training from school to life roles. The progress of society became the key concern, rather than the complete human development of individual students.

These tenets of New Liberal thought formed the core of the educational philosophy advanced in textbooks for teachers written in the first decades of the twentieth century. Paul H. Hanus of Harvard University identified the discovery and development of each pupil's dominant interests as the special aim of secondary education and, therefore, the teacher's greatest responsibility.[14] David Snedden went further in his 1913 text in a defense of the differentiated curriculum. Rather than speaking of adapting curriculum to each student's interests, Snedden argued for group classification: "A uniform program of education is no longer possible. To an indefinite extent programs must be adapted to varying groups."[15] The choice of program was not to be made by the student; decisions were to be reached according to "expert" evaluation of which students might profit from various educational opportunities: "Prescription and forced classification there must of necessity be; but only as determined by the incapacity of the individual to profit from a given type of opportunity."[16] Edward Thorndike, arguably the most influential force in teacher education in the early twentieth century, also upheld the practice of choosing a special line of action *for* an individual.[17] His rationale for such action was based on the benefit to society: "When education becomes able to select the work best fitted to each individual as well as to fit the individual to his work, it will not only increase economic productivity, but also the health, morality, and culture of society."[18] Thorndike illuminated the alteration in school philosophy brought to bear by the implementation of the differentiated curriculum. The purpose of schooling was now to create a specialist, not one equipped with an education that reflected the breadth of the liberal arts: " . . . education beyond certain fundamentals should narrow itself to fit every man for a certain probable course of life, not for all life's possibilities."[19] This specialization, which highlighted preparation for the world of work, also included specific preparation in social, civic, and recreational arenas.[20] In short, teachers were advised to train students for specialized roles in their complex society. It was suggested that this required an increased emphasis on "practical" studies.

Unmistakably, twentieth-century educators argued that social efficiency required schooling that emphasized citizenship, job preparation, and the effective use of leisure time. Every discipline came to be evaluated by this standard. Professor Alexander Inglis of Harvard

University articulated this position in his 1918 text, *Principles of Secondary Education*: "Hence the value of any subject of study is to be measured according to the degree in which it may contribute directly or indirectly to the attainment of [socio-civic, economic-vocational, and individualistic-avocational aims], and the aims or purposes of any accepted subject of study in the secondary school are to be determined accordingly."[21] Inglis went on to declare that all of the subjects included in the secondary-school curriculum *could not* and *should not* be studied by all students.[22] In reconfiguring the secondary-school curriculum, a line was drawn between the "practical" subjects and those that, traditionally, had been championed in the cause of mental discipline. Perhaps George H. Betts, professor of psychology at Cornell College, Iowa, captured this precept best: "Such values as *knowledge, culture, power*, no longer satisfy the educational ideal; these must in some way combine to spell *efficiency*."[23] It was widely held that the classics as well as the modern languages, mathematics, and history, did not factor into the efficiency equation for most students. In his lectures on the theme, "Education for a Changing Civilization," William Heard Kilpatrick prescribed the following:

> For most pupils, Latin can and should follow Greek into the discard. Likewise with most of mathematics for most pupils. Much of present history study should give way to study of social problems. . . . Modern foreign languages can hardly be defended for most who now study them.[24]

University of Illinois professor William C. Bagley also wrote that the study of higher mathematics was appropriate only for future engineers. Teachers who read his text met with the opinion that the average high-school student had little need for algebra, geometry, and trigonometry.[25] In 1912, Betts traced the school response to public demand for practical subjects, noting the proportional reduction of academic subjects. He concluded that social efficiency was soon to become the "ruling concept throughout the whole range of the curriculum."[26]

As the twentieth-century high school turned its attention to training students for differentiated roles in society, then, "practical" courses came to occupy a larger portion of the curriculum. Throughout this transformation, individualism was held subordinate to the perceived good of society. Scholars such as George Counts and William H.

Kilpatrick reminded teachers that "interdependence has replaced individualism" in the U.S. political economy.[27] Thorndike was more bold with his assertion that each "child should have as much high-school work as the common good requires."[28] For New Liberal educators, a primary objective of schooling was social stability, as Inglis indicated with his definition of the school as a social institution. The school was to be "maintained by society for the purpose of assisting in the maintenance of its own stability and in the direction of its own progress."[29] In New Liberal thinking, social stability required role specialization.

NEW LIBERALISM: HUMAN RATIONALITY

A corresponding tenet of New Liberal ideology was the notion that all but an elite few individuals were incapable of rational thought. Paul Violas' scholarship provides many examples of prominent New Liberal intellectuals who emphasized the nonrationality of the masses. In *Democracy and Social Ethics*, Jane Addams wrote:

> Ethics as well as political opinions may be discussed and disseminated among the sophisticated by lectures and printed pages, but to the common people, they can only come through example— through a personality which seizes the popular imagination. The advantage of an unsophisticated neighborhood is, that the inhabitants do not keep their ideas as treasures.[30]

Sociology Professor Charles Cooley argued that "Rationality . . . is, and perhaps always must be, confined to a small minority of even the most intelligent populations. . . . the scientific point of view can never be that of most of mankind."[31]

Many came to believe that the traditional academic curriculum was out of step with the intellectual capacities of most students. In 1925 Psychologist Winifred Richmond commented on the appropriate curriculum for *The Adolescent Girl*.

> The older classical and academic courses do not fit the girl of average ability, and this is not to be wondered at when we reflect that the classical high-school course of today is far heavier than that of the college of a hundred years ago. It requires intellectual tastes and aptitudes which the average person does not possess.[32]

The new science of psychology taught that most persons were controlled by emotional and nonrational means, rather than by reason. This assumption effectively eroded one of the fundamental underpinnings of the traditional academic curriculum. Academic subjects had been defended by many on the grounds that higher mathematics and the classics were essential for their disciplinary value. Faculty psychology, which was the accepted theory on epistemology for centuries, suggested that the human mind worked like a muscle. The exercise obtained, for example, through the study of trigonometry or Latin, was expected to strengthen the mind and equip it to deal effectively with difficult situations of any type. This concept of "transfer of training" did not constitute the entire philosophy of faculty psychology, however, it bore the brunt of the twentieth-century assault by practitioners of educational psychology.

Teachers in St. Louis, apparently, did not readily abandon their faith in faculty psychology. In 1914, Superintendent Blewett acknowledged that there

> still remain some traces of a belief formerly quite prevalent. Some still think that Arithmetic, or Algebra, or Latin, or other studies have peculiar merit as discipline studies or as culture studies; but recent psychology denies that any specific virtue of this kind is inherent in and peculiar to certain studies. [33]

With a new generation of teachers, however, new psychology won the day. By 1926, the *St. Louis Board of Education Curriculum Bulletin* officially stated "While transfer of training may take place under certain conditions, it is neither automatic nor inevitable."[34] Stripped of much of the traditional rationale for requiring academic subjects in the high-school curriculum, teachers found themselves having to defend the existence of their studies.

NEW LIBERALISM: PROGRESS

In the midst of turbulent changes in the United States political economy between 1870 and 1920, New Liberals did not believe that social progress was guaranteed. If progress was to occur, according to New Liberal ideology, the elite few who were capable of harnessing reason must use their expertise to bring order to society. New Liberals sought a state organization that would "put the wise minority in the saddle," as sociologist Edward A. Ross argued.[35] Experts were to determine the capacity of each individual, who would then perform his or her role in the name of social progress. The analogy of the individual person as a cell in the social body, interdependent and subservient to the whole, was central to the New Liberal hope for progress.

These ideas contradict any notion of a society governed by the people as surely as New Liberals rejected belief in equality among persons. There was no inconsistency, however, with the New Liberal definition of democracy. Edward L. Thorndike reasoned that the "argument for democracy is not that it gives power to all men without distinction, but that it gives greater freedom for ability and character to attain power."[36] This skewed conception of democracy undergirded the differentiated curriculum in high schools. In *Public Education in the United States: A Study and Interpretation of American Educational History*, prominent educator Ellwood P. Cubberley stressed

> Instead of being born free and equal, we are born free and unequal, and unequal we shall ever remain. The school, we now see, cannot make intelligence; it can only train and develop and make useful the intelligence which the child brings with him to school. This is a matter of his racial and family inheritance, and nothing within the gift of the schools or our democratic form of government.[37]

New Liberal educators drew the wrong-headed conclusion that differences among persons were so great as to require differential education. As Cubberley's statement indicates, New Liberals often based distinctions in schooling on race. Racist ideology supported the philosophy of schooling that Booker T. Washington learned at Hampton Institute and instituted at Tuskegee. In his 1895 Atlanta Compromise speech, Washington asserted, "No race can prosper till it learns that there is as much dignity in tilling a field as in writing a poem. It is at the bottom of life we must begin, and not at the top."[38] Washington's message was echoed by Willard W. Beatty, president of the Progressive Education Society and director of the Education Division of the Bureau of Indian Affairs. Writing on Native-American education, Beatty implored

> Indian young people must be taught to do the things that will make them self-sufficient. . . . If this much can be accomplished and Indians freed from their present dependence upon charity and direct

relief, they will have been placed on a plane of economic equality with half their fellow white citizens and more than half the population of Europe. [39]

Cubberley did not deny that the differentiated curriculum institutionalized superior educational experiences for the elite. Rather, he argued that such unequal schooling opportunities were in the best interest of a democracy.

The prime idea underlying these differentiated courses has been that of providing better advantages for gifted children, and as such they are among the most interesting experiments for the improvement of democracy that have been made. . . . A democracy, too, is especially in need of leaders to guide the mass, and it is from among its gifted children that the leaders must be drawn. [40]

Lewis M. Terman was one of the most vigorous proponents of the practices of classifying and sorting individuals in order to achieve "social progress." Responding to objections to the further differentiation of studies in 1924, Terman declared,

I have no patience with those who condemn this plan as undemocratic. The abandonment of the single-track, pre-high-school curriculum is in fact the first necessary step toward educational democracy. . . . The educational sentimentalists who defend [the single track], who fear mental tests and ignore or deny individual differences, are of a class with those who stake their life on a coue formula, fear doctors and deny the actuality of disease. [41]

In the search for progress, New Liberal scholars such as Cubberley, Thorndike, and Terman redefined the meaning of democracy. Given this philosophical climate, one wonders just what Charles H. Judd's survey team was describing in 1918 when they reported that the "cosmopolitan high school is the school of democracy, and in St. Louis such schools are admirably organized." [42]

NEW LIBERALISM: SOCIAL EFFICIENCY

Edward A. Krug notes that, as every society must decide whether to endure or embrace the societal necessity of management of the individual for the benefit of the group, the United States embraced this form of social control in the early years of the twentieth century.[43] Indeed, the submission of the individual to the State became a key theme in the social-efficiency movement in the United States during the Progressive Era, and the doctrine found ample expression in educational literature. Cubberley listed the training of children for citizenship among four great tasks of the modern school in 1919. Stephen Sheldon Colvin's 1917 *Introduction to High School Teaching* marked citizenship training in sharp relief to education for personal development.

> The most generally recognized aim of the American secondary school is to train boys and girls to become useful members of the communities in which they are to live, in other words to promote good citizenship in the broadest sense of the term. This aim is so comprehensive that it includes all other aims that are ordinarily advanced as reasons why a boy or girl should take a high school course, with the exception of the *narrow and unjustifiable aims* of mere self-advancement, and personal pleasure.[44]

William D. Lewis, in a 1914 publication entitled *Democracy's High School*, conceded that the community had become "wisely selfish in recognizing in its schools not a philanthropy but a cooperative agency for social service."[45] He went on to praise the nonacademic nature of differentiated courses of study for preparing students for the various types of trained service for which the public was in need. Lewis consistently argued that the justification for public expense for high schools was the production of an improved citizenry. He went on to state that only those subjects that contributed to citizenship training should be required—English, civics, physical training, home arts (for girls), and manual training (for boys.)[46]

Evidently, this message was absorbed into the St. Louis school system with few objections. The 1914 *Annual Report* contained the warning that any subject in the curriculum could justify its presence there only by its proved value in working out the purpose for which

> the schools exist. . . . If they cannot prove that they aid in the purpose of the State, they should not be given place. Then, too, in so far as their relative aid to the purpose can be ascertained, this should be the

measure of the relative emphasis placed upon them and of the relative time accorded them.[47]

In light of this philosophy, the declining numbers of students in academic courses of study is understandable. Further, the same report reflects the New Liberal perspective of a protean society and the school's responsibility to adapt.

The work of the school must change with the changing needs of the state. . . . The school's guiding conscience at all times is the purpose of the state in its establishment.[48]

School assemblies were suggested in order to impress the idea of universality upon the "pliable" consciences of students. The Judd survey praised the daily assembly for emphasizing the "fact that a school is not a mere collection of classroom units but that it has a social unity."[49] In 1926, the St. Louis Board of Education clarified the focus of the schools for any who remained in doubt: "Schools serve two interests: those of the individual and those of society; wherever the two come into conflict those of society take precedence."[50]

The New Liberal desire to create a functional society by schooling youth for particular life roles, together with little respect for students' rational capacity, produced an educational philosophy that emphasized the control of human behavior. Increased attention to the differentiated curriculum, with its transition away from academic subjects requiring cognitive skills, paralleled growing support for schooling as a means of social control. George S. Counts believed that the early 1920s marked a crucial time in the history of the high school. He urged that academic training be supplemented with subject matter designed to bring about "desirable changes in the behavior of children and in social life."[51] At the beginning of the century, sociologist Ross determined that education was to succeed religion "as the method of indirect social restraint," describing education as "an economical system of police."[52] In point of fact, Ross believed education as a form of social control was so potent that this knowledge was not to be widely shared, for "To betray the secrets of ascendancy [was] to forearm the individual in his struggle with society."[53] Seeking support for the domestic-science movement, Ellen Richards asked in 1908, "Who can doubt that . . . the domestic science course offers the best means to influence the lives of people and influence them quickly?"[54] Behavior control reached a prominent position among objectives for St. Louis schools by at least 1914. Principal John W. Withers proclaimed the primary purpose of education to be the

> determination or control of behavior; knowledge and other organized forms of mental life are only of secondary importance, and even of no importance at all unless they actually or conceivably influence behavior in some desirable way. The principles, then, which should control the organization and direction of public education must be derived from the study of human behavior and the means of determining and controlling it. [55]

Through the 1920s, educators in St. Louis continued to focus on citizenship, vocational training, and character development for their students. The paucity of references to intellectual development in the annual reports reflected the New Liberal faith in nonrational means of shaping one's "character." The *Seventy-Fourth Annual Report* in 1928 proclaimed the "next great forward move in education will doubtless be in this field of the training of the emotions—the development of desirable ideals, attitudes, tastes, and appreciations."[56] In 1930, the annual report included a summary of St. Louis educators' replies to a questionnaire on character education distributed by the National Education Association, Department of Superintendence. Those who responded indicated that, in addition to organizations such as student government and a variety of extracurricular clubs and activities that stressed character formation, "regular class work is consciously directed towards the development of desirable character traits."[57] In some schools, students were rated on industry, cooperation, and other character traits. High-school teachers, "no matter what their subject, find opportunities for character training in their class work."[58]

The events in St. Louis paralleled a development in United States secondary schools that Krug details in *The Shaping of the American High School*. Beginning around 1910, nonacademic activities and courses of study were regarded with equal or greater importance than academic studies.[59] The drive for social efficiency was the impetus behind this transformation, a notion captured most colorfully by Cubberley.

> The public schools of the United States are, in a sense, a manufactory, doing a half-billion dollar business each year in trying

to prepare future citizens for usefulness and efficiency in life. As such we have recently been engaged in applying to it some of the same principles of specialized production and manufacturing efficiency which control in other lines of the manufacturing business. [60]

THE DIFFERENTIATED CURRICULUM: A NEW LIBERAL APPARATUS

New Liberal educators retooled the high-school curriculum in the early years of the twentieth century, to sort individuals, presumably by ability, in order to most effectively train each person for his or her place in the social order. There was no pretense that each position would be equal, but each was considered necessary for the smooth running of society. Educators argued that the differentiated curriculum, based on assumed individual abilities and needs, would result in increased choice on the part of the individual. Karier has called this one of the great educational myths of the twentieth century. He writes that from its inception, the differentiated curriculum has served to "channel, control and limit the choice of individuals."[61] In his day, Cubberley acknowledged that the "essential idea underlying each [experiment in differentiated courses of study] is that children are different not only in mental capacity but in future possibilities as well. . . . "[62] Indeed, future life opportunities were limited by the New Liberal belief that intellectual differences that exist among people are so great as to require divergent educational experiences. Rather than help students develop their abilities and expand the range of life choices, many were content to simply train children to accept inequalities that the school perpetuated. Frank N. Freeman of the University of Chicago explained it was the "business of the school to help the child to acquire such an attitude toward the inequalities of life, whether in accomplishment or in reward, that he may adjust himself to its conditions with the least possible friction."[63] Freeman's statement exposed the New Liberal priority to eliminate social conflict through the schools.

The notion of individual differences served as the primary rationale for the differentiated curriculum. In 1926, St. Louis school officials affirmed that the "fact of individual differences conditions the results that may be expected from the educative process."[64] Individual differences as justification for the differentiated curriculum, however, may have masked a deeper concern for social stability. In 1909,

Woodrow Wilson, speaking of United States society, explained, "We want one class of persons to have a liberal education and we want another class of persons, a very much larger class, of necessity, in every society, to forego the privileges of a liberal education and fit themselves to perform specific difficult manual tasks."[65] If Wilson's model materialized, a majority of students would be denied a traditional academic education, regardless of their perceived individual abilities.

Wrapped in the New Liberal rhetoric of "democracy" and "equal educational opportunity," school men and women in the early twentieth century required some measure of validity to support the "sort-and-train" mission they had accepted. This was provided by scientific experts in the field of educational psychology. The most prominent of those who endorsed intelligence tests, Edward L. Thorndike, asserted that "exact and complete knowledge about the correlations of mental traits will be of enormous importance for the utilization of man-power by schools, churches, employers, and the state."[66] Using IQ tests constructed on a foundation of unproved suppositions and racist, nativist, and sexist biases, psychologists assumed a positive correlation between social class and native intelligence. Thorndike went as far as to say that "Intellectual ability and moral worth hang together."[67] This idea was also supported by Lewis M. Terman, developer of the Stanford-Binet IQ tests. He wrote,

> . . . not all criminals are feeble-minded, but all feeble-minded are at least potential criminals. That every feeble-minded woman is a potential prostitute would hardly be disputed by any one. Moral judgment, like business judgment, social judgment, or any other kind of higher thought process, is a function of intelligence.[68]

There were powerful, contemporary arguments against the misuse of IQ tests, yet the tests were a crucial component in bringing about the New Liberal social order. Terman was on the mark in 1916 when he proclaimed that the time "is probably not far distant when intelligence tests will become a recognized and widely used instrument for determining vocational fitness."[69] His tests would soon be used by the U.S. Army in World War I to classify officer candidates; shortly thereafter, the tests were used in St. Louis schools to sort children into "appropriate" channels of the differentiated curriculum.

The obsession with intelligence testing spread across the country with rapid speed. Cubberley advised

The educational significance of this new means of measuring intelligence is very large. Questions relating to proper classification in school, grading, promotion, choice of studies, schoolroom procedure, vocational guidance, and the proper handling of subnormal children on the one hand and gifted children on the other, all acquire new meaning when viewed in the light of intelligence measurement.[70]

Indeed, the impact of IQ testing on American school children would be tremendous. IQ testing supplied a "scientific" surge to the retreat from high-school academic courses of study that had been set in motion by the adoption of the differentiated curriculum. A teacher at Erasmus Hall High School in Brooklyn concluded that either the "Terman test was not valid . . . 'or the programming of so many students into mathematics is a blunder, if not a crime, and should be discontinued.'"[71] The crime that occurred, however, was the classification of children as lacking the ability to pursue academic studies. This transgression was accentuated by the prejudices that permeated the composition and application of the intelligence tests.

Thorndike and Terman both claimed that intellectual abilities were determined by race. Their intelligence scale placed northwestern Europeans at the top, followed by distinct and progressively lower ranges for southeastern Europeans, Mexicans, Native Americans, and Africans. While abilities were expected to vary within each racial group, scientists of Thorndike and Terman's ilk assumed that individual destinies were circumscribed by genetic forces linked to race. Except for the occasional "sport," no one was believed to be able to transcend the limits set by the scientific elite for his or her race. "Experts" in all areas of U.S. society—government, education, religion, the economy— ascribed to this racist dogma, and set policy accordingly. Thorndike preached that intellectual differences in

remote ancestry or race account for a very large percentage of differences found amongst men. . . . race directly and indirectly produces differences so great that government, business, industry, marriage, friendship, and almost every other feature of human instinctive and civilized life have to take account of a man's race.[72]

Terman was among those who argued for restricted immigration laws as a measure to keep the germ plasm in the United States "pure."

The immigrants who have recently come to us in such large numbers from Southern and Southeastern Europe are distinctly inferior mentally to the Nordic and Alpine strains we have received from Scandinavia, Germany, Great Britain, and France. . . . No nation can afford to overlook the danger that the average quality of its germ plasm may gradually deteriorate as a result of unrestricted immigration.[73]

Thorndike also claimed that the sexes differed in mental qualities. He wrote that, whether from native tendencies or differences in training, girls were more subjective, personal, emotional, accurate, indirect, and deceitful than boys. Thorndike taught that girls were more apt to judge a situation by its effect on their own feelings and affairs, and maintained a narrower range of information and interests than boys. He found girls to be less active, violent, and insubordinate than boys, but girls were the neater of the two sexes. Thorndike argued that male and female types were similar in intellectual capacities, with one important difference. Males, he suspected, deviated more from the type. This meant that the highest-scoring male in any quality would always be more talented than the highest-scoring female, while the lowest-scoring male would have less ability than the lowest-scoring female. It appears as if Thorndike held higher expectations for "overlap" between men and women than between members of particular races. Nevertheless, he concluded that

if men differ in intelligence and energy by wider extremes than do women, eminence in and leadership of the world's affairs of whatever sort will inevitably belong oftener to men. They will oftener deserve it.[74]

The St. Louis Board of Education established a Division of Tests and Measurements on 12 July 1921. Some three hundred teachers and principals were sent to Harris Teachers College and Sumner Teachers College to be trained in Educational Measurements. Although St. Louis educators used these tests in all levels of the school system, it was decided early on that

one of the profitable uses of intelligence testing would be in rating the eighth grade graduates coming to the high schools. . . . the results of the examinations were used quite generally in determining the initial organization of the first year classes.[75]

Results of the tests given in January 1922 suggest that African-American students fared no better in St. Louis with the racially biased tests than students in other parts of the country. Higher percentages of incoming students at Sumner High School scored in the 70 and 80 IQ ranges than new students at Central, Cleveland, McKinley, and Yeatman. At the same time, lower percentages of ninth-grade students at Sumner scored in the ten-degree ranges from 90 to 130 than their fellows at the other St. Louis high schools.[76]

There was some correlation between IQ test scores of 1922 and 1923 for students entering Central, Cleveland, McKinley, and Yeatman High Schools and the courses of study taken by the students. (Sumner High School was not listed with the others on this chart in the *Annual Report*, nor was its omission addressed.) The course of study with the highest student median IQ score was the Scientific Course. This was followed by the General, Classical, Commercial, Manual Training, Art, and Home Economics Courses.[77] The total range of median IQ scores was less than ten points, however, the ordering of courses paralleled the occupational association with IQ scores established by Terman. He predicted that persons with higher IQ scores would be best adapted for the professional classes of workers. Following, in order, down the IQ scale were the semiprofessional, skilled, semiskilled, and unskilled classes. Perhaps the biases inherent in intelligence testing were transmitted through the use of IQ tests to the differentiated curriculum in St. Louis. The entire process was circular in form. IQ tests, which had been developed to benefit the upper classes, were used to distinguish which students would have access to particular tracks in the differentiated curriculum. The academic courses of study, which led to the upper occupational stratum, primarily accepted students with top IQ scores.

St. Louis high schools continued to use IQ tests for classifying students into various courses of study throughout the 1920s. As the *Seventy-Fourth Annual Report* indicated, "The thought is to direct the child's efforts along most promising and profitable lines."[78] It does not appear that the question, "promising and profitable for whom?" was asked. Had it been presented, however, Thorndike would have been ready with a reply. Aware that intelligence tests were part of a social arrangement that enabled the elite to control the masses, the professor from Columbia University preached that, ". . . in the long run, it has paid the 'masses' to be ruled by intelligence."[79]

Aspects of New Liberal ideology proved to be a major force in bringing about the adoption of the differentiated curriculum in St. Louis. Multiple courses of study geared to the practical concerns of life allowed educational "experts" to sort and train students for particular roles in society. Social efficiency became the watchword as school objectives were dominated by concerns for behavior control, character formation, and preparation for service to the State. New psychology, first, dismantled teachers' faith in faculty psychology, which further weakened the position of academic subjects in the curriculum. Then, the development of intelligence tests created a "scientific" facade, behind which life-determining choices for children were made.

There was, however, another dominant magnetism that drew the differentiated curriculum to St. Louis high schools, and held it firmly in place. Vocationalism was more than just training for specific occupations; it was the understanding that the principal intent of secondary schooling was to discover one's function for adulthood. This perception fell over the high school like a dense fog, clouding desire to learn simply for the joy of learning. To be sure, there were teachers and students who managed to break through this heavy shroud, but too many were in agreement with Ernest C. Moore of Harvard University. In a 1917 article for *School and Society,* Moore wrote, "To teach the young that each one of them has a place and a work to do and that his main business in youth is to find out what that work is and to fit himself most diligently to do it seems to me to be the whole purpose of education."[80]

VOCATIONAL EDUCATION

There were only hints of the impending change in the high-school curriculum when C.A. Herrick warned educators of the possible impact of commercial education.

> A word of caution. Let those who make this provision see to it that they defile not the sacred temple of learning. Let them beware lest they commit crime in the name of educational progress.[81]

A bit of the melodramatic, perhaps; but, it was not long before these words were marked by a resounding veracity.

Commercial courses served as a driving wedge that opened the way for vocationalism in high schools in the United States. According to John Rury, 80 percent of all commercial instruction in the United States was conducted by private business schools up until 1890. By 1920, however, this ratio dropped to 50 percent and an almost equal number, 45 percent of all commercial students, were preparing for a business career in the public high schools. Commercial education was strongly entrenched in the differentiated curriculum by 1928 when one-sixth of all high-school students across the country were enrolled in business courses, most of them women.[82] Evidently, business leaders found the high-school graduates well-trained for work in their companies, and at public expense. Educators in St. Louis were aware of this interest as early as 1901. The *Forty-Seventh Annual Report* included notice that

> recognition by the community of the preparation for business secured by those who complete the High School course is shown by the increasingly large demand made by business houses of this city for the young men who graduate from the school. More positions are open to graduates than we are able to fill, and the reports from those who have employed them are conclusive evidence as to their character and readiness for work.[83]

The feminization of clerical work had not yet reached St. Louis; no doubt, school officials hoped announcements of this sort would lure more boys to continue their education at the high school.

The pattern for industrial involvement in public education had been firmly established by the beginning of the twentieth century; it has yet to abate. The National Education Association's Committee of Nine on the Articulation of High School and College, a forerunner to the well-known group that produced *The Cardinal Principles of Secondary Education*, reported in 1911 that the

> high school should in a real sense reflect the major industries of the community which supports it. The high school, as the local educational institution, should reveal to boys and girls the higher possibilities for more efficient service along the lines in which their own community is industrially organized.[84]

This message fit the Zeitgeist of the emerging corporate American state well. And it was well received. Also in 1911, Paul H. Hanus, in an introduction to a text entitled *The Vocational Guidance of Youth*, stated that the "establishment of schools at public expense for the training of workers in our industries, on our farms, and in commerce is making decided progress."[85] The concern for vocationalism in public high schools reached the upper echelons of U.S. society rather quickly. In 1913, a presidential commission was organized to investigate vocational schooling and report on the desirability and feasibility of national aid for vocational training. Eventually this led to the passage of the Smith-Hughes Bill of 1917. The commission announced that American industry required one million new workers annually, explicitly calling for three years of vocational training beyond elementary school in order to attain efficient service.[86] The differentiated curriculum, already paving the "royal road to the practical," became a federal works project.[87] Educators and industrialists alike were called upon to convince the public to accept the new school curriculum. In 1919, officials in the Department of the Interior Bureau of Education issued the following:

> The general public will need to be educated to the importance of
> schooling, and particularly to the necessity of differentiated courses.
> Employers and labor leaders will need to be utilized as cooperating
> factors in bringing the school and industry together in such a way as
> to result in better industry and a better school.[88]

This statement suggests that there was some measure of resistance to the adoption of the differentiated curriculum. Yet, what resistance that did develop did not often issue from those in high positions of educational, industrial, or governmental leadership. Others, however, did note the precarious nature of the alliance being forged between industry and education. William McAndrew, principal of Washington Irving High School in New York City, admonished in 1908

> Industrial wealth has proved itself no special friend of children, or of
> their education. The greed that lures children to the coal mine and
> cotton mill by the seductive temptation of early wage-earning would
> be a sorry influence in schools detached from the old system. The
> business avarice that first brought Africans as slaves to our shores,
> and then Chinese, and now Italians, because their labor is cheap, is

scarcely a power to be trusted with the direction of any public schools.[89]

Regardless of such warnings, school systems pushed ahead in the drive toward vocationalism. Apparently, the mandate of business and industry was difficult to ignore. A few years after the differentiated curriculum had replaced the traditional academic curriculum in St. Louis, school officials timorously revealed that the vocational course "should not pretend to be more than it is, but it would doubtless meet a very insistent demand that is now met by private enterprises."[90] With these most recent demands came a reconstructed emphasis on work skills. In *The Vocational Guidance of Youth,* Hanus advised schools to underscore "the importance and the dignity of *work* of all kinds as the foundation of all individual and social welfare."[91] Efforts at building respect for work increased with the incorporation of Taylorism in U.S. factories. As the principles of Scientific Management were put into place, designed to reduce the amount of skill required and control wielded by workers on the assembly line, worker dissatisfaction mounted. Capitalists decreed that a more expedient type of intelligence be nurtured in the public schools. Nationally prominent educator David Snedden defined this "industrial intelligence" as he illuminated the strong connection between industry and vocational education: "Employers desire habits of industry, application, thrift, orderliness, and speed; therefore vocational education must keep constantly before it the inculcation of these habits."[92] William D. Lewis, Principal of the William Penn High School in Philadelphia and author of *Democracy's High School*, concurred. He urged that the high-school course of study "be adapted to its particular community, which it should furnish with workers trained to habits of promptness, accuracy, and perseverance, as applied not only to learning lessons from books, but also to doing tasks with the hand."[93]

Admittedly, schooling devoted to "industrial intelligence" would require a transformation from the academic curriculum of the past. On this point, the NEA's Committee of Nine was clear: "The universal education to which our institutions are now committed is radically different from the education for a literary class to which we were formally devoted."[94] The pathway to the differentiated curriculum was even cleared by President Theodore Roosevelt, who used his bully pulpit to preach the virtues of a "practical" education. In a message to Congress on 3 December 1907, he stated, "Our school system is gravely defective in so far as it puts a premium upon mere literacy training and tends therefore to train the boy away from the farm and the workshop."[95]

Once the differentiated curriculum had been established, economic interests reached beyond the course structure and into actual studies. In a paper for the National Education Association, Clarence D. Kingsley prophesied that when the "social sciences—history, civics, and economics—are better adapted to the needs of high-school pupils, they will teach more about the history of industries, the social significance of commerce, and the newer vocations connected with public utilities and social service."[96] A parallel concern of monopoly capitalists in this era was the need to produce consumers as well as workers, in order to maintain the economic structure they were designing. Schools were to be useful in this enterprise as well. Stuart Ewen maintains that the "embellishment of public schooling with modern 'home economics' curricula is but one example of the way in which a mode of existence produced in industrial plants and publicized by advertising was being woven into the web of daily life."[97] The differentiated curriculum was designed to benefit industry, even in the courses of study that were not directed toward the production of wage earners.

St. Louis high schools exhibited similar patterns of industrial involvement. In 1918, the Judd survey team suggested that an industrial survey be made of the city to ascertain the leading vocations and trades. The purpose was to better relate the work of the school to the fundamental industries in St. Louis. Further, the authors of the Judd report commented that commercial subjects were

> essentially vocational in their purpose and should be taught with this aim in mind and the results measured by the standards of actual business use. What the public demands in these subjects the school should furnish . . . .[98]

The survey team praised the practice in which St. Louis teachers served as vocational guidance counselors for high-school students, and suggested that the faculty consider beginning this work at an earlier point in the schooling experience. Here teachers aided students in selecting "appropriate" courses of study based on the child's presumed future.[99]

Ellwood Cubberley pointed to the elevated plane of importance assumed by vocational guidance in schools, contributing it to the growing complexity of industrial society and the minute subdivision of the old trades.[100] The St. Louis *Annual Report* for 1926 noted a high degree of interest in the district's Division of Vocational Counseling, in the form of 617 calls from industrial and commercial employers.[101] Indeed, vocational guidance programs did much to bring industrial interests into the school curricula. The development of the vocational guidance campaign was, itself, something of a metamorphosis, chronicled by the U.S. Bureau of Education.

> Those who have watched the vocational guidance movement have seen it broadening out until, originally signifying little more than the giving of limited counsel to individual seekers for employment, it has come to mean an important program affecting fundamentally both education and industry. . . . vocational guidance . . . presupposes a complete remaking of education on the basis of occupational demands.[102]

Many hoped that along with satisfying demands of business and industry, vocational education would solve the problem of a high drop-out rate in St. Louis high schools. As in other schools, St. Louis graduated only a minority of its high-school students. Although the logic failed to account for the many students who left school because of the necessity to work, school officials hoped the promise of a "practical" education would keep students in school. The St. Louis Board of Education minutes for 14 September 1909 preserve board members' expectations that vocational courses would "increase materially the enrollment and persistence in attendance in the high schools. . . . "[103] William Henry Black, president of the Missouri State Teachers' Association, had addressed this point regarding commercial education in 1900. Speaking against the inclusion of commercial courses in the high-school curriculum, Black cautioned,

> Of course, they succeed in getting more students into school because of this course than they had otherwise, but at the same time where they seem to be gaining in one respect, they are losing in another respect. For the sake of numbers, it is always a question whether genuine educational methods should be jeopardized.[104]

Nearly two decades later it was considered common wisdom among educators that vocational education was a key means of keeping students in school. Stephen Colvin assured teachers who read his book, *An Introduction to High School Teaching*, if "the pupil regards a high school course as definitely connected with his future career he is more likely to enter and to remain than if he goes with no very definite object in view."[105] The students whom educators hoped would be drawn to school by vocational education, however, were not expected, by New Liberal thinkers, to possess much cognitive ability. If vocational education was important for keeping students in school, it was even more important that the curriculum "prepare the youth to render intelligent and valuable service to the world of trade."[106] An implicit message made its way to educators: children from working-class backgrounds were to be educated for working-class futures. Those who read *An Introduction to High School Teaching* learned that the

> high school is aiming to give an education to a large number of pupils of varied home training, tastes, and abilities. . . . more and more the demand for vocational and practical education will be voiced, and . . . the older ideas of a cultural and a disciplinary education will be pushed to one side to satisfy the demands of the present day.[107]

Of course, it was the educational policy makers, governmental officials, and business leaders who were doing much of the pushing, but in any case, the high-school curriculum shifted.

The great theme of the differentiated curriculum was that it would enable each student to prepare specifically for the future that was best adapted to his or her individual circumstances. The promise of material prosperity undergirded the rationale for vocational education. But in his essay, "Of the Wings of Atalanta," W.E.B. DuBois unveiled the fatality that awaits a society that proclaims material prosperity as the touchstone of all success. One might have applied his critique to the way in which vocational education was developing in the public schools. DuBois decried the notion that wealth is to be the panacea of every social ill—"wealth as the end and aim of politics, and as the legal tender for law and order; and, finally, instead of Truth, Beauty, and Goodness, wealth as the ideal of the Public School."[108] DuBois revealed the division between academic education and vocational preparation as the false duality it is.

> . . . how foolish to ask what is the best education . . . shall we teach them trades, or train them in liberal arts? . . .the final product of our

training must be neither a psychologist nor a brickmason, but a man. And to make men, we must have ideals, broad, pure, and inspiring ends of living,—not sordid money-getting, not apples of gold.[109]

Vocationalism not only sent students chasing after apples of gold, it implanted the notion that the main purpose of secondary schooling was to find one's role in the great social organism and to prepare for that function. The business of the public school was to "teach the young that each one of them has a place" and to fit the student for it.[110]

THE "BOY PROBLEM"

In 1900, the editors of *School Review* published an article entitled, "Where Are All the High School Boys?" Authors DeYoe and Thurber addressed the phenomenon that had come to be known in education circles as the "boy problem."

> . . . if we are not to have a comparatively ignorant male proletariat opposed to a female aristocracy, it is time to pause and devise ways and means for getting more of our boys to attend high school."[111]

The enrollment pattern that was established in St. Louis high schools in the last decades of the nineteenth century and into the twentieth century was occurring in public high schools throughout the United States. Girls outnumbered boys, often by considerable numbers. In 1888 only one-quarter of the high-school enrollment in the nation's ten largest cities were boys, a fact that then-U.S. Commissioner of Education William Torrey Harris declared "a matter of grave concern."[112] Commissioner Harris' statistics, which showed 20,344 male high-school graduates in 1899, compared to 36,124 female graduates, prompted the editors of the *St. Louis Post-Dispatch* to ask if education was to be abandoned to women.[113] The "boy problem" screamed out at St. Louis readers through the 1902 headline: "SENIORS AT HIGH ARE MOSTLY GIRLS: Young Men Are In Minority In Midwinter Class." After noting that nearly two-thirds of the St. Louis high-school graduates were women, the reporter called attention to the gender disparity in the various courses of study.

> In the classical and scientific courses the young men are hopelessly outnumbered, and in the normal course not a male name appears. In

the business course only do their numbers exceed those of the young women. [114]

In 1892, a year in which girls constituted 72 percent of St. Louis high-school enrollment, the *Annual Report* contained an assessment of the cause, and a possible solution, to the problem. Both highlight the nexus between school and work.

> The prospect of becoming teachers after completing the High and Normal School course seems to be a much stronger incentive than the mere individual training derived from the course. The desire and in many cases the necessity, on the part of boys, to begin remunerative labor influences much more strongly the boy's decision than does [sic] the apparent advantages of a more complete education. . . . Various methods have been tried with the view of making the course apparently more practical, and in this way securing the attendance of a greater number of boys at the High School. [115]

The incidence of boys leaving school to go to work often pointed to the beginning of their careers, which were not dependent upon high-school completion. But in St. Louis, teaching did require that one finish a high-school course of study; thus, a high-school diploma represented a means of entry into one of the few professional options available to women. As John Rury writes, the very feminization of the high school that male critics deplored was a direct consequence of the gender differentiation that they advocated for society in general.[116]

The mere existence of the "boy problem" exposed the illogic of rigid gender differentiation. Although secondary schools had been structured initially for the benefit of boys, girls compiled impressive high-school records in the late nineteenth century while educators worried that boys remained a minority in public high schools. Rather than interpret this situation as a sign that the premise supporting the prevalent gender theory was flawed, schoolmen targeted the "boy problem" as abnormal. DeYoe and Thurber warned, "If our girls continue to outnumber our boys . . . then we have the anomaly of schools attended chiefly by girls, though planned exclusively for boys. . . . "[117] Tyack and Hansot point out that, ironically, in this age of wild "scientific" accusations based on the composite of one's germ plasm, those who wrote about "the 'boy problem' assumed that the cause of male academic failings lay not in the male genes but in a defective school system."[118]

The answer everywhere offered as the solution to the "boy problem" was to make the high-school course of study more practical through the variation of the curriculum. St. Louis school officials announced in 1892,

> Another very desirable reform is suggested by the abnormally small attendance of boys in the High School. This attendance could undoubtedly be increased by adding to the course of study a comprehensive system of manual training.[119]

Although keeping boys in school was the original motive in adding the "practical" courses to the high-school curriculum, changes were made for girls as well, in spite of the fact that they had responded to the academic curriculum quite well. Calvin M. Woodward, a leader in the manual-training movement, argued that withdrawals from the high school were caused by a lack of interest or appreciation for education on the part of students and their parents, ignoring students who left school for work due to economic necessity. Woodward, who served as president of the St. Louis Board of Education, believed that a "hands-on" approach to learning would draw these students to school. He anticipated distinct learning interests for boys and girls.[120]

St. Louis school officials were pleased with the results of the curriculum adjustments. More boys were attending high school and educators were quick to credit the "practical" courses for the progress. The minutes from the Board of Education meeting of 13 June 1899 read: "Manual training, including woodwork and domestic science, does make school more attractive and does increase the attendance. The evidence on this point is strong and uniform."[121] Annual reports continued to include comments on the satisfactory developments concerning the increase in boys' enrollment in the high schools. In 1900, the *St. Louis Post-Dispatch* reported that the proportion of boys in the high school had increased from one-seventh to one-third. The writer of this staff editorial expressed pleasure that the "boys of St. Louis have been waked up at last to their great peril," but warned that a ratio of one to three was still too small. "Unless there is a Jack for every Jill in the High School education will be lopsided and partial."[122] In his study of the St. Louis school system, Selwyn Troen found that an important shift in the distribution of the student population was directly related to new offerings in the high schools. He stated that the new courses substantially increased the relative number of male graduates, from 29.7 percent in 1900 to 42.7 percent in 1920. [123]

Although adding "practical" courses to the differentiated curriculum was the most common approach to ending the "boy problem," some advocated complete segregation of the sexes in the public high school. Course segregation by gender was not a foreign idea to educators in St. Louis. In 1907, Principal Morrison rejected the notion of separate schools for girls and boys, but he was not ready to rule out differentiation within the comprehensive high school, stating, "If with a fuller knowledge of the intellectual needs of boys and girls it can be shown that they should be taught separately in a part or all in their studies and exercises, the question will not be one of building separate schools; it will be simply a question of internal classification." [124] This concept of sex segregation was tried out in only a few places, St. Louis not among them, but the rationale for a sex-segregated program was interesting. Principal J.E. Armstrong of Englewood High School in Chicago explained the advantages of sex segregation in a 1910 article for *The School Review.*

> I fully believe I am justified in the conclusion that the segregation of the sexes during the first and second years of high school holds more boys in school, greatly improves their scholarship, and removes from them the feeling of unfair comparisons due to differences in degree of maturity of children of the same age but opposite sex; and that the possibility of adapting the work to the needs of each sex will make it easy to train each sex for a higher degree of efficiency. [125]

While Armstrong lauded the potential the sex-segregated curriculum held for boys, and duly noted the advantages such a system promised for training students, by gender, for social efficiency, he failed to mention the effects of the program on girls. Would it hold more girls in school or greatly improve their scholarship? These questions did not appear to be of great concern to educators who tackled the "boy problem." To many, the real threat seemed to be that "high schools are in danger of losing their coeducational character and becoming exclusively female seminaries." [126] Educators' response to the "boy problem" was yet another indication that producing female scholars was not a function for the twentieth-century high school.

DOMESTIC FEMINISM

Women were active agents in the transformation of the high-school curriculum. Jane Bernard Powers describes the battle for vocational education for women as one of the first instances in United States history where women were instrumental in shaping educational policy.[127] Domestic feminists maintained allegiance to women's traditional family responsibilities while they sought to expand their roles as "Municipal Housekeepers." The domestic-feminist argument grew out of the nineteenth-century notion that women inhabited a separate but equal sphere, essential for social progress. In contrast to other women's-rights activists in the twentieth century who claimed legal, political, economic, and educational rights for women, domestic feminists proposed that women carry their traditional family role into uncharted social spaces. The domestic-feminist argument bolstered women's participation in a variety of reform issues such as the drive for pure air, food, and water, protective labor legislation, and vocational education.[128] For example, some supporters of female suffrage argued that women's "special" qualities equipped them with crucial civic characteristics that were lacking in the male electorate. As Millicent Rutherford details in her dissertation, "Feminism and the Secondary School Curriculum, 1890-1920," this argument also supported a school curriculum that established separate courses of study for girls and boys.[129]

Opposition to higher education for women was not quite dead at the turn of the century, and it was often countered by the domestic-feminist argument that educated women were better wives and mothers. The *St. Louis Post-Dispatch* coverage of the 1904 general meeting of the American Medical Association featured a paper by Dr. A. Lapthorn Smith, in which he argued against advanced academic study for women, echoing the thirty-year-old claims of Dr. Edward Clarke. Dr. Smith prescribed an education for girls that many supposed would prepare them for the responsibilities of motherhood, a prescription marred by racism as well as sexism. Smith urged, "If the breed that now dominates this continent is to live it must begin, and that soon, the sensible, practical training of its girls."[130] A special report on the "Benefits of College Education for Women," however, was more characteristic of the *Post-Dispatch* position on women's education. The report introduced St. Louis readers to the philosophies of noted educators who supported higher education for women because it equipped them to better occupy "women's sphere," whether in society or at home. New York University Chancellor John H. MacCracken pointed to the new work opening up for women in the emerging political economy, while President Charles F. Thwing of Western Reserve University, Dean Laura D. Gill of Barnard College, and President Thomas Hunter of the Boston Normal College all focused on the college-educated woman as a better wife, mother, and housekeeper. Together the educators presented a case for the importance of a college education in preparing the "complete, perfect women of America."[131] In another article, St. Louis educator Calvin Woodward assured readers that higher education would not diminish a woman's chances at matrimony.[132]

Domestic feminists registered their greatest impact on the differentiated curriculum in the area of home economics, "a progressive-era panacea for the reform of American society . . ."[133] As women's roles were altered in the face of turbulent industrial and urban changes in the United States, home-economic advocates lobbied for its inclusion in the high-school curriculum as a measure to preserve the traditional family. Researcher Ellen Richards, a leader in the home-economics movement, considered the curricular inclusion of domestic science as "nothing less than an effort to save our social fabric from what seems inevitable disintegration."[134] The domestic-feminist agenda included family-related issues such as divorce, money management, declining birth rates, infant mortality, and health, all of which might have been studied under the home-economics banner. Powers draws a distinction, however, between domestic feminists and other family protectionists such as Dr. Smith, Edward Ross, or Robert J. Sprague. Both groups turned to home economics as a way of strengthening the family, but domestic feminists worked from an assumption of women's superior abilities in dealing with social-reform problems and called for the empowerment of women to address the problems. Family protectionists, on the other hand, saw women as capital to be managed in a high-stakes, racist, breeding game. Sprague cast his opposition to women in the workforce in such terms in his article, "Education and Race Suicide," published in the *Journal of Heredity*.

> Women are the capital of the race. The farmer that uses his land for golf-links and deer preserves instead of for crops has but one agricultural fate; so the civilization that uses its women for

stenographers, clerks, and school-teachers instead of mothers has but one racial fate.[135]

Powers reports that domestic feminists and family protectionists agreed on fundamental principles that wielded influence on the school curriculum: the primacy of women's homemaking and mothering role, the importance of separate but equal spheres of influence, and home economics as the vehicle through which young women learned the special skills required to fulfill their predestined role in society.[136] Richards grounded her endorsement of home economics in the New Liberal doctrine of individual role specialization for the advancement of society. "Women will then choose the household as her profession, not because she sees no other way of supporting herself, not because it is a traditional inheritance; but because she will there find the means to give the best of strength and skill and knowledge for the betterment of mankind."[137]

In one sense the domestic feminists who supported home economics, primarily European-American, middle-class women, were very much of the same cloth. Many of the women who supported the domestic-feminist agenda were members of the General Federation of Women's Clubs and the American Home Economics Association.[138] In another sense the domestic feminists who supported home-economics education were a diverse lot; Powers documents the paradoxical essence of the home-economics movement as, at once, traditional and feminist. Traditional in its constancy to women's traditional roles and responsibilities, domestic feminism also encompassed those who sought to expand women's influence on society.[139] Powers discovered that in contrast to the development of vocational education for men, there were no "grand architects" of the vocational-education movement for women. Rather, the pattern of women's influence on educational policy reflected a complexity and diversity of thought shaped by varying effects of race, class, gender, and geography in the formation of vocational education for women.[140]

It is important to note that the core of women who successfully influenced federal policy regarding the institutionalization of home economics were not educators; yet neither was there any organized opposition from women in education.[141] Individual women, however, did voice opposition to the way in which home-economics advocates wanted to transform the high-school curriculum. Willystine Goodsell questioned the proposal of some educators that all girls be required to study home economics. She maintained that if education in domestic science was made obligatory, it would have the effect of training women for one vocation at a time when society demanded efficiency in a multitude of areas.[142] Latin teacher Mary Leal Harkness raised this and other objections in a piercing article published in a 1914 volume of *Atlantic Monthly*. (It is significant to note that Harkness' article appeared in a popular magazine rather than an educational journal.) In "The Education of the Girl," Harkness asked why it should be assumed that inner qualities such as character, taste, and talent in women were similar, when it was widely recognized that in the outward configuration of form and feature, women varied as much from each other as did men.[143] Harkness and Goodsell seem to have accepted the New Liberal faith in role specialization, but they clearly rejected the notion that social roles would be determined on the basis of gender.

High-school girls, too, rejected home economics as a course of study. The best explanations for the low enrollments after 1920 were that girls found the subject matter in home-economic courses was the same as that learned at home or in junior high school, and domestic science did not prepare one for desirable employment or college.[144] In 1928, only 16.5 percent of the students in 14,725 public high schools were enrolled in home-economics classes.[145] By the 1920s, some schools responded to the lack of interest in domestic science by requiring home economics for all girls, but the increasing tendency was for schools to offer elective classes in home economics in place of a prescribed curriculum. Administering home-economics classes independent of prerequisite classes became a parallel trend.[146]

Although home economics as a high-school course of study never developed into the enterprise envisioned by Ellen Richards and her colleagues, Powers reminds us that the influence domestic science brought to bear on girls' aspirations should not be understated.[147] As domestic-science courses were added to the high-school curriculum, widespread support for girls to enroll in advanced algebra, trigonometry, and the sciences faded.[148] Data in chapter 5 documented the sharp drop in St. Louis girls' participation in the Scientific Course that occurred with the introduction of the differentiated curriculum. As domestic feminists and other New Liberals had hoped, the domestic-science wing of the differentiated curriculum reminded students of women's place in the social order.[149]

GENDER IDEOLOGY

Gender ideology undergirded changes in the St. Louis high-school curriculum at the start of the twentieth century. New Liberal thought, vocationalism, the "boy problem," and domestic feminism coagulated into a way of seeing the world that accented sex differences. Just as Victoria Brown discovered in Los Angeles, educators in St. Louis made gender a more salient feature in schools with the move to the differentiated curriculum. [150]

The image of individual cells functioning in an organic body became the defining metaphor in New Liberal ideology. New Liberals tempered role specialization with controlled pluralism. As Violas shows, New Liberal pluralism did not allow each individual a separate identity to be developed according to one's own individual needs and logic, rather it was an ordered diversity in which each individual developed according to the needs and logic of the whole. The society was to be composed of groups, with each individual forging her identity from the group, and all groups connected to the larger social order. [151] Clearly, gender was one of the characteristics New Liberals used to group students. Educators on the national scene identified a course of study suitable for all girls, relegating any other interests a girl might have to secondary status. At the 1910 National Education Association conference, Mrs. W.N. Hutt explained, "Let us have all the purely cultural subjects *for which the girl has time*, but let them be accessories to the useful subjects rather than substitutes for them." [152] New Liberal thinking dictated that girls were to form their identities in accord with society's expectations of women, and that girls' development was to unfold, influenced first and foremost by the needs of society. Writers of the 1910 NEA "Report of Subcommittee on Industrial and Technical Education in the Secondary School" confirmed, "We shall be wise, then, to test every plan for the education of women, not merely with questions of immediate expediency or of *personal advantage, but always with the thought of the larger contribution to the common good*, and the higher function which woman can never surrender." [153]

The late-nineteenth-century shift in ideology had a tremendous impact on the way girls experienced schooling in the United States. As long as the high school operated from an academic center, it remained something of an oasis for girls, separate from the sexist expectations in the larger society. [154] Once the New Liberal directive mandated that schools prepare students for their expected social roles, the gender ideology that dominated society swept into the schools. Americans have long believed in the school's capacity to fashion citizens according to ideological blueprints, and modern scholars continue to document the powerful effect ideological underpinnings have on one's experiences in school. [155] Violas observed of Progressive-Era schooling, that in "all cases, the occupational orientation of the educational experiences worked to reduce the possibility of any but the school-projected future of the child." [156] His observation helps one to discern the force of gender ideology in the schools when juxtaposed against popular conceptions of women's role in the early twentieth century, such as that expressed by Hutt at the 1910 NEA convention. She declared that the

> vocation of every woman is marriage. . . . A woman may study elocution or philosophy, medicine or music, but she will, with it all, wake up some fine morning and find herself in some man's kitchen, and woe be unto her if she has not the knowledge with which to cook his breakfast. [157]

In the emerging formula that equated schooling with role specialization, many argued that stringent academic requirements for girls were superfluous.

In his 1914 text *Democracy's High School*, William D. Lewis captured the essence of New Liberal thinking as it applied to girls' schooling experiences. The following passage exposes the New Liberal concern that schooling train students for particular social roles, that a "practical" curriculum was best suited for this purpose, and that the good of society would take precedence over individualism.

> If the service of the school to the boys was vague and uncertain, its practical value to the great mass of girls approached absolute zero. It has long been evident that the girl who is graduated from the traditional high school is neither better fitted thereby for the duties of a wife, home-maker, and mother, nor efficiently trained to meet the practical problem of self-support. Society, therefore, is beginning to see that her education is very often a mistake both for itself and for the girl. [158]

Again and again educators and other social scientists emphasized the "group characteristics" shared by all girls. Psychologist Winifred

Richmond explained that although "girls differ greatly from each other, yet there are certain fundamental traits and characteristics which we may expect to find in some form in all of them."[159] New Liberals believed that these fundamental traits destined most girls for the roles of "wife, home-maker, and mother"; schooling that did not prepare girls for these roles was considered an aberration. The very operation of the social organism was dependent upon girls training for their domestic roles, according to New Liberal thinking. Psychologist Richmond claimed that women's gender-specific role was the linchpin in the social order.

> The girl of average intelligence is the feminine component of that backbone without which society would disintegrate. She does more, perhaps, than any other single factor to preserve and perpetuate such social organization as the race has worked out.[160]

With the perception that so much was riding on women's service, some demanded that girls study domestic science. Lewis proposed that the "democratic" high school require for every girl

> systematic instruction in those home arts, efficiency in which will largely determine her happiness and service. Woman's knowledge of such matters as these is of vital public concern, and the public had the same right to conserve its own interests by requiring this instruction in the schools it is supporting as the private businessman has to profit in the advancement of his business.[161]

Eighty-five percent of junior high schools in the United States made home economics a compulsory study for girls, but the practice was not generally accepted at the high-school level.[162] Nonetheless, the crusade for social efficiency changed the high-school experience in important ways for girls. John Rury points out that if social efficiency meant stripping the high school of its traditional academic approach, ironically, it also meant changing the curriculum to meet the presumed interests and needs of a group that had already established a solid record of success in the traditional high school: women.[163] In spite of this fallacy, educators were advised to weigh Latin against cooking, solid geometry against dressmaking, and algebra against household duties in the education of their female students.[164] F.J. Jeffrey, principal of the Hadley Vocational School in St. Louis, equated the study of textiles and Latin in a 1934 address before the Educational Committee of the League of Women Voters: "Textiles as taught today in the vocational schools, I believe, give a girl just as much intellectual training as the same amount of time spent on Latin, and at the same time gives her a far greater contact with life."[165] St. Louis educators embraced the notion of social efficiency, stating that the

> nearer the school can approach the healthy situations of actual life in organizing the experiences to which it subjects it pupils, the more successful will it be in fixing habits, producing skill, training judgment, and creating ideals that shall make the individual efficient in the new situation that will confront him.[166]

Given the relentless desire to match one's studies as closely as possible to the assumed situations of actual life, it is likely that many in St. Louis paused to consider the questions posed in a 1911 editorial in *Education.*

> Where does trigonometry apply in a good woman's life? Will it contribute anything toward peace, happiness and contentment in the home? Will it bake any bread, sew on any buttons or rock any cradles?[167]

That "good women" were counseled away from advanced mathematics and other academic subjects was not inconsequential; yet this direction fit nicely into the New Liberal perspective. Not only did traditional academic study seem incongruous with the expected responsibilities of young women, it required an intellectual capacity that many scholars believed to be lacking in girls. Thorndike's conclusion that men more often than women deserved eminence in and leadership of the world's affairs was surely of no small consequence. By 1925, psychologists described the "average girl" in the following light.

> What then can be expected of the average girl? There are certain things we know she cannot do; she cannot fill positions requiring the exercise of much initiative or executive ability; she has little capacity for leadership; she can think very little for herself; she follows her leaders blindly; . . . she is more easily taught and trained, more apt to make an adjustment to her immediate social environment . . . ; by

virtue of her very lack of intellectual ability she accepts things as she finds them and goes with the crowd.[168]

G. Stanley Hall argued, with great fervor, that differences between the sexes were significant. At the 1903 NEA conference, Hall asserted that in "savagery women and men are more alike in their physical structure and in their occupations, but with real progress the sexes diverge and draw apart, and the diversities always present are multiplied and accentuated."[169] Hall encouraged educators to mark these distinctions to their uttermost "to make boys more manly and girls more womanly."[170]

In 1912, a writer for the *Atlantic Monthly* noted that most men acknowledged a "woman's place in the social organism."[171] New Liberal ideology was a gender ideology. New Liberalism was not, however, the only force that reshaped the high-school curriculum. As early as the 1890s, the changing profile of women's work influenced women's secondary education. Changes in women's work, in the home and in the workplace, activated new understandings of girls' education and resulted in a more narrowly defined curriculum for girls in the high school.[172] Vocationalism was another movement that accentuated sex differences in the high school.

By 1930, educators across the United States identified helping students to determine their choice of occupation as a primary responsibility in secondary education.[173] In "Choosing a Vocation: The Origins and Transformation of Vocational Guidance in California, 1910-1930," Harvey Kantor traces the shifting emphasis from vocational guidance to educational guidance that occurred in secondary schools. Initially prompted by concern that students held occupational aspirations incongruent with workplace realities, educators' efforts transitioned from a focus on the labor market to determining course schedules within the school.[174] For many girls, aligning the course of study with workplace realities translated into commercial education. Kantor explains that the emphasis on directing students to appropriate courses of study was reinforced by two changes in the relationship between schooling and the labor market: the formalization of educational requirements for entry into the professions, and the expansion of white-collar work in stores and offices, a sector of the labor force dominated by women.[175]

Although, as Powers and Rury demonstrate, commercial education was the most successful branch of vocational education for women, industrial and domestic education were also promoted as appropriate courses of study for fitting girls for their working futures.[176] In a 1912 essay, Earl Barnes wrote that specialization in industry was destined to result in gender-specific jobs and encouraged his peers to determine "the kinds of work that are specially fitted to women's gifts and limitations."[177] Barnes' conception of the training that would "lead girls into the actualities of the life that lies before them" included industrial and professional preparation, but he concluded that most girls' work "would be connected with children and the service of the home."[178] Thus, Barnes suggested at least two years of domestic-science education for all girls after the age of fourteen.[179] The notion that a girl's education must include domestic science permeated professional educational literature as well as the popular press. A year prior to the publication of Barnes' article, the NEA Committee of Nine took special pains to address the place of women's education in the differentiated curriculum. Again, educators distanced the traditional academic curriculum from girls' educational needs.

> Our traditional ideals of preparation for higher institutions are particularly incongruous with the actual needs and future responsibilities of girls. It would seem that such high-school work as is carefully designed to develop capacity for and interest in the proper management and conduct of a home should be regarded as of importance at least equal to that of any other work. We do not understand how society can properly continue to sanction for girls high-school curricula that disregard this fundamental need. . . .[180]

Victoria Bissell Brown discerned that while educators defended manual-training programs for boys against the charge that they funneled students into specific occupations, no parallel defense was offered regarding home economics for girls. As has been shown, educators consistently prescribed study in domestic science for *all* girls, *because they were girls.* Advocates of manual training praised the program for its developmental potential and for its holistic approach to education. A contrasting philosophy supported the domestic-science course of study for girls. "The destiny of woman being marriage, she should be thoroughly prepared and educated for its duties."[181] While educators claimed to fight mightily against directing boys into some specific channel, they were committed to predicting girls' futures and to organizing schooling to fit that future.[182]

During the Progressive Era, vocationalism turned the school's agenda to preparing students for their life's work. Educators guided students to curricular choices consistent with workplace realities and schools were inoculated with the gender ideology of the labor market. Alongside the availability of job-specific training for girls in office work or industry, vocationalism brought a mandate transcending race and social class: "girls must get ready to be women."[183] It was clear to many that being a woman constituted a girl's life's work.

It is undoubtedly apparent that both the "boy problem" and domestic feminism imposed gender ideology on the high school. Brown observes that educators in the United States became "obsessed with the specter of female dominance" in the high school, worried that girls' greater enthusiasm for their studies would generate a drastic reordering of the gender system. Tyack describes the debate over women's education as transcending pedagogical issues to encompass disputes over gender relationships in the larger society. And Powers marks the treatment of women based on their special characteristics as a turning point in education, the school's contribution to the discussion of the "woman question."[184]

Brown included an explanation of the "scientific" foundation of the "boy problem" in her analysis. Experts argued that cell metabolism was different in the two sexes. "Katabolic" male cells supported active, innovative efforts while "anabolic" female cells were suited for passive, instinctive, repetitive efforts. Educators who believed that girls were, by nature, mediocre, that boys were naturally independent, and who were alarmed by the high percentages of girls in high school, deduced that the traditional high-school curriculum was, itself, weak.[185] From its beginning, the adoption of the differentiated curriculum was a step to make the high school more masculine.[186] Concerns for the effeminization of schooling, however, were not limited to discussions of the "boy problem" at the high-school level. Lynn D. Gordon documented college communities' responses to fears that women's presence on campus threatened male dominance in social and institutional life in her study of *Gender and Higher Education in the Progressive Era*. Gordon connected this activity to controversies over the changing construction of gender in society.[187]

The domestic-feminist concept that women maintained specialized roles in society translated into an argument for sex-specific courses of study in school. Prominent educators broadcast their gender-based message through popular outlets. James E. Russell, Dean of Teachers

College, Columbia University, wrote an article for *Good Housekeeping Magazine* in 1913 in which he not only predicted sex-segregated work for high-school students, but also drew clear distinctions between college-preparatory and domestic-science curricula.

> I fancy that the movement, begun with the introduction of the household arts, will continue until the high-school training for girls who do not go to college will be sharply set off from the college-preparatory course. . . . Consequently I predict a growing tendency to differentiate the work of boys and girls in our high schools.[188]

The domestic-feminist contention that "women had to be socialized and trained for their role as municipal housekeepers" did not sit well with all educators.[189] Latin teacher Mary Harkness argued strenuously against the notion that girls were destined for one occupation alone and the restricted opportunities that such thinking fomented. In 1914 she could see that the trajectory of the differentiated curriculum was off the mark.

> But my objection to the whole movement to "redirect" the education of girls is not that many very good things are not put into the redirected curriculum, but that its whole direction is wrong. . . . that one half of the human race should be "educated" for one single occupation, while the multitudinous other occupations of civilized life should all be loaded on the other half. The absurd inequality of the division should alone be enough to condemn it.[190]

The understanding that girls and boys would prepare for distinct social roles in high school did not, as it turned out, condemn the new curriculum. Powers describes the victory of home-economics education as elusive in that it did not attract a large percentage of girls. Yet its symbolic importance in sanctioning the sex-differentiated curriculum was a significant legacy.[191]

RESPONSE TO THE DIFFERENTIATED CURRICULUM

Edward Krug wrote that in the United States, the great body of secondary-school teachers and principals met the differentiated curriculum and its practical orientation with silent opposition.[192] Apparently, something close to this was the case in St. Louis. A first consideration is that teachers had little, if any, significant input into educational policy decisions. As Richard J. Altenbaugh documents in his essay on "Teachers and the Workplace," scientific management imposed a business model on schools in the early twentieth century that reduced the decision-making role of teachers and relegated all educational considerations to questions of cost. In effect, "Schools became *plants* while school boards assumed the label of the *directorate* and teachers served as the *working force*."[193] Although some early dissent among teachers did surface, most notably under the leadership of Margaret Haley in Chicago, Altenbaugh concludes that protests against the social-efficiency model of schooling were effectively suppressed. St. Louis teachers worked under a yellow-dog contract from 1919 to 1937, but teachers considered it pragmatic to remain silent on educational issues long before the efficiency model swept through the country's schools.[194] Teachers' letters to the editor of the *St. Louis Post-Dispatch*, generally unsigned, acknowledged the insecure nature of their employment and the silence which that imposed, and lamented, "Our souls are not our own. . . . "[195] One editorial referred to teachers' dissatisfaction with "fads," presumably changes in curriculum, and teachers' inabilities to share their professional points of view with school administrators.

> Silently, but, I trust, successfully have the teachers of the St. Louis public schools worked among the patrons of the schools to show how much valuable time is wasted upon fads. The teachers cannot express themselves to either the superintendent or his assistants, for that would mean dismissal. . . . Do not those who do the work, namely, the teachers, know more than either the superintendent or his very many supervisors the needs of the pupils? The teachers at present dare not call their souls their own, but follow blindly and against their intelligence.[196]

Yet high-school teachers' protests against the differentiated curriculum were not totally muffled. Gilbert B. Morrison, who left as principal of the Manual Training High School in Kansas City to become the first principal of the McKinley High School in St. Louis in 1903, wrote on teachers' reactions to the new courses of study with the passion of one committed to ushering in a new system. Morrison's experience, that high-school teachers whose own education had been purely academic were opposed to the "practical" courses of study, should come as no surprise.[197] In a paper written for the Kansas State Teachers' Association, Morrison offered his observations as a seasoned veteran in the curriculum battle: "To advocate Manual Training as a necessary part of a school curriculum has been, until very recent years, to invite the most emphatic opposition of a large majority of our teachers."[198] In another paper prepared for the Missouri State Teachers' Association, Morrison shared some of the issues teachers raised about manual training. They questioned its educational value and its place in the high-school curriculum. Teachers raised concerns about the costs of the newer programs of study and how the additional courses could fit into an already overcrowded curriculum. Teachers were also wary of pedagogical problems involving teaching methods and the new courses of study.[199]

Morrison's perspective on manual-training programs paralleled Calvin Woodward's ideas on the subject. Woodward's support of Morrison was, surely, an influential factor in Morrison's move to St. Louis. In June 1903, Woodward wrote Morrison a letter praising Morrison's recent article in *Manual Training Magazine*, calling it one of the best articles ever written. Woodward went on say, "Of course some people do not like it, the people whom it hits and hits hard, the 'book' people, the 'expression' people, the 'originality' people, the people who want something or anything that is not exact workmanship."[200] Morrison and Woodward teamed up to write a pamphlet in response to the resistance of manual-training programs at NEA conferences, leveling their sights on teachers.

> The question of improvement is a question of educating teachers. We can not change these conditions in a day, a year or a decade. We will do well when we get the teaching fraternity headed in the right direction.[201]

The messages that teachers received in the next few years, in their preparation programs, in their professional literature, and even in the popular press, supported the concept of the differentiated curriculum and headed them in Morrison's "right" direction. St. Louis teachers could read about the new educational theory in their local papers. The *St. Louis Post-Dispatch*, for example, reported that University of Chicago professor George Herbert Locke did not wonder that most boys left high school, given the traditional academic curriculum. Locke's theory exposed a critical question for teachers.

For a great many people Latin, Greek, algebra and kindred subjects have no conceivable practical application. If a teacher is unable to answer the query often made by boys, "What good is this study?" the study ought to be dropped.[202]

Another special article to the *Post-Dispatch* gave attention to Dr. A. Lapthorn Smith's ideas on education.

I would have girls taught the elements in the same manner and to the same degree as boys, but I would cut out algebra, astronomy and all the higher subjects. In their stead I would substitute outdoor sports, cooking, sewing, care of the child, instruction in all that pertains to the marriage relation.[203]

School administrators in St. Louis expressed strong support of the differentiated curriculum in the local press. In 1913, Dr. Calvin O. Davis, "a Harvard educational expert," indicted the St. Louis school system for failing to meet new educational standards. St. Louis school superintendent Ben Blewett jumped to the defense of the system, stating,

Dr. Davis is a theoretical expert, who is very much misinformed as to conditions in St. Louis. Here we have 11 elective courses, designed to meet as wide a range of demand as is possible.[204]

Superintendent Blewett declared that the range of courses offered in St. Louis exceeded that of most cities and emphasized the practicality of the courses of study. Teachers were less enthusiastic about changes in the high-school curriculum.

When Charles Judd's survey team came to the city in the late 1910s, they were, overall, pleased with the condition of the district. Their recommendations, however, indicated that St. Louis educators had not yet fully accepted the doctrine of social efficiency. For instance, school men and women still considered education largely a matter of mental discipline rather than adjusting the pupil to his or her material, social, and spiritual environment. The survey team considered this a distressing example of lack of adaptation to individual needs. High-school physics provided a case in point. "This subject is treated in the same manner for all pupils, boys and girls alike, and with no regard to the particular curriculum followed, and moreover, is required of all pupils."[205]

Some ideas disseminated by *The Cardinal Principles of Secondary Education*, however, were expressed by St. Louis high-school faculty and picked up by the Judd survey team.[206] Many teachers of modern language believed that demanding two years of language study for all students would result in "a general lowering of the quality of instruction" and would prove to be a waste of time for many. Some teachers opposed requiring algebra and plane geometry for graduation. Many mathematics teachers favored differentiated courses in mathematics connected to the students' courses of study, suggesting, as an example, a course in practical arithmetic, algebra, and constructive geometry as part of the Domestic Arts curriculum.[207] School surveys became a celebrated tool of the New Liberal educator. George D. Strayer of Teachers College, Columbia University, conducted another St. Louis survey in 1939. Strayer found that by then a majority of high-school teachers agreed that "the entire curriculum of both elementary and high school should be organized around life problems."[208] Strayer's finding is an indication that national policy trends filtered to St. Louis and, eventually, were accepted by teachers.

Teachers who were slow to accept curriculum transformation were faced with the issue at every professional turn. Attendants at the Missouri State Teachers' Association in 1915 heard C.A. Greene speak on "Desirable Changes in the Present Organization of the Public Schools—The High School." His thesis represented so clearly the wanton attitude that bound children to class-, race-, and sex-biased destinies that a lengthy quotation is appropriate.

> As before mentioned universal education is both recent and still in the experimental stage. Is it to become our weal or woe? Shall we educate the washerwoman's daughter to leave the wash tub? Shall we educate the ditcher's son to leave the ditch? Shall we educate the miner's son to leave the mine? Is this the mission of the teacher or the function of education? If so, who will do our washings in the near future? Who will dig our ditches and lay our sewer and water mains so we may have the modern conveniences and sanitation? Who will work in the mines and bring forth the precious metals and the coal that is now one of the necessities of life? Or shall we keep some ignorant so that this work may be done?. . . May not education in these communities prove a two-edged sword when laborers are

needed in the near future? If education is to be universal we should emphasize the fact that the *needful* activities of one vocation are as important as another, and the educational system should enrich them all.[209]

If newspaper coverage reflected public opinion, schooling for work was an accepted notion in St. Louis, in spite of, perhaps due to, its racist connections. The Sunday Magazine of the *St. Louis Globe-Democrat* featured an article, "Where Waiters Are Trained," on 5 February 1933. Highlighting classes in restaurant service that had been added to the Vashon High School curriculum, the reporter explained that the "art of correct table service has been reduced to a science, has been removed from the old and more or less haphazard manner and placed in the class room."[210] In the course of two decades "scientific table service" overshadowed a tradition of academic study in African American high schools in St. Louis.

Evidence suggests that students' movement to the "practical" courses of study did not reflect student disappointment with their academic studies. Birdie Arbuckle Price collected memories of Sumner High School graduates of the class of 1909 and published them in a volume entitled, *Down Memory Lane: 50th Anniversary Celebration Charles Sumner High School*. Decades after their graduation Sumner high-school students recalled their experiences with mathematics, Latin, science, and rhetoric teachers. The educational philosophy of Principal Oscar M. Waring made a lasting impression: "None can do his best work in all its richness without a sound fundamental education and greatest of all a sterling character."[211] St. Louis Central High School graduate Emily L. Shields won the Washington University scholarship in 1901. When asked about her schooling, seventeen-year-old Shields replied,

I liked all my studies, but found Latin and Greek and literature more attractive than the others. Latin and Greek were particularly easy to me.[212]

The pull to the "practical" studies increased throughout the decade, however, and by 1912 only a small percentage of students remained in the Classical or Scientific Courses of study. In 1909, Principal Morrison reported that 60 percent of the students at McKinley High School were enrolled in the Manual Training or Commercial Courses of study. Some students moved from one course to another at semester's end, with most moving from academic courses to vocational courses. [213] Jeffrey Hirsh noted that the L'Ouverture school exhibit at the 1893 Columbian Exhibition in Chicago spurred an increased interest in manual training. At the same time, African-American boys in St. Louis requested that manual training be implemented at the high-school level. [214] Early school reports that followed the introduction of the manual-training curriculum at Sumner High School documented strong support by students and their parents. [215] But Principal Waring, noted as a "scholar of the old school," considered Latin an indispensable element of education. Unlike many of his St. Louis administrative colleagues, Waring supported classical education after more practical courses were added to the high-school curriculum and Manual Training became a popular course of study. [216]

Morrison attributed the triumph of manual training to popular demand, in contrast to the lack of support from teachers whom, he implied, occupied the farthest outposts of scholarly dissent to the "practical" studies. Morrison contended that manual training courses in schools had been

> brought into being by the people themselves whose instincts are truer
> to their needs than are the learned abstractions of scholasticism. . . .
> The people build and maintain and defend these schools because the
> old ones are inadequate to their needs. [217]

Some members of the St. Louis community did expect the differentiated curriculum to meet students' needs better than the traditional academic curriculum. "A Mother" commended the St. Louis schools on the addition of domestic science to the grammar-school curriculum in her letter to the editor of the *St. Louis Post-Dispatch* dated 1903. She noted that parents of the students who had taken the domestic-science courses were "loud in their praises of the department" and hoped it would be added to all schools. The writer also explained that many students wished to study domestic science instead of the classical or other courses of study in the high school. [218] One Missouri loyalist merged two educational innovations with strong ties to St. Louis, the kindergarten and manual training, into "Show-Me Education" in another 1903 editorial. This writer praised Calvin Woodward and F. Louis Soldan for introducing manual training to the St. Louis curriculum. Arguing that manual training brought the pedagogical strengths of the kindergarten (learning by doing, incorporating fun into learning) to the high school, this citizen urged that the idea of manual training permeate the curriculum through applications in economics, literature, geography, history, physics, botany, geology, natural history, anatomy, and sociology.[219]

African-American support in St. Louis for industrial education similar to that advocated by Booker T. Washington can be traced at least to 1880 when Philip H. Murray established the *St. Louis Advance*, a paper dedicated to "the industrial education of the Negro."[220] Editor Murray dismissed classical education in favor of trade training, writing:

> the engineer had replaced the scholar. . . . The Greek grammarian has been supplanted by the machinist, and the man who would hunt for a hundred years to find out the meaning of a Hebrew dot only illustrates the intellectual fool of our modern times. . . . the great need of the race to-day is a thorough knowledge and the skillful training in the various fields of mechanism and labor.[221]

Some African Americans in St. Louis also supported commercial education. David V. Bohannon edited *The Negro Educational Review: A Monthly Magazine Devoted to the History, Science, Art and Philosophy of Education and to the Professional and Business Interests of the American Negro*, a journal that echoed some strains of the Washingtonian philosophy. E. W. Newsome, chair of the Educational Committee of the YMCA in St. Louis, published an article on commercial education in the journal in which he argued for a business education as an essential part of the school curriculum "and by it see the establishment of our race as essential and important factors in the great business of the world."[222] The new additions to the high-school curriculum, commercial education, domestic science, manual training (and its related component, industrial education), found support across the St. Louis community.

Morrison was convinced that arguments against manual training were not taken seriously by the general population: "Pedagogical vaccination against progress doesn't take with practical people."[223] As a New Liberal educator, Morrison was quick to link the differentiated curriculum to social progress. Perhaps the New Liberal influence on Morrison's work was most apparent, however, in his rationale for the public acceptance of manual training.

Hand training has come into our schools because the social and industrial conditions demanded it. It is being forced by the laity, and not by the teaching profession. They take to it by instinct as one of the necessary means of self preservation. It is only another instance of the universal law of natural selection. [224]

The public support for differentiation at the high-school level that Morrison documented was still apparent in St. Louis two decades later. In 1926, George Counts pointed to elements in St. Louis, both within the school system and without, that favored the establishment of a limited number of highly specialized schools. [225] Although the comprehensive high school had, by then, become a permanent feature of the St. Louis school system, vocational courses flourished and vocational high schools were instituted. In February 1917, the Board of Education recorded its approval of vocational education in an endorsement of the Smith-Hughes Bill. [226] In the late 1920s, organizations such as the St. Louis Radio Trades Association and the Carpenters' District Council offered technical assistance and cooperation in the training of apprentice workers to the St. Louis Board of Education. In 1928 and 1929, parent-teacher associations and the Urban League of St. Louis requested that the Board of Education make provisions for a vocational school open to African Americans. [227] The St. Louis Board of Education finally voted to establish a vocational school for African-American students in 1934, following extensive lobbying efforts led by Reverend George E. Stevens. Stevens addressed the Board on behalf of a General Education Committee, representing eleven African-American organizations, asking for standardized vocational courses and a standardized vocational-education faculty to provide technical training equal to that offered at the Hadley Vocational School for European-American students. European-American opposition to the school, voiced by Edward A. Ferrenbach, centered on anticipated depreciation of property values in the neighborhood designated for the vocational school. It is important to note that Stevens' statement on 10 April 1934 to the Board of Education made reference to mixed opinion regarding vocational education among both African-American and European-American St. Louis citizens. Those opposing the establishment of a vocational school for African Americans had pointed to a lack of unity on the issue from the African-American community in the attempt to stall the efforts of vocational school supporters. But Stevens dismantled that position and pointed to the fundamental concern of the African-American coalition, the racist double-standard in St. Louis schools:

> When the Board decided on Hadley school, it was not the result of their getting a unified statement from the hundreds of thousands of our White citizens. . . . Why, therefore, should there be a unified statement required from the tens of thousands of Colored citizens before we get our school?

> . . . the Board knows that there is a wide-spread, deepening and reasonable unrest among the Colored people due to two things:

> FIRST—The fact that Vocational training for Colored youth at Vashon is not to be compared with that given at Hadley.

> SECOND—They seem to see the stealthy approach and fixity of a double standard in our Public school system as involving the Colored youth. There will be no unrest among us at all necessitating a united expression of complaint and needs if the Board will treat all of the city's children alike. [228]

In 1914, a representative of the Central Trades and Labor Union petitioned the Board of Education, requesting the establishment and maintenance of separate high schools for boys and girls. The board responded by informing the petitioners that

> probably unwittingly, they are giving ear to a gross slander of the sons and daughters of themselves and other citizens. It is recommended further that they be requested to give no heed to the council that seeks to pull to pieces the organization of the high schools which has been justified by a half century of success; but to stand together with other good and intelligent citizens in its support and defense. [229]

The board, solid in its defense of the coeducational high school, considered the differentiated curriculum sufficient in addressing the educational needs of St. Louis youth. It was not sufficient, however, for Mrs. George A. Bass, chair[person] of the Federal Home Demonstration Bureau. In 1920 she urged the Board of Education to make training in home economics compulsory for girls for at least one year in the high schools. Her request was referred to the Superintendent of Instruction. A year later, Jennie Hildenbrandt offered to give the school district a house and lot in the city to be used for a "Home Making School for Girls." The Board of Education, appreciative of the "deep interest in the proper training of young women" that prompted the proffered gift, rejected the property due to the expense that would be entailed to upgrade the building to a satisfactory condition. [230]

The St. Louis community was supportive of vocational education. Few opponents of the differentiated curriculum made their objections a matter of the public printed record. One individual, Charles E. Stetler, addressed the Board of Education regarding the elimination of certain subjects in the high-school curriculum. This happened in the fall of 1927, prior to the collapse of the various courses of study into a single, multitracked curriculum. Stetler was concerned that the further deterioration of academic standards would inhibit the college selection of St. Louis high-school graduates. The Board's response, three months later, was that algebra had not been eliminated from the high schools. The Board further assured that entrance to all colleges in the North Central Association of Colleges and Secondary Schools was granted to high-school graduates without examination, provided they met other requirements. [231]

Stetler's concerns notwithstanding, changes in the high-school curriculum stirred up little in the way of organized protest from the St. Louis community. In the early years of the transition to the differentiated curriculum, an occasional staff editorial in the *St. Louis Post-Dispatch* would lob critical analyses of the developing courses of study into the public arena. A 1901 piece questioned the efficacy of any commercial course of study to provide the essential resources, breadth and vigor of mind, for a successful career in commerce. The writer asked, why not classical and scientific training to erect a broad foundation for general commercial knowledge? [232] The *Post-Dispatch* editorial staff also found fault with industrial training devoid of academic study, arguing that schools devoted to "work and unity" would not be able to turn out "men." [233] The construction of McKinley High School, with its state-of-the-art cooking school and model laundry, prompted another critique of the emerging high-school curriculum. Racist conviction perforated the writer's satirical commentary on domestic science in the high school.

We are going to try all the modern educational experiments, of course. We cannot afford to miss one of them, even though when they are all over we may find that Ah Lee is a better laundryman than our best biologist and Dinah Washington a better cook than our best chemist.[234]

Race was a key factor in public response to the implementation of domestic-science curricula. In October 1900, the *Post-Dispatch* ran an editorial stating that cutting down or changing the education of girls in order to insure a supply of domestic workers would not result in progress.

Girls have begun to learn typewriting and a thousand other things besides cooking, and they will continue to learn them. Why should they be confined to cooking and housework any more than men to gardening and stable duties?[235]

The newspaper staff, however, expressed no concern in constricting African-American girls' education. The next month the *St. Louis Post-Dispatch* carried a story, "Negro Girls Learn Agriculture At Tuskegee Institute," detailing women's work at Tuskegee in dairying, poultry raising, horticulture, gardening, and livestock. Author Isabel C. Barrows explicitly noted that the objective in this course of study was not to prepare students to become "expert" farmers, or to manage large farms. Rather, the young women were expected to apply their knowledge to their own homes. Barrows wrote that the Tuskegee program was "suggestive to other schools, for what colored girls can do. . ."[236] Interestingly, the article included mention of the first group of Tuskegee students rebelling against being forced to work as field hands. But, readers were assured, others were happy to join the class in which "strong, sensible, earnest young women are busy at work learning the mysteries of chicken life."[237] The message to the St. Louis community was that girls, presumably of European descent, must continue to learn "a thousand other things besides cooking," but the "sensible" African-American girl could devote her schooling to agricultural study.

The *Post-Dispatch* ran other editorials and stories on the benefits of bringing the "practical" studies into the curriculum. The writer of a 1901 editorial described manual training as a "triumph of educational effort" in a piece that recaptured Calvin Woodward's initial expectations for schooling that integrated hand and head skills.[238] The rhetoric of supporters of the home-economics movement that swept the nation reached St. Louis, as evidenced by a parent's description of a course in which "How to cook well and with the greatest economy is scientifically explained. . . . "[239] But the contesting headlines and first paragraph of a 1903 *Post-Dispatch* article on domestic science portended the failure of home economics in terms of its own curriculum goals as delineated by Jane Bernard Powers in *The "Girl Question" in Education*. The *Post-Dispatch* writer represented cookery as "the long neglected science," and compared it to "other important scientific subjects," emphasizing the academic foundation of home economics that Ellen Richards worked so intently to have recognized.[240] Yet the headlines belied the claim that home-economics classes would provide opportunity for girls to apply disciplines such as chemistry or environmental science to their work: "HIGH SCHOOL GIRLS LEARN DISHWASHING—Heaviest Kitchen Tasks Come First in Lessons Now Being Given.—FUDGE AND CAKE COME LAST—Pupils Carefully Instructed How to Tell Whether Eggs Are All They Should Be."[241] Teaching dishwashing and egg inspection missed the mark set by home-economics advocates of domestic-science courses.

A review of the St. Louis response to the differentiated curriculum at the turn of the century revealed a lack of strong, organized opposition. The only group identified as resisting the curriculum transformation, teachers, were in no position to press their case. Threat of dismissal served, effectively, to silence teacher opposition. Principal Morrison understood that, with time, the old guard would be replaced by a teaching corps trained to accept the differentiated curriculum. Other groups left evidence that they favored the adoption of the differentiated curriculum. New Liberal ideology surfaced in arguments that schools should help students fit into shifting social and industrial conditions, as expressed by representatives of trade associations and community organizations. The expectation that school should prepare students for their working futures was common to what one might consider the well-meaning efforts of the Carpenters' District Council, the Federal Home Demonstration Bureau, or the Urban League of St. Louis, as well as bolder positions taken by the intellectual elite and like-minded citizens. The letter to the editor of the *St. Louis Post-Dispatch* that put forward the statement that the "country needs its masses trained to work rather than books," differed little from Woodrow Wilson's statement against liberal education for the working class.[242] Historians believe that student and parental support of the differentiated curriculum was connected to vocational aspirations and economic conditions. One parent's letter to the editor of the *Post-Dispatch* expressed concern that the addition of commercial education to the St. Louis high-school curriculum would result in the elimination of the Normal Course, and thereby reduce job opportunities for young women.[243] Although the Commercial Course itself became a popular avenue to jobs for high-school girls, the parent's response is evidence of the strong nexus between schooling and work that developed in the Progressive Era. In short, there was little opposition to the differentiated curriculum because students and parents thought it might meet the economic needs of students while industrial and community groups anticipated benefits for the larger society. Initially, teachers resisted the differentiated curriculum, but their silent opposition was no match against the force of social efficiency spawned by New Liberal ideology. Opponents of the differentiated curriculum came to realize, as one critic of the *Cardinal Principles* noted, "The demand for efficiency borrowed from the world that deals with material things is to govern the educational process. . . . "[244]

CONCLUSION

Educators in St. Louis and across the United States transformed the high-school curriculum in the first years of the twentieth century, setting the stage for secondary schooling for decades to come. The differentiated curriculum was energized by New Liberal ideology, hammered into place by vocationalism, incited by the "boy problem," and sanctioned by domestic feminists. New Liberal thinkers envisaged that "ideal feminine qualities change with changing social ideals" and argued that traditional academic education was an anachronistic ideal for girls.[245] After educators retracked schools to fit students for vocations, educational guidance was on a par with vocational guidance. The message to girls was that they should approach their studies from the perspectives of future wives and mothers most certainly, and perhaps as teachers, office workers, or domestics. The family directive held regardless of the course of study a girl might take, as indicated in an editorial published in the *St. Louis Post-Dispatch*. The writer supported education for women precisely because it was expected to help them prepare for the domestic vocation.

> How can any thinking person say that the higher education is of little use to woman as wives and mothers?. . . Is the life of the home and the family of less importance than the pursuit of some art or industry?[246]

If not contributing to a more explicitly sexist environment, New Liberal ideology, vocationalism, and domestic feminism created a hidden curriculum in schools that taught girls and boys were destined for divergent social roles. Reaction to the "boy problem," however, was never hidden. Only the least perceptive student would have missed the significance of the discussion on the feminization of the high school. A *Post-Dispatch* writer warned the St. Louis community in 1904, "If the boy quits school to go to work before he reaches the eighth grade, while the girl goes forward to the High school, intelligence itself is pretty sure to smack of feminity."[247] The problem brought to mind for this writer by the two-to-one ratio of girls to boys among St. Louis high-school graduates was that women's influence was likely to seep beyond the school: "If to feminize education is deplorable what word of woe will adequately describe the feminization of all social interests."[248] New Liberal thinking, vocationalism, the "boy problem," and domestic feminism accentuated gender differences and forged an ideology that altered girls' experiences in high school.

The differentiated curriculum launched the ascent of domesticated citizen in St. Louis schools. The domesticated citizen represented the quintessential "cell" in the public organism, the citizen schooled for her place in the social order. Her place might radiate from the home to the municipality, but her role was demarcated by women's "special" qualities. A conversion in course of study patterns provided one measure of the shifting emphasis from female scholar to domesticated citizen in St. Louis high schools. Two girls and fifty-four boys graduated from the Scientific Course in St. Louis high schools in 1916, whereas ninety-eight girls and thirty-nine boys had finished the Scientific Course of study in 1903 (table 15). Together the Scientific and Classical Courses claimed 48.9 percent of the European-American girl graduates in St. Louis in 1900, 36.2 percent in 1904, only 9.8 percent in 1908, and 5 percent by 1912. Courses of study designed to prepare girls for "women's place" in society maintained substantial numbers of female graduates after 1908. Together the Commercial and Domestic Art and Science Courses in St. Louis accounted for 15.8 percent of European-American female graduates in 1908, 21.8 percent in 1912, 35.3 percent in 1916, 24.9 percent in 1920, 31.6 percent in 1924, and 22.9 percent in 1928. The percentages were even higher for African-American female graduates for most years: 62.1 percent in 1912, 22.1 percent in 1916, 51 percent in 1920, 47.9 percent in 1924, and 25.1 percent in 1928 (tables 13 and 14). While a student might elect a class in mathematics or science, even if such a class was not required in one's course of study, anecdotal evidence suggests that it was the rare high school girl who did so. The 19 September 1924 issue of *Scrippage*, Soldan High School's student newspaper, included a report on the "fairly large enrollment" of the Chemistry 3 and Physics 3 classes. The writer found it noteworthy to record that three of the twenty-two students in Chemistry 3 were girls; Physics 3 was composed of twenty boys.[249]

This study adds to the recent literature on the history of girls' secondary schooling in the United States. It follows in the wake of the first wave of critical histories of public schools, which focused primarily on class issues. Working from this foundation, historians in the 1980s expanded their analyses to include gender, ethnic, and regional factors. Historians now recognize gender as an analytical variable as important to educational history as class or ethnicity.[250] Rury's work on the connections between the labor market and girls' schooling and Powers' research on the complexities within the vocational education movement for women are excellent national studies. *From Female Scholar to Domesticated Citizen* narrows the scope on the history of girls' high-school experiences by examining the impact of Progressive Era educational policy within one school district. This research complements Brown's study of the Los Angeles High School, allowing for regional comparisons. The St. Louis study broadens the historical analysis by assessing changes across the curriculum, beyond vocational courses, and by comparing the effects of curriculum change on African-American and European-American students. A central emphasis in this text, which distinguishes it from earlier work in the history of women's education, is the function of New Liberal ideology in justifying curriculum changes in the high school as they applied to girls. New Liberal thinkers adjusted schooling to fit students for specialized roles in society; the ideal roles for women absorbed a good amount of attention among those framing the high-school course of study for girls.

While it would be a mistake to write students off simply as pawns of an intellectual elite, in effect retreating to the earlier position of "women as victims" in history, one cannot discount the power of dominant ideology in education. As Geraldine Jonçich Clifford and others have written, "images possess power in their own right."[251] During the Progressive Era, students and teachers made their way through the high-school curriculum, influenced by strong public perceptions of the ideal woman. Tyack and Hansot's comprehensive account of the history of coeducation in American schools appears to overlook this point. They describe schools as places where "gender distinctions were less salient" than in other social environments, due to similar classroom structures of demands and rewards for girls and boys.[252] But as Victoria Bissell Brown indicates, girls and boys were not always in the same classrooms, they did not experience school only in the classroom, and they did not bring the same attitudes, goals, and expectations with them to the classrooms.[253] Students' newspaper reports preserved pieces of the ethos that pervaded the high-school environment. A 1924 issue of Soldan High School's *Scrippage*, for example, relayed visiting principal Merle C. Prunty's comment that ". . . it didn't take much powder to 'catch a man' in St. Louis."[254] An earlier issue covered a meeting of the Round Table Girls in which the members held a formal debate on the question, "Resolved, that the virtues of Apple Sauce far surpass those of Banana Oil."[255] Sources of humor, attitudes, goals, and expectations, including those in the academic arena, are shaped by one's perspective of reality. During the Progressive Era, New Liberal thought generated a gender ideology that, powerfully, shaped students' goals and academic behavior, as well as the attitudes and plans of their parents and teachers.[256] In order to understand the full impact of the differentiated curriculum on girls' high-school experiences at the turn of the century, one must consider the curriculum shift in the context of New Liberal ideology.

The differentiated curriculum conformed to the New Liberal perception of schooling so well that it provoked little discord in St. Louis. Evidence suggests that, aside from some initial resistance from teachers, no other group including students, parents, or community members put forward a sustained effort to oppose the implementation of the differentiated curriculum. This is not to say that no individual rejected the differentiated curriculum and its consequences. Perhaps there were those in St. Louis who agreed with Latin teacher Mary Leal Harkness' evaluation.

The thing against which I pray to see a mighty popular protest is the wasting of children's time, and the dissipation of all their innate powers of concentration, through the great number of studies of minor . . . educational value, which is now one of the serious evils in our schools. And I think that this evil is bearing rather more heavily upon the girls than upon the boys. . . .[257]

In St. Louis, a city proud of the quality of its public education, there was no "mighty popular protest" against the educational evil that disproportionately affected girls.

NOTES

1. *Cardinal Principles of Secondary Education*, Department of the Interior, Bureau of Education, Bulletin 1919, No. 88, (Washington, DC: U.S. Government Printing Office, 1918), 12.

2. John L. Rury, *Education and Women's Work: Female Schooling and the Division of Labor in Urban America, 1870-1930* (Albany: State University of New York Press, 1991), 6; Myra Sadker and David Sadker, *Failing at Fairness: How America's Schools Cheat Girls* (New York: Charles Scribner's Sons, 1994), 32-41; Elisabeth Hansot, "Historical and Contemporary Views of Gender and Education," in *Gender and Education: Ninety-Second Yearbook of the National Society for the Study of Education, Part I*, Sari Knopp Biklen and Diane Pollard, eds. (Chicago: University of Chicago Press, 1993): 12-24; John Modell and J. Trent Alexander, "High School in Transition: Community, School, and Peer Group in Abilene, Kansas, 1939," *History of Education Quarterly* 37 (Spring 1997): 10-11.

3. Victoria Bissell Brown, "The Fear of Feminization: Los Angeles High Schools in the Progressive Era," *Feminist Studies* 16 (Fall 1990): 502, 504-505.

4. For a comprehensive understanding of New Liberalism, see Clarence J. Karier, Paul Violas, and Joel Spring, *Roots of Crisis: American Education in the Twentieth Century* (Chicago: Rand McNally College Publishing Co., 1973), especially Violas, "Progressive Social Philosophy: Charles Horton Cooley and Edward Alsworth Ross," pp. 40-65; Violas, "Jane Addams and the New Liberalism," pp. 66-83; Karier, "Liberal Ideology and the Quest for Orderly Change," pp. 84-107; and Karier, "Testing for Order and Control in the Corporate Liberal State," pp. 108-137; and, Steven E. Tozer, Paul C. Violas, and Guy B. Senese, *School and Society: Historical and Contemporary Perspectives*, 2d ed. (New York: McGraw-Hill, 1995), pp. 102-107. Karier's unparalleled intellectual history, *The Individual, Society, and Education: A*

History of American Educational Ideas, 2d ed. (Urbana: University of Illinois Press, 1986) puts New Liberalism in the context of educational thought throughout United States history. Violas assesses the impact of New Liberal intellectuals and educators on schooling in *The Training of the Urban Working Class: A History of Twentieth-Century American Education* (Chicago: Rand McNally College Publishing Co., 1978).

5. Tozer, Violas, and Senese, *School and Society*, 105.

6. Karier, "Liberal Ideology and Orderly Change," 87.

7. Historians acknowledge that New Liberal efforts for more effective means of social control emerged, in part, from a genuine concern for poverty-induced human suffering in urban America. See Violas, "Jane Addams and the New Liberalism," 68, and Jane Bernard Powers, *The "Girl Question" in Education: Vocational Education for Young Women in the Progressive Era* (London: The Falmer Press, 1992), 1.

8. Karier, "Liberal Ideology and Orderly Change," 105-106; Violas, *Training of the Working Class*, 230.

9. Karier, "Liberal Ideology and Orderly Change,"105-106; Violas, "Jane Addams and the New Liberalism," 83.

10. Karier, Violas, and Spring, *Roots of Crisis*, 3.

11. Gail P. Kelly, "Response to Angus's 'Conflict, Class, and the Nineteenth-Century Public High School in the Cities of the Midwest, 1845-1900,'" *Curriculum Inquiry* 18 (1988): 87. See also Michael Apple, *Ideology and Curriculum* (London: Routledge and Kegan Paul, 1979); Samuel Bowles and Herbert Gintis, *Schooling in Capitalist America: Educational Reform and the Contradictions of Economic Life* (New York: Basic Books, 1976); Michael Katz, *Class, Bureaucracy and Schools: The Illusion of Educational Change in America* (New York: Praeger, 1971); Edward A. Krug, *The Shaping of the American High School, 1880-1920* (Madison: University of Wisconsin Press, 1964); Joel Spring, *Education and the Rise of the Corporate State* (Boston: Beacon Press, 1972). Other educational historians who take a critical perspective on schools include James D. Anderson, *The Education of Blacks in the South, 1860-1935* (Chapel Hill: University of North Carolina Press, 1988); Brown, "The Fear of Feminization"; Harvey A. Kantor, *Learning to Earn: School, Work, and Vocational Reform in California, 1880-1930* (Madison: University of Wisconsin Press, 1988); and William J. Reese, *The Origins of the American High School* (New Haven: Yale University Press, 1995).

12. *On the Origin of Species* marked a watershed in western intellectual thought. Darwin's theory, that life is in a constant state of flux, permeated areas of scholarly activity other than biology such as philosophy, religion, law, and education. The Enlightenment belief in an orderly, mechanical universe gave

way to a new vision of the world as a living, evolving organism. The organic metaphor was used frequently in the early twentieth century in reference to the organization of society. The St. Louis *Annual Report* of 1908, in a discussion on the function of the high school, noted that social institutions "are not the *a priori* creations of the philosophers and statesmen, but shape themselves through a slow process of development. They never can transcend in spirit or in practice the intellectual and moral state of the community of whose social life they are the organs." (*Fifty-Fourth Annual Report of the Board of Education of the City of St. Louis, Mo. for the Year Ending June 30, 1908* [St. Louis: Buxton & Skinner Stationery Company, 1909], 54:121.) In 1914, Superintendent Ben Blewett, writing on the importance of the school taking on other social functions, stated the "analogy between the process of development of social institutions and of the organs in plant or animal life is not a strained analogy." (*Sixtieth Annual Report of the Board of Education of the City of St. Louis, Mo., for the Year Ending June 30, 1914* [N.p., n.d.], 60: 303-304.)

13. For a complete discussion of Cooley's and Ross's social theories, see Violas, "Progressive Social Philosophy," *Roots of Crisis*, 40-65.

14. Paul H. Hanus, *Educational Aims and Educational Values* (New York: Macmillan, 1908), 19.

15. David Snedden, *Problems of Educational Readjustment* (Boston: Houghton Mifflin , 1913), 19.

16. Ibid., 21.

17. Edward L. Thorndike and Arthur I. Gates, *Elementary Principles of Education* (New York: Macmillan, 1929), 26. See Clarence J. Karier's assessment of Thorndike's influence in *Scientists of the Mind: Intellectual Founders of Modern Psychology* (Urbana: University of Illinois Press, 1986), 91.

18. Thorndike and Gates, *Elementary Principles*, 36.

19. Ibid., 26.

20. Ibid., 305-306.

21. Alexander Inglis, *Principles of Secondary Education* (Boston: Houghton Mifflin , 1918), 387.

22. Ibid., 417.

23. George Herbert Betts, *Social Principles of Education* (New York: Charles Scribner's Sons, 1912), vii.

24. William Heard Kilpatrick, *Education for a Changing Civilization: Three Lectures Delivered on the Luther Laflin Kellogg Foundation at Rutgers University, 1926* (New York: Macmillan, 1931), 111-112.

25. William Chandler Bagley, *Educational Values* (New York: Macmillan, 1912), 146-147.

26. Betts, *Social Principles,* 267-268, 275.

27. George S. Counts, *The Social Foundations of Education* (New York: Charles Scribner's Sons, 1934), 538; Kilpatrick, *Education for a Changing Civilization*, 21.

28. Thorndike and Gates, *Elementary Principles*, 320.

29. Inglis, *Principles of Secondary Education*, 3.

30. Quoted in Violas, "Jane Addams and the New Liberalism," 82.

31. Quoted in Violas, "Progressive Social Philosophy," 48.

32. Quoted in James W. Lichtenberg, "The Adolescent Girl—1925," *Journal of Counseling and Development* 63 (February 1985): 342.

33. *St. Louis Annual Report* 60: 309.

34. *St. Louis Board of Education Curriculum Bulletin* no. 1 (N.p. 1926), 7.

35. Quoted in Violas, "Progressive Social Philosophy," 48.

36. Edward L. Thorndike, "Intelligence and Its Uses," in *Shaping the American Educational State: 1900 to the Present*, Clarence J. Karier, ed. (New York: The Free Press, 1975), 232.

37. Ellwood P. Cubberley, *Public Education in the United States: A Study and Interpretation of American Educational History* (Boston: Houghton Mifflin, 1919), 451.

38. Booker T. Washington, "Atlanta Exposition Address of 1895," in Tozer, Violas, and Senese, *School and Society*, (New York: McGraw-Hill, 1995), 179.

39. Quoted in Tozer, Violas, and Senese, *School and Society*, 206-207.

40. Cubberley, *Public Education in the United States*, 377.

41. Lewis M. Terman, "The Conservation of Talent," in *Shaping the American Educational State: 1900 to the Present*, Clarence J. Karier, ed. (New York: The Free Press, 1975), 189.

42. Charles H. Judd, *Survey of the St. Louis Public Schools*, 3 vols. (Yonkers-on-Hudson, NY: World Book Company, 1918), 2: 355.

43. Krug, *Shaping of the American High School*, (Madison: University of Wisconsin Press, 1964), 1: 250.

44. Cubberley, *Public Education in the United States*, 368; Stephen Sheldon Colvin, *An Introduction to High School Teaching* (New York: Macmillan, 1917), 5. Emphasis added.

45. William D. Lewis, *Democracy's High School* (Boston: Houghton Mifflin, 1914), 5, 20.

46. Ibid., 5, 20, 111-113.

47. *St. Louis Annual Report* 60: 309.

48. Ibid., 311.

49. Judd, *Survey of the St. Louis Public Schools*, 2: 314.

50. *St. Louis Board of Education Curriculum Bulletin*, 7.

51. George S. Counts, *The Senior High School Curriculum* (Chicago: University of Chicago, 1926), 149.

52. Quoted in Krug, *Shaping of the American High School, 1920-1941*, 2 vols. (Madison: University of Wisconsin Press, 1972), 1: 252.

53. Quoted in Krug, 1: 252.

54. Quoted in Krug, 1: 277.

55. *St. Louis Annual Report* 60: 317.

56. *Seventy-Fourth Annual Report of the Board of Education of the City of St. Louis, Mo., for the Year Ending June 30, 1928* (N.p., n.d.), 74: 35.

57. *Seventy-Sixth Annual Report of the Board of Education of the City of St. Louis, Mo., for the Year Ending June 30, 1930* (N.p., n.d.), 76: 40-42.

58. Ibid.

59. Edward A. Krug, *The Shaping of the American High School* 2: 136.

60. Cubberley, *Public Education in the United States*, (Boston: Houghton Mifflin, 1919), 378-379.

61. Karier, *Shaping the American Educational State*, (New York: The Free Press, 1975), 233.

62. Cubberley, *Public Education in the United States*, 376.

63. Quoted in Karier, *Shaping the American Educational State*, 163.

64. *St. Louis Board of Education Curriculum Bulletin*, 7.

65. Quoted in Krug, *Shaping of the American High School*, 1: 294.

66. Thorndike, "Intelligence and Its Uses," in *Shaping the American Educational State*, 230.

67. Karier, *Shaping the American Educational State*, 162; Edward L. Thorndike, *Individuality* (Boston: Houghton Mifflin, 1911), 27.

68. Lewis M. Terman, *The Measurement of Intelligence: An Explanation of and a Complete Guide for the Use of the Stanford Revision and Extension of the Binet-Simon Intelligence Scale* (Boston: Houghton Mifflin, 1916), 11.

69. Ibid., 17. For a critical examination of primary documents relating to intelligence testing in United States schools, see Karier, *Shaping the American Educational State*, especially chapter 5, "Testing, Predicting, Sorting and Tracking," chapter 6, "IQ, Dysgenics and Racism," and chapter 9, "The Nature-Nurture Debate: Towards a False Consciousness." Also see Horace Mann Bond's analyses of IQ testing, including "Some Exceptional Negro Children," *The Crisis* 34 (1927): 257-259, 278, 280 and "Intelligence Tests and Propaganda," *The Crisis* 15 (1924): 61-64.

70. Cubberley, *Public Education in the United States*, 452.

71. Quoted in Krug, *Shaping of the American High School*, 2: 95.

72. Thorndike, *Individuality*, 33-34.

73. Lewis M. Terman, "Were We Born That Way?" in Karier, *Shaping the American Educational State*, 206.

74. Edward L. Thorndike, *Educational Psychology*, 2d ed. (New York: Teachers College, Columbia University, 1910), 35.

75. *Sixty-Eighth Annual Report of the Board of Education of the City of St. Louis, Mo., for the Year Ending June 30 1922* (N.p., n.d.), 68: 31-49.

76. Ibid., 53.

77. *Seventy-First Annual Report of the Board of Education of the City of St. Louis, Mo., for the Year Ending June 30 1925* (N.p., n.d.), 71: 46.

78. *St. Louis Annual Report* 74: 28.

79. Thorndike, "Intelligence and Its Uses," 232.

80. Ernest C. Moore, "Is the Stress Which Is Now Being Put upon the Practical Interfering with the Idealistic Training of Our Boys and Girls?" *School and Society* 5 (1917): 366.

81. Quoted in William Henry Black, "Present Educational Problems in Missouri" (President's Address at the Meeting of the State Teachers' Association, Jefferson City, Missouri, 1900), 6.

82. Rury, *Education and Women's Work*, 149-151.

83. *Forty-Seventh Annual Report of the Board of Education of the City of St. Louis, Mo., for the Year Ending June 30, 1901* (St. Louis: Nixon-Jones Printing Company, 1902), 47: 64-65.

84. Clarence D. Kingsley, "Report of the Committee of Nine on the Articulation of High School and College," *National Education Association Journal of Proceedings and Addresses* 49 (1911): 561.

85. Hanus, in introduction to Meyer Bloomfield, *The Vocational Guidance of Youth* (Boston: Houghton Mifflin, 1911), viii-ix. Marvin Lazerson and W. Norton Grubb's edited volume, *American Education and Vocationalism: A Documentary History 1870-1970* (New York: Teachers College Press, 1974), is a cornerstone document in vocational educational history in the United States. Other key secondary sources are Walter Feinberg and Henry Rosemont, eds., *Work, Technology, and Education: Dissenting Essays in the Intellectual Foundations of American Education* (Urbana: University of Illinois Press, 1976); Harvey Kantor and David B. Tyack, eds., *Work, Youth, and Schooling: Historical Perspectives on Vocationalism in American Education* (Stanford: Stanford University Press, 1982); Kantor, *Learning to Earn* (Madison: University of Wisconsin Press, 1988); Kantor, "Work, Education, and Vocational Reform: The Ideological Origins of Vocational Education, 1890-1920," *American Journal of Education* 94 (August 1986): 401-426; Kantor, "Choosing a Vocation: The Origins and Transformation of Vocational Guidance in California, 1910-1930," *History of Education Quarterly* 26 (Fall

1986): 351-375; Marvin Lazerson, *Origins of the Urban School: Public Education in Massachusetts, 1870-1915* (Cambridge: Harvard University Press, 1971); Spring, *Education and the Corporate State,* and Violas, *Training of the Urban Working Class.* Vocational education is also addressed in Raymond Callahan, *Education and the Cult of Efficiency* (Chicago: University of Chicago Press, 1962); Lawrence Cremin, *Transformation of the School: Progressivism in American Education, 1876-1957* (New York: Alfred A. Knopf, 1961); Berenice M. Fisher, *Industrial Education: American Ideals and Institutions* (Madison: University of Wisconsin Press, 1967); Jurgen Herbst, *The Once and Future School: Three Hundred and Fifty Years of American Secondary Education* (New York: Routledge, 1996); Krug, *Shaping of the American High School*; David Nasaw, *Schooled to Order: A Social History of Public Schooling in the United States* (New York: Oxford University Press, 1979); Spring, *The American School 1642-1993*, 3d ed. (New York: McGraw-Hill, 1994); Tozer, Violas, and Senese, *School and Society*; (New York: McGraw-Hill, 1995); and, David B. Tyack, *The One Best System* (Cambridge: Harvard University Press, 1974). See the governmental documents "Progress in Vocational Education," *Report of the Commissioner of Education, 1914* (Washington, DC: U.S. Government Printing Office, 1915), U.S. Bureau of Education, "Vocational Secondary Education," *Bulletin* no. 21 (Washington, DC: U.S. GPO, 1916), and W. Carson Ryan, *Vocational Guidance and the Schools*, U.S. Bureau of Education, Bulletin no. 24, 1918 (Washington, DC: U.S. GPO, 1919), and Vocational *Education Magazine* for primary sources, along with David Snedden, *Problems of Educational Readjustment* (Boston: Houghton Mifflin, 1913) and Snedden, *Vocational Education* (New York: Houghton Mifflin, 1920). Albert H. Leake's, *The Vocational Education of Girls and Women* (New York: MacMillan, 1918), is a helpful primary source on vocational education for women. The Gerritsen Collection of Women's History contains a number of sources regarding vocational education: Vocation Office for Girls, *Bulletin* (Boston: Girls Trade Education League, 1911-1913); Anna Steese Sausser Richardson, *The Girl Who Earns Her Own Living* (New York: B.W. Dodge, 1909); William Arch McKeever, *The Industrial Training of the Girl* (New York: Macmillan, 1914); New York Bureau of Vocational Education, *News-Bulletin*; Women's Educational and Industrial Union, Boston, Dept. of Research, *The Public Schools and Women in Office Service* (Boston: The Union, 1914); Edith A. Barnett, *The Training of Girls for Work: An Expression of Opinions* (London: Macmillan, 1894); and, Marguerite Stockman Dickson, *Vocational Guidance for Girls* (Chicago: Rand McNally, 1919). Secondary sources on vocational education for women include Powers, *The "Girl Question" in Education*; (London: The Falmer Press, 1992); John L. Rury,

Education and Women's Work: Female Schooling and the Division of Labor in Urban America, 1870-1930 (Albany: State University of New York Press, 1991); Rury, "Vocationalism for Home and Work: Women's Education in the United States 1880-1930," in *The Social History of American Education*, B. Edward McClellan and William J. Reese, eds. (Urbana: University of Illinois Press, 1988); David Tyack and Elisabeth Hansot, *Learning Together: A History of Coeducation in American Public Schools* (New Haven: Yale University Press, 1990); and Geraldine Jonçich Clifford, "'Marry, Stitch, Die, or Do Worse': Educating Women for Work," in Kantor and Tyack, *Work, Youth, and Schooling* (Stanford: Stanford University Press, 1982).

86. Cubberley, *Public Education in the United States*, (Boston: Houghton Mifflin, 1919), 416.

87. In 1882, an editorial writer noted that "The profession of teaching has fairly run mad in search of the royal road which leads to the practical." (Quoted in Krug, *Shaping of the American High School*, 1: 15.) The differentiated curriculum became the "royal road to the practical" in U.S. schools during the twentieth century.

88. W. Carson Ryan, Jr., *Vocational Guidance and the Public Schools*, prepared for the Bureau of Education of the Department of the Interior (Washington, DC: U.S. GPO, 1919), 100.

89. Quoted in Krug, *Shaping of the American High School*, 1: 246.

90. *Fifty-Seventh Annual Report of the Board of Education of the City of St. Louis, Mo. , for the Year Ending June 30, 1911* (N.p., n.d.), 57:67.

91. Hanus, in Bloomfield, *Vocational Guidance*, x.

92. Quoted in Willystine Goodsell, *The Education of Women: Its Social Background and Its Problems* (New York: Macmillan, 1923), 193.

93. Lewis, *Democracy's High School*, (Boston: Houghton Mifflin, 1914), 75.

94. Kingsley, "Report of the Committee of Nine," 565.

95. Quoted in Krug, *Shaping of the American High School*, 1: 225.

96. Clarence D. Kingsley, "The High-School Period as a Testing-Time," *National Education Association Addresses and Proceedings* 51 (1913): 51.

97. Stuart Ewen, *Captains of Consciousness: Advertising and the Social Roots of the Consumer Culture* (New York: McGraw-Hill, 1976), 203.

98. Judd, *Survey of the St. Louis Public Schools*, 2: 310, 355.

99. Ibid., 303.

100. Cubberley, *Public Education in the United States*, (Boston: Houghton Mifflin, 1919), 419-420.

101. *Seventy-Second Annual Report of the Board of Education of the City of St. Louis, Mo., for the Year Ending June 30, 1926* (N.p., n.d.), 72: 53.

102. Ryan, *Vocational Guidance and the Public Schools*, 98.

103. *Official Proceedings of the Board of Education of St. Louis* 16 (July 1st, 1909 to June 30th, 1910), 16: 175.

104. Black, "Present Educational Problems in Missouri," president's address at the meeting of the State Teachers' Association, Jefferson City, Mo., 1900, 6.

105. Colvin, *Introduction to High School Teaching*, (New York: Macmillan, 1917), 38.

106. J.J. Sheppard, "The New Departure in Secondary Education," *National Education Association Addresses and Proceedings* 43 (1904): 114.

107. Colvin, *Introduction to High School Teaching*, 19-20.

108. W.E.B. DuBois, "Of the Wings of Atalanta," in *The Souls of Black Folk* (New York: Vintage Books, 1990), 61.

109. Ibid., 67.

110. Moore, "Stress upon the Practical," 366.

111. Quoted in Tyack and Hansot, *Learning Together*, (New Haven: Yale University Press, 1990), 174. See chapter 7, "Differentiating the High School: The "Boy Problem," pp. 165-200 for Tyack and Hansot's comprehensive analysis of the "boy problem."

112. Quoted in Rury, *Education and Women's Work*, (Albany: State University of New York Press, 1991), 19.

113. "Women and Education," *St. Louis Post-Dispatch*, 23 Feb. 1901.

114. "SENIORS AT HIGH ARE MOSTLY GIRLS: Young Men Are In Minority In Midwinter Class," *St. Louis Post-Dispatch*, 19 Jan. 1902.

115. *Thirty-Eighth Annual Report of the Board of President and Directors of the St. Louis Public Schools for the Year Ending June 30, 1892* (St. Louis: The Mekeel Press, 1893), 38: 41-42.

116. Rury, *Education and Women's Work*, 24.

117. F.E. DeYoe and C.H. Thurber, "Where Are the High-School Boys?" *The School Review: A Journal of Secondary Education* 8 (April 1900): 241.

118. Tyack and Hansot, *Learning Together*, 170.

119. "Facts Concerning One Hundred Years of Progress in the Public Schools of St. Louis 1838-1938," *Public School Messenger* 35 (3 January 1938): 63.

120. A distinction should be made between Woodward's original conception of manual training and the movement that was later labeled as "industrial training" or "vocational education." Woodward intended manual training to be a supplement to, rather than a replacement for, academic learning. Also, manual training was to enhance the education of all students, unlike vocational training, which as part of the differentiated curriculum was reserved for those students whom educators deemed incapable of academic study. See

C.M. Woodward, *Manual Training in Education* (London: Walter Scott, Charles Scribner's Sons, 1892); Selwyn K. Troen, *The Public and the Schools: Shaping the St. Louis System, 1838-1920* (Columbia: University of Missouri Press, 1975), 166-174; *Forty-Sixth Annual Report of the Board of Education of the City of St. Louis, Mo., for the Year Ending June 30, 1900* (St. Louis: Buxton & Skinner Stationery Co., 1901), 46: 27.

121. *Printed Record of the Board of Education of the City of St. Louis* 11 (April 11th, 1899 to June 11th, 1901): 124.

122. "Jack and Jill In the High School," *St. Louis Post-Dispatch*, 8 Feb. 1900.

123. Troen, *The Public and the Schools*, (Columbia: University of Missouri Press, 1975), 188.

124. Gilbert B. Morrison, "The Scope and Content of the District High School" (Paper delivered at the Pennsylvania Teachers' Association, Philadelphia, February 1907), 11. Gilbert Morrison Papers.

125. J.E. Armstrong, "The Advantages of Limited Sex Segregation in the High School," *The School Review: A Journal of Secondary Education* 18 (May 1910): 350.

126. DeYoe and Thurber, "Where Are the High-School Boys?" 236.

127. Powers, *The "Girl Question" in Education*, (London: The Falmer Press, 1992), 49; Millicent Rutherford, "Feminism and the Secondary School Curriculum, 1890-1920" (Ph.D. diss., Stanford University, 1977), 2.

128. Powers, *The "Girl Question" in Education*, 16, 24; Rury, *Education and Women's Work*, 12-13, 136.

129. Rutherford, "Feminism and the Secondary School Curriculum," 26.

130. "Higher Education Ruinous To Women," *St. Louis Post-Dispatch*, 9 June 1904.

131. "Benefits of College Education for Women," *St. Louis Post-Dispatch*, 23 June 1901.

132. Rose Marion, "College Girls and Dan Cupid," *St. Louis Post-Dispatch*, 24 June 1902.

133. Powers, *The "Girl Question" in Education*, 13. Powers' text is the best source for learning about the origin and development of vocational education for women in the United States in the years between 1900 and 1930. John Rury's *Education and Women's Work, 1870-1930* is also invaluable for a study of women's vocational education. For a study of home economics, these texts can be supplemented with Tyack and Hansot, *Learning Together*; Clifford, "'Marry, Stitch, Die, or Do Worse'"; and Emma Seifrit Weigley, "It Might Have Been Euthenics: The Lake Placid Conferences and the Home Economics Movement," *American Quarterly* 27 (Spring 1975): 79-86. For primary sources

on home economics during the Progressive era consult the *Journal of Home Economics* and publications of the National Society for the Promotion of Industrial Education (later known as the National Society for the Promotion of Vocational Education.) A reader might find the following governmental publications useful: *Annual Report of the Commissioner of Education, 1909*, vol. 1; *Education of the Home*, Bulletin No. 18, Bureau of Education, 1911; "Homemaking as a Vocation for Girls," in *Cooking in the Vocational School*, Bulletin No. 1, U.S. Bureau of Education, 1915; *Home Economics Education Organization and Administration*, Bulletin No 28, Home Economics Series No. 2, (Washington, DC: U.S. GPO, 1919); "Manual Arts and Homemaking Subjects," *Annual Report of the Commissioner of Education, 1920* (Washington, DC: U.S. GPO, 1921); and, *Vocational Education in Home Economics* (Washington, DC: U.S. GPO, 1930). Other primary sources on home economics include P.I. Ellis, *Americanization through Homemaking* (Los Angeles: Wetzel, 1929); Leake, *Vocational Education of Girls*; Harkness, "The Education of the Girl"; Ellen Richards, "The Present Status and Future Development of Domestic Science Courses in High School," in *Fourth Yearbook of the National Society for the Scientific Study of Education* (Bloomington: Pantagraph Printing and Stationery Company, 1903): 39-52; and, Richards, "The Social Significance of the Home Economics Movement," *Journal of Home Economics* 3 (1911): 116-122.

134. Quoted in Rury, *Education and Women's Work*,(Albany: State University of New York Press, 1991), 140; Powers, *The "Girl Question" in Education,* 12, 17.

135. Quoted in Goodsell, *Education of Women*, (New York: Macmillan, 1923), 34; Powers, *The "Girl Question" in Education,* 17-19.

136. Powers, *The "Girl Question" in Education,* 19.

137. Quoted in Krug, *Shaping of the American High School*, (Madison: University of Wisconsin Press, 1969), 1: 230.

138. Ibid., 16-17.

139. Powers, *The "Girl Question" in Education*, 4, 13.

140. Ibid., 10, 22-23.

141. Ibid., 80; Rutherford, "Feminism and the Secondary School Curriculum," Ph.D. diss., Stanford University, 1977, 86.

142. Goodsell, *Education of Women*, 110-112.

143. Mary Leal Harkness, "The Education of the Girl," *Atlantic Monthly* 113 (March 1914): 325.

144. Powers, *The "Girl Question" in Education,* 95; Rury, *Education and Women's Work*, 164-168.

145. Powers, *The "Girl Question" in Education,* 95.

146. Henrietta W. Calvin, *Home Economics Education*, prepared for the Bureau of Education of the Department of the Interior (Washington, DC: U.S. GPO, 1923), 6.

147. Powers, *The "Girl Question" in Education,* 83, 94-95, 97.

148. Rutherford, "Feminism and the Secondary School Curriculum," 173.

149. Powers, *The "Girl Question" in Education*, 97.

150. Brown, "Fear of Feminization," *Feminist Studies* 16 (Fall 1990): 511.

151. Violas, "Progressive Social Philosophy," *Roots of Crisis* (Chicago: Rand McNally, 1973), 57. See the section, "Controlled Pluralism," pp. 56-60, for in-depth treatment of this concept.

152. Mrs. W.N. Hutt, "The Education of Women for Home-Making," *Journal of Proceedings and Addresses of the National Education Association* 48 (1910): 48: 132. Emphasis added.

153. "Report of the Subcommittee on Industrial and Technical Education in the Secondary School," *NEA Proceedings*, 48: 761. Emphasis added.

154. Rury, *Education and Women's Work*, 4-10; 211-216; Tyack and Hansot, *Learning Together*.

155. See, for example, American Association of University Women, *How Schools Shortchange Girls* (Wellesley: American Association of University Women Educational Foundation and National Education Association, 1992); Jean Anyon, "Social Class and School Knowledge," in *Curriculum Inquiry* (Ontario: John Wiley & Sons, 1981); Michael W. Apple, *Ideology and Curriculum* (London: Routledge & Kegan Paul, 1979); Michael W. Apple and Lois Weis, eds., *Ideology & Practice in Schooling* (Philadelphia: Temple University Press, 1983); Mary Field Belenky, Blythe McVicker Clinchy, Nancy Rule Goldberger, and Jill Mattuck Tarule, *Women's Ways of Knowing: The Development of Self, Voice, and Mind* (New York: Basic Books, 1986); Kathleen P. Bennett and Margaret D. LeCompte, *How Schools Work: A Sociological Analysis of Education* (New York: Longman, 1990); Sari Knopp Biklen and Diane Pollard, eds., *Gender and Education, Ninety-second Yearbook of the National Society for the Study of Education* Part I (Chicago: University of Chicago Press, 1993); Paulo Freire, *Pedagogy of the Oppressed* (New York: Herder and Herder, 1972); Henry A. Giroux, *Ideology, Culture, and the Process of Schooling* (Philadelphia: Temple University Press, 1981); bell hooks, *Teaching to Transgress: Education as the Practice of Freedom* (New York: Routledge, 1994); Jane Roland Martin, *Reclaiming a Conversation: The Ideal of the Educated Woman* (New Haven: Yale University Press, 1985); Jane Roland Martin, *Changing the Educational Landscape: Philosophy, Women, and Curriculum* (New York: Routledge, 1994); Sonia Nieto, *Affirming Diversity: The Sociopolitical Context of Multicultural*

Education (New York: Longman, 1992); Jeanne Oakes, *Keeping Track: How Schools Structure Inequality* (New Haven: Yale University Press, 1985); John U. Ogbu and Margaret Gibson, eds., *Minority Status and Schooling: A Comparative Study of Immigrant and Involuntary Minorities* (New York: Garland, 1991); William Peters, *A Class Divided: Then and Now* (New Haven: Yale University Press, 1987); Sanford W. Reitman, *The Educational Messiah Complex: American Faith in the Culturally Redemptive Power of Schooling* (Sacramento: Caddo Gap Press, 1992); Eric Rofes, "Opening Up the Classroom Closet: Responding to the Educational Needs of Gay and Lesbian Youth," *Harvard Educational Review* 59 (November 1989): 444-453; Myra Sadker and David Sadker, *Failing at Fairness: How America's Schools Cheat Girls* (New York: Charles Scribner's Sons, 1994); and, Lois Weis and Michelle Fine, eds., *Beyond Silenced Voices: Class, Race, and Gender in United States Schools* (Albany: State University of New York Press, 1993).

156. Violas, *Training of the Urban Working Class*, 182-183.

157. Hutt, "Education of Women," 48: 128.

158. Lewis, *Democracy's High School*, (Boston: Houghton Miffling, 1914), 4.

159. Quoted in Lichtenberg, "The Adolescent Girl," *Journal of Counseling and Development* 63 (February 1985): 342.

160. Ibid.

161. Lewis, *Democracy's High School*, 111-113.

162. Powers, *The "Girl Question" in Education*, 95-96.

163. Rury, *Education and Women's Work*, (Albany: State University of New York Press, 1991), 8.

164. Krug, *Shaping of the American High School*, (Madison: University of Wisconsin Press, 1969), 1: 275-279.

165. "Views of Teachers and Students Out of Tune, Jeffrey Says," *St. Louis Globe-Democrat*, 8 Mar. 1934. League of Women Voters of St. Louis papers, Western Historical Manuscript Collection, University of Missouri-St. Louis.

166. *St. Louis Annual Report* 60: 310.

167. Quoted in Krug, *Shaping of the American High School* 1: 282.

168. Quoted in Lichtenberg, "The Adolescent Girl," 342.

169. G. Stanley Hall, "Coeducation in the High School," *National Education Association Journal of Proceedings and Addresses* 42 (1903): 446.

170. Ibid. Tyack and Hansot note that women psychologists, contemporaries of Hall and Thorndike, refuted the idea of mental differences between men and women. Willystine Goodsell, for example, offered a sound critique of Hall's work: "Obviously Dr. Hall has elevated regard for the sex and maternal functions of woman into a cult which profoundly affects his

conception of her entire education. . . . Yet with entire seriousness, the theory is advanced as modern, being garbed in a dubiously scientific dress of biology and psychology." The point here is that Thorndike's and Hall's theories *were* advanced as modern, scientific knowledge, in spite of the work of Goodsell, and psychologists Helen T. Wooley and Leta S. Hollingsworth. It does not discredit Wooley's and Hollingsworth's work to acknowledge the overwhelming influence of Thorndike, "America's most influential educational psychologist," and Hall, founder of the field of child psychology, founder of the psychological laboratory at Johns Hopkins, founder of the American Psychological Association, and the originator of the *American Journal of Psychology* and the *Journal of Applied Psychology*. See Tyack and Hansot, *Learning Together*, (New Haven: Yale University Press, 1990), 168-170; Goodsell, *Education of Women*, (New York: Macmillan, 1923), 68; Clarence J. Karier, *Scientists of the Mind: Intellectual Founders of Modern Psychology* (Urbana: University of Illinois Press, 1986): 89, 160-161.

171. Earl Barnes, "Women in Industry," *Atlantic Monthly* 110 (July 1912): 118.

172. Rury, *Education and Women's Work*, 74, 132.

173. Harvey Kantor, "Choosing a Vocation: The Origins and Transformation of Vocational Guidance in California, 1910-1930," *History of Education Quarterly* 26 (Fall 1986): 352.

174. Ibid., 359, 369-370, 375.

175. Ibid., 374.

176. See Power, *The "Girl Question" in Education* (London: The Falmer Press, 1992) and Rury, *Education and Women's Work,* (Albany: State University of New York Press, 1991), for a comprehensive contrast of commercial education, industrial education, and domestic education.

177. Barnes, "Women in Industry," 122.

178. Ibid., 121.

179. Ibid.

180. Kingsley, "Report of the Committee of Nine," *NEA Journal of Proceedings and Addresses* 49 (1911): 561.

181. Quoted in Brown, "Fear of Feminization," *Feminist Studies* 16 (Fall 1990): 509.

182. Brown, "Fear of Feminization," 509-510.

183. Barnes, "Women in Industry," 121.

184. Brown, "Fear of Feminization," 496; Tyack, in Powers, *The "Girl Question" in Education*, ix; Powers, *The "Girl Question" in Education*, 2. Powers explains that the "woman question" centered on women's economic, political, and social roles and their psychological, intellectual, and physical

capacities. Suffrage, economic independence, the perceived demise of the home, and general demands for equity were some central issues addressed by the "woman question."

185. Brown, "Fear of Feminization," 497-499.

186. Tyack, in Powers, *The "Girl Question" in Education*, ix.

187. Lynn D. Gordon, *Gender and Higher Education in the Progressive Era* (New Haven: Yale University Press, 1990), 2, 4-5, 11.

188. James E. Russell, "Co-Education in High Schools: Is It a Failure?," *Good Housekeeping Magazine* 57 (October 1913): 493-495.

189. Powers, *The "Girl Question" in Education*, 16.

190. Harkness, "Education of the Girl," *Atlantic Monthly* 113 (March 1914): 328.

191. Powers, *The "Girl Question" in Education*, 50, 128-129.

192. Krug, *Shaping of the American High School*, (Madison: University of Wisconsin Press, 1969), 1: 323.

193. Richard J. Altenbaugh, "Teachers and the Workplace," in *The Teacher's Voice: A Social History of Teaching in Twentieth-Century America*, Richard J. Altenbaugh, ed. (London: The Falmer Press, 1992), 157-159.

194. Ibid., 159-161.

195. Letters to the editor, *St. Louis Post-Dispatch*, 8 Jan. 1901; 15 Jan. 1901. An incident in 1933 accentuated the degree to which teachers' lives were controlled by the St. Louis Board of Education. J. Clark Waldron, economics teacher at the night school at Beaumont High School, was dismissed by Superintendent of Instruction, Henry J. Gerling, following Waldron's arrest for picketing a clothing firm. Although Waldron was released for lack of evidence, Gerling upheld the dismissal, stating,

> The manner in which he was acting brought the St. Louis schools into disrepute. . . . a school teacher has no right to place himself in a position inviting arrest. . . . My point is that the system was unable and unwilling to tolerate unfortunate notoriety.

("Gerling Releases Economics Teacher," unidentified news clipping in League of Women Voters papers, Western Historical Manuscript Collection, University of Missouri-St. Louis.) Waldron responded that Gerling's action

> menaces such freedom in the schools as there has been. It smacks of the growing tendency toward absolute control of education by the privileged classes.

("J. Clark Waldron Protests Dismissal," *St. Louis Globe-Democrat*, 27 Oct. 1933. League of Women Voters papers, Western Historical Manuscript

Collection, University of Missouri-St. Louis.) The *St. Louis Post-Dispatch* editorial staff sided with Waldron in protesting the Board of Education's strict control of teachers:

> The Waldron dismissal is a blow to academic freedom. It serves notice on St. Louis teachers that their opinions and behavior, though wholly outside of the classroom, are subject to censorship and punishment.

("Mr. Waldron's Dismissal," *St. Louis Post-Dispatch*, n.d. League of Women Voters papers, Western Historical Manuscript Collection, University of Missouri-St. Louis.) Mrs. Schuyler Smith, president of the St. Louis League of Women Voters, wrote a letter to Gerling dated 1 November 1933, protesting the Waldron dismissal. The League of Women Voters considered the incident

> too great interference with the personal, private activities of teachers, who should be entitled to precisely the same freedom and subject to the same responsibilities as attach to other citizens. Suppression of such rights, we believe, can only have a detrimental effect upon teacher morale and therefore upon the efficiency of the school system.

(Schuyler to Gerling, 1 Nov. 1933, League of Women Voters papers, Western Historical Manuscript Collection, University of Missouri-St. Louis.) Apparently, Waldron's dismissal was not reversed.

196. K. Schulz, "A Teacher's Standpoint," *St. Louis Post-Dispatch*, 13 Jan. 1901.

197. Morrison to the Kansas City Board of Education, 18 Dec. 1903, Gilbert Morrison Papers, Missouri Historical Society Archives.

198. Gilbert B. Morrison, "The Significance of the Manual Training Movement," (Paper delivered at the Kansas State Teachers' Association, Topeka, 31 December 1903.) Gilbert Morrison Papers, Missouri Historical Society Archives.

199. Gilbert B. Morrison, "Manual Training in the Public Schools," (Paper delivered at the Missouri State Teachers' Association, n.d.) Gilbert Morrison Papers, Missouri Historical Society Archives.

200. Woodward to Morrison, 2 June 1903, Gilbert Morrison Papers, Missouri Historical Society Archives.

201. Morrison and Woodward pamphlet, Gilbert Morrison Papers, Missouri Historical Society Archives.

202. "Common Schools Behind The Age," *St. Louis Post-Dispatch*, 23 July 1903.

203. "Higher Education Ruinous To Women," *St. Louis Post-Dispatch*, 9 June 1904.

204. News clipping (paper not identified) dated 21 March 1913. Vertical files. St. Louis Public Library.

205. Judd, *Survey of the St. Louis Public Schools*, 2: 296-297.

206. U.S. Department of the Interior, Bureau of Education, *Cardinal Principles of Secondary Education*, Bulletin 1919, no. 88 (Washington, DC: U.S. Government Printing Office, 1918).

207. Judd, *Survey of the St. Louis Public Schools*, 2: 325-327.

208. George D. Strayer, *A Report of a Survey of the Public Schools of St. Louis, Missouri* (Bureau of Publications, Teachers College, Columbia University, 1939), 28.

209. C.A. Greene, "Desirable Changes in the Present Organization of the Public Schools—The High School," *Bulletin Missouri State Teachers' Association* 1 (April 1915): 63.

210. *St. Louis Globe-Democrat*, 5 Feb. 1933, Sunday Magazine section.

211. Birdie Arbuckle Price, *Down Memory Lane: 50th Anniversary Celebration Charles Sumner High School* (N.p., 1959), 6.

212. "Won Coveted Scholarship," *St. Louis Post-Dispatch*, 24 Jan. 1901.

213. "From the Committee on Increase of High School Accommodations," *Official Bulletin High School Teachers New York City* no. 21 (6 November 1909): 4.

214. Jeffrey Hirsh, "Manual Training and the Negro in St. Louis, 1880-1898," unpublished paper, Missouri Historical Society, 1974, 13.

215. *Forty-Ninth Annual Report of the Board of Education of the City of St. Louis, Mo., for the Year Ending June 30, 1903* (St. Louis: Nixon-Jones Printing Co., 1904), 49: 160-161.

216. "Waring Principal of Sumner High for 32 Years," *St. Louis Globe-Democrat*, undated news clipping, St. Louis Schools Scrapbook, Missouri Historical Society.

217. Morrison and Woodward pamphlet, Gilbert Morrison Papers, Missouri Historical Society Archives.

218. "Domestic Science," *St. Louis Post-Dispatch*, 23 Jan. 1903.

219. "Show-Me Education," *St. Louis Post-Dispatch*, 20 Jan. 1903.

220. Quoted in Hirsh, "Manual Training and the Negro in St. Louis," 4.

221. Quoted in Hirsh, 4-5.

222. E.W. Newsome, "Commercial Education," *The Negro Educational Review: A Monthly Magazine Devoted to the History, Science, Art and Philosophy of Education and to the Professional and Business Interests of the*

American Negro 4 (August 1909): 2. Nina P. Lewis Collection, Western Historical Manuscript Collection, University of Missouri-St. Louis.

223. Morrison and Woodward pamphlet, Gilbert Morrison Papers, Missouri Historical Society Archives.

224. Gilbert Morrison, "Industrial Education—A Discussion of Dr. Jesse's Paper" (Delivered at the Missouri State Teachers' Association), Gilbert Morrison Papers, Missouri Historical Society Archives.

225. Counts, *The Senior High School Curriculum*, (Chicago: University of Chicago, 1926), 10.

226. *Printed Record of the Board of Education of the City of St. Louis* 23 (July 1st, 1916 to June 30th, 1917), 23: 629.

227. *Printed Record of the Board of Education of the City of St. Louis* 33 (July 1st, 1926 to June 30th, 1927), 33: 810; *Printed Record of the Board of Education of the City of St. Louis* 34 (July 1st, 1927 to June 30th, 1928), 34: 981; *Printed Record of the Board of Education of the City of St. Louis* 35 (July 1st, 1928 to June 30th, 1929), 35: 587, 987.

228. Reverend George E. Stevens to St. Louis Board of Education, 10 April 1934. League of Women Voters of St. Louis papers, Western Historical Manuscript Collection, University of Missouri-St. Louis. See also "Board Votes for Negro Training at Franklin School," unidentified news clipping dated 13 June 1934 in League of Women Voters of St. Louis papers, Western Historical Manuscript Collection, University of Missouri-St. Louis.

229. *Printed Record of the Board of Education of the City of St. Louis* 20 (July 1st, 1913 to June 30th, 1914), 20: 994.

230. *Printed Record of the Board of Education of the City of St. Louis* 27 (July 1st, 1920 to June 30th, 1921), 27: 2, 676.

231. *Printed Record*, 34: 325, 806.

232. "Commercial Education," *St. Louis Post-Dispatch*, 2 Apr. 1901.

233. "An Educational Advertiser," *St. Louis Post-Dispatch*, 4 Nov. 1904.

234. "Our Comprehensive Curriculum," *St. Louis Post-Dispatch*, 5 Sept. 1903.

235. "Coming To Her Own," *St. Louis Post-Dispatch*, 6 Oct. 1900.

236. Isabel C. Barrows, "Negro Girls Learn Agriculture At Tuskegee Institute," *St. Louis Post-Dispatch*, 11 Nov. 1900.

237. Ibid.

238. "Manual Training Exhibit," *St. Louis Post-Dispatch*, 19 June 1901.

239. "Domestic Science," *St. Louis Post-Dispatch*, 23 Jan. 1903.

240. "HIGH SCHOOL GIRLS LEARN DISHWASHING," *St. Louis Post-Dispatch*, 28 Dec. 1903. See Powers, *The "Girl Question" in Education*, 93-97.

241. "HIGH SCHOOL GIRLS LEARN DISHWASHING," *St. Louis Post-Dispatch*, 28 Dec. 1903.

242. "Opposed to Kindergartens," *St. Louis Post-Dispatch*, 9 May 1900. See page 238 in this chapter for Wilson's statement.

243. "St. Louis' Future School Teachers," *St. Louis Post-Dispatch*, 26 Sept. 1900. See Powers, *The "Girl Question" in Education* (London: The Falmer Press, 1992) and Rury, *Education and Women's Work* (Albany: State University of New York Press, 1991), for family support of the differentiated curriculum for girls.

244. "Review on *Cardinal Principles of Secondary Education*," *Educational Review* 59 (February 1920): 165.

245. "Masculine and Feminine Qualities," *St. Louis Post-Dispatch*, 30 June 1904.

246. "Women Should Be Educated," *St. Louis Post-Dispatch*, 25 Aug. 1901.

247. "The Process of Feminization," *St. Louis Post-Dispatch*, 19 June 1904.

248. Ibid.

249. "Advance Chemistry and Physics Classes Full," *Scrippage*, 19 Sept. 1924. Soldan High School Collection, 1923-1931, Western Historical Manuscript Collection, University of Missouri-St. Louis.

250. Powers, *The "Girl Question" in Education*, 2-3. See also Tyack's statement in Geraldine Jonçich Clifford, "Man/Woman/Teacher: Gender, Family, and Career in American Educational History," in *American Teachers: Histories of a Profession at Work*, Donald Warren, ed. (New York: Macmillan, 1989), 294.

251. Clifford, "Man/Woman/Teacher," 311. See also Brown, "Fear of Feminization," *Feminist Studies* 16 (Fall 1990) and Powers, *The "Girl Question" in Education*.

252. Quoted in Brown, "Fear of Feminization," 511. See Elizabeth Hansot and David Tyack, "Gender in American Public Schools: Thinking Institutionally," *Signs: Journal of Women in Culture and Society* 13 (Summer 1988), and Tyack and Hansot, *Learning Together*.

253. Brown, "Fear of Feminization," 511.

254. "Oklahoma Principal Enjoys Visit to Soldan," *Scrippage*, 17 Oct. 1924. Soldan High School Collection, 1923-1931, Western Historical Manuscript Collection, University of Missouri-St. Louis.

255. "Round Table Girls Give Two Humorous Debates," *Scrippage*, 26 Sept. 1924. Soldan High School Collection, 1923-1931, Western Historical Manuscript Collection, University of Missouri-St. Louis.

256. Brown, "Fear of Feminization," 511.

257. Harkness, "Education of the Girl," *Atlantic Monthly* 113 (March 1914): 326.

Epilogue

"... whatever variation is made in the present plan of [girls']
education, it should not be based upon the narrow foundation of
preconceived ideas of differences inherent in sex."[1]
　　　　　—Mary Leal Harkness, "The Education of the Girl," 1914

"... whatever public opinion has demanded, schools have never been
able to turn out merely educated human beings, but always boys and
girls, prospective men and women. And so they must continue to do
so.... we must continue to 'make women.'"[2]
　　　　　　　　　　　—Marguerite Stockman Dickson,
　　　　　　　　　　　Vocational Guidance for Girls, 1919

"Young women in the United States today are still not participating
equally in our educational system."[3]
　　—*The AAUW Report. How Schools Shortchange Girls: A Study of
　　　　　　　　　Major Findings on Girls and Education* 1992

A decade ago Sally Schwager assessed the state of women's
educational history and concluded that curricular reform, a traditional
concern in the history of American education, had not yet been
addressed from a feminist perspective. Excluding girls and women
from academic thought distorted that which was known about
curriculum history, according to feminist theory.[4] Following Millicent
Rutherford's 1977 dissertation, "Feminism and the Secondary School
Curriculum, 1890-1920," David Tyack and Elisabeth Hansot, Victoria
Bissell Brown, John L. Rury, and Jane Bernard Powers advanced
scholarly knowledge of the high-school curriculum and girls' schooling

during the Progressive Era.[5] Many scholars now recognize that feminist theory is flawed unless it attends to the intersections of gender, race, and class in society; feminist theorists call for scholarship that approaches race, class, and gender in relational ways.[6] In charting the transition *From Female Scholar to Domesticated Citizen,* I have endeavored to present the consequences of the adoption of the differentiated curriculum in St. Louis, to see how gender, race, and class combined to affect girls' curriculum choices.

One should not be surprised to learn that girls and boys tended to complete different courses of study after 1900, for the ideological underpinnings that justified the adoption of the differentiated curriculum were saturated with a gender bias that pervaded social thought. The idea of sex-determined civic, work, and domestic roles could be identified as a common element among the fundamental doctrines of New Liberalism, vocationalism, the "boy problem," and domestic feminism. These forces created a gendered ideology that prepared the way for the differentiated curriculum as a vehicle for specialized instruction. Teachers recognized that schooling geared to gender-specific futures was a departure from earlier educational practice, even as it was being developed. In her 1919 text, *Vocational Guidance for Girls*, Marguerite Stockman Dickson noted that

> For years, and in fact until very recently, the whole tendency in education for girls has been toward a training which ignores sex and ultimate destiny. The teachers themselves were so trained and are therefore the less prepared to see the necessity for any special teaching along these lines. They may even resent any demand for specialized instruction for girls.[7]

Indeed, teachers in St. Louis left subtle evidence that they resented the turn to specialized instruction inherent in the differentiated curriculum. Others, such as Mary Leal Harkness, were more direct in their protest. But opponents of the differentiated curriculum were up against the long tradition of women's "special" qualities that served as a foundation for the domestic-feminist agenda, as well as the New Liberal conceptions of citizenship that spread throughout the country as that ideology surged into a position of dominance. Once educators took on the responsibility of citizenship and work preparation as defined by the New Liberal agenda, in place of an educational philosophy dedicated to students' intellectual and moral development, school became a different place for girls. In what ways could schooling for citizenship and work develop for girls in a society in which women were disfranchised and faced gender discrimination in the labor market? Many concluded that the "state which 'trains for citizenship' cannot logically ignore the necessity for training the mothers of future citizens."[8] To be sure, there were girls well enough "intoxicated" with personal freedom and ambition to reject the prescribed courses for girls.[9] That some chose other paths in the emerging educational structure, however, was in spite of wide-ranging support for gender-specific courses in the differentiated curriculum. That educators described such choices as the result of "intoxication" (of any sort) exposes a clear picture of the general expectations they held for girls.

One question that arises when scholars consider gender as an important variable in curriculum history is: Why did girls' academic prospects in high school diminish at a time that appeared to signal expanding social, political, and economic opportunities for women? First one must evaluate the degree to which women's status was, in fact, improving during the Progressive Era. Certainly, new positions in the workforce opened for women, more women finished high school and pursued higher education, women took leading roles in creating and maintaining public policy, and women finally obtained the right to vote. These gains were not shared equally or experienced in the same way by all women, however; institutional racism and blatant bigotry stood in the way of African-American women who sought better-paying jobs, college admission, and the ballot. Historian Elsa Barkley Brown shared her mother's experience as one example. In an essay in which Brown delineated the considerable life contributions of working-class African-American women, she explained that her mother was fortunate to have been the youngest of eight children, for her family provided each child with as much education as was available to them. By the time Brown's mother finished high school, the Louisville Municipal College for Negroes put higher education within reach. Brown's mother graduated with a bachelor's degree in mathematics in the 1930s. Not disposed to teaching, the young woman described by Brown as the pride of her community searched for a job congruous with her abilities and achievements. Brown writes that, finally, her mother found a position "with an employer who was suitably impressed with all that this young African American girl had accomplished; yes, it would be so refreshing to have an intelligent maid for a change."[10] Yet even as they battled race and gender discrimination, African-American women did not define themselves as victims. They developed new definitions of womanhood out of the complex dialectics of their lives.[11] As more history is written from a perspective that affords oppressed women the dignity of being actors in their own lives and communities, our understanding of women's status and women's accomplishments during the Progressive Era will be enhanced.[12]

The women whose access to jobs, education, and political participation were not obstructed by racism still had to measure their gains against changes in the economic, educational, and political systems. Historians have documented how women's entry into a field often preceded a decline in power and status in the related positions. For example, as women gained access to college, prestige in education shifted to graduate school where women remained in the minority. And by the time women gained the right to vote, the United States political system had been transformed to reduce the effectiveness of the individual ballot.[13] Clearly, a linear model of progress does not fit with women's experiences in the United States during the Progressive Era. Nonetheless, women's increasing public participation in economic, political, and social arenas placed the "woman question" at center stage in public debate during this period.[14]

Changes in women's status intensified concerns that schooling should help students prepare for traditional or newly formed gender roles. As more women entered college and the workforce, many began to fear for the stability of the home. In the public mind, rising divorce rates and declining birth rates presented twin threats. A popular response was to encourage girls to incorporate home economics into their school work. Dickson wrote:

> In spite of the "uneasy women" who feel that the home offers insufficient scope for their intellectual powers, the executive ability required to run a home smoothly and well is of no mean order. . . . We must then consider "guidance toward homemaking" as a necessary part of a girl's education and as a possible solution of the home problems on every hand.[15]

Supporters of women's participation in the workforce looked to the school also, for job training. Commercial education became a huge success in high schools as office work became a feminized profession. Changes in women's status as workers, then, led diverse groups to embrace the differentiated curriculum. Whether the increase in women's employment was perceived as cause to teach girls the finer points of women's traditional familial responsibilities from a modern perspective, or as reason to train girls in occupations "suited for women," it had a part in emphasizing gender distinctions in school.

In the second decade of the twentieth century, as arguments from the radical sector of the women's movement raised the issue of women's equality with men, one writer punctuated her remarks on education for American girls by asserting that girls will learn that "equality of the sexes means in no sense similarity."[16] The differentiated curriculum enabled educators to distance themselves from schooling practices of the nineteenth century when girls and boys had studied the same curricula. Most often public schools have operated as conservative institutions. The emphasis on the school's responsibility to turn out "prospective men and women" in the first decades of the twentieth century may be interpreted as a conservative institution's response to the radical idea of gender equality.[17]

The differentiated curriculum served to strengthen the process of gender identification in high school. Gender lines appeared in the curriculum once students were instructed to choose a course of study in alignment with their projected futures. In St. Louis, some courses of study quickly became identified as girls' or boys' domains: Normal, Art, Domestic Art and Science, and Manual Training. The differentiated curriculum had been in place for about thirteen years before boys dominated enrollment in the Scientific Course. It took another ten years before girls maintained a predominant position in the Commercial Course. Certainly by 1920 students and teachers could tag most courses of study as "girls" or "boys" courses. This behavior provided a sharp contrast to student's course-taking pattern in the nineteenth-century high school.[18]

This evidence suggests that students were beginning to make distinctions between girls' and boys' schooling in a manner consistent with dominant ideas of their day. Educational leaders professed overwhelming support for the differentiated curriculum, so much so that arguments against it are difficult to find in professional literature after the turn of the century. The St. Louis community mounted no significant opposition to the differentiated curriculum, indicating local acceptance of the new educational philosophy. Gendered ideology became a powerful influence on girls' education. Educators, psychologists, and sociologists denounced the value of mathematics and science in women's lives, and girls' enrollment in the Scientific

Course in St. Louis plummeted. Eight decades after girls' participation in the scientific course of study dropped most severely, research has confirmed that gender stereotyping is correlated with girls' persistence in mathematics classes. Based on data from the National Assessment of Educational Progress, girls who reject traditional gender roles have higher mathematics achievement than girls who have more stereotyped expectations.[19] Proponents of the change in the high-school curriculum during the Progressive Era declared the cultivation of gender roles as a central principle of their educational philosophy. The resulting decline in girls' participation in the Scientific Course foreshadowed recent research on the effects of gender on girls' schooling.

The differentiated curriculum, with its emphasis on role specialization, cut into the traditional academic curriculum, allowing stereotypical views of women's abilities and women's responsibilities to surge through the school structure. To interpret the differentiated curriculum as an institutional device that limited women's opportunities, however, is not to imply that all girls were victimized as a result. Historians know well that power is never completely monopolized—it has always been contested and flowed into unintended places.[20] Nevertheless, the introduction of the differentiated curriculum at the beginning of the twentieth century allowed gender distinctions to gain a foothold in a space that had been protected during the nineteenth century, the public high school.

Myra Sadker and David Sadker's study, *Failing at Fairness: How America's Schools Cheat Girls*, contains excerpts of interviews with women and girls across the United States. Women who attended high school in the 1940s, 1950s, and 1960s recall being counseled by school officials not to take classes in physics or being written off by mathematics teachers as not being able to learn. Research from the 1980s and 1990s finds that girls still battle sexist teaching and counseling in the high school. One high-school girl reports

> In my science class the teacher never calls on me, and I feel like I don't exist. The other night I had a dream that I vanished.[21]

There is a connection between the type of schooling this student describes and the fact that the "female scholar" has vanished from public consciousness. Educational developments since the advent of the differentiated curriculum have eclipsed the estimable academic legacy established by high-school girls in the nineteenth century. The efforts to

reshape schooling around "women's destiny" nearly a century ago have
had long-lasting consequences.

NOTES

1. Mary Leal Harkness, "The Education of the Girl," *Atlantic Monthly*
113 (March 1914): 325.

2. Marguerite Stockman Dickson, *Vocational Guidance for Girls*
(Chicago: Rand McNally, 1919), 75.

3. *The AAUW Report. How Schools Shortchange Girls: A Study of Major
Findings on Girls and Education* (Washington, DC: AAUW Educational
Foundation and National Education Association, 1992), 84.

4. Sally Schwager, "Educating Women in America," *Signs: Journal of
Women in Culture and Society* 12 (Winter 1987): 372; Margaret L. Andersen,
Thinking about Women: Sociological Perspectives on Sex and Gender, 3d ed.
(New York: Macmillan, 1993), 344.

5. Millicent Rutherford, "Feminism and the Secondary School
Curriculum, 1890-1920," Ph.D. diss., Stanford University, 1977; David Tyack
and Elisabeth Hansot, *Learning Together: A History of Coeducation in
American Public Schools* (New Haven: Yale University Press, 1990); Victoria
Bissell Brown, "The Fear of Feminization: Los Angeles High Schools in the
Progressive Era," *Feminist Studies* 16 (Fall 1990): 493-518; John L. Rury,
*Education and Women's Work: Female Schooling and the Division of Labor in
Urban America, 1870-1930* (Albany: State University of New York Press,
1991); Jane Bernard Powers, *The "Girl Question" in Education: Vocational
Education for Young Women in the Progressive Era* (London: The Falmer
Press, 1992).

6. Andersen, *Thinking about Women*, 348-350.

7. Dickson, *Vocational Guidance for Girls*, 75-76.

8. Ibid., 76.

9. Ibid., 16.

10. Elsa Barkley Brown, "Mothers of Mind," in *Double Stitch: Black
Women Write About Mothers and Daughters*, Patricia Bell-Scott, Beverly Guy
Sheftall, Jacqueline Jones Royster, Janet Sims-Wood, Miriam DeCosta-Willis,
and Lucille P. Fultz, eds. (New York: Harper Perennial, 1993), 80-81.

11. Ibid., 84.

12. Audrey T. McCluskey, "The Current Status of Black Women's
History: Telling Our Story Ourselves," in *Black Women in the Middle West
Project: A Comprehensive Resource Guide. Illinois and Indiana: Historical
Essays, Oral Histories, Biographical Profiles, and Document Collections,*

Darlene Clark Hine, Patrick Kay Bidelman, Shirley M. Herd, and Donald West, eds. (West Lafayette, IN: Purdue Research Foundation, 1986), 16.

13. See Patricia Albjerg Graham, "Expansion and Exclusion: A History of Women in American Higher Education," *Signs: Journal of Women in Culture and Society* 3 (Summer 1978): 759-773; and Paula Baker, "The Domestication of Politics: Women and American Political Society, 1780-1920," *American Historical Review* 89 (June 1984): 620-647.

14. Powers, *The "Girl Question" in Education*, 2; Tyack and Hansot, *Learning Together*, 201-208.

15. Dickson, *Vocational Guidance for Girls*, 72.

16. Anne Morgan, *The American Girl; Her Education, Her Responsibility, Her Recreation, Her Future* (New York: Harper & Bros., 1915), 15.

17. Dickson, *Vocational Guidance for Girls*, 75.

18. Girls constituted almost 100 percent of the student enrollment in the Normal Course from its inception. Other courses of study were not marked as the province of either sex in the nineteenth century.

19. *The AAUW Report*, 30.

20. Linda K. Kerber, Alice Kessler-Harris, and Kathryn Kish Sklar, eds., *U.S. History as Women's History: New Feminist Essays*, (Chapel Hill: University of North Carolina Press, 1995), 9.

21. Quoted in Myra Sadker and David Sadker, *Failing at Fairness: How America's Schools Cheat Girls*, (New York: Charles Scribner's Sons, 1994), 134. See also pp. 33-35; 120-121.

Index